Complex Economic Dynamics

Studies in Dynamical Economic Science
Richard H. Day, series editor

Complex Economic Dynamics, Volume I: An Introduction to Dynamical Systems and Market Mechanisms
Richard H. Day, 1994

Prices, Cycles, and Growth
Hakukane Nikaido, 1995

Dynamic Macroeconomics: Instability, Fluctuation, and Growth in Monetary Economies
Peter Flaschel, Reiner Franke, and Willi Semmler, 1997

Complex Economic Dynamics, Volume II: An Introduction to Macroeconomic Dynamics
Richard H. Day, 1999

Complex Economic Dynamics
Volume II
An Introduction to Macroeconomic Dynamics

Richard H. Day

with contributions by
Tzong-Yau Lin, Zhang Min, and Oleg Pavlov

The MIT Press
Cambridge, Massachusetts
London, England

This book was set in Times New Roman by Asco Typesetters, Hong Kong, and was printed and bound in the United States of America.

Library of Congress Cataloging-in-Publication Data

Day, Richard Hollis, 1933–
  Complex economic dynamics / Richard H. Day
      p.   cm.
  Includes bibliographical references and index.
  Contents: v. 1. An introduction to dynamical systems and market mechanisms.—v. 2. An introduction to macroeconomic dynamics
  ISBN 0-262-04141-3 (v. 1).—ISBN 0-262-04172-3 (v. 2)
  1. Economics, Mathematical. 2. Statics and dynamics (Social sciences). I. Title.
HB135.D389   1994
330'.01'51—dc20   93-30291
                                                           CIP

Pythagoras' assertion that things behave as they do because of their structure, which can be described in mathematical terms, was one of the basic propositions without which science as we know it would be impossible.
—W. H. Auden, *The Greeks and Us* (paraphrased)

Contents

List of Figures

Preface to Volume II

This book contains an introduction to dynamical systems theory and to the theory of market mechanisms, business cycles, economic growth, and economic development. It presents fundamental and essential concepts in terms of classic economic ideas while emphasizing new insights one gains when nonlinearity is incorporated explicitly and complex behavior included among the possible modes of change.

Volume I contains a nontechnical introduction to the basic facts of economic change and to the theoretical ideas used for describing them (part I), a technical survey of the relevant mathematical tools (part II), and an introduction to the dynamic theory of competitive markets (part III).

Volume II is concerned with macroeconomic dynamics. It deals with business cycles (part IV), with economic growth (part V), and with economic development (part VI). The models of cycles pertain to relatively short-term forces; the models of growth provide partial explanations of longer-term fluctuations; the models of development shed light on the episodic ups and downs of human culture. This volume concludes (part VII) with a brief history of economic dynamics, a guide to current developments, and a summary and reflection on the significance and limitations of dynamic economics for both theory and policy.

The purpose of theory in general, and economic theory in particular, is not to describe experience in detail but rather to identify salient aspects of reality that can be understood in terms of interacting structures and forces. Theoretical understanding can never be complete, and practical economic decision making should always take as much account of experience and history as it does of economic theory. But the analysis of carefully specified models can supply insights that may be difficult or impossible to attain in any other way. To ignore these insights is as foolish as to ignore the evident facts. It is my hope, therefore, that the present work will be useful for understanding the past, for anticipating possibilities for the future, and for shaping events in the present.

An important feature of my approach is the focus on global analysis: that is, what can happen for all allowable initial conditions and what can happen when key structural parameters of technology, preference, and behavior vary over wide ranges. Given the theorems reviewed in parts I and II, the mathematics required to do this is not advanced. Most of the results depend on basic concepts: the Intermediate Value and Mean Value theorems, the necessary conditions for a maximum, standard limiting arguments, and the manipulation of inequality expressions. The main mathematical concepts from part II of volume I are listed in the appendix.

To maintain continuity with the first volume, the chapters in this book are numbered sequentially beginning with chapter 13, there being 12 chapters in volume I. For convenience of reference, passages are designated by chapter, section, and subsection. Thus, "§4.2.1" is chapter 4, section 2.1, "Iterated Maps and Semiflow." Theorems or propositions are referred to by chapter and sequential number; thus Theorem 7.3 refers to the third theorem in chapter 7. Terms introduced for the first time are italicized.

The reader should be reminded of the acknowledgments recorded in volume I. I will not reproduce them here except to say that various portions of the following chapters have greatly benefited from the contributions of several of my students, former students, and colleagues, especially T. Y. Lin (in parts IV and V), Zhang Min (parts V and VI), Jean-Luc Walter (part VI), Wayne Shafer (chapters 13 and 14), Herbert Dawid (chapter 16), and Massimo Di Matteo (chapters 13 and 16). If, in spite of their help, some errors remain, these are my own fault. Most of the diagrams for this volume were prepared by Oleg Pavlov. The manuscript in all its versions was prepared by Barbara Gordon Day. Finally, I would like to thank Terry Vaughn for his patience in seeing this work through to publication, and Matthew Abbate for his meticulous job of copyediting.

Notations

Within a given chapter, equations and diagrams are numbered sequentially. References to equations or diagrams are preceded by the appropriate chapter number. For example, equation (15.6) is equation (6) in chapter 15. Likewise, figure 13.7b is diagram b in figure 7 in chapter 13.

References to sections within chapters is made by the notation, §X.Y, which means chapter X, section Y.

$=$	equals
$\equiv$	is identically equal to
$:=$	is defined to be
$\in$	"is an element of" or "belongs to"
$\subset$	is contained in
$\supset$	contains
$\backslash$	set subtraction: $A \backslash B$ the set of points in A that are not in B
$\backslash$	complement: $\backslash A$ is the set of points not in A
$\mathbb{N}$	the set of integers
$\mathbb{N}^+$	the set of nonnegative integers
$\mathbb{N}^{++}$	the set of positive integers
$\mathbb{R}$	the set of real numbers
$\mathbb{R}^+$	the set of nonnegative real numbers
$\mathbb{R}^{++}$	the set of positive real numbers
$]a, b[$	the complement of (a, b)
$)a, b($	the complement of $[a, b]$
$\tilde{x}$	a stationary state of the variable x
$\tilde{x}^p$	a periodic or cyclic point of period p
$\bar{x}$	a fixed value of the variable x
x^e	estimate or forecast of the variable x
$E(\cdot)$	statistical expectation of the terms in parentheses
λ	price adjustment parameter or the natural rate of population growth
$\max\{a, b\}$	the larger of the terms a and b
$\min\{a, b\}$	the smaller of terms a and b
$\chi_S(x)$	the indicator function $= 1$ if $x \in S$ and $= 0$ if $x \notin S$

M	the supremum or maximum of a function
m	the minimum or infimum of a function
$\lambda(\cdot)$	Lebesgue measure
$\mu(\cdot)$	a measure function
$c\ell(S)$	closure of the set S, namely, the set of its limit points
$\text{supp}_X f$	the support of a function on a set $X : \text{supp}_X f := c\ell\{x \mid f(x) > 0\}$
$\text{supp}_X \mu$	the support of a measure on the set X = the smallest closed subset of X with positive measure
$\text{supp}\, \mu$	the smallest closed set in the domain of the process with full measure $(= \mu(D))$
$\mathcal{P}(S)$	the power set of a set S: the set of all subsets of S. Also denoted 2^S

IV BUSINESS CYCLES

... high hopes
surging wealth
shattered dreams
frantic search
recovered lives
again ...

13 The Real/Monetary Business Cycle Theory

> *... the presence or absence of a fluctuation* inherent to the economic process *is practically and scientifically the fundamental problem.*
> —Joseph A. Schumpeter

> *Thus our conditions together explain the outstanding features of our actual experience;—namely, that we oscillate, avoiding the gravest extremes of fluctuation in both directions, round an intermediate position appreciably below full employment.*
> —John Maynard Keynes, *The General Theory*

The forces of demand and supply, which operate on the microeconomic level, accumulate to bring about changes in the economy as a whole. From the macroeconomic point of view it is not individual markets but this general level of economic activity and its fluctuations that are of primary interest.

Over the years during which decentralized markets have played a major role in economics, a host of business cycle theories purporting to explain aggregate output and employment have been advanced. Among the most influential of these is the one first expressed in Keynes's *General Theory of Interest, Money and Unemployment.* In an explicitly dynamic telling of the story, rising production, employment, and capacity utilization during the upswing of the cycle increases the demand for money. If the supply of money is inelastic, interest rates rise. This increases the opportunity cost of capital, but it need not depress investment initially because of the positive impact of rising production and profits. But the growing transactions demand for cash eventually crowds the money markets. Interest rates continue to rise until they impinge on investment demand. The depressing effect of the cost of capital overwhelms the stimulating influence of rising levels of output. Investment is reduced. A decline in employment, aggregate demand, and interest rates follows. Lower interest rates will eventually stimulate investment and consumption, but a recovery may take some time because of excess capacity and lowered profits. Fluctuations over more than two centuries in the industrial economies suggest that this model is a reasonable first approximation of reality.[1]

The flow of cause and effect just described is represented in figure 13.1. Changes in aggregate production have two effects on investment demand. One is a direct, positive connection through income and profits. The other is an indirect, negative connection through the monetary sector. If the relative importance of the two effects reverses when national income changes enough, then fluctuations can occur. The central elements of this

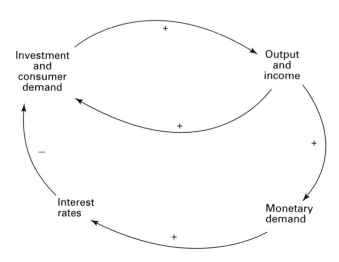

Figure 13.1
The real/monetary business cycle. The arrows indicate the flow of causal effect. The signs show the correlation of effect. The inner loop is the positive real feedback loop. The outer loop is the negative monetary feedback loop.

process are: (i) that the monetary sector interacts with the real economy in a crucial manner through the interest rate and the supply of money; (ii) that the monetary sector adjusts quickly to bring about a balance in supply and demand for money; (iii) that macroeconomic change is explained (at least in part) by out-of-equilibrium adjustments to imbalances in aggregate supply and demand for goods; and (iv) that the primary (short-run) response to disequilibrium is through quantity rather than price adjustments.

All of these assumptions can and have been challenged, and a huge literature exists about the issues in dispute. Briefly, it is said that prices and wages do adjust and that economic theory should assume that they do so instantaneously on all markets so that the economy always works in equilibrium. It has been argued that this must be the case because if it weren't, opportunities for profit would exist which arbitragers would eliminate. Moreover, it has been argued that money's primary role in equilibrium is as a numeraire so that only relative prices matter. The corollary is that the economy is neutral to the supply of money and to the general level of prices. Although these equilibrium arguments predate those of the Keynesian disequilibrium theory, they reemerged in the distinctly different theoretical garb of optimal growth theory in the 1970s and have often been represented as "modern" or "new." I shall consider this growth-oriented cycle theory in part V.[2] However, the realistic and practically important real/monetary theory shall be the focus of analysis in this chapter and in chapters 14 and 15.

The original formulation of this theory occurred at a time when mathematical analysis was just being introduced into the study of economic cycles and long before there was any detailed knowledge of complex dynamics at all.[3] It is only now, after the mathematical tools have been developed, that a full understanding of the possibilities inherent in that theory can be derived.

13.1 Aggregate Demand and the Adjustment Process

13.1.1 The Model

The analysis begins with the aggregation of all of the various commodities and instruments of exchange in society into "money," "labor," and "goods." It continues by assuming that all prices, including the wages of labor, are fixed, so that aggregate national income can be presented by a single index. This simplifying assumption can be justified as a first, crude approximation under conditions in which prices change relatively slowly compared to the other variables.

Let m, g, and l be indexes denoting money, goods, and labor respectively; r and Y denote the real interest rate and aggregate real income ($\equiv$ aggregate real output), respectively; $D^m(r, Y)$ and $S^m(r, Y)$ the aggregate demand and supply functions for money; $D^g(r, Y)$ and $S^g(r, Y)$ the aggregate demand and supply functions for goods; and $D^l(r, Y)$ and $S^l(r, Y)$ the aggregate demand and supply function for labor.

Consider the money market first. Short-run market clearing will be assumed to occur on the money markets so that r and Y satisfy the condition

$$D^m(r, Y) = S^m(r, Y). \tag{13.1}$$

This temporary equilibrium condition determines an implicit function $r = f(Y)$ which gives for each Y the rate of interest that clears the money market at this level of aggregate real income.[4] If Y_t is the given level of income, then

$$r_t = f(Y_t) \tag{13.2}$$

and $D^m(f(Y_t), Y_t) = S^m(f(Y_t), Y_t)$. The existence of the implicit function $f(\cdot)$ requires that the conditions of the implicit function theorem are satisfied, namely that the partial derivatives of D^m and S^m exist, are continuous, and that $\frac{\partial D^m}{\partial Y} - \frac{\partial S^m}{\partial Y} \neq 0$, $Y \geq 0$.[5]

The Keynesian theory focuses on short-run forces that involve adjustments in output and employment to changes in the level of aggregate demand. While the supply of money can depend on the interest rate and current income even in the short run, the potential work force and production capacity are considered to be determined by long-run forces and are treated as parameters. Thus, the labor force depends on population numbers, on education, on customs concerning the work day and the work week, and so forth, and is more or less independent of the current interest rate and aggregate income level. Let l be the amount of labor employed and $\bar{l}$ be the potential labor force at full employment. Then, within the scope of the present theory, $S^l(r, Y) \equiv \bar{l}$.

The *potential supply of goods*, $\bar{Y}$, depends on the aggregate capital stock, the normal capacity utilization rate (related to the customary work day and work week), the level of technological efficiency, and so forth. Levels of demand that do not exceed potential supply satisfy the constraint

$$D^g(r_t, Y_t) \leq \bar{Y}. \tag{13.3}$$

At a given level of income Y_t and using (13.2), the effective demand for goods to be produced in the succeeding period $t+1$ is

$$0(Y_t) := D^g(f(Y_t), Y_t). \tag{13.4}$$

Income enters with a lag because expenditures are based on preceding receipts and because orders for durable consumer goods and capital must be made on the basis of the currently known past interest rate, not on the one that emerges from the current period's market. Expectations must adjust to experience and output must also.[6]

We assume that effective supply is independent of the current rate of interest and aggregate income level and that it is adjusted to satisfy demand. Thus,

$$S^g(r_t, Y_t) \equiv Y_{t+1} = D^g(f(X_t), Y_t),$$

or simply the difference equation

$$Y_{t+1} = \theta(Y_t). \tag{13.5}$$

The effective demand for labor in a given period depends on output and the conditions of production, which, assuming that the supply of goods is adjusted to demand with a lag, means that it depends on r and Y with a lag. Let $Y = F(l)$ be a production function relating output to actual employment l, given the available capital stock, etc. Using the production function, we get

$$l_{t+1} = F^{-1}(Y_{t+1}) = F^{-1}(D^g(r_t, Y_t)) := D^l(r_t, Y_t) \tag{13.6}$$

which defines the short-run demand for labor. If $F'(l)$ exists, is continuous, and is positive for all $l \geq 0$, then the existence of the inverse function $F^{-1}(\cdot)$ follows.[7] Focusing on the excess supply, we get

$$l_{t+1} = D^l(r_t, Y_t) \leq \bar{l}. \tag{13.7}$$

The Keynesian regime is the set of (r, Y) pairs that satisfy the condition (13.3) or, equivalently, (13.7). Systems could be considered that would allow output above the potential as defined here. This would require more intensive labor and capital utilization than "normal." Such possibilities will not be taken up here.

Given an initial income level Y_0, (13.5) determines a sequence of successive real aggregate income levels; (13.2) determines a sequence of real interest rates; and (13.6) determines the sequence of employment levels. A sequence $(r_t, Y_t, l_t)_{t=1}^{\infty}$ generated in this way, given the initial condition Y_0, is a *trajectory*. A triple $(\tilde{r}, \tilde{Y}, \tilde{l})$ such that $\tilde{Y} = \theta(\tilde{Y}) \leq \bar{Y}$, $\tilde{r} = f(\tilde{Y})$, and $\tilde{l} = D^l(\tilde{r}, \tilde{Y}) = F^{-1}(D^g(\tilde{r}, \tilde{Y})) \leq \bar{l}$ is a *fixed price equilibrium*. Obviously, such an equilibrium is a stationary state of the underlying dynamic model.[8]

The simplifying assumptions that have been made so far block out the influence of a host of important variables at work in the actual economy. Nonetheless, as shall be seen, this process does yield some clues about why the macro economy behaves as it does.[9]

13.1.2 The Wave of Aggregate Demand

To make sure that a stationary state exists and that it is positive, the following conditions are assumed:

$\theta(0) > 0$ and $\lim_{Y\to\infty} \theta(Y)/Y < 1$.   (13.8)

The first of these means that there is a source of aggregate demand that is positive even at zero income. The second means that when income is high enough, the demand for goods falls below real income. Existence follows from Theorem 5.1.

In order to infer how aggregate income can behave as a consequence of the adjustment process when the economy is not at a stationary state, we must examine the profile of the mapping $\theta(\cdot)$, which is given (in terms of first-order effects) by the slope of the aggregate demand function

$$\theta'(Y) = \frac{\partial D^g}{\partial r} \cdot f'(Y) + \frac{\partial D^g}{\partial Y}.$$ (13.9)

For example, recall that if $|\theta'(\tilde{Y})| < 1$, then the stationary state $\tilde{Y}$ is asymptotically stable; or, if $\theta'(\tilde{Y}) < -1$, then $\tilde{Y}$ is unstable and expanding fluctuations must occur in the neighborhood of $\tilde{Y}$, and so on.[10] The first term on the right side of (13.9) is the *monetary interaction term*; the second term on the right is the *income effect*. The ratio of these two terms has a crucial bearing on which of the several possibilities can occur.

Consider the aggregate demand for goods. Assume that

$\partial D^g/\partial r < 0$, $\partial D^g/\partial Y > 0$, $Y > 0$.   (13.10)

The first expression reflects the *substitution effect* of a rising opportunity cost of expenditure on goods when the interest rate increases; that is, as r increases, the desirability of financial assets increases. The second is the marginal income effect; as income increases, the demand for goods increases. When these conditions are satisfied, we shall say that *the demand for goods is normal*.

For money demand, assume that

$\partial D^m/\partial r < 0$ and $\partial D^m/\partial Y > 0$.   (13.11)

The first expression reflects the substitution effect caused by a change in the opportunity cost of holding money. When the interest that can be earned in financial and real investments rises, the opportunity cost of holding money in the most liquid form rises. The second effect is caused by the transaction requirements for a changing level of economic activity. When the general level of economic activity increases, the amount of cash balances required to service these transactions also increases.

For the supply of money, it is assumed that

$$\partial S^m/\partial r \geq 0, \quad \partial S^m/\partial Y \geq 0. \tag{13.12}$$

The first of these reflects the influence of interest rates on the use of free reserves; as rates of return on investment rise, banks are willing to increase the supply of loans. The second reflects an assumption that banks may be willing and able to expand loans as deposits rise with the general level of economic activity.[11]

From (13.2), one finds that

$$f'(Y) = -\left(\frac{\partial D^m}{\partial Y} - \frac{\partial S^m}{\partial Y}\right) \bigg/ \left(\frac{\partial D^m}{\partial r} - \frac{\partial S^m}{\partial r}\right).$$

Given the marginal interest rate effects just assumed in (13.11)–(13.12), the denominator is negative for all Y. The marginal income effects assumed are both positive. Consequently, if

$$\frac{\partial D^m}{\partial Y} > \frac{\partial S^m}{\partial Y}, \tag{13.13}$$

then the temporary equilibrium interest rate increases with increases in income, that is,

$$f'(Y) > 0, \quad Y \geq 0. \tag{13.14}$$

When (13.11)–(13.13) hold, we shall say *the money market is normal*. The function $f(\cdot)$ is illustrated in figure 13.2, where it is also assumed that $f''(Y) > 0$. We will take a closer look at this assumption below. Taking it as given, however, something can be said about aggregate demand as income changes.

Returning to the slope of the aggregate demand function, it can be seen from (13.9) that if the slope of $f(\cdot)$ becomes small enough at relatively low income levels and if the interest rate is low enough at some initially low income level, then the influence of income will dominate; aggregate demand will be upward sloping. In graphical terms the positive feedback loop in figure 13.1 is dominant. As income increases enough, the interest rate rises because $f(\cdot)$ slopes upward at an increasing rate; the negative influence could then come into play, possibly reducing the demand for goods. If this happens, the negative feedback loop in figure 13.1 becomes dominant and aggregate demand will have a nonlinear profile. In particular it may have a range in which the interest effect becomes so pronounced

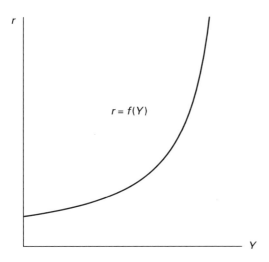

$r = f(Y)$

Figure 13.2
The temporary equilibrium interest rate as a function of aggregate income (LM curve)

that the slope of aggregate demand is negative. Here is a clear example of the possible emergence of *causal effect reversal* described in §3.1.4.

The monetary effect depends both on the influence of income on interest rates and on the sensitivity of the demand for goods to the opportunity cost of finance. Given a rising interest rate, the stronger the interest effect on the demand for goods, the stronger the monetary "crowding out" effect and the more negative the slope of aggregate demand will be when income becomes large enough.

We shall say that the monetary effect is *weak* if *for all* Y,

$$0 < \frac{\partial D^g}{\partial r} \cdot f'(Y) + \frac{\partial D^g}{\partial Y}; \tag{13.15}$$

it is *strong* if there exist values of Y such that

$$\frac{\partial D^g}{\partial r} \cdot f'(Y) + \frac{\partial D^g}{\partial Y} < 0; \tag{13.16}$$

and it is *very strong* if the slope of aggregate demand at a stationary state $\tilde{Y}$ is less than -1, that is,

$$\left[\frac{\partial D^g}{\partial r} \cdot f'(Y) + \frac{\partial D^g}{\partial Y} \right]_{\tilde{r}, \tilde{Y}} < -1. \tag{13.17}$$

If, in addition to the assumptions of normality of goods and money markets, the monetary interaction term behaves as follows,

$$\lim_{Y \to 0} \frac{\partial D^g(f(Y), Y)}{\partial r} \cdot f'(Y) = 0, \tag{13.18}$$

then the monetary influence at low income levels is negligible. The slope of aggregate demand will be positive; it may increase as Y increases and it may decrease if the monetary effect is strong. Suppose in addition that there exists Y^v such that

$$\lim_{Y \to Y^v} \frac{\partial D^g(f(Y), Y)}{\partial r} f'(Y) = 0, \tag{13.19}$$

then the income effect must again come to dominate the monetary interaction term and, as Y approaches Y^v, the slope of aggregate demand must be positive. Evidently, the slope of the aggregate demand function must change sign, implying the existence of a local minimizer Y^*. If this minimum is less than $\bar{Y}$, the potential supply, then the slope of aggregate demand will be positive when income is close enough to full employment income.

If the money and goods markets are normal, if the monetary effect is strong, and if the monetary interaction dies out at both small enough and large enough income levels, as given by (13.18) and (13.19), then we shall say that *the goods and money markets are Keynesian*. Later in this chapter we give sufficient conditions for normal markets to be Keynesian.

Let us summarize all this as:

PROPOSITION 13.1 (The Wave of Aggregate Demand)   *If the goods and money markets are Keynesian, then there is a wave of aggregate demand for goods. That is, $\theta'(Y)$ is positive when income is small enough. It may increase but it must subsequently decrease and become negative. It must increase again as income increases and be positive as income approaches a large enough income level denoted by Y^v.*

13.1.3   Persistent Fluctuations

Aggregate demand functions based on Keynesian markets are illustrated in figure 13.3, which illustrates some of the possibilities for aggregate behavior. Because there is a wave of aggregate demand, the sign of $\theta'(\cdot)$ must change twice, implying the existence of a local maximizer $Y^{**} < \tilde{Y}$

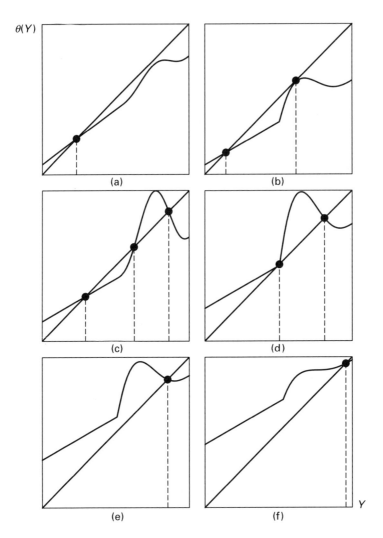

Figure 13.3
Examples of Keynesian aggregate demand functions with strong monetary effect

with local maximum $Y^M = \theta(Y^{**})$ as well as the local minimizer $Y^* > \tilde{Y}$ with local minimum $Y^m = \theta(Y^*)$. For values of Y below Y^{**}, $\theta'(Y)$ is positive because the income effect on demand dominates. For values of Y above Y^{**} but below Y^*, $\theta'(Y)$ is negative because the interest effect on aggregate demand dominates. The local minimum occurs because the interest effect dies out, so above Y^* the income effect again dominates. Let

$$V := (Y^m, Y^M).$$

Clearly, there exists a stationary state

$$\tilde{Y} \in V. \tag{13.20}$$

Assume that $Y^m < Y^{**} < Y^* < Y^M$, as shown in figure 13.4a. For values of Y below $\tilde{Y}$, $\theta(Y) > Y$. Aggregate income must expand monotonically until it reaches or exceeds $\tilde{Y}$. In particular $\theta(Y^m) > Y^m$, so once a trajectory exceeds Y^m, it cannot fall below. For values of Y above $\tilde{Y}$, $\theta(Y) < Y$, so aggregate income must contract monotonically until it reaches or falls below $\tilde{Y}$. But $\theta(Y) < Y^M$ for all $Y < Y^M$, so once a trajectory falls below Y^M it cannot rise above it. If

$$Y^M < Y^u = \min\{\overline{Y}, Y^v\}, \tag{13.21}$$

then no trajectory that enters V can escape. If the monetary effect is very strong $(\theta'(\tilde{Y}) < -1)$, then fluctuations persist for all trajectories that do not hit $\tilde{Y}$ exactly in finite time.

If $Y^m < Y^{**} < Y^M < Y^*$, then no fluctuations can fall below $\theta(Y^M)$ and fluctuations will persist in the set

$$V^M := (\theta(Y^M), Y^M),$$

as shown in figure 13.4b. Alternatively, if

$$Y^{**} < Y^m \quad \text{and} \quad \theta(Y^m) < Y^u,$$

then $\theta'(Y)$ is falling and $Y^m < \theta(Y) < \theta(Y^m)$ for all $Y \in (Y^m, \theta(Y^m))$. Consequently, fluctuations persist in the set

$$V^m := (Y^m, \theta(Y^m)),$$

as shown in figure 13.4c.

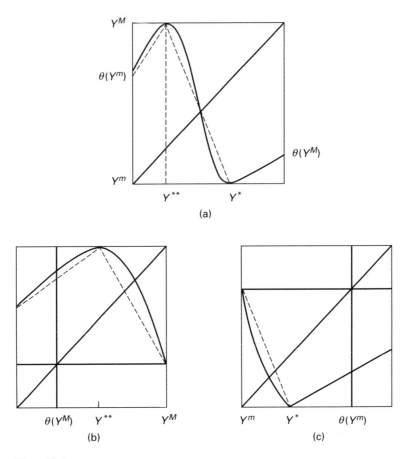

Figure 13.4
Three cases with persistent fluctuations

Given the market conditions assumed, there can be more than a single equilibrium. Indeed, there can be two, three, or more. Let us consider here cases for which the largest stationary state $\tilde{Y}$ belongs to V. The additional stationary states occur in the increasing part of aggregate demand where the income effect is dominant, as shown in figure 13.5c. Note that Y^2 must be unstable and Y^1 asymptotically stable. Assume (without loss of generality) that the other stationary states, if they exist, occur below Y^1. Now it is possible that trajectories that start above Y^m could fall below Y^2, in which case they would have to converge to a stationary state below this level, such as Y^1. Here again there are three basic possibilities for fluctuations to persist. In addition to a condition preventing an escape above $\bar{Y}$, trajectories must not fall below Y^2. The reasoning is analogous to the single equilibrium case.

These results say nothing about the qualitative character of the fluctuations when they exist. They might be periodic or, possibly, nonperiodic and irregular. If any of the chaos overshoot conditions given in theorems 7.1, 7.2, or 7.3 obtain (see the appendix), then unstable, nonperiodic (chaotic) trajectories and periodic trajectories of various orders will exist. For example, it is easy to construct conditions for which

$$\theta(Y^M) \le \theta^{-1}(Y^{**}) < Y^{**} < Y^M.$$

Then we have successive values that satisfy the Li-Yorke overshoot conditions of Theorem 7.1, as shown in figure 13.5.

If in addition the Misiurewicz expansivity conditions of Theorem 8.6 attain, then trajectories will be nonperiodic almost surely and by Theorem 8.8 will be unstable and chaotic almost surely. For details the reader should review chapters 7 and 8. What should be emphasized here is that *in the real/monetary macro theory it is the nonlinearities in the demand for goods and money and the interaction between the two markets that produce the preconditions for cycles or persistent irregular fluctuations.*

Putting all this together, we have:

PROPOSITION 13.2 (Persistent Fluctuations) *If markets are Keynesian, then*

(i) bounded fluctuations of aggregate income persist almost surely in a trapping set given by the following conditions.
Case I: *If $\tilde{Y}$ is unique or if $Y^2 < Y^m$, if $Y^M \le \bar{Y}$, and if*

$$Y^m < Y^{**} < Y^* < Y^M,$$

then V traps all fluctuations.
Case II: *If $\tilde{Y}$ is unique or if $\theta(Y^M) > Y^2$, if $Y^M < \bar{Y}$, and if*

$$Y^m < Y^{**} < Y^M < Y^*,$$

then V^M traps all fluctuations.
Case III: *If $\tilde{Y}$ is unique or if $Y^m > Y^2$, if $\theta(Y^m) < \bar{Y}$, and if*

$$Y^{**} < Y^m < Y^*,$$

then V^m traps all fluctuations.

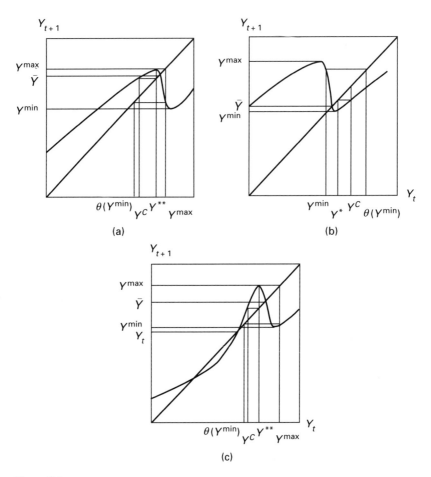

Figure 13.5
The Li-Yorke chaos conditions. Source: Day and Shafer (1985, 283).

(ii) If the chaos overshoot conditions of Theorem 7.1 are satisfied, both cyclic and chaotic trajectories will exist in the trapping set.

(iii) If the ergodic expansivity conditions of Theorem 8.6 hold, chaotic trajectories will emerge and persist for almost all initial conditions in the trapping set, frequencies of aggregate income values will converge to densities, averages of income values will obey the central limit theorem, and the macroeconomic model economy will generate data that looks very much like a stochastic process even in the absence of random shocks.

13.1.4 Escape from Chaos

If $Y^M > \overline{Y}$ and fluctuations exist in the neighborhood of the largest stationary state $\tilde{Y}$, then aggregate demand can rise above $\overline{Y}$. As $\theta(\cdot)$ is continuous, there exists an interval $E \subset V$ such that $\theta(E) = [\overline{Y}, Y^M]$. Any trajectory that enters E therefore "escapes" in one period, as shown in figure 13.6. Now consider the set of income levels in V that map into E. This is

$$E^2 = \theta^{-1}(E^1) \cap V.$$

Any trajectory that enters E^2 escapes in two periods. Let

$$E^3 = \theta^{-1}(E^2) \cap V.$$

Trajectories that enter E^3 escape in three periods. In general, let

$$E^n = \theta^{-1}(E^{n-1}) \cap V.$$

These are the points in V that escape in n periods. Let

$$U = \bigcup_{n=0}^{\infty} \theta^{-n}(E) \cap V.$$

Then U is an unstable set and all trajectories that begin in or enter U escape in a finite number of periods by exceeding $\overline{Y}$.

Escape from V can also occur if $Y^m < Y^2$ because there will exist $Y \in V$ such that $\theta(Y) < Y^2$. Just as before, the continuity of $\theta(\cdot)$ guarantees that there will be an interval E in V such that $\theta(Y) < Y^2$ for all $Y \in E$. Then an unstable set U can be constructed in the same manner as before.

The above reasoning leaves open the questions as to whether all or almost all trajectories will escape V. The answer to these questions requires some technical concepts, which were developed in chapter 8.

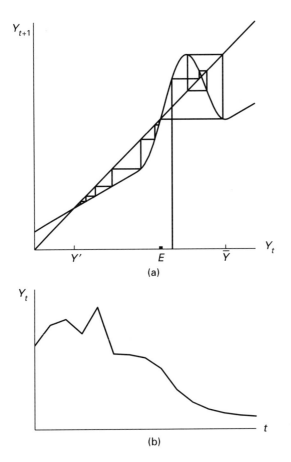

(a)

(b)

Figure 13.6
Escape from chaos. (a) The escape set. (b) Irregular fluctuations followed by a "free fall" to a low-level equilibrium.

Recall that if a map $\theta(\cdot)$ is *expansive* on a given set, say S, then $|\theta'(Y)| > 1$ for all $Y \in S$. It is *strongly* expansive if several additional technical conditions are met, as described in Theorem 8.9. If $\theta(\cdot)$ is strongly expansive on $V \backslash E$, then Theorem 8.10 tells us that escape will occur almost surely.

The following summarizes these findings.

PROPOSITION 13.3 (Escape) *Suppose markets are Keynesian.*

(i) If

$$Y^M > Y^u \quad with \quad Y^m > Y^2,$$

then some fluctuating trajectories will escape the Keynesian regime. If θ is expansive on $V \backslash E$, then trajectories escape almost surely.

(ii) If $Y^m < Y^2$ with $Y^M < Y^u$, then some fluctuating trajectories in V will fall below Y^2 and converge to Y^1. If θ is strongly expansive on $V \backslash E$, then trajectories will converge to Y^1 almost surely.

(iii) If $Y^M > Y^u$ and $Y^m < Y^2$, then some fluctuating trajectories will eventually escape the Keynesian regime, and some will eventually converge to Y^1. If θ is strongly expansive on E where E is the set of points that map above $\overline{Y}$ or below Y^2, then both of these two eventualities will occur with positive measure and one or the other of them will occur almost surely.

When the conditions described in this proposition occur, then some trajectories in V may exhibit nonperiodic, possibly chaotic-appearing fluctuations, but then escape, either converging to a low-level Keynesian equilibrium (Y^1), as shown in figure 13.6, or jumping outside the Keynesian regime altogether.

13.2 An IY-LM Model

Most expositors, including Keynes himself, generally cast the real/monetary theory in somewhat less general terms than has been done above.[12] They did this in order to facilitate a graphical exposition of comparative statics, but the assumptions they used for this purpose are also convenient in the dynamic context we are pursuing. They enable us to give stronger conditions on the various possible qualitative behaviors and to see more clearly how the causal-effect-reversing wave of aggregate demand emerges.

13.2.1   The Model

For the monetary sector, suppose the demand for money can be decomposed into separable transactions and liquidity components,

$$D^m(r, Y) := \kappa Y + \mathscr{L}(r), \tag{13.22}$$

which is defined for all $Y \geq 0$, for all $r \geq r^0$, where $r^0 \geq 0$, and $\kappa > 0$. The first term on the right is called the *transactions demand for money*, and $1/\kappa$ is called the *transactions velocity* of money. The second term on the right is called the *liquidity demand for money*, and $\mathscr{L}(\cdot)$ is called the *liquidity preference* function. If the liquidity preference function is downward sloping and convex, that is, if

$$\mathscr{L}'(r) < 0, \mathscr{L}''(r) > 0 \quad \text{for all} \quad r > r^0, \tag{13.23}$$

then liquidity demand for money increases at an increasing rate with decreases in the interest rate.

Assume also that the supply of money is constant at a fixed value M so that

$$S^m(r, Y) \equiv M. \tag{13.24}$$

Then the temporary equilibrium interest rate $r = f(Y)$ satisfies

$$\mathscr{L}(r) + \kappa Y = M. \tag{13.25}$$

In this context $f(\cdot)$ is called the *LM function*. Taking the total derivative, we get

$$f'(Y) = -\frac{\frac{\partial D^m}{\partial Y}}{\frac{\partial D^m}{\partial r}} = -\frac{\kappa}{\mathscr{L}'(r)} > 0. \tag{13.26}$$

It follows that $f(\cdot)$ is convex, that is, $f''(Y) > 0$. This means that the money market is normal. Assume that

$$\lim_{r \to r^0+} \mathscr{L}(r) = \infty \quad \text{and} \quad \lim_{r \to \infty} \mathscr{L}(r) = L^{00}. \tag{13.27}$$

Then for some $r' > r^0$,

$$f(0) = r' \quad \text{and} \quad \lim_{Y \to \bar{\bar{Y}}} f(Y) = \infty \tag{13.28}$$

where $\bar{\bar{Y}} = (M - L^0)/\kappa$.

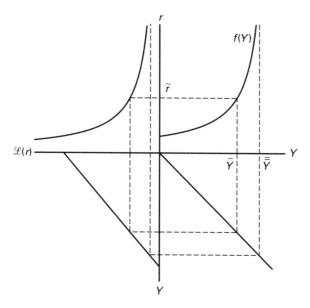

Figure 13.7
The components of money demand and temporary money market equilibrium

The relationship between $\mathscr{L}(\cdot)$ and $f(\cdot)$ is shown in figure 13.7. Notice that $\bar{\bar{Y}}$ places a new bound on the Keynesian regime because for incomes above $\bar{\bar{Y}}$ there would not be enough money to meet transaction demand. Such a bound need not arise in the general formulation above (though it is consistent with that case) because the supply of money was assumed to be endogenous. Let us define

$$Y^u = \min\{\bar{Y}, \bar{\bar{Y}}\}.$$

Aggregate income in the Keynesian regime with money demand defined by (13.22)–(13.28) is confined to $[0, Y^u]$.

Next, assume that the demand for goods is comprised of separate consumption and investment components and that these in turn consist of autonomous and induced components as follows. Let E be the sum of *autonomous* consumption and *autonomous* investment; that is, the private sector expenditures that would be made independently of current aggregate income and interest rates. Let G be autonomous government expenditure that is, likewise, independent of current aggregate income. Suppose

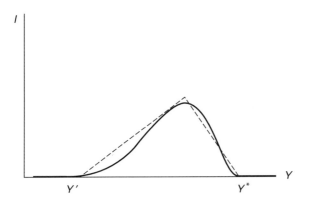

Figure 13.8
The wave of induced investment. The IY curve. The dashed lines indicate piecewise linear
forms to be discussed in chapter 14.

next that *induced* consumption is given by the *induced consumption function*, which is assumed to be

$$C(r, Y) := (1 - \tau)\alpha Y \tag{13.29}$$

where α is the *marginal propensity to consume*, $0 < \alpha < 1$, $(1 - \tau)Y$ is *dis-
posable* income, and τ is the income tax rate. Assume that induced investment is given by the *induced investment function*

$$I(r, Y) \equiv 0, 0 \leq Y \leq Y' \quad \text{and} \quad \lim_{r \to \infty} I(r, Y) = 0. \tag{13.30}$$

Assume also that

$$\partial I / \partial r \leq 0 \quad \text{and} \quad \partial I / \partial Y > 0. \tag{13.31}$$

When income is sufficiently low (and excess capacity and unemployment sufficiently high), no induced investment takes place. But when income exceeds the threshold $Y' \geq 0$, investment is stimulated by falling
interest rates or by increasing income levels. However, when interest
rates increase enough, the demand for investment goods goes to zero.
There is a wave of induced investment. This property is illustrated in figure 13.8.

The aggregate demand for goods is

$$D^g(r, Y) := E + G + \alpha(1 - \tau)Y + \mu I(r, Y) \tag{13.32}$$

where $\mu \geq 0$ is the investment *intensity parameter* or investment demand "shifter" that indicates how important induced investment is.

The temporary equilibrium condition on the money market given by the LM curve can be used to eliminate the interest rate term in the investment demand function and to obtain an *investment-income* (IY) function defined by

$$h(Y) := I(f(Y), Y). \tag{13.33}$$

The aggregate demand for goods can now be expressed by

$$\theta(Y) := D^g(f(Y), Y) = E + G + aY + \mu h(Y) \tag{13.34}$$

where $a = (1 - \tau)\alpha$. Then the aggregate output adjustment equation (13.5) becomes

$$Y_{t+1} = \theta(Y_t) := E + G + aY_t + \mu h(Y_t). \tag{13.35}$$

13.2.2 The Intensity of Investment

The parameter μ mirrors past controversies concerning the importance of induced investment. If $\mu = 0$, *induced* investment plays no role and the "real" economy is independent of the monetary sector. In this case equation (13.35) reduces to a linear equation with slope $a = (1 - \tau)\alpha$ such that $0 < a < 1$. The adjustment process must be asymptotically stable, and the unique, stable stationary state is $\tilde{Y} = (E + G)/(1 - a)$. If, on the other hand, μ is positive, then induced investment matters and so does money. The interaction between the monetary and real sectors can lead to complications. The task of exploring the various possibilities is somewhat simplified now. The only nonlinear component is the induced investment function $I(r, Y)$.

The slope of the aggregate demand function is

$$\theta'(Y) = a + \mu h'(Y) = a + \mu \left[\frac{\partial I}{\partial r} f'(Y) + \frac{\partial I}{\partial Y} \right]. \tag{13.36}$$

The term $\partial I / \partial r$ is negative by hypothesis and $f'(Y)$ was found above to be positive, so the second term on the right is negative. However, the third term on the right is positive. From this expression the counterparts of the monetary effect conditions given in (13.15)–(13.17) can be derived. The monetary effect is *weak* if for all Y,

$$\theta'(Y) > 0 \quad \text{or} \quad \frac{k}{|\mathscr{L}'(r)|} < \frac{a + \mu \frac{\partial I}{\partial Y}}{\mu |\frac{\partial I}{\partial r}|}. \tag{13.37}$$

The monetary effect is *strong* if there exist Y such that

$$\theta'(Y) < 0 \quad \text{or} \quad \frac{a + \mu \frac{\partial I}{\partial Y}}{\mu |\frac{\partial I}{\partial r}|} < \frac{k}{|\mathscr{L}'(r)|}. \tag{13.38}$$

The monetary effect is *very strong* if

$$\theta'(\tilde{Y}) < -1 \quad \text{or} \quad \left[\frac{a + \mu \frac{\partial I}{\partial Y} + 1}{\mu |\frac{\partial I}{\partial r}|}\right]_{\tilde{r}, \tilde{Y}} < \left[\frac{k}{|\mathscr{L}'(r)|}\right]_{\tilde{r}, \tilde{Y}}. \tag{13.39}$$

From these expressions Proposition 13.1 follows.

13.2.3   Macroeconomic Adjustments: Generic Properties

The largest stationary state, $\tilde{Y}$, depends on all the parameters of the model. In particular it depends on μ. Write this dependence as $\tilde{Y}(\mu)$. Obviously, $\tilde{Y}(0) = (E + G)/(1 - a)$. When μ is very small, $\tilde{Y}(\mu)$ must be close to $\tilde{Y}(0)$ and the dynamics are little affected. When μ increases enough, however, the maximum $\tilde{Y}(\mu)$ can change a lot, depending, of course, on the nature of induced investment and demand for money.

This dependence can display two canonical forms, as shown in figure 13.9. In the first case (a), the single maximum stationary state increases monotonically as μ increases. In the second case (b), a bifurcation point μ is reached at $\theta'(Y) = a + \mu^s h'(Y) = 1$, and a second stationary state Y^2 emerges for this value. For $\mu > \mu^s$, there must be three stationary states in which the larger one, $\tilde{Y}$, falls in the range for which aggregate demand is downward sloping and for which the monetary effect is strong. For still larger values of μ, the monetary effect must become very strong.

To clarify this, we observe that as the IY function has a maximizer $Y^\# \in (Y', Y^v)$, it must be that

$$h'(Y) \begin{cases} > 0, & Y' < Y < Y^\# \\ = 0, & Y = Y^\# \\ \leq 0, & Y^\# < Y < Y^u. \end{cases}$$

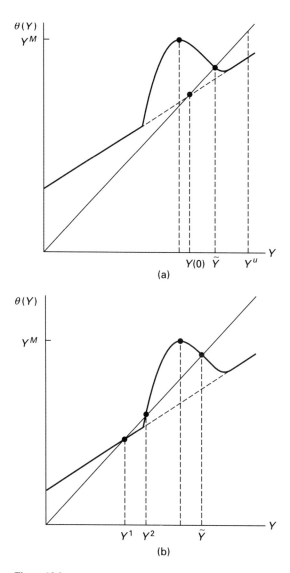

Figure 13.9
Canonical forms for aggregate demand. (a) Only a single stationary state can occur. (b) One, two, or three stationary states can occur.

For $Y \neq Y^{\#}$, the term $\mu|h'(Y)|$ can be made as large as we please. In particular there must exist a value of μ, say $\mu_1 \geq \mu_0$, such that

$$\mu h'(\tilde{Y}) \begin{cases} > -(1+a), & \mu_0 < \mu < \mu_1 \\ = -(1+a), & \mu = \mu_1 \\ < -(1+a), & \mu > \mu_1 \end{cases}$$

In the first case $\tilde{Y}$ is asymptotically stable; in the third case $\tilde{Y}$ is unstable and fluctuations emerge near $\tilde{Y}$.

Can fluctuations persist? To answer this, note that the local maximum value of Y^M increases monotonically with μ, so there exists a value, say μ^e, such that

$$Y^M(\mu^e) = Y^u.$$

For any $\mu > \mu^e$, therefore, an escape interval exists and some trajectories can escape the Keynesian regime. In the three-stationary-state case it could happen that values of μ exist for which $\theta(Y) < Y^2$, so that convergence to Y^1 will occur.

To summarize, we have:

PROPOSITION 13.4 (Convergence, Fluctuations, and Escape) *Given the Keynesian aggregate demand functions for money and goods described above, there exist values of μ, say μ^1, μ^2, μ^e, with $\mu^1 \leq \mu^2 < \mu^e$, such that*

(i) for all $\mu \in [0, \mu^1]$, the adjustment process converges asymptotically to a unique stationary state;

(ii) for all $\mu > \mu^2$, expanding fluctuations in aggregate demand occur near $\tilde{Y}$;

(iii) for all $\mu > \mu^e$ some trajectories in V escape the Keynesian regime.

(iv) If there are three stationary states Y^1, Y^2, $\tilde{Y}$ and if there exists a value μ^f such that $\theta(Y^M(\mu^f)) < Y^2$, then some trajectories in V escape V and converge asymptotically to Y^1.

(v) For values of $\mu^2 < \mu < \min\{\mu^e, \mu^f\}$, there exists a trapping set in V and all trajectories that enter V remain in V. For almost all such trajectories fluctuations persist. The persistent fluctuations can converge to cycles or they may be strongly chaotic, depending on the exact character of the underlying functions and whether or not they satisfy the strong chaos conditions referred to in Proposition 13.3.

13.3   Numerical Experiments

All of the possibilities that have been derived in theory can be obtained using explicit functional forms. First, let the liquidity demand for money be represented by the equation

$$\mathscr{L}(r) := L^{00} + \lambda/(r - r^0), \quad r > r^0 \tag{13.40}$$

where λ is a parameter. For simplicity, assume that $r^0 = 0$. If the transactions demand is κY where κ is a parameter, then the LM curve is

$$r = f(Y) = \lambda/(M - \kappa Y - L^{00}). \tag{13.41}$$

It is defined on the open interval $(0, Y^v)$ where $Y^v = (M - L^{00})/\kappa$. These functions were illustrated in figure 13.7. Clearly, the money market is normal and Keynesian.

For the investment function use

$$I(r, Y) := \begin{cases} 0, & 0 \le Y \le Y' \\ b(Y - Y')^\beta (\rho/r)^\gamma, & Y \ge Y' \end{cases} \tag{13.42}$$

where Y', b, ρ, β, and γ are parameters. For income below Y' there would be no induced investment. As Y rises above Y', capacity utilization rises and stimulates investment.

Think of ρ as a target rate of return. If $r = \rho$ investment is governed by the capacity utilization term; if the $r < \rho$ the effect is stimulating. If $r < \rho$, then the effect is depressing. The larger the parameter γ is, the more pronounced are these influences. With this investment function it is easy to see that the goods market is normal and Keynesian.

Substituting (13.41) into (13.42), we obtain the IY function

$$I = h(Y) := \begin{cases} 0, & 0 \le Y \le Y' \\ B(Y - Y')^\beta (Y^v - Y)^\gamma, & Y' \le Y \le Y^v, \end{cases} \tag{13.43}$$

where $B = b(\rho\kappa/\lambda)^\gamma$, $Y^v = (M - L^{00})/\kappa$. This function has the "cocked hat" shape shown in figure 13.8.

Using the linear consumption function (13.29) with (13.43), the adjustment equation (13.35) becomes

$$Y_{t+1} = \begin{cases} E + G + aY_t, & 0 \le Y \le Y' \\ E + G + aY_t + \mu B(Y_t - Y')^\beta (Y^v - Y)^\gamma, & Y' \le Y \le Y^u \end{cases} \tag{13.44}$$

where $Y^u = \min\{\bar{Y}, Y^v\}$.

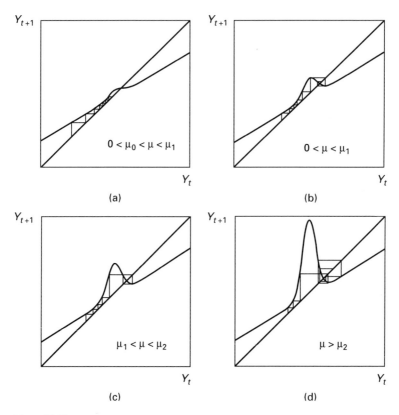

Figure 13.10
Comparative Keynesian dynamics. Qualitative changes caused by shifts in the intensity of induced investment. (a) Monotonic convergence. (b) Cyclic convergence. (c) Stable two-period cycle. (d) Conditions for nonperiodic fluctuations satisfied.

For trajectories to be confined to a trapping set, the conditions of Proposition 13.2 must be met. Otherwise, trajectories can escape the Keynesian regime as discussed in Proposition 13.3 and Proposition 13.4. Phase diagrams of equation (13.44) are shown in figure 13.10 for four different positive values of μ. If μ is very small, as shown in figure 13.10a, then induced investment cannot change the picture very much from what it is when $\mu = 0$. Any sequence of output adjustments converges monotonically to an income level somewhat bigger than $\tilde{Y}(0) = (E + G)/(1 - a)$. As μ is increased, however, the dynamics of aggregate income can change a very great deal, as shown in figures 13.10b, 13.10c, and 13.10d.

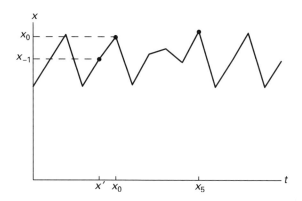

Figure 13.11
An aggregate income trajectory that passes the LIMPY chaos test, $x_1 < x_0 < x_5$

Thus, in figure 13.10b cycles emerge but converge to a stable, stationary state, while in figure 13.10c a stable two-period cycle occurs. As μ increases still more, this cycle increases in complexity, as shown in figure 13.10d.

Consider, for example, the value of aggregate income labeled x_0 in figure 13.11. Clearly

$$\theta(x_0) < \theta^4(x_0) < \theta^2(x_0) < \theta^3(x_0) < x_0 < \theta^5(x_0). \tag{13.45}$$

Hence,

$$\theta(x_0) < x_0 < \theta^5(x_0), \tag{13.46}$$

which satisfies the sufficient condition for chaos given by Theorem 7.3. Also note,

$$\theta^6(x_{-1}) = (\theta^2)^3(x_{-1}) > \theta^2(x_{-1}) \tag{13.47}$$

so the map $\theta^2(\cdot)$ also satisfies Theorem 7.3.

To see if chaos occurs almost everywhere, Theorem 8.6 must be considered. The criterion $1/|\theta'(y)|^{\frac{1}{2}}$ has been computed for one such curve. Its graph, which is shown in figure 13.12, has the required convex segments on the intervals corresponding to the monotonic segments of the map. This suggests that Theorem 8.6 may hold. If so, the process possesses an absolutely continuous invariant measure and behaves like a stationary stochastic process for at least some parameter values. This conjecture is illustrated in figure 13.13, which gives the computed density function for a sample trajectory and its sample means.

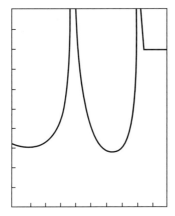

Figure 13.12
The criteria for the Schwartzian derivative condition

13.4   The Static IS-LM Framework

To see how the present dynamic theory is related to the earlier IS-LM model,[13] define a function $g(\cdot)$ with $r = g(Y)$ such that

$$D^g(g(Y), Y) = Y. \qquad (13.48)$$

This gives the locus of (r, Y) pairs that bring about equilibrium on the goods market. The function $g(y)$ is called the *IS curve*. Suppose that $f'(Y) > 0$ and $g'(Y) < 0$. Then Keynesian equilibrium lies at the intersection of the two curves shown in figure 13.14. The IS curve can have a positive slope at high levels of income; there could then be three distinct Keynesian equilibria, as shown in figure 13.14b.

We have assumed that the LM curve, which plays an explicit role in the dynamic analysis, has the conventional upward-sloping shape shown in figure 13.2. A further question of interest is what the shape of the IS curve would be, were we to assume equilibrium (instead of adjustment) on the goods market. Wouldn't it have to have bizarre shapes in order to be consistent with instability, especially in the extreme case of chaos?

To answer this question, consider the criterion for a very strong monetary effect (13.39) for determining local instability of the maximum stationary state, $\tilde{Y}$. This inequality implies that

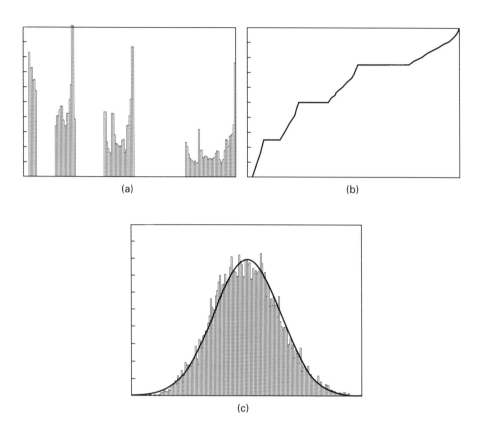

Figure 13.13
Ergodic behavior. (a) Histogram of GNP values. (b) Cumulative distribution. (c) Histogram
of sample means and the normal curve. Source: Day and Shafer (1987).

$$f'(\tilde{Y}) > \left. \frac{\frac{(1+a)}{\mu} + \frac{\partial I}{\partial Y}}{-\frac{\partial I}{\partial r}} \right|_{\substack{r=\tilde{r} \\ Y=\tilde{Y}}}, \tag{13.49}$$

which states that the slope of the LM function must be great enough at $\tilde{Y}$. Substituting $g(Y)$ into (13.32) to obtain (13.48) and taking total differentials, the slope of the IS curve is

$$g'(Y) = \frac{\frac{1-a}{\mu} - \frac{\partial I}{\partial Y}}{\frac{\partial I}{\partial r}}. \tag{13.50}$$

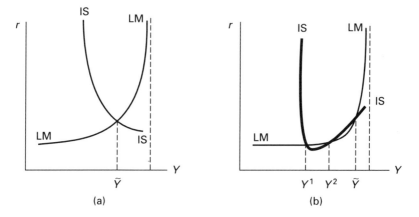

Figure 13.14
The IS-LM model of real/monetary equilibrium. (a) A unique equilibrium. (b) Multiple equilibria.

By hypothesis, $\partial I/\partial r < 0$ and $\partial I/\partial Y > 0$. Evidently, the slope can be positive if there are points where the income effect and the intensity of induced investment are large enough. The income effect dominates the interest effect at low income levels but the interest effect dominates at high levels. Consequently, if the slope of the IS curve is positive, it must occur at relatively high levels, giving the fishhook shape illustrated in figure 13.14b. In this case, there can be three stationary states. These correspond to the situation illustrated already in figures 13.3c and again in 13.5c.

Adding the term $\frac{2}{\partial I/\partial r}$ to both sides of (13.51), the very strong monetary effect condition (13.49) can be reexpressed as

$$f'(Y) > g'(Y) - \frac{2}{\mu \frac{\partial I}{\partial r}}. \tag{13.51}$$

Clearly, the larger the intensity of induced investment and/or the larger the interest effect on induced investment, μ, the less steep the LM curve need be to produce instability, regardless of whether the IS curve is upward or downward sloping. If $\partial I/\partial Y \equiv 0$, as is often assumed in the early Keynesian literature, then the IS curve is always downward sloping and as μ increases it becomes progressively flatter, thus eventually insuring the emergence of fluctuations. To summarize, *locally expanding but bounded periodic or nonperiodic fluctuations occur generically with conventional-looking IS and LM curves.*

13.5 Summary and Conclusions

The analysis of this chapter has shown that all the fundamental modes of dynamic behavior can occur in the real/monetary macro model of the economy when supply adjusts to demand in the goods market, when nonlinearities are present in aggregate demands for money and goods, and when the interaction between real and monetary sectors is strong enough. Convergence to stationary states, convergence to cycles, persistent unstable, nonperiodic (chaotic) fluctuations, and nonperiodic fluctuations followed by an escape above potential demand or by a free fall to a low-level stationary state—all of these types of behavior can occur and all are generic for intuitively and economically plausible aggregate demand functions.

It was emphasized that the derivation of these comprehensive results rests on strong simplifying assumptions that block out the potential role of other important variables, such as capital accumulation, price changes, money supply changes, and so forth. In particular, growth in these variables could have the effect of dampening or even suppressing fluctuations so that aggregate income would grow at fluctuating rates or even more or less smoothly, as does happen in reality during some periods of relative stability. But fluctuations could still be a latent potentiality that could reemerge when these variables slowed their rates of change. Because real world empirical macroeconomic data do fluctuate irregularly much of the time, the present theory may very well provide a part of the explanation.

14 Plausible Parameters, Counterfactual Histories, and the Robustness of Chaos

Dynamic ... analysis ... liberates economists from the necessity of having separate theories of the "turning points." ... Even a simple [dynamic] theory ... can explain all four phases of an idealized cycle.
—Paul A. Samuelson, "Dynamic Process Analysis"

Linear functions are used in many standard macroeconomic textbooks, quantitative policy analyses, and theoretical studies. They are particularly convenient for calculating the multiplier effects of changes in policy instruments.[1] But such comparative static multiplier analyses rest on the asymptotic stability of equilibria. If the fixprice equilibrium is unstable, the fluctuations that arise are explosive and unbounded. Such trajectories would have to escape the Keynesian regime because they must eventually violate the labor or capacity constraints (equations (13.3) and (13.4)), or because some variables would be forced to become negative. Consequently, the simple multiplier model cannot be used to study fluctuations. If, however, the non-negativity restrictions usually ignored in such treatments are made explicit, then the aggregate demand functions take on "kinked" or piecewise linear forms. The kinks bound any fluctuations, so the constraints are not violated. Cycles and chaos, as well as stable, convergent behavior, can occur.

The piecewise linear version has three advantages. First, direct use can be made of plausible parameter values that have been developed for the linear model to find out which types of qualitative behavior are empirically relevant. Second, the piecewise linear model enables an especially precise and comprehensive analysis of stability, cycles, chaos, and ergodicity. It can then be seen exactly how various modes of aggregate behavior depend on the underlying parameters of demand and supply. Third, it involves an especially clear-cut example of multiple—phase dynamics.[2]

14.1 Aggregate Demand and the Adjustment Process

14.1.1 The Monetary Sector

Suppose the demand for money has the Keynesian form given in equation (13.27), but let the liquidity demand function $\mathscr{L}(\cdot)$ be given a piecewise linear form defined in

$$\mathscr{L}(r) := \begin{cases} \infty, & r < r^0 \\ L^0, & r = r^0 \\ L^0 - \lambda(r - r^0), & r^0 < r < r^{00} \\ L^{00}, & r^{00} \le r \end{cases} \tag{14.1}$$

where $L^{00} = L^0 - \lambda(r^{00} - r^0)$. This form indicates that liquidity demand can absorb any amount of money for interest rates below r^0; for interest rates above r^0, it declines in a linear dependence on r determined by λ, the marginal influence of interest above r^0. The parameter L^0 is the minimum level of money demand compatible with $r = r^0$. The liquidity demand falls from this level as the interest rate increases until it reaches its lower bound L^{00} at the interest rate r^{00}.

Substitute (14.1) into the money demand function (equation 13.22). Assume a fixed money supply M. If income is large enough, then, setting demand equal to supply and solving for the market-clearing interest rate, we get $r = r^0 + (\kappa/\lambda)(Y - Y^{**})$, where $Y^{**} = (M - L^0)/\kappa$ is the income level at which the interest rate is equal to its minimum level, r^0. Consequently, the LM curve has two segments corresponding to the second and third segments of $\mathscr{L}(\cdot)$ in (14.1). Thus,

$$r = f(Y) := \begin{cases} r^0, & 0 \le Y \le Y^{**} \\ r^0 + (\kappa/\lambda)(Y - Y^{**}), & Y^{**} \le Y < \bar{\bar{Y}}. \end{cases} \tag{14.2}$$

The function is unbounded at $\bar{\bar{Y}} := (M - L^{00})/\kappa$ and undefined above $\bar{\bar{Y}}$. *In what follows we shall, for simplicity and without loss of generality, assume that $r^0 = 0$.*

The derivation of the LM curve is illustrated in figure 14.1. The liquidity demand curve is shown in the upper left quadrant. The market-clearing equation linking liquidity demand, transactions demand, and the supply of money is shown in the lower left quadrant. The 45° line shown in the lower right quadrant translates liquidity demand from the lower vertical axis to the right horizontal axis. The derived LM curve, which is upward sloping for incomes above Y^{**}, is shown in the upper right quadrant. Notice that the axis in each direction indicates increasing positive values.

The interval $(0, Y^{**})$ is the *liquidity trap* where changes in aggregate income have little impact on interest rates. Above Y^{**} the interest rate is sensitive and the crowding-out effect of the transactions demand for cash drives interest rates upward in a linear dependence on income. When income exceeds $\bar{\bar{Y}}$, the model breaks down. A switch in regime would be

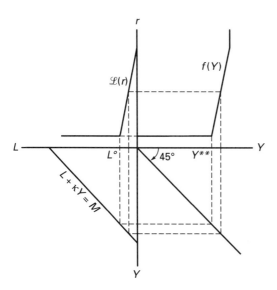

Figure 14.1
Derivation of the LM curve

necessary then to explain how changes in the price level, the transaction velocity, or the money supply take place so as to permit continued functioning of the system.

The piecewise or kinked linear profile of the LM curve approximates its smooth counterpart shown in figure 13.2. It should be noted that the goodness of the approximation depends on where the linear segments are placed (by choosing κ, λ, and L^0).

14.1.2 Investment Demand

Now turn to the induced demand for investment goods. Suppose that below a threshold Y', excess capacity is so great that orders for investment goods are zero even though interest rates may be very low. Above the threshold Y', suppose income has a stimulating effect on investment. Suppose also that the real interest rate, which is the opportunity cost of investing in new capacity, has a depressing effect on investment. If disinvestment is not important in the short run, induced investment can be represented by[3]

$$I(r, Y) := \max\{0, \beta(Y - Y') - \gamma r\}. \tag{14.3}$$

Recall that at incomes below Y^{**}, interest rates are not influenced by the income level. If

$$Y^{**} = (M - L^0)/\kappa > Y', \tag{14.4}$$

then investment is not depressed by the interest effect in the income range $[Y', Y^{**}]$ because the money market rate of interest does not change in this interval. These conditions mean that *investment begins to be stimulated by income increases before money market crowding raises interest rates.*

Substituting the LM function (14.2) into the investment function (14.3) so as to eliminate the interest rate, we get the IY relation that incorporates both investment multiplier and monetary crowding-out effects. It has three or four branches depending on the strength of the monetary interaction. The first branch occurs in the range $0 \leq Y \leq Y'$ when induced investment is zero because of excess capacity. (Autonomous investment may still be positive.) The second branch occurs for incomes between the investment threshold Y' and Y^{**}, where interest is at its lower bound but the stimulating effect of income on induced investment is operating. Thus,

$$\begin{aligned} h(Y) &= \beta(Y - Y') - \gamma r^0 \\ &= \beta(Y - Y') \quad \text{since} \quad r^0 = 0. \end{aligned} \tag{14.5}$$

The slope of the IY function in this income range is β.

The third branch occurs after the transactions demand pushes the interest rate up out of the liquidity trap and the investment-depressing effect of interest comes into play. Then we have

$$\begin{aligned} h(Y) &= \beta(Y - Y') - \gamma[r^0 + (\kappa/\lambda)(Y - Y^{**})] \\ &= (\gamma\kappa/\lambda)Y^{**} - \beta Y' + [\beta - (\kappa\gamma/\lambda)]Y \quad \text{if} \quad r^0 = 0. \end{aligned} \tag{14.6}$$

The slope here is

$$\sigma := \beta - \kappa\gamma/\lambda, \tag{14.7}$$

so it must be less than the slope in the preceding regime. The level of interest required to clear the money market rises when income increases beyond Y^{**}. This depresses investment by reducing the stimulating effect of income increases. This crowding out is enhanced by increases in κ or γ or by decreases in λ or β. Alternatively, we can say that crowding out is enhanced if the ratio of interest rate effects γ/λ is greater than the ratio of income effects β/κ. I shall call σ the *monetary effect*.

If σ is positive, then the marginal response of investment to changes in income is smaller above the threshold Y^{**} because of the depressing interest rate effect, but it is still positive. Set $h(Y) = 0$ and solve for Y. We get

$$Y^* := \beta Y' - [\kappa(\gamma/\lambda)\,Y^{**}]/\sigma$$

$$:= [\beta Y' - (\gamma/\lambda)(M - L^0)]/\sigma. \tag{14.8}$$

Then the investment function can be written as

$$I = h(Y) := \begin{cases} 0, & Y \in \mathscr{R}^1 := [0, Y') \\ \beta(Y - Y'), & Y \in \mathscr{R}^2 := [Y', Y^{**}) \\ \sigma(Y - Y^*), & Y \in \mathscr{R}^3 := [Y^{**}, Y^u]. \end{cases} \tag{14.9}$$

The bound Y^u that figures in $\mathscr{R}^3$ is the smaller of full employment income $\bar{Y}$ or $\bar{\bar{Y}} = (M - L^{00})/\kappa$, which is the income level that would be possible if the entire money supply, net of the minimal liquidity requirement L^{00}, is devoted to transactions. If σ is positive, the investment function has the appearance shown in figure 14.2a.

When σ is negative, investment *declines* where aggregate income exceeds Y^{**} and is driven to zero at Y^*. For incomes above this point, induced investment is eliminated and only autonomous investment remains; just as in the smooth model of §13.2, there is a *wave of induced investment*. Instead of three regimes, there are four, and the investment-income IY function can be written

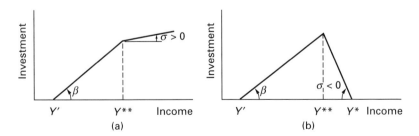

Figure 14.2
The IY function with weak (a) and strong (b) monetary effects.

$$I = h(Y) := \begin{cases} 0, & Y \in R_1 := [0, Y'] \\ \beta(Y - Y'), & Y \in R_2 := [Y', Y^{**}] \\ \sigma(Y - Y^*), & Y \in R_3 := [Y^{**}, Y^*] \\ 0, & Y \in R_4 := [Y^*, Y^u], \end{cases} \tag{14.10}$$

which has the appearance shown in figure 14.2b. The sets R_i, $i = 1, \ldots, 4$ are the phase zones that determine which branch of the investment function is active.

The regime-switching character of the IY function is a consequence of the linear forms for money and investment demand (14.1) and (14.3). We could think of it as approximating a smooth function where the marginal income effect is fairly stable over wide ranges but changes more rapidly in certain critical regions. The interval $[0, Y']$ approximates a situation when investment is very low due to extreme excess capacity. The "liquidity trap" range of income $[0, Y^{**}]$ approximates a region where the interest rate changes very little with changes in Y, so the interval $[Y', Y^{**}]$ approximates a range where investment responds directly to increasing income and without the depressing effect of increasing interest rates; the range $[Y^{**}, Y^*]$ corresponds to a region where the interest rate is sensitive to growing money demand and has a crowding effect on investment; the range above Y^* is the area where endogenous investment is severely reduced because of high interest rates.

14.1.3 Consumption and Autonomous Demand

The model is completed by the consumption function and the components of autonomous demand assumed in §13.2. The induced consumption demand was assumed to be $C(r, Y) := aY$ where $a = (1 - \tau)\alpha$, in which as before α is the marginal propensity to consume and τ is the average tax rate. Define the constant expenditure term $A = E + G$, where E is the sum of autonomous investment and autonomous consumption, and where G is government expenditure.

14.1.4 Aggregate Demand and the Monetary Effect

Just as in the model of §13.2, let μ be an intensity parameter that enables us to vary exogenously the importance of induced investment in aggregate demand. Substituting equation (14.10) into equation (13.35), we see that aggregate demand has four branches corresponding to the branches of the investment function. Thus,

$$\theta(Y) = E + G + (1 - \tau)\alpha Y + \mu h(Y)$$
$$= \theta_i(Y) := A_i + a_i Y, \quad Y \in \mathscr{R}^i, \tag{14.11}$$

where

$$a_1 := (1 - \tau)\alpha, \qquad A_1 := E + G$$
$$a_2 := (1 - \tau)\alpha + \mu\beta, \quad A_2 := E + G - \mu\beta Y'$$
$$a_3 := (1 - \tau)\alpha + \mu\sigma, \quad A_3 := E + G - \mu\sigma Y^*$$
$$a_4 := (1 - \tau)\alpha, \qquad A_4 := E + G.$$

If σ is positive, remember that $\mathscr{R}^4 = \varnothing$ and that $\mathscr{R}^3$ depends on whether σ is positive *or* negative. A positive change in the investment intensity parameter μ has the effect of shifting aggregate demand upward in regimes 2 and 3.

The slope of aggregate demand must be positive in regimes 1, 2, and 4 but can be negative in regime 3. Corresponding to the three conditions in (13.37)–(13.38), the monetary effect is *weak* if

$$a_3 > 0 \quad \text{or} \quad \frac{\kappa}{\lambda} < \frac{(1 - \tau)\alpha + \mu\beta}{\mu\gamma}; \tag{14.12}$$

it is *strong* if

$$a_3 < 0 \quad \text{or} \quad \frac{\kappa}{\lambda} > \frac{(1 - \tau)\alpha + \mu\beta}{\mu\gamma}; \tag{14.13}$$

it is *very strong* if

$$a_3 < -1 \quad \text{or} \quad \frac{\kappa}{\lambda} > \frac{1 + (1 - \tau)\alpha + \mu\beta}{\mu\gamma} \tag{14.14}$$

and if

$$\tilde{Y} = \frac{A_3}{1 - a_3} > 0 \quad \text{and} \quad Y^{**} < \tilde{Y} < Y^*, \tag{14.15}$$

or if

$$\frac{M - L^0}{\kappa} < \frac{E + G - \mu\sigma Y^*}{1 - [(1 - \tau)\alpha - \mu\sigma]} < \left[\beta Y' - \frac{\gamma}{\lambda}(M - L^0) \right] \cdot \frac{1}{\sigma}. \tag{14.16}$$

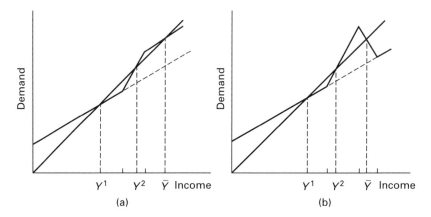

Figure 14.3
Aggregate demand with weak (a) and strong (b) monetary effects.

The implications of these conditions are analogous to the more general models of chapter 13. If the monetary effect is weak, the positive income loop of figure 13.1 dominates for all Y. Aggregate demand is therefore upward sloping. If the monetary effect is strong, the slope in $\mathscr{R}^3$ is negative, as shown in figure 14.3b.

14.2   The Quantity Adjustment Process

Continuing to assume that supply adjusts to demand, we get the multiple-phase adjustment process

$$Y_{t+1} = \theta(Y_t) = \theta_i(Y_t), \quad Y_t \in \mathscr{R}^i. \tag{14.17}$$

Four examples of trajectories for this process are shown in figure 14.4. The changes in qualitative behavior that occur when μ increases are analogous to the smooth model illustrated in figure 13.10.

14.2.1   Stationary States in the Keynesian Regime

If an equilibrium exists in a given regime, say $\tilde{Y}^i$, then a necessary condition is that

$$\tilde{Y}^i = \frac{A_i}{1 - a_i} \in \mathscr{R}^i,$$

$i = 1, 2, 3$ if the monetary effect is weak and $i = 1, 2, 3, 4$ if the monetary effect is strong. This translates into the following inequalities:

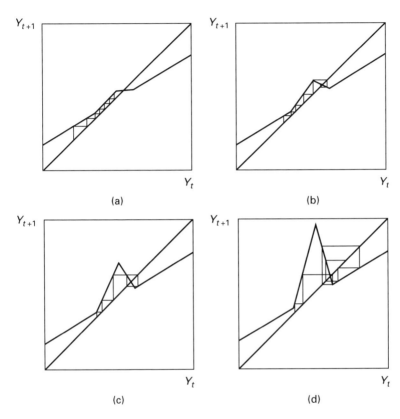

Figure 14.4
Comparative Keynesian dynamics for the piecewise linear model. (a) Monotonic convergence. (b) Cyclic convergence. (c) Stable two-period cycle. (d) Nonperiodic fluctuations. The investment demand shifter μ is small in (a) and increases successively through (d).

$$0 < \tilde{Y}^1 = \frac{A}{1-a} < Y', \tag{14.18}$$

$$Y' < \tilde{Y}^2 = \frac{A - \mu\beta Y'}{1 - a - \mu\beta} < Y^{**} = \frac{M - L^0}{\kappa}. \tag{14.19}$$

If σ is negative, then Y^* is positive and

$$Y^{**} = \frac{M - L^0}{\kappa} < \tilde{Y}^3 = \frac{A - \mu\sigma Y^*}{1 - a - \mu\sigma} < Y^* = \frac{\kappa(\gamma/\lambda) Y^{**} - \beta Y'}{\sigma} \tag{14.20}$$

is a condition sufficient for a stationary state in $\mathcal{R}^3$.

A stationary state in $\mathscr{R}^4$ implies that the monetary effect is strong but that

$$Y^* < \frac{A}{1-a} < Y^u. \tag{14.21}$$

Notice that both the stationary state $\tilde{Y}^i$ and the threshold Y^* depend on both μ and σ for $i = 2, 3$. Thus, if either or both of the parameters of investment demand β, γ and/or either or both of the parameters of money demand κ, λ and/or the intensity of induced investment μ change, then the possible existence and levels of the stationary states in $\mathscr{R}^2$ and $\mathscr{R}^3$ are modified.

14.2.2 Stability Analysis

Obviously, any stationary state in $\mathscr{R}^1$ or $\mathscr{R}^4$ will be asymptotically stable because

$$0 < \theta'(\tilde{Y}^1) = \theta'(\tilde{Y}^4) = (1-\tau)\alpha < 1. \tag{14.22}$$

If the monetary effect is strong and (14.20) is satisfied, then $\theta'(\tilde{Y}^2) = (1-\tau)\alpha + \mu\beta$. Consequently, $\tilde{Y}^2$ exists. It will be asymptotically stable if

$$\mu < \frac{1 - (1-\tau)\alpha}{\beta} \tag{14.23}$$

and unstable if

$$\mu > \frac{1 - (1-\tau)\alpha}{\beta}. \tag{14.24}$$

Finally, if the monetary effect is very strong, then the stationary state $\tilde{Y}^3 \in \mathscr{R}^3$ exists. It will be asymptotically stable if

$$\mu < \frac{1 - (1-\tau)\alpha}{|\beta - \kappa\gamma/\lambda|} \tag{14.25}$$

and unstable if

$$\mu > \frac{1 - (1-\tau)\alpha}{|\beta - \kappa\gamma/\lambda|}. \tag{14.26}$$

In the latter case, expanding fluctuations occur in trajectories that pass close to $\tilde{Y}^3$.

These inequality conditions imply all the results given in Proposition 13.3. Let us state it more succinctly as:

PROPOSITION 14.1   *All the possibilities of asymptotically stable and unstable stationary states, cycles, and fluctuations occur robustly in the piecewise linear real/monetary macro model.*

14.3   Plausible Parameters and Counterfactual Histories

Because linear aggregate demand functions for goods and money have frequently been used in policy and in econometric discussions over the years, various authorities have estimated their parameters. These estimates provide a basis for constructing examples of the Keynesian business cycle in the piecewise linear form under consideration here.

14.3.1   Parameter Values

The parameters of the model can be divided into two groups. The first group gives the "marginal" influences of income and the interest rate on consumption (α), investment (β, γ), and the demand for money (κ, λ). These are constant in the present model but correspond to the partial derivatives of the demand functions given for the more general models of chapter 13. Also included in this group is the income tax rate (τ), which is assumed also to be a constant.[4] The second set of parameters are *exogenous variables* that measure "autonomous" or "outside" influences, which play an important role but are not explained within the present theory. Included in this group are autonomous private consumption and investment expenditures (E), government expenditures (G), the investment threshold (Y'), and the exogenous demand for liquidity (L^0) at which the liquidity trap begins. (It is assumed that the minimum interest rate $r^0 = 0$.) Potential output is $\bar{Y}$.

Parameters in the first group can be based on econometric estimates reported in the literature. Those in the second group can be calibrated so as to represent average conditions prevailing in a given historical period. For this purpose, three widely separated base periods were chosen: Period I: 1930–1934, the bottom of the Great Depression, Period II: 1960–1965, a period of stable growth, and Period III: 1975–1978, a period of stagflation. Using averaged data for C, I, G, r, and M for these periods, the structural equations can be solved to get L^0 and Y'. For example, to es-

Table 14.1
Parameter Values for Counterfactual Simulations

Slope Parameter	Base Period		
	I	II	III
Marginal propensity to consume (α)	.75	.75	.75
Average tax rate (τ)	.20	.20	.20
Investenat intensity (μ)	.60	.60	.60
Marginal propensity to invest from income (β)	1.16	1.16	1.16
Marginal propensity to invest due to interest rates (γ)	10.61	20.83	26.88
Marginal transactions demand for money (κ)	.135	.135	.135
Marginal liquidity money (λ)	.95	.665	.191
Autonomous consumption (E)	32.02	3.63	41.42
Government expenditure (G)	46.30	204.90	298.68
Investment threshold (Y')	177.28	600.30	936.15
Investment maximizer (Y^{**})	243.95	821.01	1354.99
Investment crowded out (Y^*)	250.56	908.95	1383.35
Full capital output (Y^u)	340.00	1180.00	1450.00
Money supply (M)	81.22	214.13	228.61

timate L^0 we use $L^0 = M + \lambda r - \kappa Y$ where M and Y are the average values for the given period. The resulting parameter values are given in table 14.1.[5]

Using the data in table 14.1, the slope coefficient for aggregate demand in each regime can be calculated. These are given in table 14.2. The parameter σ is negative and the monetary effect is strong in all of the regimes, i.e., $a_3 < 0$. The slope in the third regime is quite steep for Base Periods I and III. This is due in part to the rather steep LM curve in this regime. This segment rises from the flat segment of the LM curve which occurs in the range (Y', Y^{**}); this range is very wide. In Base Period II the LM curve is flatter in its upward-sloping range than in Period I or III.

The three aggregate demand functions are illustrated in figure 14.5. The shift upward in aggregate demand as one progresses from Period I through Periods II and III is the result of capital accumulation, population growth, increase in the money supply, and the long-run forces of development, that is, in the exogenous "level" parameters E, G, Y', κ, L^0, and M.

Our estimates imply that interest is insensitive over a wide range of income, but that it is very sensitive when income gets relatively high. This,

Table 14.2
Slope Coefficients for the Linear Regimes of Aggregate Demand

	Base Period		
Slope Parameter	I	II	III
Regime I and IV (a)	.60	.60	.60
Regime II (b)	1.30	1.30	1.30
Regime III (c)	−7.02	−1.16	−9.74

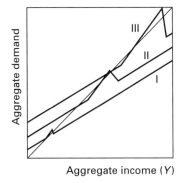

Figure 14.5
Estimated aggregate demand functions for the three base periods

of course, is exactly the nonlinearity that helps drive the business cycle, as was seen in chapter 13.[6]

14.3.2   Qualifications

There are several reasons why we must be cautious in attributing too much realism to such examples. First, as noted in chapter 13, many variables assumed constant in the theory actually vary in the real economy. Second, the range of parameter values reported in the literature is surprisingly wide. Third is the practice followed by most econometricians of ignoring the fundamental nonlinearities in the model. This practice biases the parameter estimates. To see how this can happen, recall figure 13.2, which showed the smooth nonlinear curve. If the true relationship is nonlinear, then the slope of any linear approximation will depend on which part of the general nonlinear relationship is to be closely approximated by the linear model.

The first problem can be alleviated by conducting comparative dynamic or numerical bifurcation studies for differing parameter values. We shall give an example of this approach below. The second problem can also be dealt with by comparing model behavior for various alternative parameter values throughout the full range of those reported. For the third problem, new statistical methods could facilitate the identification and estimation of nonlinear relationships. Such a development would, however, carry us far beyond the purpose of this study. For the illustrative purpose of the theory developed in this book we shall simply make use of the parameter values in the literature, but adapt them to the multiple-regime character of the structural equations in the present model. They will at least give us a clue as to whether or not the theory has any relevance at all.

14.3.3   Counterfactual Histories

Model histories can be generated using each of these sets of parameter values. The "counterfactual histories" show how aggregate income would have behaved *if the assumptions of the model had been approximated in reality* and indicate the kind of dynamic forces that might be operating within a broader context. The simulated counterfactual histories for the three parameter sets are shown graphically in figure 14.6. The behavior

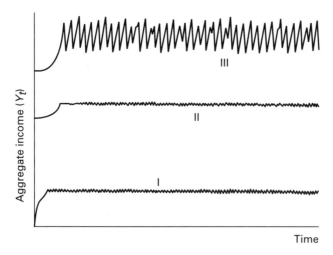

Figure 14.6
Sample trajectories for the counterfactual histories

for the three base periods is strikingly different. Periods I and II show fluctuations with relatively small amplitudes while Period III exhibits wide swings in aggregate income.

To give a picture of the long-run qualitative properties of the trajectories, the histograms of aggregate income values for each example are reproduced in figure 14.7. Here, too, we see that the results are strikingly different. For Period I the trajectory of aggregate income appears to converge rapidly to a two-period fluctuation; the histogram of aggregate income values has two spikes corresponding to these periodic values. For Base Period II a two-period fluctuation is also present. In this case, the amplitudes are irregular, that is, irregular but almost periodic in the sense that income values fall into two very narrow ranges. The

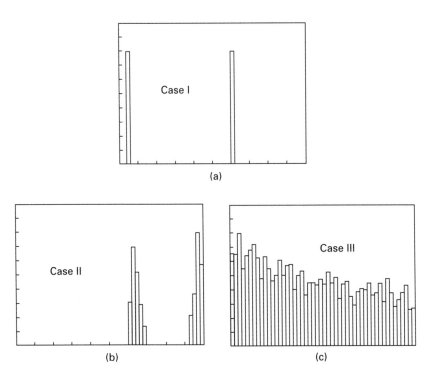

Figure 14.7
Numerical probability distributions for the counterfactual histories. (a) Case I: a stable two-period cycle. (b) Case II: a two-period fluctuation with random amplitude. (c) Case III: random period and random amplitude. In Cases II and III the frequencies in 50 equally spaced intervals were obtained from 30,000 iterates. Note that the scales have been reduced in (b) and (c) to facilitate comparison.

behavior appears something like a two-period cycle with a random shock from a finite distribution added. Actually, however, the fluctuation is deterministic. For Base Period III the fluctuations vary from 2 to 5 periods from peak to peak or trough to trough. They also exhibit highly irregular amplitudes throughout the entire interval. The histogram reflects this by showing positive frequencies throughout the range of variation.

14.3.4 Comparative Dynamics: The Robustness of Fluctuations

How robust are these results? Do they occur just for the parameter values chosen or will similar behavior occur for others?

Certainly fluctuations are not necessary. For example, if we set $\mu = .25$, the monetary effect will not be very strong, so any cycles must be damped. In such a case fluctuations could persist only through the continual impulse of shocks. Contrastingly, in each of the three cases considered here, intrinsic cycles do occur.

To see if this behavior is robust, a bifurcation diagram has been computed for each of the three periods by varying μ (and implicitly β, λ, κ, or δ) continuously. Values of μ at even intervals of .005 ranging from 0 to 1 were picked. For each value the model was simulated for 450 iterates. So as to avoid transient behavior, only the values later than iteration 325 were plotted. The results are shown in figure 14.8.

The bifurcation diagram for Base Period I reflects an orderly but very complex dependence in qualitative behavior on the importance of induced investment (and by implication on the parameters of money and investment demand). Qualitative behavior changes drastically from stable periodic to unstable, stochastic behavior and back again through different periodicities.

The bifurcation diagram for Case II, based on the parameters for Base Period II, is not so remarkable. Still, as μ increases, the variation in the amplitude of the two-cycle increases, then merges into a zone of random-like behavior, switches to a three-cycle which shows increasing random amplitudes as μ continues to increase, and finally merges into a zone suggesting chaotic fluctuations.

In Case III the random distribution of aggregate income values throughout the range of fluctuations does not appear to change as μ shifts. The central feature of both random amplitude and random periodicity seems to persist throughout.

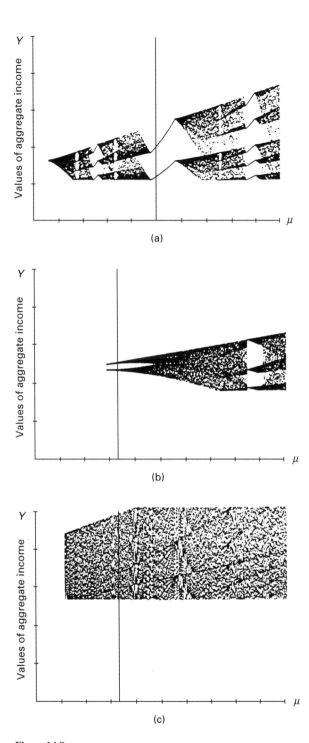

Figure 14.8
Bifurcation diagrams for the investment intensity. (a) Case I. (b) Case II. (c) Case III.
Vertical lines indicate base values of μ.

14.4   The Algebra of Cycles and Chaos

14.4.1   Conditions for Persistent Fluctuations

To see what the scope for instability is, consider the criterion (14.14). Rearranging terms, we find that instability occurs if

$$\mu > [1 + (1 - \tau)\alpha]/[\gamma\kappa/\lambda - \beta]. \qquad (14.27)$$

Substituting values for α, β, κ, and τ from table 14.1, we get

$$\mu > 1.6/[.135\gamma/\lambda - 1.16] = \mu^c \qquad (14.28)$$

as a sufficient condition for persistent cycles. Obviously, if the monetary effect is strong, asymptotic stability will occur for all $0 < \mu < \mu^c$ and persistent cycles or chaos for all $\mu \geq \mu^c$. Using the table 14.1 values, we get $\mu_I^c = .35$, $\mu_{II}^c = .52$, and $\mu_{III}^c = .9$ for the three cases, all relatively small numbers.

Or turn things around. Rearrange equation (14.14) so that we get a condition for the more controversial ratio γ/λ as follows:

$$\gamma/\lambda > \beta/\kappa + [1 + (1 - \tau)\alpha]/\kappa\mu. \qquad (14.29)$$

Using the table 14.1 parameters on the right, we get

$$\gamma/\lambda > 28.35 \qquad (14.30)$$

as the condition for persistent fluctuations. The values for γ/λ in each of the base periods are 111, 31, and 141, respectively. Thus, in our illustration, Cases I and III fluctuations would persist even if the ratio were reduced by a very large amount (either by increasing λ or reducing γ).

Such results hold only for the counterfactual conditions assumed. They only reveal cyclical *tendencies* that may be repressed or exaggerated (we can't say which) when prices, capacity, and various supply-side effects are allowed to play an explicit role. The fact that fluctuations are highly robust suggests that quite wide swings in other variables could be required to flatten changes in aggregate income. Certainly, it is clear that qualitative changes in macrobehavior and randomlike fluctuations in aggregate income can be induced by intrinsic properties of economic structure.

14.4.2   Transforming the Trapping Set

In order to get a more precise understanding of the conditions under which cycles and chaotic fluctuations occur, we shall proceed as we did in the analysis of the general case in chapter 13 by constructing the trapping set within which all fluctuations must eventually occur. As before, three distinct cases occur exactly like those given in Proposition 13.3. It simplifies the task if we transform the map to the unit interval.

For our present purposes, let us define

$$a = a_1 = (1 - \tau)\alpha$$

$$b = a_2 = (1 - \tau)\alpha + \mu\beta$$

$$c = a_3 = (1 - \tau)\alpha + \mu\sigma.$$

Case I: Use the transformation

$$y = (Y - Y^m)/(Y^M - Y^m).$$

Then aggregate demand transformed to the unit interval becomes a tilted-Z form

$$T(y) := \begin{cases} 1 + b(y^{**} - y), & y \in [0, y^{**}) \\ 1 + c(y - y^{**}), & y \in [y^{**}, y^*) \\ a(y - y^*), & y \in [y^*, 1] \end{cases} \qquad (14.31)$$

where $y^{**} = (Y^{**} - Y^m)/(Y^M - Y^m)$ and $y^* = (Y^* - Y^m)/(Y^M - Y^m)$. Note that $y^{**} - y^* = \frac{1}{c}$.

Case II: Use the transformation

$$y = [Y - \theta(Y^M)]/[Y^M - \theta(Y^M)].$$

Then aggregate demand transformed to the unit interval is a shack map

$$T(y) := \begin{cases} 1 + b(y - y^{**}), & y \in [0, y^{**}) \\ 1 + c(y - y^{**}), & y \in [y^{**}, 1] \end{cases} \qquad (14.32)$$

where $y^{**} = 1 - \frac{1}{c}$.

Case III: Use the transformation

$$y = (Y - Y^m)/[\theta(Y^m) - Y^m]$$

to get a check map

$$T(y) := \begin{cases} c(y - y^*), & y \in [0, y^*) \\ a(y - y^*), & y \in [y^*, 1) \end{cases} \qquad (14.33)$$

where $y^* = -\frac{1}{c}$.

14.4.3 Cycles, Chaos, and Strong Chaos

The most complete analysis can be given for Case II; Case III is essentially equivalent.[7]

PROPOSITION 14.2 (Day and Shafer 1987) *Let θ be given by the piecewise linear model (14.11) with parameters satisfying (14.20). The restriction of θ to the trapping set is a (Type II) map. Let k be the minimum integer such that*

$$T^{k-1}(0) < y^{**} \leq T^k(0) \tag{14.34}$$

where $T(y)$ is obtained from $\theta(y)$ by the linear transformation given in (14.33).

(i) If

$$b^k c > 1, \tag{14.35}$$

nonperiodic trajectories occur almost surely; all cycles are unstable and there exists an absolutely continuous invariant measure; the support of this measure is an attractor for almost all trajectories that enter the trapping set.

(ii) If

$$b^k c < 1, \tag{14.36}$$

there exists a unique asymptotically stable cycle of least period $k + 1$ which attracts almost all trajectories that enter the trapping set. If $k + 1$ is odd, then nonperiodic fluctuations exist, but these occur with measure zero.

Proof

(i) The simplest situation is when both b and $|c|$ are greater than unity. Then the map $T(y)$ given by (14.33) is expansive, so we know from Theorem 8.4 that all cycles are unstable and a unique absolutely continuous invariant measure exists whose support is the attractor for almost all trajectories in $[0,1]$. Figure 14.9 shows how this case arises.

When $0 < b < 1$, the map $T(y)$ is not expansive, so the above argument does not hold. But consider the set $\mathbb{C} = [y^{**}, 1]$ on which the map *is* expansive (because $|c| > 1$) and take a point y in $\mathbb{B} := (0, y^{**})$. Either $T(y) \in \mathbb{C}$ or not. Suppose the latter and take $T^2(y)$. Either it belongs to $\mathbb{C}$ or not. Eventually, there must exist a smallest positive integer k, such that

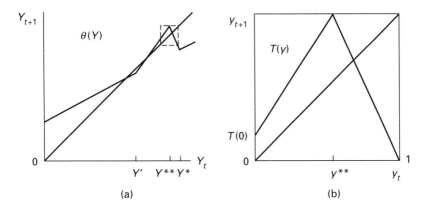

Figure 14.9
Expansivity for the Type II map. (a) The basic map. The trapping set is indicated by the
dashed lines. (b) The map on the trapping set transformed to the unit interval.

$$T^{k-1}(y) < y^{**} \leq T^k(y). \tag{14.37}$$

The minimum exponent such that (14.35) holds for $y = 0$ is clearly the
maximum period from trough to peak of any fluctuation that can occur.
Figure 14.10 gives an example where T is nonexpansive and $k = 2$.

Consider the map $T^k(\cdot)$. The derivative at any point y is

$$\frac{dT^k(y)}{dy} = T'(T^{k-1}(y)) \cdot T'(T^{k-2}(y)) \ldots T'(y). \tag{14.38}$$

Some points will lie in $\mathbb{B}$ and some in $\mathbb{C}$. Suppose k_1 points lie in $\mathbb{B}$ with
$k_1 \geq 1$. Then

$$\frac{dT^k(y)}{dy} = b^{k_1} c^{k_2}, \quad k_2 = k + 1 - k_1.$$

Because $c > 1$ and $0 < b < 1$ by hypothesis, this derivative is minimized
at $y = 0$ where

$$\frac{dT^k(0)}{dy} = b^k c.$$

Consequently, $T^k(y)$ will be an expansive map if $b^k c > 1$.

(ii) If $b^k c < 1$, then $T^k(\cdot)$ is contractive. Consider the left open interval
$S := (0, \min\{T(0), y^{**}\}]$. Because T is continuous, there must exist a
point z in S such that $T^{k-1}(z) = y^{**}$ where k is the maximum trough-

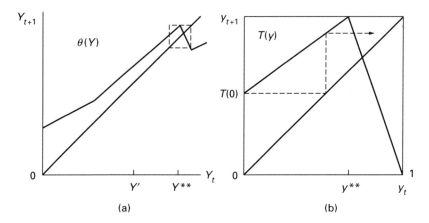

Figure 14.10
Nonexpansive Type II map. (a) The basic map. (b) The map on the trapping set transformed
to the unit interval.

to-peak period given by (14.35) for $y = 0$. Note that $T^{k+1}(z) = 0$. Define
$F(x) = T^{k+1}(x) - x$. Then $F(0) > 0$ and $F(z) < 0$, so by Theorem 5.4
there exists a fixpoint, say $u \in S$. By hypothesis $T^j(z) < y^{**}$, $j = 0, \dots,$
$k - 1$. As $u < z$ it must be the case that $T^j(u) < y^{**}$ for $j = 0, \dots, k - 1$
and that $T^k(u) > y^{**}$. Consequently,

$$\frac{dT^{k+1}(y)}{dy}\bigg|_{y=u} = b^k c.$$

If $b^k c > 1$ the cycle is unstable. If $b^k c < 1$ then u is stable and there must
exist a finite integer p such that either $T^p(0) = u$ or $T^p(1) = u$. Moreover,
u is unique. Of course, $T(y^{**}) = 1$ and $T(1) = 0$ so u attracts 0, y^{**}, and
1. Therefore, by the Misiurewicz Theorem 8.6 almost all trajectories converge to the cyclic orbit $\gamma(u)$. Note that if k is even, $\gamma(u)$ is an odd cycle
so by the LIMPY Theorem a scrambled set exists but, because almost all
trajectories converge to $\omega(u)$, chaotic fluctuations occur with Lebesgue
measure zero.   ■

Remembering that $b = (1 - \tau)\alpha + \mu\beta$ and that $c = (1 - \tau)\alpha +$
$\mu(\beta - \kappa\gamma/\lambda)$, it is clear that *strong chaos can occur for a very large set of*
parameter values that enter the Keynesian business cycle model. Note that
$b - c = \mu\gamma k/\lambda$. Suppose we fix b. Then by varying c we are in effect
varying $\gamma k/\lambda$. Because μ appears in b, the three "independent" economic

parameters $\gamma, k,$ and λ determine c. Hence, for any given value of b the variation in y^{**} implies a corresponding variation in $\gamma k/\lambda$.

Of course, similar results can also occur for the Type I map, but the analysis is considerably complicated by the additional turning point in the map T on the trapping set. These details can be considered by the ambitious student with a capacity for some tedious calculations.

14.4.4 The Complete Comparative Dynamics for Case II

Our results can be summarized in a convenient form by taking advantage of the linearity of $T(\cdot)$ restricted to $[0, y^{**}]$. Assume (14.37); then the explicit solution of $y_{t+1} = T(y_t)$ for $y_0 = 0$ is

$$yk = T^k(0) = T(0)(1 + b + \cdots + b^{k-1}). \tag{14.39}$$

Now let

$$f_k(b) := \frac{1 + b + \cdots + b^{k-1}}{1 + b + \cdots + b^k}. \tag{14.40}$$

Then, observing that $T(0) = 1 - by^{**}$, we get the equivalent expression for the $k + 1$ cycle

$$f_k(b) \le y^{**} = 1 - \frac{1}{c} \le f_{k+1}(b). \tag{14.41}$$

Let $\mathbb{C}_n := \{(b, c) \text{ such that } (14.41) \text{ is satisfied for } n = k + 1\}$. Then for all parameter values in $\mathbb{C}_n$, fluctuations with maximum duration n occur in the trapping set.

Now define

$$S_n := \{(b, c) \mid b^k c \le 1\} \cap \mathbb{C}_n,$$

and

$$E_n := \{(b, c) \mid b^k c \ge 1\} \cap \mathbb{C}_n.$$

Let $g_k(b) = 1 - b^k$. Using the fact that $y^* = 1 - \frac{1}{c}$, we find that

$$b^k c < 1 \Leftrightarrow y^* < g_k(b) := 1 - b^k \tag{14.42}$$

$$b^k c > 1 \Leftrightarrow y^* > g_k(b) = 1 - b^k. \tag{14.43}$$

Consequently, S_n contains all parameters (b, c) that satisfy (14.41) and (14.42) while E_n contains all parameters that satisfy (14.41) and (14.43).

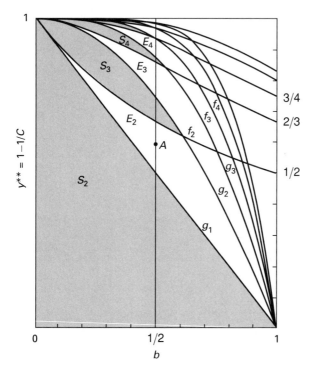

Figure 14.11
Parameter zones of stable cycles, thin chaos, and ergodic behavior. Source: Day and Shafer (1987).

Note that

$$f_k(1) = \frac{k}{k+1}.$$

Using this fact and the definitions of S_n and E_n we obtain a complete graphical equivalence for Proposition 14.2. This is done in figure 14.11. The functions $f_1, \ldots, f_6$ are shown. The numbers give the maximum peak-to-peak (or trough-to-trough) period of any fluctuation.

The $g_k(b)$ lines for $g_1, \ldots, g_6$ have been superimposed. According to the theorem we are exploiting, the shaded areas S_{k+1} are those satisfying both (14.41) and (14.42). Then for all (b, c) combinations that fall in these sets, unique, stable cycles emerge. For the odd sets, $S_3, S_5, \ldots$, the model will possess weak chaos; that is, chaotic trajectories exist but the probability of

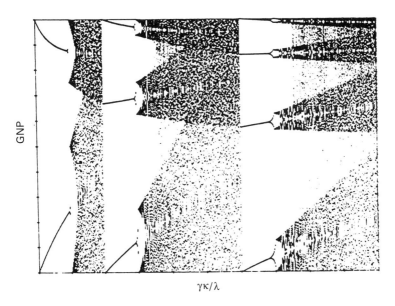

Figure 14.12
Bifurcation diagram for the parameter $\gamma\kappa/\lambda$. Note that aggregate income values have been transferred to the unit interval.

finding one is zero. The unshaded sets E_{k+1} are those for which non-periodic fluctuations occur almost surely.

14.4.5 Numerical Bifurcation Analysis

To get a better picture of how the qualitative behavior of the model changes as a parameter is varied, a numerical simulation for a slice through the (b, y^{**}) space is shown in figure 14.12 for $b = \frac{1}{2}$. The horizontal axis in this figure is $y^{**} = 1 - 1/c$. The parameter c is varied in increments of 0.1 from 1 to 11. For each value of c the Case II map was iterated 250 times and the last 125 values plotted on the vertical axis, giving an approximate picture of the long-run dynamics and how the pattern of behavior shifts with y^{**} (and hence with $\gamma\kappa/\lambda$).

14.4.6 Statistical Behavior

In figure 14.13a a histogram has been constructed for 10,000 iterates of (14.32) for given parameter values corresponding to point A in figure 14.11, using 150 subintervals of the unit interval. The sequence of model-generated values can be regarded as the realization of a stochastic process

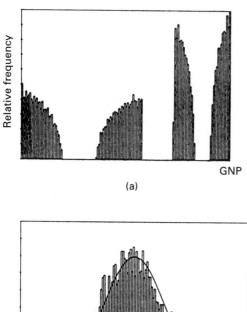

(a)

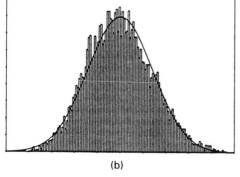

(b)

Figure 14.13
Statistical behavior of aggregate income. (a) Histogram of GNP values. (b) Histogram of sample means and the normal curve.

that obeys the central limit theorem. Thus, successive runs of, say, n values can be thought of as samples from this process, the means of which are distributed normally. Figure 14.13b shows the computed histogram of the sample means. The smooth curve is the normal distribution whose moments are equated with those of the numerical distribution.

14.5   Comparison with the Static IS-LM Framework

As in the smooth, nonlinear theory of chapter 13, it is interesting to consider the relationship of the dynamic IY-LM model to the static, IS-LM version.

The fixprice equilibria on the goods market are given by the locus of non-negative (r, Y) pairs that solve

$$Y = A + aY + \mu \max\{0, \beta(Y - Y') - \gamma r\}.$$

When $Y < Y'$, the goods market is independent of the money market because real interest rates (by assumption) cannot become negative. If a stationary state exists below Y', it must satisfy $\tilde{Y}^1 = A/(1 - a) < Y'$ for all positive r. This equilibrium value will not change with r, so the IS curve can be thought of as a vertical spike over the value $\tilde{Y}^1$. It is undefined elsewhere in the interval $(0, Y')$.

Recall that when the monetary effect is strong, there exists a value $Y^* > Y^{**}$ where the interest rate drives induced investment to zero. In this case, the IS curve is also undefined above Y^* except if a fixpoint occurs at $A/(1 - a)$, which can happen if $A/(1 - a) > Y^{**}$.

When $Y > Y'$ the market-clearing interest rate which gives the IS curve is

$$r = \frac{A - \mu\beta Y' + (a + \mu\beta - 1)Y}{\mu\gamma}, \quad Y > Y'.$$

Because $0 < a < 1$, the IS curve is downward sloping when μ is small enough, that is, when $\mu < (1 - a)/\beta$. As μ increases, the IS curve becomes flatter and then becomes positive. Rearranging terms of the instability condition $c < -1$ given in (14.14), we have

$$\frac{a + \mu\beta}{\mu\gamma} < \frac{\kappa}{\lambda} - \frac{1}{\mu\gamma}.$$

Subtracting $1/(\mu\gamma)$ from both sides and rearranging, we get

$$\frac{a + \mu\beta - 1}{\mu\gamma} + \frac{2}{\mu\gamma} < \frac{\kappa}{\lambda}.$$

The first term on the left is the slope of the IS curve. The term on the right is the slope of the LM curve. Thus, the slope of the LM curve $f'(Y)$ must be steep relative to the slope of the IS curve $g'(Y)$ as in the general theory. If the IS curve is positively sloped, there can be three stationary states, with the smaller one occurring below Y' where the goods market is independent of the money market. If the IS curve is negatively sloped the LM curve need not be so steep for locally expanding cycles to occur, but there can only be one stationary state.

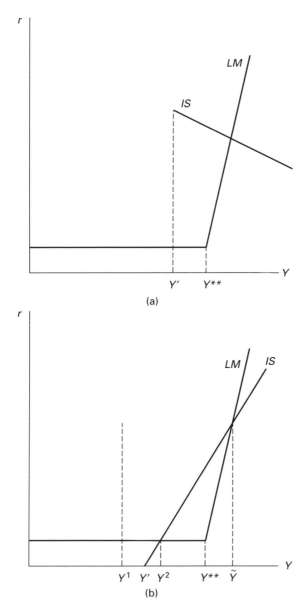

Figure 14.14
The IS-LM representation of real/monetary equilibrium for the piecewise linear model. (a)
Induced investment is relatively unimportant. (b) The monetary effect is strong and induced
investment is relatively important.

These results are roughly analogous to those for the smooth IY function of §13.2 and are illustrated in figure 14.14.

14.6 Summary and Conclusions

The piecewise linear model produces all the qualitative features of the more general nonlinear real/monetary theory. It has enabled us to trace the conditions for stability, cycles, and chaos very precisely to the underlying parameters of demand. Finally, it has enabled us to specify numerical examples based on empirically plausible parameter values. A wide variety of qualitatively different aggregate behaviors can be generated by choosing parameters within the range of values reported by various experts. These include stable stationary states, stable cycles of various orders, and chaotic fluctuations that behave like stochastic processes. The implication of this is that when many of the variables and parameters held constant in the present theory are allowed to vary, the qualitative behavior of the system can be changed drastically. The amplitude and periodicity of cycles can change, nonperiodic behavior can emerge from previously stationary or cyclic situations, or highly unstable chaotic behavior can be stabilized. As before, all of these results are generic for the class of normal demand schedules.

15 Comparative Monetary and Fiscal Policy

The phenomena ... are better described as disequilibrium dynamics.
—James Tobin, "Keynesian Models of Recession and Depression"

Within the framework of the real/monetary business cycle theory in both its general and piecewise linear versions, we have seen that rising aggregate income during the upswing of the business cycle leads eventually to rising interest rates caused by the crowding out on money markets as the transactions demand for money rises. If investment is sensitive enough to interest rates, this causes a decline in aggregate demand and employment. Interest rates then fall, which stimulates investment and consumption. But a recovery may take some time because of excess capacity and unemployment.

How are these events influenced by monetary and fiscal policy?

This question is usually investigated, using the comparative static method,[1] under the assumption that any fluctuations will be strongly damped so that time paths are unimportant and only stationary states need be considered. This can be misleading when adjustments do not converge and when fluctuations are perpetuated. We have seen in chapter 13 that unstable fluctuations are generic, and chapter 14 presented crude evidence that strong tendencies toward instabilities are present when "plausible" parameter values are used for three widely spaced historical periods. It would seem that a policy analysis in the presence of intrinsic fluctuations would be of interest.

For this purpose a comparative dynamic method is needed. Although such a method is distinctly different from its comparative static counterpart, it is analogous. In comparative statics one studies how stationary states change in response to shifts in a parameter. Such stationary states, if stable, give the asymptotic behavior of the dynamic model. If the stationary states are unstable, the asymptotic behavior will be given by the attractor. This set will be finite if the asymptotic behavior is a strictly periodic cycle; it will be an uncountable set with positive measure that can be represented by an absolutely continuous distribution function if the long-run behavior is strongly ergodic. In the latter case the model behaves something like a stochastic process. Sometimes these trajectories have periodic turning points but random amplitudes; sometimes both are essentially random.

The general procedure for comparative dynamic policy analysis then is to compare, using a bifurcation analysis, the asymptotic performance of the model as policy instruments are shifted. We shall do this for shifts in government expenditure, G, the tax rate, τ, and the money supply, M. All this will be perfectly analogous to the bifurcation analysis of the previous two chapters using the investment demand shifter, where it was found that the qualitative character of the business cycle depends in a complex way on all the parameters of demand. Changes in policy instruments can have similar effects. It will be seen that they can trigger the economy into or out of stable stationary, periodic, or nonperiodic behavior in an analogous manner. Moreover, we will show that a policy change in a given direction can have switching directions of influence. For example, a steady increase in government expenditure could shift the economy from a stable stationary state through cycles of varying periods and non-periodic fluctuations and back into a stable stationary state.

This fact introduces a source of uncertainty that arises not from the erratic nature of political and other exogenous influences, but entirely from intrinsic, nonlinear interactions of the financial and real sectors. It provides a new hypothesis concerning the notorious difficulty of antici-pating in the real world the effects of given monetary or fiscal changes.

Before proceeding, an important caveat. Policy analysis based on the real/monetary business cycle theory should not be taken literally. A number of variables are fixed that should be allowed to vary in a more complete analysis; it leaves out all multisectoral interactions except that between the coarsely representative aggregate demand functions for money and goods; and it assumes that the money supply is independent of the tax rate and government expenditure, which cannot be true in a world of reserve banking where government deficits and surpluses imply changes in the stock of bonds and hence the money supply. Nonetheless, there is something of interest to be learned from the basic model about the effects of policy, and, as an exercise in method, it is worth working through as a starting point for more general and more realistic investigations. [2]

15.1 Model Summary

The comparative dynamic analysis can be conducted most conveniently and completely using the piecewise linear version of the model discussed in the preceding chapter. Because the levels and slopes of the four linear segments or regimes depend on the underlying parameters, it is obvious that changes in the policy parameters will have the effect of shifting the aggregate demand curve. To see this conveniently, let us reproduce the equation for aggregate demand here with all of the parameters represented explicitly,

$$Y_{t+1} = \theta(Y_t) := \begin{cases} A + aY_t, & Y_t \in R_1 := [0, Y') \\ B + bY_t, & Y_t \in R_2 := [Y', Y^{**}) \\ C + cY_t, & Y_t \in R_3 := [Y^{**}, Y^*) \\ A + aY_t, & Y_t \in R_4 := [Y^*, Y^u) \end{cases} \tag{15.1}$$

where

$a = (1 - \tau)\alpha$

$b = a + \mu\beta$

$c = a + \mu\sigma \quad \sigma = \beta - \gamma\kappa/\lambda$

$A = E + G$

$B = A - \mu\beta Y'$

$C = A - \mu\sigma Y^*.$

Remember that when c is negative,

$$Y^{**} = (M - L^0)/\kappa \tag{15.2}$$

is the local maximizer of $\theta(Y)$, so that

$$Y^M = \theta(Y^{**}) \tag{15.3}$$

is an upper bound on fluctuations in aggregate income. Likewise, when c is negative,

$$Y^* = [\beta Y' - (\gamma/\lambda)(M - L^0)]/\sigma \tag{15.4}$$

is a local minimizer of $\theta(Y)$, so that

$$Y^m = \theta(Y^*) \tag{15.5}$$

is a lower bound on fluctuations in aggregate income. Aggregate income values below Y^{**} do not influence interest rates, but above it they do because of crowding out. Below Y^* changes in Y induce changes in investment, but not above. This, recall, is because induced investment has been crowded out. Only autonomous investment, which is included in E, remains.

We need to use the fact, shown in §14.4.2, that the profile of aggregate demand in the trapping set takes three canonical forms determined by the values defined in (15.2)–(15.5), as follows:

the *tilted Z*: $Y^m < Y^{**} < Y^* < Y^M$ (15.6)

the *shack*: $Y^m < Y^{**} < Y^M < Y^*$ (15.7)

the *check*: $Y^{**} < Y^m < Y^* < Y^M$.   (15.8)

In addition to these three cases, there are four situations in which the trapping set disappears. In one, designated a *super peak*, induced demand is greater than aggregate income in the second and third regimes. That is,

$$\theta(Y) > Y \quad \text{all} \quad Y \in R_2 \cup R_3.$$

It is easy to see that the condition for this is

super peak: $Y^* < Y^m$.   (15.9)

When

$$\theta(Y) < Y \quad \text{all} \quad Y \in R_2 \cup R_3,$$

we get a *sub peak*; the condition for which is

sub peak: $Y^M < Y^{**}$.   (15.10)

It can also happen when three stationary states exist that

$$\theta(Y^M) < Y^2 \tag{15.11}$$

where Y^2 is the middle (and unstable) stationary state. Then an escape interval exists and if $\theta(\cdot)$ is expansive for $Y \in R_2 \cup R_3$ (i.e., b and $c < -1$), then trajectories in $R_2 \cup R_3$ must eventually escape and converge to Y^1, the smallest stationary state. Of course, if

$$Y^M > Y^u, \tag{15.12}$$

then fluctuating trajectories in $R_2 \cup R_3$ must also escape, but in this case they jump from the Keynesian regime altogether.

Given a base situation that exhibits one of these forms, a parameter change, in particular a change in one of the policy instruments G, τ, or M, not only can shift aggregate demand without changing its form, but also can cause a change from one form to another. Both the transitory and the asymptotic behavior of aggregate income will be affected.

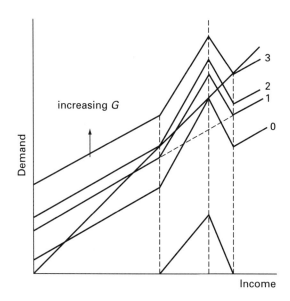

Figure 15.1
Changes in government expenditure

15.2 Government Expenditure

15.2.1 Changes in the Profile of Aggregate Demand

First, consider shifts in government spending. The parameter G only influences the constant term representing autonomous expenditure in aggregate demand. It must, therefore, have the effect of shifting aggregate demand and, correspondingly, the intercepts A, B, and C vertically, as shown in figure 15.1.[3]

Let Δ_g indicate the change in the parameter that follows it with respect to a change in G. Using (15.2)–(15.5) it is easy to see that

$$\Delta_g Y^m = \Delta G$$

$$\Delta_g Y^{**} = 0$$

$$\Delta_g Y^* = 0 \tag{15.13}$$

$$\Delta_g Y^M = \Delta G.$$

For example, $\Delta_g Y^m$ is the change in Y^m caused by a change in government expenditure. It equals the change in G itself. (Remember that Y^m is the lower bound on any fluctuations that might occur.)

Now look at the conditions (15.6)–(15.8) that determine the three canonical forms for fluctuations. Start with the tilted-Z form. Suppose G is reduced by an amount that changes Y^M, so that

$$Y^M + \Delta_g Y^M = Y^M + \Delta G < Y^*. \tag{15.14}$$

Then this change in government expenditure triggers a qualitative shift in form from the tilted-Z to the shack form. If G is reduced still more, so much that

$$\Delta G < Y^{**} - Y^M, \quad \text{then} \quad Y^M + \Delta_g Y^M < Y^{**}.$$

The trapping set and the two larger stationary states disappear. Fluctuations can't occur and all aggregate income trajectories converge to a unique stationary state in the first regime. No induced investment takes place in this instance—a rather extreme situation—but it must be included for completeness. In between these bifurcation points is a value of ΔG that allows for fluctuations but for which trajectories eventually converge to the stationary state Y^1. This possibility is of special interest and §15.2.3 below is devoted to it.

Now consider *increases* in G. If

$$\Delta G > Y^{**} - Y^m, \tag{15.15}$$

then

$$Y^m + \Delta_g Y^m = Y^m + \Delta G > Y^{**} \tag{15.16}$$

and the tilted Z switches to the check map form. If G increases so much that

$$\Delta G > Y^* - Y^m, \quad \text{then} \quad Y^m + \Delta Y^m > Y^*.$$

The trapping set disappears; all aggregate income trajectories have to converge asymptotically to a (unique) stationary state in the fourth regime where there is no induced investment. In either of the above situations, if

$$Y^M + \Delta G > Y^u,$$

then fluctuations could occur (if $Y^* > Y^m$) but trajectories can escape the Keynesian zone.

To see how these possibilities arise as G is changed, consider figure 15.1 and let graph 1 be the base situation, a tilted-Z form like that derived in chapter 14. Suppose aggregate income is stuck on the smallest of the three stationary states Y^1. It is stable. Therefore, a small increase in G will have a stable multiplier effect. It will shift the stationary state Y^1 gradually upward. When the total autonomous expenditure reaches the level G^2, aggregate demand curve 2 results. Here a qualitative jump occurs. When G increases above G^2 there is only one stationary state. Because the slope of aggregate demand is negative in regime R_3 with absolute value greater than one, fluctuations must emerge and be perpetuated. Periodic cycles or chaotic fluctuations could occur. Further increases in G will be associated with changing long-run distributions of aggregate income, and irregular fluctuations will continue to occur. If G is increased beyond G^3, the unstable stationary state will disappear. Instead, a stable stationary state is reached and further changes in expenditure will again be associated with the conventional stable multiplier processes.

Suppose that, instead of starting at a low level of G and increasing it, we begin with a high level and decrease it. For example, begin at a point with G above G^3. Assume also that aggregate income is stuck at the stationary state, which in this case is unique. Decreases in G will be associated with stable decreases in stationary aggregate income until the point G^3 associated with demand curve 3 is reached. With further decreases, stochastic fluctuations will appear. If G is decreased continuously these may persist until G^0 is reached, which is the level of government expenditure that yields aggregate demand curve 0. Then the stable multiplier process will reemerge. Note that changes in G have entirely different impacts on the qualitative behavior of aggregate income in the range (G^0, G^3) than for values outside this range. These values, therefore, are critical bifurcation points. Actually, as we will see, there is a bifurcation point between G^0 and G^1, say G^{00}, where transitory fluctuations are possible but ultimately we get an escape and monotonic convergence to Y^1 from above. Note also that qualitative changes that occur when G is decreased from an initially high level are not all exactly the same as those that occur when G is increased from a low level.

15.2.2 Numerical Bifurcation Analysis

These findings can be illustrated in much more detail by computing bifurcation diagrams. In §14.3, three sets of parameters were specified corresponding to three base periods: the Great Depression, the early 1960s, and the late 1970s. Using these base situations, three bifurcation diagrams

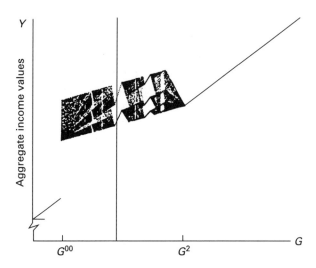

Figure 15.2
Comparative dynamics of government expenditure (or autonomous investment and consumption)

can be derived for changes in G. The results have been reported in detail elsewhere.[4] Here I shall give one example, the bifurcation diagram for Period I shown in figure 15.2. The computations show the emergence of complex behavior throughout a finite range of expenditure, (G^{00}, G^2). Within this range the multiplier process is, of course, unstable. The base level of G is shown by the vertical line. Note the discrete jump that occurs at G^{00} in conformity with the analysis above. As G is increased above G^{00}, persistent fluctuations shift from ergodic behavior, where aggregate income is distributed throughout an interval, to stable cycles, to periodic cycles that have random amplitudes, and back to ergodic behavior.

The patterns shown in the shading give an indication of how the density of aggregate income values changes with changing G. Where the shading is dark the density is larger; where it is light the density is smaller. The average GNP for any given level of government expenditure will lie between the upper and lower bounds of the fluctuations that occur for that level of G. When the model is asymptotically stable, average GNP is the same as the equilibrium value.

From the diagram, another perhaps startling result emerges. Average GNP must trend upward if G increases through much of the interval (G^{00}, G^2). However, close to G^2 *average* GNP *falls*; then beyond G^2 it resumes increasing. Moreover, there will be an even wider range of values of G where fluctuations occur for which average GNP will be greater than it is for a range of values associated with stable and increasing equilibrium values.

This finding suggests the following possible inference. The disorder in chaotic fluctuations guarantees the impossibility of accurately forecasting events far in the future. *Such an unpredictable, "chaotic" situation, however, may be preferable to a completely stable situation for which prediction is perfect.*

15.2.3 Chaos and Catastrophe: Escape from Chaos

This point can be illustrated even more dramatically. Consider the example for Base Period III and recall the chaotic fluctuations shown in the numerical trajectory of figure 14.6. The map $\theta(\cdot)$ for this case is shown by graph III in figure 14.5. It has three stationary states that have been denoted $Y^1, Y^2, \tilde{Y}$ with $Y^1 < Y^2 < \tilde{Y}$.

As was noted already, it is not difficult to see that if G decreases then Y^2 increases and $\theta(Y^*)$ decreases. This means that if G decreases enough, we could satisfy (15.11). This will happen if

$$E + G + \Delta G < \frac{-\mu(b-1)}{b(c-a)} \left[\left(\frac{a-c}{b-1} \right) \beta Y' + \frac{a}{c} \sigma Y^* \right], \tag{15.17}$$

a result that can be obtained by using the definitions and rearranging terms. In this case an initial condition above Y^2 could lead to fluctuations that eventually escape and contract to Y^1. Using the data from tables 14.1 and 14.2 in the right side of the previous inequality, we get

$$E + G + \Delta G < 286.47 \tag{15.18}$$

for this condition. In Case III, $E + G = 340.10$. Imagine now reductions in government expenditure (and/or autonomous expenditures) of \$54 billion. Then $A + \Delta_g A = 286.10$, which satisfies (15.18).

Figure 15.3 gives a trajectory that begins above Y^2. Irregular fluctuations appear as in the base situation, but now after a period of erratic behavior an aggregate income value is generated below the middle stationary state and a contraction sets in, first very moderate, then precipitous, finally converging to the smallest of the three stationary states. *Although the economy is now stable, unemployment is much higher and average income much lower than in the previous case when chaos prevailed.*

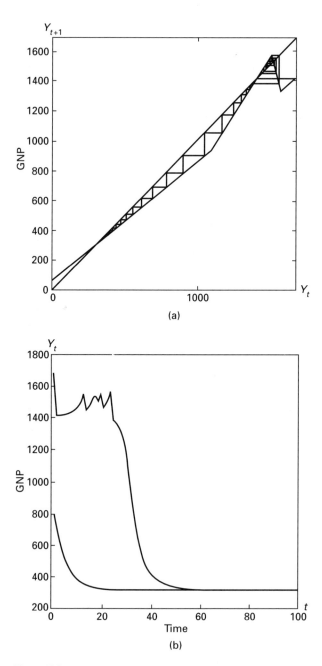

Figure 15.3
Escape from chaos. (a) The phase diagram. (b) Time path of GNP.

Using Theorem 8.9, we could show that no matter where in the original trapping set the process starts, the probability of escape is 1. Or, to put the matter differently, the attractor that describes the dynamics of the system in the long run changes from an interval to a point. Such sudden or discrete jumps in behavior brought about by a change in a parameter are sometimes called "catastrophes" in the mathematical literature. Here the mathematical phenomenon is interpreted within our model economy as a catastrophic decline in aggregate income.

Another way in which an escape can occur is from the Keynesian regime altogether if $Y^M > Y^u$. Here, too, transitory fluctuations could occur for some time and then aggregate income would jump above the level Y^u, signaling a change from a sticky-price economy to an inflationary situation.

15.3 Changes in the Tax Rate

Changes in the tax rate, as can be seen from equation (15.1), tilt or rotate aggregate demand by changing the slope of the aggregate consumption function. Beginning with the same base situation as in figure 15.1, critical bifurcation points for τ are readily identified, as shown in figure 15.4.

Because induced investment is not directly influenced by the tax rate, the switching points Y', Y^*, and Y^{**} are unchanged but the value of aggregate income at these points does change. Recall that α is the marginal propensity to consume unadjusted for the average income tax, i.e., $a = (1 - \tau)\alpha$. A change in the tax rate in amount $\Delta\tau$ induces a change in the adjusted marginal propensity to consume of $-\alpha\Delta\tau$. We find, therefore, that

$$\Delta_\tau Y^m = -\alpha\Delta\tau Y^*$$

$$\Delta_\tau Y^{**} = 0$$

$$\Delta_\tau Y^* = 0 \tag{15.19}$$

$$\Delta_\tau Y^M = -\alpha\Delta\tau Y^{**}.$$

Changes in the tax rate can, therefore, cause switches in the profile of aggregate demand within the trapping set in a manner analogous to changes in expenditure as derived in equations (15.14)–(15.18). Corresponding qualitative changes in the behavior of aggregate income then occur.

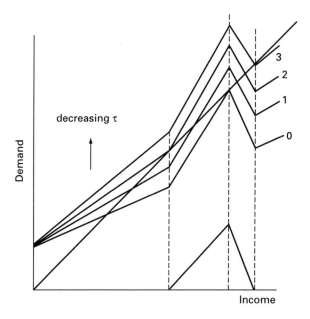

Figure 15.4
Changes in the tax rate

   The algebraic derivation of these bifurcation points can be left as an exercise, but it is perhaps instructive to look at the numerical bifurcation diagram for one of the three empirical cases. This is done in figure 15.5. There it is seen that complex changes in the qualitative behavior of model-generated aggregate income occur in response to increases or decreases in the tax rate. Apparently, changes in the qualitative pattern of aggregate income behavior caused by tax policy are roughly like those caused by expenditure policy, as can be seen by comparing the two bifurcation diagrams (figures 15.2, 15.5). This is because increases in G and decreases in τ shift aggregate demand upward. The effects are not exactly the same, however. The former shift is vertical and preserves the slopes of the various demand segments while the latter shift is a rotation; it increases the slopes of the first, second, and fourth segments while decreasing the slope of the third. But this doesn't appear to make much difference for Case I.
   The comparative desirability of a fluctuating economy or one in stable equilibrium can also be considered in this situation. Obviously, a jump up

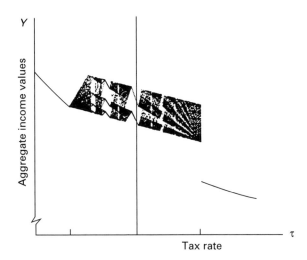

Figure 15.5
Comparative dynamics for the tax rate (or on the marginal propensity to consume)

in the average GNP occurs when the tax rate is reduced enough; even though fluctuations are induced, the average level will continue to trend upward as the tax rate is reduced. When a sufficiently low level is reached, however, the amplitude of fluctuation will fall (so the economy becomes more stable) and the average GNP level will also fall, a perhaps counterintuitive feature of less wide economic swings. Then as the tax rate is reduced still further, the economy becomes asymptotically stable again and the average (equilibrium) GNP resumes an upward response.

15.4 Monetary Policy

Monetary policy is represented by an exogenous change, ΔM, in the money supply M. Let Δ_m indicate the change in the variable it precedes caused by a change in the money supply, ΔM. Then it is easy to see that

$$\Delta_m Y^m = a\gamma/(\lambda\sigma)\Delta M$$

$$\Delta_m Y^{**} = (1/\kappa)\Delta M$$

$$\Delta_m Y^* = \gamma/(\lambda\sigma)\Delta M$$

$$\Delta_m Y^M = (b/\kappa)\Delta M$$

(15.20)

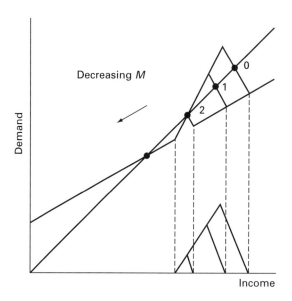

Figure 15.6
Changes in the money supply

where $b = a + \mu\beta$ as before. The parameters Y', a, b, and c are unaffected, so a change in the money supply involves a parallel shift in the third segment of the aggregate demand function (15.1), now defined in the interval $[Y^{**} + \Delta_m Y^{**}, Y^* + \Delta_m Y^*]$. That is, the investment-income (IY) function changes in the third regime where induced investment is sensitive to changes in the interest rate.

This is shown in figure 15.6. The three segments labeled 0, 1, and 2 correspond to money supplies M^0, M^1, M^2 where $M^2 < M^1 < M^0$. When the money supply is so small that induced investment is driven out altogether, the downward-sloping segment of aggregate demand disappears. Only the first regime is relevant in the range $[0, M^2/\kappa]$. Two bifurcation points are readily identified. When M is big enough (above M^0), the maximum potential value of aggregate demand exceeds Y^u and the model must shift to a non-Keynesian regime. When $M < M^2$ only a single, stable, stationary state exists. In between these values, cycles or chaos reign.

For the tilted-Z form to hold, the inequality expressions in (15.6) must be satisfied, so for the new money supply $M + \Delta M$ we must have

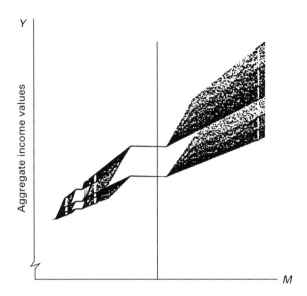

Figure 15.7
Comparative dynamics for the money supply

$$Y^m + a\gamma/(\lambda\sigma)\Delta M < Y^{**} + \kappa^{-1}\Delta M < Y^* + \gamma/(\lambda\sigma)\Delta M$$

$$< Y^M + b\kappa^{-1}\Delta M. \qquad (15.21)$$

If the last inequality on the right is reversed or replaced by an equality, the tilted-Z shape gives way to a single-peaked or tent shape. If b and c are greater than unity then $\theta(\cdot)$ is expansive on the trapping set, so aggregate income trajectories would be ergodic—a situation that prevails in each of the examples we have been using. On the other hand, if the left-most inequality in (15.21) is reversed or changed to an equality, then the tilted Z gives way to a check shape. Because $0 < a < 1$, $\theta(\cdot)$ is not expansive in R_3. But it is possible that a higher-order iterate is expansive on the entire trapping set if $ac < -1$. (See chapter 14.)

In figure 15.7 the bifurcation diagram is given for changes in the money supply using our familiar "empirical" example for Case I. Starting with its average value of M for the period 1930–1934, *increases or decreases have no influence at all until they are large enough. Then they set in train a growing complexity of behavior.* When the money supply decreases, the amplitude of fluctuation decreases but not complexity. When the money

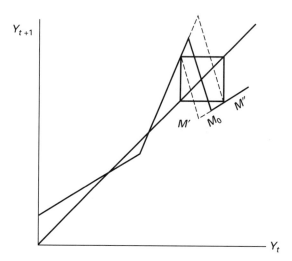

Figure 15.8
Changing into and out of chaos by changing the money supply

supply increases, the amplitude increases. In both cases the qualitative behavior switches from cycles to chaos over and over again as M changes.

To see exactly how such a perhaps counterintuitive relationship can emerge, consider the elaboration of figure 15.6 in figure 15.8. Suppose the initial money supply is M. Shifts in the money supply between M' and M'' yield aggregate demand functions that shift between the lines indicated in the diagram. The two-period cycle that exists for M is unchanged throughout this range. Beyond these points changes in the money supply induce chaotic fluctuations.

15.5   Summary and Conclusions

Some striking new insights have emerged from this reconsideration of the standard real/monetary macro theory in dynamic terms.

(i) Changes in policy instruments can trigger drastically different patterns of response depending on the preexisting policy instruments and their direction of change.

(ii) A policy may have no effect for small changes and then, after a threshold is reached, trigger great changes in behavior.

(iii) Complex dynamics can occur for a wide range of behavioral parameters and instrumental variable values; that is, intrinsic, chaotic fluctuations can occur robustly with respect to varying policy situations.

(iv) Situations may occur in which a change in a policy instrument can eliminate fluctuations but at the cost of a lower GNP—or, putting it the other way around, a change in policy instrument can trigger unstable fluctuations but with a higher average GNP over the cycle than before. A fluctuating economy might be more desirable than an asymptotically stable one.

(v) When variables treated as constants in the theory are allowed to change, such as autonomous expenditure, prices, and capital accumulation, the qualitative response of aggregate income to policy can change, even when all the policy parameters are fixed.

Evidently, policy makers may have even more to contend with in attempting to guide an economy than has already been recognized by macroeconomists. Comparative policy analysis needs to be concerned not just with the effects of monetary and fiscal parameters on the long-run level of output and employment; it also needs to recognize the potential ability of policy changes to shift output adjustments into cyclical or nonperiodic fluctuations in addition to possibly stabilizing such instabilities when they emerge. In addition, it needs to recognize the disconcerting possibility that the direction of influence on the economy of a given policy instrument under one set of conditions may be different than under another set of conditions.

For several reasons the analyses of chapters 13–15 are limited in applicability. Actual price and wage levels are seldom if ever stationary, and the aggregate supply of goods, money, and labor, capital accumulation, and the government budget constraint must all be brought into the picture in a nontrivial way in order to get a satisfactory understanding of macroeconomics. Nonetheless, the real/monetary theory remains of contemporary interest. First, it involves both monetary and "real" variables in a nontrivial way. Second, it provides an explanation of aggregate output when markets are not perfectly coordinated. Third, when the general price level is changing rather modestly, when output, employment, and especially interest rates and investment are changing relatively rapidly, and when the phenomenon of "crowding out" on money markets is at play—

all phenomena characteristic of some historical periods—then the model is useful as a first approximation of the real-world economy.

Certainly, the central place of the real/monetary analysis in economic policy gives it continuing significance whatever the current fashion in business cycle research might be. As we have seen, it is an instructive pedagogical vehicle for surveying the concepts and machinery of dynamic analysis. In any case, we have uncovered properties of the dynamic macro model that were unnoticed for more than half a century since the classic statement of the concepts on which it rests was published. That Keynes's basic ideas should have such intricate, nontrivial, yet newly perceived implications would seem to be a surprising and fitting testament to their inherent richness and continuing interest.

V ECONOMIC GROWTH

Growth—obeying
the iron law
—or breaking it
in chaotic flow

16 Capital Accumulation, Balanced Growth, and Growth Cycles

The development of the real gross national product of a country does not follow a smooth path but shows irregularities ...
—Erik Lundberg, *Instability and Economic Growth*

In this and the next two chapters the theory of growth trends and growth cycles is introduced. In contrast to the real/monetary business cycle theory investigated in part IV, emphasis here is on the long run. The business cycle theory provided clues about what can happen to aggregate economic variables such as national income, employment, and monetary interest rates in the short run as a result of adjustments in output and the interaction between product and money markets. For purposes of longer-run analysis, variables that play a central role include capital accumulation or decay, the rate of return on investment, the influence of time preference on savings, and changes in technology. In contrast to the models of part IV, monetary factors are here ignored and the labor and goods markets are assumed to clear. For simplicity, population is assumed to grow at a steady "natural" rate.

The discussion begins with the "one-sector" model in which the savings rate is a constant fraction of income and in which a production function with aggregate capital and labor as inputs allows for continuous factor substitution. It is perhaps the simplest possible model that can explain the growth trend of the nineteenth and twentieth centuries. Then a variable savings rate that exhibits "wealth saturation" is considered. The plot thickens. Either simple or complex dynamics can occur around a unique balanced-growth path. In addition to an asymptotically stable steady state, unstable fluctuations in the capital/labor ratio can occur. Coupled with the positive trends in population and technology, the implication is one of expanding oscillations in GNP fluctuating around a trend. A version of the model when savings is constrained by caution is given. The qualitative results are similar, but the effect of caution is to reduce the growth rate for a while and to moderate fluctuations when they occur. Examples of the model-generated growth cycles have a graphical appearance somewhat like actual data.[1]

In chapter 17 variable savings behavior is derived from an explicit economizing tradeoff between current consumption and an anticipated future sustainable standard of living. Agents are forward looking but consider their opportunities and tradeoffs anew in each period; they do not take account of the entire future in an intertemporally optimal manner. Their incomplete knowledge leads to wealth saturation and to the causal-effect-reversing nonlinearity illustrated in chapter 16. All of the possible kinds of simple and complex dynamics in the capital/labor ratio can occur, stable steady balanced growth being at one extreme and ergodic, irregular fluctuations at the other.[2]

Chapter 18 is devoted to concepts of optimal growth and their relationship to adaptive economizing behavior. Two characterizations of optimal growth are considered. The *Golden Rule of growth* involves the maximum sustainable level of per capita well-being. The dynamic *principle of optimality* requires that an infinite sequence of future savings and consumption decisions maximize an infinite sum of discounted future utilities, and that current consumption be representable by a strategy that is optimal with respect to the entire future regardless of what has happened in the past.[3] We consider how these two concepts are related to each other and to the adaptive economizing version of the growth theory analyzed in chapter 17. It is found that, at best, adaptive economizing trajectories may converge to the optimal path; at worst, they may fluctuate about it. In the latter event caution keeps the economy closer to the optimal path.

In the simplest optimal growth model, trajectories must be monotonic, but for a large class of viable bounded dynamical systems there can be specified an intertemporally optimal economy that will generate cyclic or chaotic trajectories. This result says that a very large class of growth paths can be rationalized.[4] Chapter 18 concludes with reflections on the meaning of this.

16.1 Production

Let aggregate output be determined by the production function

$$Y = BF(K, L) \tag{16.1}$$

where K is the aggregate capital stock, L is the available supply of labor, and B represents the level of technology. It will be convenient to interpret the labor supply as originating in two-adult households. One adult equivalent from each household is contributed to the labor force. In this way, the supply of labor is measured in adult equivalents, which is the same as the number of households.

It is assumed that $F(\cdot)$ is strictly concave, twice differentiable, and homogeneous of the first degree, that is, that for all $K, L > 0$,

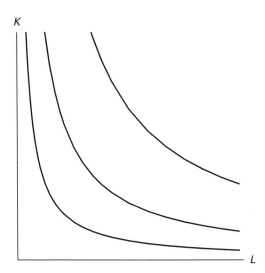

Figure 16.1
Production isoquants in (K, L) space

$$\frac{\partial F}{\partial L} > 0, \quad \frac{\partial F}{\partial K} > 0, \quad \frac{\partial^2 F}{\partial L^2} < 0, \quad \frac{\partial^2 F}{\partial K^2} < 0, \tag{16.2}$$

and that for any constant $\lambda > 0$,

$$F(\lambda K, \lambda L) = \lambda F(K, L). \tag{16.3}$$

It is also assumed that

$$F(0, L) = F(K, 0) = 0, \tag{16.4}$$

and that

$$\lim_{K \to 0} \frac{\partial F}{\partial K} = \infty = \lim_{L \to 0} \frac{\partial F}{\partial L}. \tag{16.5}$$

Isoquants of the production function are shown in figure 16.1. Such a production function is commonly said to be *neoclassical*.[5]

Given its homogeneity, the production function can be rewritten in terms of output per family by setting $\lambda = 1/L$ and substituting into (16.3). We get

$$y = Bf(k) := BF(K/L, 1) \tag{16.6}$$

where $y := Y/L$ (per family real aggregate output) and $k := K/L$ (per family real capital stock or the capital/labor ratio). The properties of this function that are important for what follows are given in

LEMMA 16.1 (Properties of Production)

(i) $f'(k) > 0, f''(k) < 0$ *for all* $k > 0$;

(ii) $f(0) = 0, \lim_{k \to 0} f'(k) = \infty$, *and* $\lim_{k \to \infty} f'(k) = 0$;

(iii) $f'(k) < f(k)/k$ *for all* $k > 0$;

(iv) $\lim_{k \to 0} f(k)/k = \infty$ *and* $\lim_{k \to \infty} f(k)/k = 0$;

(v) $y = w + rk$ *where* $r = Bf'(k)$ *is the (gross) rate of return on capital and* w *is the marginal product of labor, i.e.,* $w = B(\partial F/\partial L)$.

Proof Statements (i) and (ii) follow directly from the assumed conditions on F and its partials; (iii) follows from the Mean Value Theorem[6] and (i). The second expression in (ii) together with (iii) implies the first expression in (iv). The second expression in (iv) is obtained by using the homogeneity of F to get, for all $K > 0$,

$$\lim_{L \to 0} F(K, L) = K \lim_{L \to 0} \frac{L}{K} F(K/L, 1)$$

$$= K \lim_{k \to \infty} [1/(K/L)]F(K/L, 1) = K \lim_{k \to \infty} \frac{f(k)}{k} = 0.$$

For (v), take the derivative of both sides of (16.3) with respect to λ, set $\lambda = 1$, and multiply by B to get $B[(\partial F/\partial K)K + (\partial F/\partial L)L] = Y$. Dividing by L gives $y = w + rk$. ∎

The average product of capital is everywhere greater than the marginal product, a consequence of the assumed diminishing productivity of capital. The average income distribution Y/L is equivalent to saying that labor and capital receive their marginal products.

16.2 Economic Growth with Constant Savings Rates

16.2.1 Capital Accumulation

The capital accumulation identity is

$$K_{t+1} = (1 - \delta)K_t + I_t \tag{16.7}$$

where K_t is the capital stock available for production in period t, δ is the real depreciation rate so that $(1 - \delta)K_t$ is the amount of capital stock carried forward to the next period, and I_t is new investment.

To keep matters simple—at least for the time being—suppose that the work force grows exponentially[7] at a rate n so that

$$L_{t+1} = (1 + n)L_t. \tag{16.8}$$

Dividing (16.7) by this expression, we get the capital accumulation identity in per family terms

$$k_{t+1} = \frac{1}{1+n}[(1 - \delta)k_t + i_t] \tag{16.9}$$

where $i_t := I_t/L_t$ is per family investment.

Suppose that induced consumption is a constant fraction, say $(1 - \mu)$, of income. Then savings is also a constant fraction, μ, of income. The consumption function is therefore

$$c = (1 - \mu)y = h(k) := (1 - \mu)Bf(k) \tag{16.10}$$

and the savings function is

$$s = \mu y = s(k) := \mu Bf(k). \tag{16.11}$$

The functions $Bf(\cdot)$, $h(\cdot)$, and $s(\cdot)$ are illustrated in figure 16.2.

Assuming that savings equals investment, we get the difference equation

$$k_{t+1} = \theta(k_t) := \frac{1}{1+n}[(1 - \delta)k_t + \mu Bf(k_t)]. \tag{16.12}$$

It completely describes the dynamics of the capital/labor ratio from which the trajectories of labor utilization, the aggregate capital stock, and real aggregate output can be recovered. Thus, from (16.8)

$$L_t = (1 + n)^t L_0, \tag{16.13}$$

so that

$$K_t = k_t(1 + n)^t L_0 \tag{16.14}$$

and

$$Y_t = Bf(k_t)(1 + n)^t L_0. \tag{16.15}$$

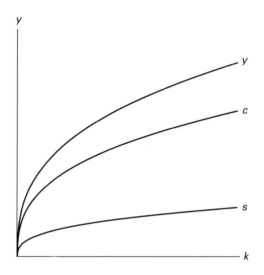

Figure 16.2
Production, consumption, and savings as functions of wealth

Population follows an exponential growth path. To determine the time path of capital and aggregate output, the behavior of k_t must be derived.

16.2.2   Qualitative Dynamics: Balanced Growth and the Steady State

A stationary state for the growth process is a capital/labor ratio $\tilde{k}$ that satisfies

$$k_{t+1} = k_t = \tilde{k} \quad \text{or} \quad (n+\delta)\tilde{k} = \mu B f(\tilde{k}). \tag{16.16}$$

If $k_0 = \tilde{k}$, then from the preceding equations for capital and output, $K_t = \tilde{k}(1+n)^t L_0$ and $Y_t = B f(\tilde{k})(1+n)^t L_0$, which means that capital stock and real aggregate output grow exponentially. The stationary capital/labor ratio is therefore associated with an economy where all the variables grow steadily in fixed proportion to one another. For this reason $\tilde{k}$ is called a *steady state* and in such a state the economy is said to follow a *balanced growth path*. The following shows that this path describes the long-run behavior of the model economy under consideration:

PROPOSITION 16.1   *Given a neoclassical production function, a constant rate of population growth, $n > 0$, and a constant savings fraction of real aggregate output, $0 < \mu < 1$, the capital/labor ratio converges monotonically to a unique, positive steady state,*

$k_t \to \tilde{k}$;

aggregate capital stock and real aggregate output converge to balanced exponential growth paths proportional to population growth. Thus,

$$K_t \to \tilde{k}(1+n)^t L_0 \quad \text{and} \quad Y_t \to Bf(\tilde{k})(1+n)^t L_0.$$

Proof Notice first that for all $k > 0$,

$$0 < \theta(k) = \frac{1}{1+n}[(1-\delta)k + \mu Bf(k)] < \frac{1}{1+n}[(1-\delta)k + Bf(k)],$$

which implies that viable trajectories exist for all positive initial conditions.

The existence of a steady state follows from Lemma 16.1, for, as $\mu B \frac{f(k)}{k}$ falls monotonically from $+\infty$ to 0 as k goes from 0 to ∞, it must pass through a unique positive value $\tilde{k}$ such that $\mu Bf(\tilde{k})/\tilde{k} = n + \delta$ (from Theorem 5.6).

For the steady state to be asymptotically stable, the following conditions must prevail:

$$-1 < \theta'(\tilde{k}) = \frac{1}{1+n}[(1-\delta) + \mu Bf'(\tilde{k})] < 1. \tag{16.17}$$

Because $f'(\tilde{k})$ is positive, $\theta'(\tilde{k})$ is always positive. From Lemma 16.1 (iii), $f'(\tilde{k}) < \frac{f(\tilde{k})}{\tilde{k}}$. Therefore,

$$\frac{1}{1+n}[1 - \delta + \mu Bf'(\tilde{k})] < \frac{1}{1+n}\left[1 - \delta + \mu B \frac{f(\tilde{k})}{\tilde{k}}\right]$$

$$= \frac{1}{1+n}[1 - \delta + n + \delta] = 1,$$

so the right inequality in (16.17) always holds. By Theorem 5.7, trajectories that come close enough to the steady state converge to it.

In this case, *all* trajectories that begin with positive initial conditions converge. The reason is that $\theta(x) > x$ for all $x < \tilde{x}$ and, as $\theta(x)$ is increasing, $\{\theta^t(x)\}_t$ is an increasing sequence bounded above by $\tilde{x}$. Likewise, $\theta(x) < x$ for all $x > \tilde{x}$ so $\{\theta^t(x)\}_t$ must form a decreasing sequence bounded below by $\tilde{x}$. ∎

These conclusions are illustrated in figure 16.3. Figure 16.3a shows the dynamic process in terms of the capital/labor ratio, and figure 16.3b illustrates the asymptotically stable balanced-growth path in the (K, L)

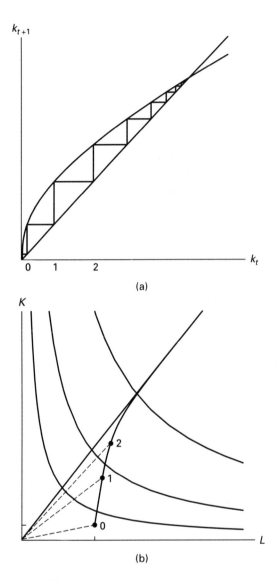

Figure 16.3
Convergence to the steady state and balanced growth. (a) The phase diagram. (b) (K, L)
space.

space. In this world, fluctuations in real aggregate output would have to be caused by shocks to the system—shocks to productivity, to the savings rate, to the depreciation rate, to the capital stock, or to the population growth rate.

16.2.3 Example

Suppose that

$$F(K, L) = K^\beta L^{1-\beta}. \tag{16.18}$$

Then

$$f(k) = k^\beta. \tag{16.19}$$

It is easy to show that the conditions of production (16.2)–(16.6) are satisfied.

16.2.4 Technological Change

Suppose technological change is introduced in the form of a *labor-augmenting productivity factor, E*, according to

$$E_{t+1} = (1 + \tau)E_t. \tag{16.20}$$

Rewrite (16.1) as

$$Y = BF(K, EL). \tag{16.21}$$

Dividing both sides by EL, we get

$$y = Bf(z) := BF[K/(EL), 1] \tag{16.22}$$

where $y := Y/(EL)$ and $z := K/(EL)$. Refer to the variable EL as a *labor productivity unit*. Then y and z are measured not in labor units (as before), but in labor productivity units. Dividing the capital accumulation identity (16.7) by the population equation (16.8) and by the productivity equation (16.20), we get the analogue of equation (16.12), but now in terms of the capital/labor productivity unit ratio. The form of the equation is identical except for the change in units and the extra constant that accounts for the increase in productivity:

$$z_{t+1} = \frac{1}{(1 + \tau)(1 + n)}[(1 - \delta)z_t + \mu Bf(z_t)]. \tag{16.23}$$

The preceding analysis applies with little change. The exponential growth of the work force remains the same, but now

$$K_t = z_t[(1+n)(1+\tau)]^t L_0 E_0 \tag{16.24}$$

and

$$Y_t = Bf(z_t)[(1+n)(1+\tau)]^t L_0 E_0. \tag{16.25}$$

The same stability argument goes through, so Proposition 16.1 is modified only slightly to get

PROPOSITION 16.2   *Given a neoclassical production function that incorporates labor-augmenting technological change at a constant rate, τ, and a constant population rate of growth, n, the capital/labor productivity ratio converges asymptotically to a positive steady state,*

$$z_t \to \tilde{z};$$

aggregate capital stock and real aggregate output converge to steady exponential growth paths proportional to the product of the initial work force and initial productivity factor, thus,

$$K_t \to [(1+n)(1+\tau)]^t \tilde{z} L_0 E_0$$

and

$$Y_t \to [(1+n)(1+\tau)]^t Bf(\tilde{z}) L_0 E_0.$$

The effect of technological advance is, therefore, to speed up the rate of growth.

16.2.5   Example

Replace (16.18) by

$$F(K,L) = K^\beta (EL)^{1-\beta}. \tag{16.26}$$

Then the results of Proposition 16.2 are readily verified.

16.3   Variable Savings Rates

In the remainder of this chapter, variable consumption and savings rates are considered. Continuous productivity improvement will be taken up after we see what happens when technology is constant.

16.3.1 Wealth Saturation

It is reasonable to suppose that current consumption, c, and savings, s, are not constant fractions of income but depend on income, y, wealth, k, and the rate of return on investment, r. Consider, for example, a consumption relationship

$$c = c(y, k, r).$$

Drawing on the representation of production as in (16.6) with $y = Bf(k)$ and setting $r = Bf'(k)$, we can define an *unconstrained consumption/wealth function*

$$g(k) := c(Bf(k), k, Bf'(k)). \tag{16.27}$$

Let us assume that it is a monotonically increasing function of k, as shown by

$$g'(k) = \frac{\partial c}{\partial y}r + \frac{\partial c}{\partial k} + \frac{\partial c}{\partial r}r'(k) > 0. \tag{16.28}$$

Suppose there exists a wealth level, k^s, which, if exceeded, would lead to a level of consumption that would exceed current income. Let $y^s = Bf(k^s)$ and $r^s = Bf'(k^s)$. Such a situation implies that when income and wealth are great enough and when the opportunity cost of consumption (or, what is the same thing, when the return to savings) is small enough, then consumption would exceed income *if it could*. Within the present model this could occur only if capital is fungible, for, once production capacity is fully utilized and total output consumed, that is the only source of further consumption. However, I shall assume that capital stock cannot be consumed once it is in place but can only be used to generate income. This implies that c and s are bounded above and below, respectively, by y and 0; that is,

$$0 < c < y \quad \text{and} \quad 0 < s = y - c < y. \tag{16.29}$$

Define

$$K^s := (0, k^s), \quad K^d := [k^s, \infty).$$

Assume that

$$g(0) = 0, \quad 0 < g(k) < Bf(k), \quad k \in K^s$$

and $$\qquad\qquad g(k) \geq Bf(k), \quad k \in \mathcal{K}^d. \tag{16.30}$$

The *constrained consumption/wealth function* defined by

$$c = h(k) = \begin{cases} g(k), & k \in \mathcal{K}^s \\ Bf(k), & k \in \mathcal{K}^d \end{cases} \tag{16.31}$$

satisfies the income constraint (16.29).

Now consider the savings function $s(k) := Bf(k) - h(k)$. We know that when $k < k^s$, $g(k)$ is monotonically increasing but less than $f(k)$ which is also monotonically increasing, so $s(k)$ must increase when k is small enough. Since $g(k) > Bf(k)$ when k exceeds k^s, the savings/wealth function satisfies

$$s = s(k) := \begin{cases} Bf(k) - h(k) > 0, & k \in \mathcal{K}^s \\ 0, & k \in \mathcal{K}^d. \end{cases} \tag{16.32}$$

I shall say that consumption/savings behavior that satisfies the properties shown in (16.30)–(16.32) exhibits *wealth saturation*.

What is the profile of $s(k)$? From Lemma 16.1 and (16.29), $s(0) = 0$. Certainly, $0 < s(k) < Bf(k)$, $k \in \mathcal{K}^s$. The fact that $s(k) = 0$ for $k \geq k^s$ implies that $s(k)$ must decrease for k close enough to k^s. That is all that can be said without placing further restrictions. But that is enough to infer a significant potential influence on the dynamics of capital accumulation.

Possible profiles for the consumption and savings functions are shown in figure 16.4. These may be compared with the constant savings rate case illustrated in figure 16.2. Clearly, the introduction of wealth saturation brings about an entirely different set of possibilities for the accumulation of capital and the growth path of per family income and real aggregate output.

16.3.2 Qualitative Dynamics

Assuming that savings equals investment as before, the process of capital accumulation is now a two-phase system:

$$k_{t+1} = \begin{cases} \theta_s(k_t) := \frac{1}{1+n}[(1-\delta)k_t + s(k_t)], & k_t \in \mathcal{K}^s \\ \theta_d(k_t) := \frac{1}{1+n}(1-\delta)k_t, & k_t \in \mathcal{K}^d. \end{cases} \tag{16.33}$$

Assume that $s(k)$ is concave and that

$$s(k) > (n+\delta)k \quad \text{for some} \quad k \in \mathcal{K}^s.$$

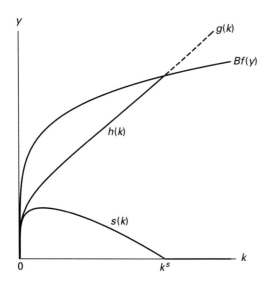

Figure 16.4
Consumption and savings as functions of wealth: the case of wealth saturation

Then there exists a unique positive steady state $\tilde{k} \in \mathcal{K}^s$ such that

$$s(\tilde{k}) = (n + \delta)\tilde{k}.$$

It could be either asymptotically stable or unstable, depending on the character of $s(k)$ for $k \in \mathcal{K}^s$. For example, if $s'(k) < -2 - n + \delta$, the stationary state would be unstable. Trajectories will eventually overshoot the steady state and fluctuations will take place. To see what will happen then, the trapping set, V, must be considered. It can take one of three forms shown in figure 16.5. These are constructed in a manner analogous to that carried out for the real/monetary business cycle model in §13.1.3. Let

$$k^M := \max_{k \in \mathcal{K}^s} \theta(k) \quad \text{and} \quad k^m := \theta(k^s).$$

Then the three cases are:

Case I: $\quad V^{\mathrm{I}} = [k^m, k^M]$

Case II: $\quad V^{\mathrm{II}} = [\theta(k^M), k^M]$ (16.34)

Case III: $\quad V^{\mathrm{III}} = [k^m, \theta(k^m)]$

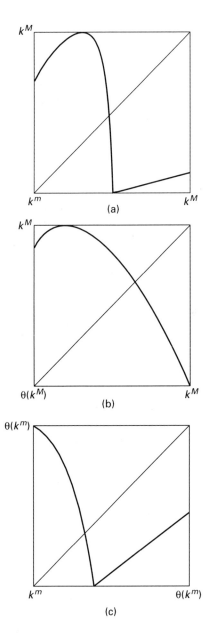

Figure 16.5
Profiles of the trapping set. (a) Case I. (b) Case II. (c) Case III.

Certainly, there are many continuous concave functions $s(\cdot)$ that satisfy the chaos conditions and ergodicity theorems (Theorems 7.1, 7.3, or 7.4 and 8.4 or 8.6). By assumption $f(\cdot)$ is concave, and it was shown that $g(\cdot)$ is monotonically increasing. These are not enough to insure that $s(k)$ is concave. In chapter 17 a concave savings function will be derived for which the chaos and ergodic conditions are generic, thus providing a constructive proof of the following informal result.

PROPOSITION 16.3 *Given the one-sector growth model with a neoclassical production function, there exist savings/capital relationships with wealth saturation such that all the types of simple and complex dynamics are potential possibilities.*

By "potential" is meant here that none of the various possibilities—asymptotic convergent, cyclic, chaotic, and strongly chaotic trajectories—can be ruled out a priori. Figure 16.6 illustrates an example in which chaotic growth fluctuations occur.

16.4   Caution and Restrained Growth

16.4.1   A Behavioral Hypothesis

Suppose now that the substitution of capital for labor is restrained by a *maximal potential growth rate*, say λ. Such restraint would arise if agents had an absolute preference for limiting the rate of expansion, (i) for purely psychological reasons; (ii) because of a cost of adjustment; or (iii) as a tactic for avoiding the uncertainties inherent in a changing way of life. Specifically, assume that $g(k)$ is defined as before but that

$$c = h(k) := \begin{cases} Bf(k) - \lambda k, & k \in \mathcal{K}^{\lambda} \\ g(k), & k \in \mathcal{K}^{s'} \\ Bf(k), & k \in \mathcal{K}^{d}. \end{cases} \tag{16.35}$$

Where

$$\mathcal{K}^{s'} := \{k \in \mathcal{K}^{s} \,|\, 0 < Bf(k) - g(k) < \lambda k\}$$

and

$$\mathcal{K}^{\lambda} := \{k \in \mathcal{K}^{s} \,|\, \lambda k \leq Bf(k) - g(k)\},$$

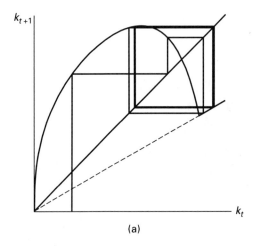

(a)

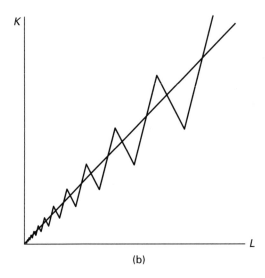

(b)

Figure 16.6
Growth fluctuations. (a) The phase diagram. (b) (K, L) space.

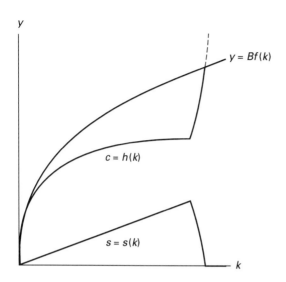

Figure 16.7
Caution-constrained growth

(16.32) then becomes

$$s = s(k) := \begin{cases} \lambda k, & k \in \mathcal{K}^\lambda \\ Bf(k) - g(k), & k \in \mathcal{K}^{s'} \\ 0, & k \in \mathcal{K}^d. \end{cases} \quad (16.36)$$

The process of capital accumulation is now represented by the three-phase system

$$k_{t+1} = \theta(k_t) := \begin{cases} \theta_s(k_t) = \frac{1}{1+n}[(1-\delta)k_t + Bf(k) - g(k)], & k_t \in \mathcal{K}^{s'} \\ \theta_\lambda(k_t) = \frac{1}{1+n}(1-\delta+\lambda)k_t, & k_t \in \mathcal{K}^\lambda \\ \theta_d(k_t) = \frac{1}{1+n}(1-\delta)k_t, & k_t \in \mathcal{K}^d. \end{cases}$$
(16.37)

Thus, when caution is not a concern, $k_t \in \mathcal{K}^{s'}$. When it is a concern, $k_t \in \mathcal{K}^\lambda$. In effect, caution about the future implies higher consumption in the present than would be chosen strictly on the basis of current income, wealth, and the rate of return on savings. The caution-constrained consumption and savings function with wealth saturation are shown in figure 16.7.

16.4.2   Qualitative Dynamics

Assume that $s(k)$ is concave and there exists a capital/labor ratio, $k' > 0$, such that

$$\frac{s(k')}{k'} > \lambda > n + \delta.$$

Then there exists a capital/labor ratio, say k^{λ}, such that

$$\mathcal{K}^{\lambda} = (0, k^{\lambda}], \quad \mathcal{K}^{s'} = (k^{\lambda}, k^{s}), \quad \mathcal{K}^{d} = [k^{s}, \infty).$$

This result follows from the continuity and concavity of $s(k)$ on $\mathcal{K}^{s} = (0, k^{s})$, which also implies that there exists a unique positive stationary state, $\tilde{k}$, such that $s(\tilde{k}) = (n + \delta)\tilde{k}$, as shown figure 16.8.

Asymptotic stability and instability follow as in the incautious case. If the rate-of-return effect is very strong and if λ is small enough that $s'(k^{\lambda}) < -2 + n - \delta$, then (because of concavity) $\theta'(k) < -1$ for all $k \in \mathcal{K}^{s}$. Obviously, $\theta'(k) = 1 - \delta + \lambda$ for all $k \in \mathcal{K}^{\lambda}$, which by hypothesis is greater than unity. Consequently, $\theta'(k)$ will be expansive for all $k \in (0, k^{s})$.

If λ is large enough, the trapping sets can have the forms given in figure 16.5. If λ is small enough, two additional cases occur as shown in figure 16.8. For Case II$'$ the expansivity tells us that ergodic fluctuations occur almost surely. Notice, however, that expansivity throughout $\mathcal{K}^{s'}$ can only occur if λ is small enough.

In Case I$'$ expansivity for $\theta(\cdot)$ cannot occur because $0 < \theta'(k) < 1$ for all $k \in \mathcal{K}^{d}$. However, it can be shown that if $\theta'(k^{\lambda})$ is strongly negative enough, then there will exist an integer such that the map $\theta^{n}(k)$ is expansive, again implying strongly ergotic fluctuations. Here we are appealing to the Lasota-Yorke Theorem 8.4. When the Case II map is nonexpansive (which happens surely when $k^{M} > k^{\lambda}$), then strong ergodicity could still occur when the Misiurewicz Theorem 8.6 is satisfied.

One or the other of the Li-Yorke or LIMPY chaos conditions can also clearly be satisfied for λ small and $\theta'(\tilde{k})$ strongly negative. For example, in Case II$'$ let the capital/labor ratio k^{**}, where

$$(1 + n)k^{M} = (1 - \delta + \lambda)k^{**} = (1 - \delta)k^{**} + s(k^{**}),$$

satisfy $k^{**} = k^{\lambda}$. Let $k^{c} = \frac{1+n}{1+\lambda-\delta}k^{**}$. The inequalities $k^{c} < k^{**} < k^{M}$ will hold because $\lambda > n + \delta$. Assuming this restriction, the Li-Yorke sufficient

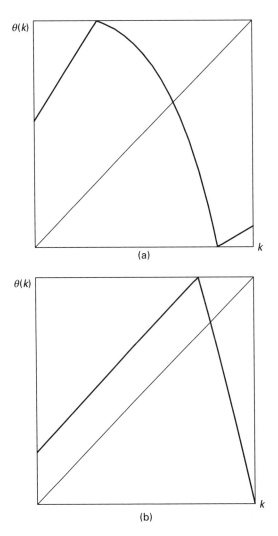

Figure 16.8
Profiles of the trapping set when caution is effective. (a) Case I′. (b) Case II′.

conditions for chaos reduce to the inequality

$$s\left[\frac{1 - \delta + \lambda}{1 + n} k^{**}\right] \leq \left[\frac{(1 + n)^2}{1 - \delta + \lambda} \frac{1 - \delta}{1 + n}(1 - \delta + \lambda)\right] k^{**}. \tag{16.38}$$

The upshot then of wealth saturation in the restrained growth case is similar to that in the unrestrained case and we can assert:

PROPOSITION 16.4 *All types of simple and complex dynamics occur generically in the model of restrained growth.*

The effect of caution in the form introduced here is not to eliminate complex dynamics but rather to slow down growth and, if the steady state is unstable, to moderate the fluctuations. Figure 16.9 gives an example based on the savings function used for figure 16.6.

16.5 Technological Change and Growth Cycles

Suppose labor-augmenting productivity advances at the rate τ as assumed above in §16.4. Suppose also that the consumption function, $c(y, k, r)$, is homogeneous of degree one in income and wealth. Define the capital/labor ratio in efficiency units so that

$$z = k/E.$$

Then it can be shown that

$$s(k)/E = s(z).$$

In the case of the unrestrained growth model with wealth saturation, the difference equation corresponding to (16.34) is

$$z_{t+1} = \begin{cases} \theta_s(z_t) := \frac{1}{(1+n)(1+\tau)}[(1 - \delta)z_t + s(z_t)], & z_t \in \mathscr{Z}^s \\ \theta_d(z_t) := \frac{1}{(1+n)(1+\tau)}(1 - \delta)z_t, & z_t \in \mathscr{Z}^d, \end{cases}$$

while in the restrained growth case it is

$$z_{t+1} = \begin{cases} \theta_s(z_t) := \frac{1}{(1+n)(1+\tau)}[(1 - \delta)z_t + s(z_t)], & z_t \in \mathscr{Z}^{s'} \\ \theta_\lambda(z_t) := \frac{1}{(1+n)(1+\tau)}(1 - \delta + \lambda)z_t, & z_t \in \mathscr{Z}^\lambda \\ \theta_d(z_t) := \frac{1}{(1+n)(1+\tau)}(1 - \delta)z_t, & z_t \in \mathscr{Z}^d. \end{cases}$$

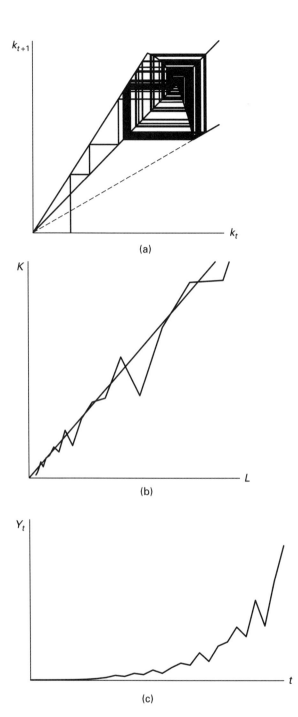

Figure 16.9
Cautious growth fluctuations. (a) The phase diagram. (b) The trajectory in (K, L) space.
(c) The trajectory of GNP.

Obviously, there exists a steady state and all types of simple and complex dynamics occur generically. When growth fluctuations occur, they do so around a rising trend, and from the definitions of K_t and Y_t the amplitude of the fluctuations increase over time. The effect of technological change, then, is not only to increase the rate of growth of this trend, but to increase the rate of growth in the amplitude of the fluctuations. In short, we have:

PROPOSITION 16.5   *The effects of a positive trend in labor-augmenting productivity in the (unrestrained or restrained) growth model with wealth saturation are: (i) to increase the rate of growth in the steady state; and (ii) if the steady state is unstable, to induce expansion in the amplitude of fluctuations at a faster rate than would occur in the absence of technological advance.*

17 Adaptive Economizing: Generic Properties

Dynamic theory ... shows how certain changes in the variables can be explained on the basis of ... structural characteristics of the system. ... The economy, of course, does not necessarily find an equilibrium position.
—Wassily Leontief, *Studies in the Structure of the American Economy* and "Theoretical Note on Time Preference"

A model of adaptive economizing is now investigated that incorporates an explicit tradeoff between current satisfaction and future benefits—but in conditions where agents cannot foresee the future and must try to forecast the consequence of present choice. Such an economy exhibits wealth saturation and can generate all the possibilities of simple and complex dynamics.

17.1 The Model

17.1.1 Adaptive Economizing

Think of an overlapping-generations framework for a private ownership economy. Adults of a given generation are manager-worker-owners to whom all proceeds of production are distributed in the form of wages or salary and dividends or real interest. They determine consumption and savings for themselves and their children. The savings are invested, and the capital stock that results, allowing for depreciation in the meantime, is the bequest that constitutes the endowment for the next generation of adults. Suppose the adults explicitly consider the tradeoff between their own consumption and the standard of living their heirs can potentially enjoy, and determine their behavior accordingly. The adults of the next period then repeat the same economizing decision but on the basis of the capital stock inherited from their predecessors.[1]

The agents do not know exactly what their future incomes will be on the basis of their current actions. They base their decisions on the current rate of return, which enables them to estimate the effect on future income of current savings.

Our boundedly rational agents also do not account for the possibility that the succeeding generation will face a similar problem and will weigh the opportunity cost and satisfaction of current savings on its own terms. Each bequest is, therefore, merely a *potential* consumption level, which could be enjoyed forever if each generation chose to maintain the stock of capital at its inherited level. In effect each generation bestows a *flexible asset*, the potential income in perpetuity, leaving it up to its heirs to decide what to do with it when they take control.[2] An intertemporally optimal model would have to incorporate the entire sequence of choices in a way that accounted for the reconsideration of the problem in each and every future period. Such an ideal representation of aggregate capital accumulation is taken up in the next chapter. The current approach reduces the infinite horizon problem to a two-period problem, one much less demanding of information and computational capability and therefore somewhat closer to the way decisions are made in the real world.

In contrast to the long-run generational interpretation, we could have a shorter time frame in mind, such as a decade or even a year. Agents provide for the long run by endowing themselves with capital stock that can generate a flow of income in the future without trying to determine what will happen over the entire conceivable future. This income can be allocated between consumption and savings in the next period—when the time comes and when one finds out what the real rate of return turns out to be. When the next time period arrives, a new income is realized, a new rate of return on investment at the new inherited capital stock is perceived, and, if this situation is different from before, the new plan leads to a new consumption level, possibly different from the one planned in the preceding period. Regardless of the time frame of reference, the implication is the same: knowledge evolves, plans are made anew, and capital accumulates or decumulates according to an *adaptive economizing model* of consumption and savings.

17.1.2 Historical Time and Planning Time

In developing the analysis of the adaptive economizing and optimal growth models of this and the succeeding chapter, I am going to use a notation that distinguishes between *historical time*, represented by a *subscript*, as has been done all along to this point, and *planning time*, represented by a *superscript*, which represents the anticipated future. For example, if x were a decision variable, x_t^i would be the value to be acted on i periods in the future but determined "now," where "now" is at historical time t. Then x_t^0 is the value of the decision variable planned for the current period, that is, "now."

Let x_t be the value actually acted on in the current period. In what follows, I shall assume the *temporary equilibrium condition*,

$$x_t = x_t^0,$$

that is, that the act planned for the current period is actually carried out. Plans for the future, however, are not always carried out, so that it could (and usually will) happen that $x_t^i \neq x_{t+i}$.

As a further convention, when analyzing the planning problem of the forward-looking agent, I shall treat x^i as the decision variable *to be* determined at the historical time t which is "now" and x_t^i as the value that *is* determined at the historical time t. In this chapter, as discussed above, I only consider agents who plan ahead a single generation. Let c^0 be the level of current consumption to be determined "now" and c^1 be the potential future standard of living in perpetuity, also to be calculated "now." Since c_t^0 will be a temporary equilibrium, we can drop the superscript in c^0 and denote by c the current level of consumption to be determined.

Throughout this chapter, the neoclassical production function is assumed as described in §16.1.

17.1.3 Consumption and Savings Strategies

Preferences of each generation are representable by a utility function

$$u(c) + \psi u(c^1) \tag{17.1}$$

where ψ is called the *future weight*. The larger ψ, the greater the weight given to the flexible asset bestowed upon the next generation. It will be assumed that for all $c > 0$,

$$u'(c) > 0, \quad u''(c) < 0, \quad \text{and} \quad \lim_{c \to 0} u'(c) = \infty. \tag{17.2}$$

Examples of utility functions satisfying these conditions are

$$u(c) = Ac^a, \quad 0 < a < 1, A > 0 \qquad \text{(a)}$$
$$u(c) = A + a \log c, \quad 0 < a \le 1, A \ge 0. \quad \text{(b)} \tag{17.3}$$

Notice that in (a) the parameter a must be less than 1 but not in (b).

If each future generation actually endowed its heirs with enough capital stock to maintain the standard of living of its forebears, the second term of (17.1) would be equivalent to the discounted sum of the utilities of the constant stream of consumption c^1 as given in

$$\alpha u(c^1) + \alpha^2 u(c^1) + \alpha^3 u(c^1) + \cdots = \sum_{i=1}^{\infty} \alpha^i u(c^1)$$

$$= \frac{\alpha}{1-\alpha} u(c^1) = \psi u(c^1), \qquad (17.4)$$

where α is the *time preference* with $0 < \alpha < 1$ and $\psi = \alpha/(1-\alpha)$. If α is close to zero, ψ is also; the future generations are given negligible weight; time preference is strong. If α is close to 1, then ψ is very large; future generations are given strong consideration; time preference is weak. As shall be seen in the succeeding chapter, this formulation establishes a link between the present approach and that of intertemporally optimal behavior.

The sustainable standard of living must account for the maintenance of the capital stock and the need to provide an endowment for net additions to the work force. This means that savings in the future would have to equal depreciation plus an increment based on the rate of population growth in order to maintain the standard of living. Thus,

$$c^1 = y^1 - (n+\delta)k^1. \qquad (17.5)$$

The capital bequest is equal to the amount of capital remaining at the end of the period plus current gross investment. The latter must be large enough to allow for population growth. Therefore,

$$k^1 = \frac{1}{1+n}[y - c + (1-\delta)k]. \qquad (17.6)$$

Our forward-looking agents understand these connections and, as a result, know that the future standard of living depends on current consumption. If they completely understand the production function, then they can compute $y^1 = Bf(k^1)$ for any k^1 and in this way obtain an exact prediction of the effects of current action. In this case, they can base their current decisions on *perfect knowledge*.[3]

If, however, they cannot foretell the future output or future rate of return on capital because they do not have complete knowledge of the production function, then they cannot compute $Bf(k^1)$ or $Bf'(k^1)$. But suppose they do perceive current output y and the current rate of return r, and use the latter as a basis for the consumption/bequest tradeoff, setting

$$r^1 = r \qquad (17.7)$$

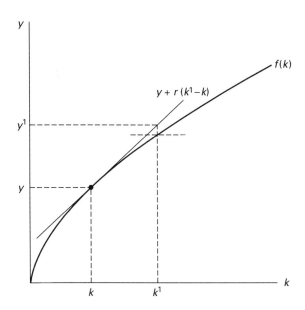

Figure 17.1
The naive adaptive forecast

where r^1 is the rate of return *anticipated* for the next period. They get a rough estimate or first-order approximation of $Bf(k^1)$ by setting

$$y^1 = y + r(k^1 - k). \tag{17.8}$$

This approximation, also called an extrapolative or "naive" adaptive forecast, is illustrated in figure 17.1.[4]

Subtracting k from both sides in (17.6) and collecting terms shows that the amount of capacity expansion that would result after depreciation and population growth are taken into account is

$$k^1 - k = \frac{y - c - (n + \delta)k}{1 + n}. \tag{17.9}$$

This amount could be negative if agents in the current generation plan to leave their heirs with a smaller capital stock than their own. Otherwise, it is positive. Combining (17.8) and (17.9), we find that

$$y^1 = y + r\frac{[y - c - (n + \delta)k]}{1 + n},$$

which implies that

$$c^1 = y + \frac{r - (n + \delta)}{1 + n}(y - c) - \frac{(r + 1 - \delta)}{1 + n}(n + \delta)k \qquad (17.10)$$

As shall be seen, it is convenient to reexpress this equation in the form

$$c^1 = c^1(c; k) := (1 + \rho)[y - (n + \delta)k] - \rho c \qquad (17.11)$$

where

$$\rho = \frac{r - (n + \delta)}{1 + n}$$

is the *current net rate of return on investment*. Let k^0 satisfy $r^0 = n + \delta$. Then

$$\rho^0 = \frac{r^0 - (n + \delta)}{1 + n} = 0. \qquad (17.12)$$

Obviously, ρ can be positive, zero, or negative, depending on whether or not r is greater than, equal to, or less than $(n + \delta)$.[5]

The most preferred combination of present consumption and future sustainable standard of living, (c_t, c_t^1), as viewed by the current generation, maximizes the utility function (17.1) subject to the relationships between present and future consumption possibilities given by (17.11) and subject to the constraint that capital cannot be consumed, i.e.,

$$0 \le c \le y. \qquad (17.13)$$

This is equivalent to (c_t, c_t^1) satisfying the maximizing relationship,

$$V^a(k) := \max_{0 \le c \le y} \{u(c) + \psi u(c^1) \mid c^1 = c^1(c; k)\}$$

where $V^a(k)$ is the *present value (or indirect utility) function*. Substituting for $c^1 = c^1(c; k)$, the preferred current consumption level must satisfy

$$V^a(k_t) = u(c_t) + \psi u([1 + \rho_t][y_t - (n + \delta)k_t] - \rho_t c_t). \qquad (17.14)$$

This is an implicit function in c_t, y_t, k_t, and ρ_t. Assuming it can be solved, we could write

$$c_t = c(y_t, k_t, \rho_t).$$

At the beginning of a given period, $k = k_t$, $y = y_t$, and $\rho = \rho_t$ where

$$\rho_t = \frac{r_t - (n + \delta)}{1 + n}.$$

Our boundedly rational agents treat r_t, k_t, and y_t as independent parameters, but *we* know that

$$r_t = Bf'(k_t), \quad y_t = Bf(k_t).$$

In theory, therefore, y_t and ρ_t depend on k_t so the current consumption c_t is a function of k_t,

$$c_t = h^a(k_t) = c\left(Bf(k_t), k_t, \frac{Bf'(k_t) - (n + \delta)}{1 + n}\right).$$

I shall call this function the (implicit) *adaptive economizing consumption strategy*. This is the analog of (16.27). The corresponding (implicit) *adaptive economizing savings strategy* is

$$s^a(k) := Bf(k) - h^a(k).$$

Assuming that savings equals investment, the *capital accumulation equation* is

$$k_{t+1} = \theta^a(k_t) := \frac{1}{1 + n}[(1 - \delta)k_t + Bf(k) - h^a(k_t)]. \tag{17.15}$$

The term "adaptive economizing" is not meant to imply that the sequences of *realized* consumptions $\{c_t\}$, $\{s_t\}$, and capital stocks $\{k_t\}$ are optimal in any sense other than that they are the result of what the *current generation* prefers, given its current wealth and the current rate of return on investment.

17.1.4   The Profile of Consumption and Savings

The behavior of the capital/labor ratio over time depends on the profile of production and on the adaptive economizing consumption strategy. The properties of the former are given in Lemma 16.1. We need to find out about the latter.

LEMMA 17.1 (The Adaptive Economizing Consumption Strategy with Incomplete Knowledge) *Given the assumptions on production (16.1)–(16.5) and preferences (17.1)–(17.2),*

(i) there exists a continuous, differentiable function, $g^a(k)$, defined on $(0, k^0)$, a constant k^s with $0 < k^s < k^0$, and sets $\mathcal{K}^s := (0, k^s)$, $\mathcal{K}^d := [k^s, \infty)$ such that

$$c = h^a(k) = \begin{cases} g^a(k) < Bf(k), & k \in \mathcal{K}^s \\ Bf(k), & k \in \mathcal{K}^d, \end{cases}$$

or equivalently

$$y - c = s^a(k) = \begin{cases} Bf(k) - g^a(k) > 0, & k \in \mathcal{K}^s \\ 0, & k \in \mathcal{K}^d \end{cases}$$

where c satisfies

$$\frac{u'(c)}{\psi u'(c^1)} \begin{cases} = \rho, & k \in \mathcal{K}^s \quad (a) \\ > \rho, & k \in \mathcal{K}^d \quad (b); \end{cases} \tag{17.16}$$

(ii) there exists a capital labor ratio, $\tilde{k} \in \mathcal{K}^s$, such that

$$\tilde{\rho} = \frac{\tilde{r} - (n + \delta)}{1 + n} = \frac{1}{\psi} \quad \left(\text{equivalently } \tilde{r} = \frac{(1 + n)}{\psi} + (n + \delta) \right)$$

and such that

$$\tilde{k} < k^s < k^0;$$

(iii)

$$s^a(k) > (n + \delta)k, \quad 0 < k < \tilde{k}$$
$$s^a(\tilde{k}) = (n + \delta)\tilde{k}$$
$$s^a(k) < (n + \delta)k, \quad \tilde{k} < k < k^s.$$

Proof

(i) To show that the function $g^a(k)$ exists, consider the first-order condition for the preferred consumption/savings decision. Suppose that both consumption and savings are positive. This implies that the preferred current consumption satisfies (17.16a). That is, the marginal substitution of current consumption for future potential income in perpetuity is equal to the net rate of return on savings.[6] The term on the left must be positive, which implies that ρ is positive also, which, in view of the decreasing returns property, implies that the capital stock is not too large. The tangency condition is illustrated in figure 17.2.

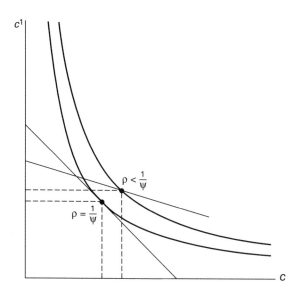

Figure 17.2
The tangency condition

Because for given k (hence y and ρ), c^1 is a function of c (given in (17.11)), the marginal utility ratio (17.16) is also a function of c. Denoting this function by

$$v(c;k) := \frac{u'(c)}{\psi u'([1+\rho][y-(n+\delta)k]-\rho c)}, \tag{17.17}$$

we can show by routine calculations that for each k

$$\lim_{c \to 0} v(c;k) = \infty \tag{a}$$

$$\lim_{c \to y} v(c;k) = \frac{u'(y)}{u'[y-(1+\rho)(n+\delta)k]} \cdot \frac{1}{\psi} < \frac{1}{\psi} \quad \text{(b)} \tag{17.18}$$

and that

$$v'(c;k) < 0. \tag{17.19}$$

This implies that for each k such that $\rho > v(y;k)$ there exists a unique present consumption that satisfies the equation $v(c;k) = \rho$ (remember the

Intermediate Value Theorem). Denote this function by $g^a(k)$. It must satisfy

$$v[g^a(k),k] = \rho = \frac{Bf'(k) - (n+\delta)}{1+n}. \tag{17.20}$$

The net rate of return ρ decreases monotonically, so $v[g^a(k),k]$ also decreases monotonically as k increases. This implies that consumption and savings are positive for each k up to a capital/labor ratio k^s defined by

$$v(y^s;k^s) = \frac{1}{\psi}\frac{u'(y^s)}{u'[y^s - (1+\rho^s)(n+\delta)k^s]} = \rho^s$$

where $y^s = Bf(k^s)$ and where $\rho^s = [Bf'(k^s) - (n+\delta)]/(1+n)$.

For all $\rho < \rho^s$, desired consumption would exceed income, which, given the assumption that capital cannot be consumed, is not possible. In this situation,

for all $\quad y \geq y^s, \quad v(y,k) \geq \rho,$

or, what is the same thing,

$s^a(k) = 0 \quad$ for all $\quad k \geq k^s.$

That is, savings are zero and the current generation spends all it earns. In this case, which is also illustrated in figure 17.2, the opportunity cost to the current generation of foregone consumption is greater than the satisfaction of preserving its own standard of living for the next generation.

Could the current generation consume nothing and invest all of its income? For this to happen, it would be necessary for the inequality

$$v(0,k) = \frac{u'(0)}{\psi u'\{(1+\rho)[y - (n+\delta)k]\}} < \rho \tag{17.21}$$

to hold for positive ρ. But $u'(0)$ is unbounded while the denominator is positive, so $v(0)$ is unbounded also. This is a contradiction. Such unreasonable behavior cannot occur in the present model. (It would imply that the children of the current generation could survive to become adults even if they have nothing to consume.)

Define the savings and no savings zones as in Lemma 17.1 by

$\mathcal{K}^s := (0, k^s), \quad \mathcal{K}^d = [k^s, \infty);$

then

$$h^a(k) = \begin{cases} g^a(k), & k \in \mathcal{K}^s \\ Bf(k), & k \in \mathcal{K}^d. \end{cases}$$

Notice that $g^a(k)$ is not strictly defined at $k = 0$, but, as $y = 0$ at $k = 0$, $h^a(0) = 0$. This completes the proofs of (i) and (iii).

(ii) The existence of $\tilde{k}$ satisfying the expressions in (ii) above follows from the Intermediate Value Theorem. As r is a declining function of k, it follows that $\tilde{r} > r^0$ and, hence, $\tilde{k} < k^0$. Moreover, as there is a unique value $\tilde{\rho} = 1/\psi$, there is a unique consumption level $\tilde{c}$ such that $v(\tilde{c}, \tilde{k}) = v(g^a(\tilde{k}), \tilde{k}) = \tilde{\rho}$. For $k = k^s$ there is no savings, but as $s(\tilde{k}) = (n + \delta)\tilde{k} > 0$, we must have $\tilde{k} < k^s < k^0$. ∎

17.2 Qualitative Dynamics

17.2.1 Existence of Trajectories and Stationary States: Global Stability

Given the piecewise nature of $h^a(k)$, the behavior of the capital/labor ratio is governed by

$$k_{t+1} = \theta(k_t) = \begin{cases} \theta_s^a(k_t) := \frac{1}{1+n}[(1-\delta)k_t + Bf(k_t) - g^a(k_t)], & k_t \in \mathcal{K}^s \\ \theta_d^a(k_t) := \frac{(1-\delta)}{1+n}k_t, & k_t \in \mathcal{K}^d. \end{cases}$$

$$(17.22)$$

The first steps in deriving the qualitative character of trajectories generated by such an economy are given in:

PROPOSITION 17.1 (The Existence of Trajectories and Stationary States)

(i) For all positive initial conditions, $k > 0$, there exist trajectories $\tau(k) = \{k, \theta(k), \theta^t(k) \cdots\}$ such that $\theta^t(k) > 0$ for all t;

(ii) trajectories are bounded and the system is globally stable, i.e., there exists a constant $k^m > 0$ such that

$\limsup\{\theta^t(k)\} < k^m;$

(iii) there exists a unique, positive steady state $\tilde{k}$ with $0 < \tilde{k} < k^m$.

Proof

(i) Consider the function

$$G(k) := \frac{1}{1+n}[(1-\delta)k + Bf(k)], \quad k \geq 0.$$

Clearly, $G(k) > 0$ for all $k > 0$. Evidently, $\theta(k) < G(k)$ for all $k > 0$. From this it follows that $0 < \theta'(k) < G'(k)$ for all $k > 0$.

(ii) Let $k^m = G(k^m)$, which exists by our well-used fixpoint argument. Using Lemma 16.1(iii), we can show that $G'(k) < 1$ for all $k \geq k^m$. This implies that $G(k) < k$ for all $k > k^m$, so $\theta(k) < k$ for all $k \geq k^m$. From this it follows that for all k there exists a time s such that

$$0 < \theta^t(k) < k^m \quad \text{for all} \quad t \geq s.$$

Consequently, for all positive initial conditions, trajectories are eventually bounded above by k^m. This is not the least upper bound, however. Since $\theta(k) < G(k)$ for all $k > 0$, there will exist a local maximum value $k^M = \theta(k^{**}) = \max_{k \in (0, k^s]} \theta(x)$. Obviously, $\theta(k) \leq k^M \leq k^m$, so $\limsup \theta^t(k) \leq k^M$. This too need not be the least upper bound, though it may be. At any rate, trajectories are globally stable.

(iii) From Lemma 17.1(ii), the capital/labor ratio $\tilde{k}$ for which $\tilde{\rho} = \frac{1}{\psi}$ determines the savings level $s^a(\tilde{k}) = (n+\delta)\tilde{k}$, is just enough to replace worn-out capital and add enough to keep capital per family constant. Substituting into (17.21), we get

$$\theta(\tilde{k}) = \theta_s^a(\tilde{k}) = \frac{1}{1+n}[(1-\delta)\tilde{k} + s^a(\tilde{k})] = \tilde{k}. \qquad \blacksquare$$

17.2.2 Generic Instability

We want to find out what qualitatively distinct types of behavior can occur in this model economy for all possible parameter values. We shall consider *any* positive B and n and *any* $\delta \in (0,1)$ and ask how the qualitative behavior changes when ψ varies throughout all positive values.

To determine the asymptotic stability or instability of balanced growth,

$$\theta_s^{a'}(k) = \frac{1}{1+n}\{(1-\delta) + Bf'(k) - g^{a'}(k)\}$$

must be evaluated at the steady state. Recalling that $1 - \delta + r = (1 + n) \cdot (1 + \rho)$, this means that we have to consider how

$$\theta_s'(k) = 1 + \rho - \frac{1}{1+n} g^{a'}(k), \tag{17.23}$$

evaluated at $\tilde{k}$, is influenced by ψ.

Take the total differential of the first-order condition (17.16a). Rearrange and collect terms to obtain the expression

$$\left[\frac{u''(c)}{\psi} + \rho^2 u''(c^1) \right] g^{a'}(k)$$

$$= \rho u''(c^1) \left\{ \rho[r + (1 - \delta)] + \frac{r'}{1+n} [y - c - (n+\delta)k] \right\} + \frac{u'(c^1)r'}{1+n}. \tag{17.24}$$

At a stationary state $\tilde{c}^1 = \tilde{c}$, $\tilde{\rho} = 1/\psi$ and $\tilde{s} = \tilde{y} - \tilde{c} = (n+\delta)\tilde{k}$. Using these facts, we find, again after some arduous but elementary algebra, that, as $(\tilde{r}' \cdot \tilde{u}')/\tilde{u}''$ is positive,

$$g^{a'}(\tilde{k}) = (1+n)\frac{1}{\psi} + \frac{\psi \tilde{r}'}{(1+\frac{1}{\psi})(1+n)} \cdot \frac{\tilde{u}'}{\tilde{u}''} > 0 \tag{17.25}$$

where all terms are evaluated at the stationary state.[7] Combining this with (17.23), we get

$$\theta_s'(\tilde{k}) = 1 - \frac{\psi^2}{1+\psi} \cdot \frac{\tilde{r}'}{(1+n)^2} \cdot \frac{\tilde{u}'}{\tilde{u}''}. \tag{17.26}$$

Certainly,

$$\lim_{\psi \to \infty} \frac{\psi^2}{1+\psi} = \infty. \tag{17.27}$$

Recalling (17.12) and (17.16a),

$$\psi \to \infty \Rightarrow \tilde{k} \to k^0 \Rightarrow \tilde{c} \to y^0 \Rightarrow u'(\tilde{c}) \quad \text{and} \quad u''(\tilde{c}) \tag{17.28}$$

are finite. Consequently,

$$\lim_{\psi \to \infty} \theta'(\tilde{k}) = -\infty. \tag{17.29}$$

The positive stationary state is surely unstable as ψ becomes large, and persisting fluctuations will emerge except for trajectories that hit $\tilde{k}$ exactly after a finite number of periods. From the conditions for positive saving (17.16a), we see that when the future weight becomes large enough, current consumption will become small relative to c^1. Except for k very close to $\tilde{k}$, savings will be close to exhausting income. Therefore, close to (but not at) $\tilde{k}$, $\theta(k)$ will be nearly equal to

$$\frac{1}{1+n}[(1-\delta)k + Bf(k)] > \tilde{k}.$$

This means the trajectories will overshoot $\tilde{k}$ and, as $\tilde{k} \to k^s \to k^0$, will fall below $\tilde{k}$; then ρ will increase, savings will be positive, and growth will resume. The phases must switch, but the fluctuations must be bounded above by $\frac{1}{1+n}[(1-\delta)k^0 + Bf(k^0)]$.

Thus, *ceteris paribus*, as ψ is increased, a trapping set emerges that eventually contains persistent fluctuating trajectories. This trapping set could have one of three canonical forms as shown in figure 16.5. We know that chaos and strongly ergodic, chaotic trajectories can exist for each of them from chapters 13 and 16. In particular, it has been shown that maps of this type can satisfy the chaos existence Theorems 7.3–7.4. Expansivity for iterates of the map θ is also easily established for Case III. The slope, $\theta'[\theta(k^s)]$, becomes as large as we want by increasing ψ. The number of periods a trajectory stays in $(k^s, \theta^2(k^s))$ must be relatively small (unless n and δ are close to zero). Even in this case, expansivity of a high-order map must occur as ψ gets arbitrarily large. In Cases I and II the Misiurewicz Theorem 8.6 must be invoked. If it holds, then chaos is strong and almost all trajectories involve irregular growth fluctuations.

So far we do not know if these findings change when ψ becomes small. Perhaps this economy is unstable for all values of ψ? We *do* know that $\tilde{k} \to 0$ as $\psi \to 0$. Thus, as ψ decreases, any oscillations that occur do so around a diminishing capital/labor ratio and must shrink in amplitude.

The upshot of this series of inferences is summarized in:

PROPOSITION 17.2 (Generic Instability)

(i) For large enough future weights, the steady state is unstable and almost all trajectories exhibit persistent bounded fluctuations; these may be cyclic or chaotic and, for some cases, may exhibit strongly ergodic, chaotic fluctuations;

(ii) as the future weight becomes small, the steady state shrinks and capital/labor ratios (which may fluctuate) approach zero amplitude.

How can agents who have a very high regard for future generations behave in such a way as to generate this kind of instability? The reason is that their extrapolative forecast of the rate of return leads them to overpredict the return to continued savings that will be available for the next generation. They would save less if they knew better. The result may be that they inadvertently "overendow" the next generation, which, as a result, experiences an extremely low rate of return on savings and invest-ment. The new generation of adults then increases its consumption above the sustainable level and allows its capital stock to decline. If we have the shorter time frame in mind, it is still the inability to anticipate real rates correctly that leads to ups and downs in investment and, hence, in investment and capital stock.

17.2.3   Conditions for Generic Asymptotic Stability and Generic Instability

By strengthening the conditions on technology and preferences, stronger results can be obtained. We can say what happens for *all* future weights ψ, not just those that are sufficiently large. Let

$$f'(k) = -\zeta_f k f''(k), \quad \zeta_f > 1 \quad \text{(a)}$$

$$u'(c) = -\zeta_u c u''(c), \quad \zeta_u \geq 1. \quad \text{(b)}$$

$$(17.30)$$

Integrating both sides of (17.30a) yields the implication that

$$f(k) = -\zeta_f(kf'(k) - f(k)) \tag{17.31}$$

which, after rearranging, implies that

$$f(k) = \frac{\zeta_f}{\zeta_f - 1} k f'(k). \tag{17.32}$$

Using (17.30a–b), the criterion (17.26) becomes

$$\theta'(k) = 1 - \frac{\psi^2}{1 + \psi} \cdot \frac{\zeta_u}{\zeta_f} \cdot \frac{1}{(1+n)^2} \cdot \frac{\tilde{r}\tilde{c}}{\tilde{k}}.$$

Using (17.32) and the facts that $\tilde{r} = \frac{1+n}{\psi} + n + \delta$ and $\tilde{c} = \tilde{y} - (n+\delta)\tilde{k}$, we find that

$$\theta'(\tilde{k}) = 1 - \frac{\psi^2}{1+\psi} \cdot \frac{1}{(1+n)^2} \cdot \frac{\zeta_u}{\zeta_f} \left[\frac{1+n}{\psi} + n + \delta \right]$$

$$\left\{ \left(\frac{\zeta_f}{\zeta_f - 1} \right) \left(\frac{1+n}{\psi} + n + \delta \right) - (n+\delta) \right\}. \qquad (17.33)$$

Note that, given the parameters ζ_u, ζ_f, n, and δ, $\theta'(\tilde{k})$ is a function of ψ. We investigate the properties of this criterion in the following.

LEMMA 17.2 (Properties of the Local Stability/Instability Criterion $\theta'(\tilde{k})$)

(i) $\displaystyle \lim_{\psi \to 0} \theta'(\tilde{k}) = 1 - \frac{\zeta_u}{\zeta_f - 1}$;

(ii) $\displaystyle \lim_{\psi \to \infty} \theta'(\tilde{k}) = -\infty$;

(iii) $\displaystyle \lim_{\psi \to 0} \frac{d\theta'(\tilde{k})}{d\psi} = \frac{[(1-\delta)\zeta_f - (n+\delta)]}{(1+n)(\zeta_f - 1)} \frac{\zeta_u}{\zeta_f}$;

(iv) $\displaystyle \lim_{\psi \to \infty} \frac{d\theta'(\tilde{k})}{d\psi} = -\left(\frac{n+\delta}{1+n} \right)^2 \frac{\zeta_u}{\zeta_f(\zeta_f - 1)}$;

(v) $\displaystyle \frac{d^2\theta'(\tilde{k})}{d\psi^2} = -2 \left(\frac{1}{1+n} \right)^2 \frac{\zeta_u}{\zeta_f} \frac{(1-\delta)}{(1+\psi)^3} \left[\frac{\zeta_f}{\zeta_f - 1} (1-\delta) + (n+\delta) \right]$,

$< 0 \quad n \geq 0, \, 0 < \delta < 1, \, \psi > 0.$

Proof

(i) Multiply the term within curly brackets through by ψ^2 to get

$$\theta'(\tilde{k}) = 1 - \frac{1}{(1+n)^2} \cdot \frac{\zeta_u}{\zeta_f} \left[\frac{1+n+\psi(n+\delta)}{1+\psi} \right]$$

$$\left\{ \frac{\zeta_f}{\zeta_{f-1}} (1+n+\psi(n+\delta)) - \psi(n+\delta) \right\}.$$

Taking the limit for $\psi \to 0$, we get the result shown.

(ii) This is known from (17.29).

(iii)–(iv) To prove the remaining properties, it is helpful to represent (17.33) in the form

$$\theta'(\tilde{k}) = 1 - ABz[Cz - (n+\delta)]$$

where

$$A := \frac{\psi^2}{1+\psi}, \quad B := \frac{1}{(1+n)^2}\frac{\zeta_u}{\zeta_f}, \quad C := \frac{\zeta_f}{\zeta_f - 1},$$

and $z := (\frac{1+n}{\psi} + n + \delta)$. Next, obtain

$$\frac{d\theta\tilde{k}}{d\tilde{k}} = -Bz[Cz - (n+\delta)]\frac{dA}{d\psi}$$

$$- AB[2Cz - (n+\delta)]\frac{dz}{d\psi}$$

where $\frac{dA}{d\psi} = \frac{\psi}{1+\psi}(2 - \frac{\psi}{1+\psi}) > 0$ for all ψ and $\frac{dz}{d\psi} = -\frac{1+n}{\psi^2}$. Using these and taking the limits, we obtain the expressions shown.

(v) Taking the second derivative of $\theta'(\tilde{k})$ with respect to ψ yields the expression

$$\frac{-2B(1-\delta)[C(1-\delta) + n + \delta]}{(1+\psi)^2} < 0.$$

Substituting for B and C gives the expression shown.   ∎

We can now determine the global behavior of the adaptive economizing model.

PROPOSITION 17.3 (Generic Asymptotic Stability and Generic Instability of Balanced Growth) *Assume that the production function satisfies (16.1–5), the utility function satisfies (17.30a–b), and $0 \le \delta \le 1$. Let $\kappa(\psi) := \theta'(\tilde{k})$.*

(i) If

$$\zeta_f \ge 1 + \zeta_u/2,$$

then there exists a unique positive number ψ' such that the steady state is asymptotically stable for all $\psi \in (0, \psi']$ and unstable for all $\psi \in (\psi', \infty)$.

(ii) If

$$\zeta_f < 1 + \zeta_u/2 \quad \text{and} \quad \zeta_f < (n+\delta)/(1-\delta),$$

then the steady state is unstable for all $\psi > 0$ and fluctuations persist almost surely.

(iii) If
$$(n+\delta)/(1-\delta) < \zeta_f < 1 + \zeta_u/2,$$

(a) then there exists a unique maximizer ψ^{**} of $\kappa(\cdot)$. If

$$\kappa(\psi^{**}) < -1,$$

then the steady state is unstable for all $\psi > 0$;

(b) however, if

$$\kappa(\psi^{**}) > -1,$$

then there exist two numbers ψ', ψ'' with $\psi' < \psi''$ such that the steady state is unstable for all $\psi \in (0, \psi') \cup (\psi'', \infty)$ and asymptotically stable for all $\psi \in (\psi', \psi'')$.

Proof Given the parameters ζ_u, ζ_f, n, and δ, the criterion function $\kappa(\psi) := \theta'(\tilde{k})$ is continuous.

(i) From Lemma 17.2, $\kappa(\cdot)$ is strictly concave. Assertion (i) of the same lemma therefore implies that for all ψ close enough to zero, $\zeta_u < 2(\zeta_f - 1) \Rightarrow |\kappa(\psi)| < 1$. From assertion (ii), however, $\kappa(\psi) < -1$ for large enough ψ. By continuity there must exist small enough and large enough values of ψ, say ψ' and ψ'', respectively, such that $|\kappa(\psi)| < 1$ for all $\psi \in (0, \psi')$ and $\kappa(\psi) < -1$ for all $\psi \in (\psi'', \infty)$.

We now show that $\psi' \equiv \psi''$. From Lemma 17.2(iii), $\kappa'(\psi)$ can be positive or negative for ψ close to 0 depending on the sign of the terms $(1 - \delta)\zeta_f - (n + \delta)$. If the former, then $\kappa(\psi)$ increases for ψ close to 0, reaches a unique maximum, and then declines monotonically for ψ beyond the maximizer. But as $\theta(k)$ is concave with a unique positive steady state, we know that $\kappa(\psi) < 1$ for all ψ. If $\kappa'(\psi)$ is negative for ψ close to zero, then by concavity it must be decreasing everywhere. This implies that $\psi' \equiv \psi''$.

(ii)–(iii) If $\zeta_u > 2(\zeta_f - 1)$, Lemma 17.2(i) implies that $\kappa(\psi)$ is unstable for ψ close to zero. Now consider Lemma 17.2(iii). It implies that

$$\text{sgn} \lim_{\psi \to 0} \kappa'(\psi) = \text{sgn}[(1 - \delta)\zeta_f - (n + \delta)]$$

(because the other terms are all positive). If $\zeta_f < (n + \delta)/(1 - \delta)$, this term is negative and by the same argument, as in (i), it must decline for all ψ. Hence, $\kappa(\psi) < -1$ for all $\psi > 0$. However, if $\zeta_f > (n + \delta)/(1 - \delta)$, then $\kappa(\psi)$ increases for small enough ψ, reaches a unique maximum, and then declines monotonically (because $\kappa(\cdot)$ is concave). Let ψ^{**} be the maximizer of $\kappa(\psi)$ in this case. Then, if $\kappa(\psi^{**}) > -1$, there must exist two values of ψ, say ψ', ψ'', such that $\kappa(\psi) < -1$ for all $\psi \in (0, \psi') \cup (\psi'', \infty)$ and $|\kappa(\psi)| < 1$ for all $\psi \in (\psi', \psi'')$. ∎

Figure 17.3 provides the qualitative picture of the function $\kappa(\psi) = \theta'(\tilde{k})$ for the four cases of the theorem.

17.3 Example

17.3.1 Complete Parametric Comparative Dynamics

If we use

$$f(k) = k^\beta \quad \text{and} \quad u(c) = a \log c,$$

then a complete qualitative comparative dynamic analysis can be given. The first-order condition when savings and consumption are both positive, (17.16a), gives

$$\frac{1}{\psi} \cdot \frac{c^1}{c} = \rho.$$

Substituting for c^1, using (17.11), and doing some rearranging, it follows that

$$g(k) := \frac{1}{1+\psi}\left[1 + \frac{1}{\rho}\right][y - (n+\delta)k].$$

This function, we recall, is defined on $k \in (0, k^0)$ where $\lim_{k \to k^0} \rho = 0$. This gives the phase structure when savings are positive,

$$\theta_s^a(k) = \frac{1}{1+n}\left\{(1-\delta)k + y - \frac{1}{1+\psi} \cdot \left(1 + \frac{1}{\rho}\right)[y-(n+\delta)k]\right\}, \quad k \in \mathcal{K}^s.$$

From this it can be shown that

$$\theta'(\tilde{k}) = 1 - A\psi(1+n)\tilde{r} - A\frac{1-\beta}{\beta}\tilde{r}^2 \tag{17.34}$$

where

$$A = \frac{(1-\beta)\psi^2}{(1+n)^2(1+\psi)} \quad \text{and} \quad \tilde{r} = \frac{1+n}{\psi} + (n+\delta).$$

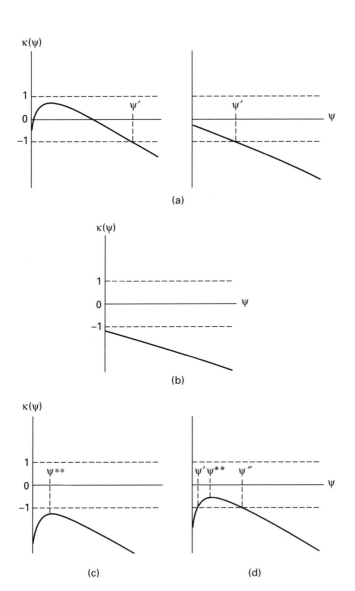

Figure 17.3
Illustrations of Theorem 17.3. (a) Case (i). (b) Case (ii). (c) Case (iii)(a). (d) Case (iii)(b).

For simplicity, let $\varrho := \theta'(\tilde{k})$. For any given value of ϱ, we get an implicit equation in (β, ψ, δ, n),

$$H_\varrho(\beta, \psi, \delta, n) := (1 - \varrho) - A(1 + n)\psi\tilde{r} - A\frac{(1 - \beta)}{\beta}\tilde{r}^2 = 0. \qquad (17.35)$$

Let $\varrho = -1$. After a certain amount of tedious calculation, it is seen that

$$H_{-1}(\beta, \psi, \delta, n) := 1 + \frac{\psi(n + \delta)}{1 + n} - \frac{-1 + \sqrt{1 + 8(1 + \psi)/\beta}}{2} \cdot \frac{\beta}{1 - \beta} = 0.$$

$$(17.36)$$

The first two terms are constant for fixed ψ, n, δ; the remaining terms constitute a continuously increasing function of β whose value goes to 0 as β goes to 0, and to infinity as β goes to 1. Consequently, for any given ψ, $H_{-1}(\psi, \beta)$ changes sign as β increases from 0. Therefore, for each ψ there exists a $\beta \in (0, 1)$, say β^u (depending on ψ), such that $H(\psi, \beta^u) = 0$ or, equivalently, such that $\theta'(\tilde{k}) = -1$.

We can therefore state:

PROPOSITION 17.4 (Lin)   *For each $\psi > 0$ there exists $\beta^u \in (0, 1)$ (depending on ψ) such that $\tilde{k}$ is unstable whenever $\beta < \beta^u$ and asymptotically stable whenever $\beta > \beta^u$.*

Figure 17.4 depicts several curves using various combinations of values of ψ and β such that (17.36) holds for given values of n and δ. To see how complex the picture is, consider points P' and P'' in the diagram. For a pair of values close to but to the left of P'', a sufficiently larger value of ψ would destabilize the system. Conversely, for a pair of values to the left of P', the system is unstable but a sufficiently large (but not too large) increase in ψ will stabilize the system. One may note that such an effect-reversal phenomenon cannot happen when $\frac{n+\delta}{1+n} > \frac{3}{5}$. In this case, there are situations where an arbitrarily small value of the future weight ψ does not suffice to ensure a globally stable steady state.

This observation can be given a general expression. To determine what the possibilities are, note that the curves satisfying (17.36) all intersect the β axis at $\beta = 1/3$; that is, $H_{-1}(1/3, 0, \delta, n) = 0$ for each $n, \delta > 0$. Now consider the slope of the locus of points satisfying (17.36), i.e.,

$$\frac{d\beta}{d\psi} = -\frac{\partial H/\partial\psi}{\partial H/\partial\beta}. \qquad (17.37)$$

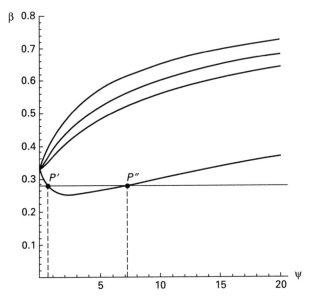

Figure 17.4
The stability/instability boundary. Three lines are given for differing values of n and δ. (β, ψ) combinations below a line give instability; combinations above give stability.

It can be seen that for $\psi = 0$ this slope is positive, zero or negative as $\frac{n+\delta}{1+n}$ is greater than, equal to or less than 3/5. But for any positive δ and any nonnegative n, this slope must become positive for ψ large enough. It must approach $(n+\delta)/(1+n)$ asymptotically. Therefore, we have

PROPOSITION 17.5 (Lin) *If*

$$2n + 5\delta > 3, \tag{17.38}$$

then for each $\beta > 0$ there exists a $\psi^u > 0$ that depends on β such that $\tilde{k}$ is stable whenever $\psi < \psi^u$ and unstable whenever $\psi > \psi^u$. Conversely, if

$$2n + 5\delta < 3, \tag{17.39}$$

then there exists a $\beta^l < \frac{1}{3}$ such that for all β satisfying $\beta^l < \beta < \frac{1}{3}$ there exist ψ^l, ψ^u depending on β such that $\tilde{k}$ is unstable for all ψ such that $0 < \psi < \psi^l$ and $\psi > \psi^u$ and stable for all ψ such that $\psi^l < \psi < \psi^u$. For all n, δ such

Table 17.1
Parameters

Case	Parameter Values		
	n	δ	β
I	0	.25	.20
II	.414	.64	.36
III	0	.64	.67
IV	0	.90	.67

that $2n + 5\delta = 3$, $\tilde{k}$ *is unstable (stable) for all* $\beta < \frac{1}{3}$ ($\beta > \frac{1}{3}$) *regardless of* ψ.

The details of the proof are given in Lin (1988, pp. 38–42). The argument can be extended by obtaining (for fixed n, δ) a sequence of functions, say $H^i(\psi, \beta)$, $i = 2, \ldots$, giving loci of bifurcation points at which cycles of order $2, 4, \ldots$ become unstable. Moreover, a function $H^c(\psi, \beta)$ exists giving the locus of bifurcation points for ψ and β below which fluctuations become ergodic. All of this requires some tedious calculation. The picture derived would be like that shown in figure 17.4 but with the interpretation correspondingly changed.

17.3.2 Numerical Experiments

In order to illustrate the theoretical findings, we shall use the four sets of parameter values given in table 17.1. Case I represents an "ancient" society with negligible population growth, durable capital structures, and a relatively low capital elasticity of output. Case II represents a U.S.-like society with rapid population growth, rapidly depreciating capital, and higher elasticity of capital. Case III represents a Europe-like society with stable population and a high capital elasticity. Case IV is like Case III except capital wears out or becomes obsolescent very quickly.[8]

The effect of alternative future weights will be studied by computing a bifurcation diagram for ψ for each of four stylized situations. Recall that

$$\psi = \frac{\alpha}{1 - \alpha} \quad \text{or} \quad \alpha = \frac{\psi}{1 + \psi}.$$

Obviously, the future weight is very small if each generation is heavily discounted (α close to 0) and becomes unbounded if each future genera-

Table 17.2
Relationship Between α and ψ

α	ψ
.09	0.10
.50	1.00
.67	2.00
.80	4.00
.90	9.00
.97	32.00
.975	40.00

tion is only modestly discounted (α close to 1). Table 17.2 gives an idea of this relationship. Small values for ψ that imply extreme discounting may not be entirely nonsensical, but large values for ψ are also plausible. Ancient civilizations produced monumental architecture, massive roads, and vast irrigation systems which were used for centuries with some remnants still in use. Such societies, *in effect*, hardly discounted the future at all. They placed a very heavy weight upon the standard of living of future generations in terms of these public goods. Modern societies have also undertaken projects of great durability, such as the Panama and Suez canals, the extensive topographical shaping for transcontinental railroads and highways, huge aqueducts, dams, etc. Evidently, from the point of view of society as a whole ψ can be quite large.

It makes sense then to consider the behavior implied by a wide range of values for ψ. In what follows we shall therefore consider values within the range given in table 17.2.

The trajectories given in figure 16.6 were computed for the case of capital saturation using the Case II figures from table 17.1 and with $\psi = 9.00$.

17.4   Caution and Technological Change

17.4.1   Caution

Caution could be introduced in the adaptive economizing model in a manner analogous to that in §16.4. It would imply a lexicographic utility function in which the society places its highest priority on being cautious (or daring) enough. As long as it stays within the bounds of flexible choice that caution permits, society "chooses" its most preferred consumption without considering uncertainty. The effects here are to moderate the rate of growth at low levels of capital and to moderate fluctuations in the unstable case. The example shown in figure 16.9 illustrates this property. It uses the Case II parameters but with $\lambda = .05$.

17.4.2 Technological Change

Technological change can also be introduced in the same way as in chapter 16 and with the same implications, namely that the steady state and the amplitude of the fluctuations increase in the unstable case.

17.5 Summary and Conclusions

The model of this chapter represents economizing as an adaptive process in which current choice rests on known current income, current wealth, and current rates of return but only on a rough forecast of future values. That rough estimate is adjusted to realized states as time passes. Knowledge evolves and plans are adapted accordingly. The model thus reflects economizing activity more or less as we experience it.

At a stationary state, if and when it is reached, anticipations are realized and the long-run behavior lies along a steady state path. Because technology and the future consequences of current decisions are perceived approximately, however, such a situation may not be reached. Indeed, depending on the parameters of time preference and productivity, the resulting trajectories of capital and real aggregate output can but need not converge to a balanced growth path. They may exhibit growth cycles or fluctuate erratically, perhaps never reaching the equilibrium path. In its extreme form, periods of excess capacity can occur in which aggregate capital stock is allowed to decay before a new period of growth sets in. The situation is one roughly like that of the relatively long cycles that occur in durable goods industries, such as construction, heavy manufacturing, petroleum refining, and electric power production. In this way the model provides a possible explanation of why growth rates and the marginal product of aggregate capital fluctuate irregularly—as they do in the data.

One may ask why agents would not learn to avoid such errors of estimation and in this way gradually avoid fluctuations. The answer is that in principle they could. But the world is complicated—too complicated to fathom, and much more complicated than our simple model of it. We use the simple model not to show how people would behave in a simple world, but rather to gain some insight into the implications of how they behave in a very complicated one. In the very complicated one in which *we* live, the assumptions of adaptive economizing and of expectations based on recent experience are not entirely unreasonable.

18 Optimal Growth

On a clear day you can see forever.
—Alan Jay Lerner, from the musical *On a Clear Day*

Instead of explaining history on the basis of bounded rational economizing behavior, suppose we wanted to know what could be the "best" economic history if the choice made at each stage were based on a complete knowledge of technology, not just an approximation of it, and on a complete consideration at each stage of the possible future sequences of consumption. This is a question of intertemporal equilibrium. This chapter is an introduction that should provide the reader with the fundamental concepts and a good starting point into the literature on optimal growth.

We begin with the *Golden Rule of savings*. This rule generates behavior that eventually leads to the maximal sustainable level of consumption generation after generation.[1] The relationship between this model and the adaptive economizing model of chapter 17 is then explored. It is shown that, as the future weight increases, the adaptive economizing *steady state* converges to that of the Golden Rule, but that non–steady state trajectories fluctuate around the Golden Rule path.

Next, the intertemporal economizing theory of optimal growth is outlined.[2] As in the adaptive economizing theory, each generation chooses between its own consumption and an endowment for its immediate heirs, but here the choice is made with reference to the preferences of future generations throughout all time on the basis of a complete understanding of the feedback structure of the problem and under the assumption that all future generations have exactly the same preferences as the current one. The rule that governs current action satisfies a principle of consistent intertemporal optimality, and the sequence of actions as a whole maximizes a utility function defined over the entire future. This is an idealization of how the economic principle could work if it worked perfectly.[3]

Again, we ask if adaptive economizing paths converge to the optimal ones. Here the answer is: yes, if utility and production functions and the time preference parameter (or future weight) satisfy certain conditions.

Within the limited framework of the one-sector model of capital accumulation explored here, optimal output, consumption, and capital trajectories converge to exponentially increasing, balanced-growth paths. The question arises whether optimal growth in more general models could display fluctuations. The answer given elsewhere is: Yes, but *only in a different class of models*. Within the setting to which our discussion here is limited, the answer is no. There are two important implications of this finding. First, if the one-sector optimal growth theory were to be used as an explanation of empirical experience, the observed fluctuation around a trend would have to be explained by exogenous perturbations or shocks, as in the constant savings rate model. Second, if the adaptive economizing model of chapter 17 were believed to give a useful approximation to reality, then fluctuating real growth trajectories could not be optimal.

A closely related question is this: Consider a fluctuating path of output and capital accumulation of the various kinds generated, for example, by the adaptive economizing theory of the preceding chapter. Does there exist an intertemporal optimizing model that could have generated that path? To rephrase the question: Does there exist a different model economy for which this path is optimal? Or, to state the issue in common parlance: Can a chaotic growth path be *rationalized*? Here the answer is yes. The chapter concludes by examining this seeming paradox. The analysis shows that to rationalize is not the same as to behave optimally.

18.1   The Golden Rule of Accumulation

Imagine an economy in which each generation endows its successor with the capital stock it would like to have received from its predecessor. What kind of savings behavior would follow from this Golden Rule?

18.1.1   The Basic Solow Model

Consider an answer to this question in terms of the Solow model of capital accumulation explored in chapter 16. The basic equation in per capita terms is

$$k_{t+1} = \frac{1}{1+n}[(1-\delta)k_t + \mu B f(k_t)] \tag{18.1}$$

where k_t is the capital/labor ratio, y_t is per capita output, B is the level of technology, μ is the savings rate, δ is the depreciation rate, and where $f(\cdot)$ possesses the properties described in §16.1.

A steady state capital/labor ratio is a stationary state, $\tilde{k}$, of (18.1), such that

$$(n+\delta)\tilde{k} = \mu\tilde{y}. \tag{18.2}$$

The steady state consumption is

$$\tilde{c} = (1 - \mu)\tilde{y} \tag{18.3}$$

where $\tilde{y} = Bf(\tilde{k})$, which depends on n, δ, μ, and the parameters of the production function. We know from Proposition 16.1 that all capital/labor ratio trajectories converge to $\tilde{k}$, so all paths of per capita consumption converge to $\tilde{c}$.

Suppose that the parameters $n, \delta, B, f(\cdot)$ are fixed. If the savings ratio could be chosen, what would be the one that would eventually lead to the most consumption per person in perpetuity? It is, of course, the value of μ, say μ^{gr}, which maximizes $\tilde{c}$. The corresponding steady state values will be denoted $\tilde{k}^{gr}, \tilde{y}^{gr}, \tilde{c}^{gr}$, and $\tilde{r}^{gr}$.

If we think of μ as a variable, then $\tilde{k}$ depends on μ. Represent this dependence by $\tilde{k}(\mu)$, so $\tilde{c}(\mu) = (1 - \mu)\tilde{y}(\mu)$. Taking the derivative with respect to μ and setting it equal to zero, we get the first-order condition for a maximum

$$\frac{d\tilde{c}}{d\mu} = 0. \tag{18.4}$$

From (18.2),

$$(n + \delta)\frac{d\tilde{k}}{d\mu} = \mu\frac{d\tilde{y}}{d\mu} + \tilde{y}.$$

Substituting into (18.4) and collecting terms,

$$\frac{d\tilde{c}}{d\mu} = \frac{d\tilde{y}}{d\mu} - (n + \delta)\frac{d\tilde{k}}{d\mu}$$

$$= [\tilde{r} - (n + \delta)]\frac{d\tilde{k}}{d\mu} = 0.$$

For this to equal zero, the interest rate must equal the growth rate of population plus the depreciation rate, i.e.,

$$\tilde{r}^{gr} = n + \delta. \tag{18.5}$$

Using the steady state condition (18.2), this becomes

$$\tilde{r}^{gr} = \mu\frac{\tilde{y}^{gr}}{\tilde{k}^{gr}}, \tag{18.6}$$

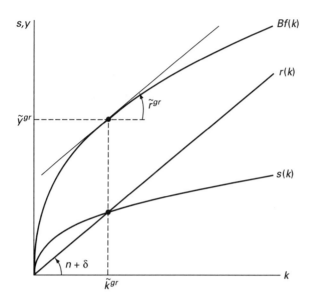

Figure 18.1
The Golden Rule savings rate

or

$$\mu^{gr} = \frac{dy/y}{dk/k}. \tag{18.7}$$

The term on the right is called the *capital elasticity of output.*
  Alternatively,

$$\mu^{gr}\tilde{y}^{gr} = \tilde{r}^{gr}\tilde{k}^{gr}. \tag{18.8}$$

That is, savings equals dividends (assuming that all profits are distributed), or

$$(1 - \mu^{gr})\tilde{y}^{gr} = \tilde{y}^{gr} - \tilde{r}^{gr}\tilde{k}^{gr} = \tilde{w}^{gr}, \tag{18.9}$$

which states that per capita consumption equals the wage income at the marginal product of labor. The relationships among $\tilde{s}, \tilde{k}, \tilde{c}, n, \delta$, and the Golden Rule μ^{gr} are shown in figure 18.1.
  To summarize:

PROPOSITION 18.1 *Given a neoclassical production function $f(\cdot)$ and given n, δ, B, there exists a unique Golden Rule savings ratio μ^{gr} that equals the* *capital elasticity of production and a unique Golden Rule steady state* $\tilde{k}^{gr} = \tilde{k}(\mu^{gr})$, *which is asymptotically stable.*

This means that, given the right savings rate μ^{gr}, the capital/labor ratio converges to the corresponding steady state, capital and labor converge to a Golden Rule balanced growth path, and consumption increases monotonically and converges to the maximum level sustainable in perpetuity.[4]

18.1.2 Example: The Cobb-Douglas Production Function

Assuming that the Cobb-Douglas production function (16.18) represents the technology, the steady state is given by

$$\tilde{k} = \left(\frac{\mu B}{n + \delta}\right)^{\frac{1}{1-\beta}}.$$

Substituting this into $f(k)$, we can show that

$$\tilde{c} = B\left(\frac{B}{n + \delta}\right)^{\frac{\beta}{1-\beta}}(1 - \mu)\mu^{\frac{\beta}{1-\beta}}.$$

We can also show that $\tilde{c}$ is a concave function of μ. Differentiating with respect to μ and solving the first-order condition, we can show that the Golden Rule savings rate equals the capital elasticity of output as was obtained in (18.7), which in this example gives

$$\mu^{gr} = \beta. \tag{18.10}$$

Since $\beta < 1$ the dynamic process converges to the steady state, $k_t \to \tilde{k}^{gr}$ and $c_t \to \tilde{c}^{gr}$.

18.1.3 Time Preference and the Golden Rule in the Adaptive Economizing Economy

Now an interesting question arises. Can an economy that discounts the future possess a Golden Rule path? More explicitly, could such an economy "choose" a future weight, ψ, so that its consumption/wealth function, say $h^{\psi}(k)$, would generate the savings rate where

$$\frac{Bf(\tilde{k}) - h^{\psi}(\tilde{k})}{Bf(\tilde{k})} = \mu^{gr}, \tag{18.11}$$

and would this value of $\tilde{k}$ be asymptotically stable?

To answer this, consider the savings function obtained for the adaptive economizing model discussed in chapter 17 indexed by the future weight ψ,

$$s^\psi(\tilde{k}) := Bf(\tilde{k}) - h^\psi(\tilde{k}). \tag{18.12}$$

From our previous analysis we know that for each ψ there exists a unique positive steady state, $\tilde{k}^\psi$, depending on ψ. Define

$$\mu^\psi := \frac{s^\psi(\tilde{k}^\psi)}{\tilde{y}^\psi}$$

where $\tilde{y}^\psi$ is the steady state income given ψ. If $\tilde{k}^\psi$ is a Golden Rule steady state, then from (18.8),

$$\mu^{gr} = f'(\tilde{k}^\psi)\tilde{k}^\psi = \tilde{r}^\psi \tilde{k}^\psi.$$

We need to know if there exists a future weight ψ such that

$$\mu^\psi = \mu^{gr}. \tag{18.13}$$

Such a ψ would be the *Golden Rule future weight*.

From (18.5), $\tilde{r}^{gr} = n + \delta$. From Lemma 17.1(ii), $\tilde{r}^\psi = n + \delta + (1 + n)/\psi$. It follows that

$$\tilde{r}(\psi) \to \tilde{r}(\mu^{gr}), \quad \text{as} \quad \psi \to \infty.$$

Evidently, *there is no finite future weight* that will generate a Golden Rule path, but the larger ψ is, the closer the adaptive steady state, $\tilde{k}(\psi)$, approaches the Golden Rule steady state, $\tilde{k}(\mu^{gr})$.

We also know from Proposition 17.3 that as ψ becomes large, $\tilde{k}(\psi)$ becomes unstable, so that for almost all initial conditions, trajectories will not converge to the Golden Rule path. The upshot is:

PROPOSITION 18.2   *The adaptive economizing steady state can only approximate a Golden Rule path. As ψ increases, the adaptive economizing steady state converges to the Golden Rule capital/labor ratio, but it eventually becomes unstable. For large enough ψ fluctuations around the Golden Rule path persist almost surely. Then capital and labor will oscillate around the balanced growth path. Consumption will fluctuate above and below the Golden Rule level. Average consumption over all generations may be higher than the Golden Rule level, but only if some generations give up almost all consumption.*

18.2 The Principle of Intertemporal Optimality

18.2.1 Optimal Trajectories

Another criterion of intertemporal optimality used in economic growth theory is that of maximizing the discounted flow of all future utilities. This criterion is the basis of the adaptive economizing analysis of capital accumulation, but in that model the problem is simplified by considering the tradeoff only between current consumption and a potentially sustainable consumption level for the future. In the present model each future generation is accounted for separately.

At a given time, t, the future sequence of consumption levels is

$$(c_t, c_{t+1}, \ldots) = (c_{t+i})_{i=0}^{\infty}.$$

An *intertemporally optimal path* from time t is one that maximizes a function of the entire path

$$U(c_t, c_{t+1}, \ldots), \tag{18.14}$$

subject to the constraints

$$k_{t+1} = \frac{1}{1+n}[(1-\delta)k_t + y_t - c_t] \quad \text{(a)}$$

$$y_t = Bf(k_t), \qquad \text{(b)} \tag{18.15}$$

$$0 \leq c_t \leq y_t, \qquad \text{(c)}$$

with k_t given. (d)

The parameters of the problem are those of the utility function, those of the production function, the technology level, and the capital stock at time t. The solution depends on all these parameters.

Such a problem can be formulated for each time t as time passes. This raises the question, Will the solution of each of these problems be consistent? That is, will each future generation want to do—when its time comes—what the current generation plans for it? Or, if we considered ourselves to be infinitely lived, would we do in every future period what we would now plan for that future period, when we consider the situation afresh each time?

18.2.2 Consistency

To get a better idea of what we are talking about, let us distinguish between the "present" historical time, t, for which the objective function (18.14) is formulated, and the anticipated "future" time periods, denote by the index i, that are considered in the calculations at time t of the optimal path.[5]

From the point of view of the "present" generation's perspective at time t, the intertemporally optimal path is one that maximizes

$$U[(c^i)_{i=0}^{\infty}]$$ (18.16)

subject to

$$k^{i+1} = \frac{1}{1+n}[(1-\delta)k^i + y^i - c^i] \quad \text{(a)}$$

$$y^i = Bf(k^i), \qquad\qquad\qquad\qquad \text{(b)}$$ (18.17)

$$0 \le c^i \le y \qquad\qquad\qquad\qquad\quad \text{(c)}$$

$$k^0 = k_t. \qquad\qquad\qquad\qquad\quad\; \text{(d)}$$

The optimal consumption stream anticipated at the "present" historical time t is

$$(c_t^0, c_t^1, c_t^2, \ldots, c_t^i, \ldots).$$

The optimal paths of capital accumulation and income anticipated at time t are

$$k_t^0, k_t^1, k_t^2, \ldots \quad \text{and} \quad y_t^0, y_t^1, y_t^2, \ldots.$$

Assume that the variable c^0 planned for the imminent period is realized and denote the realized value by c_t. Also, let k_t and y_t be realized incomes and realized capital stocks. That is, the realized consumption, capital, and income variables are

$$k_t := k_t^0, c_t := c_t^0, \quad \text{and} \quad y_t := y_t^0$$

where the k_t satisfy (18.15a). The problem of consistency is that of asking if

$$c_t^i = c_{t+i}^0 \quad \text{for all } t \text{ and for all } i.$$ (18.18)

The consistency criterion states that the "optimal" consumption level, calculated at historical time t for each anticipated future period $i \geq 0$, will be the same as the optimal level for that anticipated period when it becomes the present at historical time $t + i$.

The consistency of optimal solutions in this sense is a delicate problem that has been investigated in depth.[6] It has been found that given the assumed structure of the choice problem, a sufficient condition for consistency is that

$$U[(c^i)_{i=0}^{\infty}] = \sum_{i=0}^{\infty} \alpha^i u(c^i) \tag{18.19}$$

where $u'(c) > 0$ and $u''(c) < 0$ for all $c > 0$ and where $0 < \alpha < 1$.

In this expression the i that appears in c^i is the anticipated time index, and α^i is the ith power of the time preference parameter, α.

This is the utility function (17.4) with which we are already familiar from our discussion of the adaptive economizing model, except in that analysis only future streams $\{c^i\}_{i=1}^{\infty}$ were considered such that $c^i \equiv c^1$, $i \geq 1$. We found that only for stationary states did $c_t^1 = c_{t+1}$. In general, $c_t^1 \neq c_{t+1}$. In the asymptotically stable case, trajectories become consistent asymptotically, i.e., $c_t^1 \to \tilde{c}$ and $c_t^0 \to \tilde{c}$, so $c_t^1 \to c_{t+1}^0$. But, *in general, adaptive economizing trajectories do not converge to a steady state, and, because errors in anticipating feedback effects persist, inconsistency persists.*

If we could find consistently optimal trajectories, then we could drop the distinction between the historical time index t and the anticipated time index i. In that case the problem of optimal growth could be formulated using (18.14)–(18.15), but with the utility function explicitly in the form

$$U(c_t, c_{t+1}, \ldots) = \sum_{i=0}^{\infty} \alpha^i u(c_{t+1}). \tag{18.20}$$

18.2.3   The Principle of Optimality

To see how this can be done, return to the original intertemporal planning problem (18.16)–(18.17) but with the utility function (18.19). For the choice problem at time t, the optimal trajectory is the solution to

$$V(k_t) = \max_{(c_i)_t^\infty} \left\{ \sum_{i=t}^{\infty} \alpha^{i-t} u(c^i) \mid \text{given } k_t \text{ and (18.17)} \right\} \qquad (18.21)$$

where $V(k_t)$ is called *the indirect utility function*. Its solution is $(c_t^0, c_t^1, c_t^2, \ldots)$. The problem for the next period when historical time passes is

$$V(k_{t+1}) = \max_{(c_i)_{t+1}^\infty} \left\{ \sum_{i=t+1}^{\infty} \alpha^{i-(t+1)} u(c^i) \mid \text{given } k_{t+1} \text{ and (18.17)} \right\}. \qquad (18.22)$$

Its solution is $(c_{t+1}^0, c_{t+1}^1, c_{t+1}^2, \ldots)$. *If the solutions are consistent, the superscripts can be dropped*, i.e., we let $c_t = c_t^0$ for all t. Then,

$$V(k_t) = u(c_t) + \alpha u(c_{t+1}) + \alpha^2 u(c_{t+2}) + \cdots$$
$$= u(c_t) + \alpha[u(c_{t+1}) + \alpha u(c_{t+2}) + \cdots]$$
$$= u(c_t) + \alpha V(k_{t+1}).$$

Assuming that $k_t^i = k_{t+i}$ for all t and using the actual capital accumulation equation (18.15a) for k_{t+1}, this can be written

$$V(k_t) = u(c_t) + \alpha V\left(\frac{1}{1+n} [(1-\delta)k_t + Bf(k_t) - c_t] \right).$$

But this must be true for all t, so we can consider an arbitrary initial condition, k, and rewrite this expression as

$$V(k) = \max_{0 \le c \le Bf(k)} \left\{ u(c) + \alpha V\left(\frac{1}{1+n} [(1-\delta)k + Bf(k) - c] \right) \right\}. \qquad (18.23)$$

This expression is called *Bellman's equation* or the *principle of intertemporal optimality*, which in effect is an equivalent way of writing the consistency criterion.[7]

18.2.4 The Consistently Optimal Consumption Strategy

Recall that

$$k^0 = \frac{1}{1+n} [(1-\delta)k^0 + Bf(k^0)] \qquad (18.24)$$

is the largest reachable capital/labor ratio given the capital accumulation equation (18.15a). For each $k \in \mathcal{K} := [0, k^0]$, (18.23) is an ordinary constrained maximum problem. Suppose there exists a unique solution for each $k \in \mathcal{K}$. Then the function

$$c = h^{co}(k)$$

that satisfies

$$V(k) = u[h^{co}(k)] + \alpha V\left(\frac{1}{1+n}[(1-\delta)k + Bf(k) - h^{co}(k)]\right) \qquad (18.25)$$

is called the *(consistently) optimal consumption strategy*. This strategy determines the dynamics of capital accumulation that is optimal *with respect to the intertemporal utility function* (18.19).

The difference equation that describes the consistently optimal path of capital accumulation is

$$k_{t+1} = \theta^{co}(k_t) := \frac{1}{1+n}\{(1-\delta)k_t + Bf(k_t) - h^{co}(k_t)\}. \qquad (18.26)$$

For reference, we shall name the map $\theta^{co}(\cdot)$ a *consistently optimal dynamic structure with respect to* $u(\cdot)$, $f(\cdot)$, B, n, and δ.[8]

18.3   Consistently Optimal Dynamic Structures and Strategies

18.3.1   Consistently Optimal Dynamic Structures

The analysis of the existence and qualitative properties of consistently optimal dynamic strategies and structures involves a variety of techniques from optimization and dynamic programming theory that have not been included so far in this book, and there is not space enough to develop them here. Instead, the central results needed for our purposes will be given and the interested reader can consult the references for their background.[9]

The optimal growth problem has usually been transformed from one that defines optimality in terms of actions—here c_t—to one that defines it in terms of states—here k_t.[10] To motivate this approach, use the consumption/wealth strategy $h(\cdot)$ to define the *value function*

$$F(k_t, k_{t+1}) := u[h(k_t)] = u[(1-\delta)k_t + Bf(k_t) - (1+n)k_{t+1}]. \qquad (18.27)$$

Define the *technology set*

$$\mathcal{T} := \left\{ (k_t, k_{t+1}) \mid k_t \in \mathcal{K}, \frac{1-\delta}{1+n} k_t \leq k_{t+1} \leq \frac{1}{1+n} [(1-\delta)k_t + Bf(k_t)] \right\}.$$

$$(18.28)$$

The intertemporal optimizing problem (18.16)–(18.17) with utility function (18.19) can be rewritten as

$$W(k_t) = \max_{(k_i, k_{i+1}) \in \mathcal{T}} \left\{ \sum_{i=t}^{\infty} \alpha^{i-t} F(k_i, k_{i+1}) \mid \text{given } k_t \right\}.$$

$$(18.29)$$

That is, instead of defining the intertemporal equilibrium as an optimal sequence of consumption actions, it is defined as an optimal sequence of capital stocks or states.

Applying the principle of consistent intertemporal optimality analogously to our discussion in the preceding section, a sequence, $(k_t, k_{t+1}, \ldots)$, is *consistently optimal* and $\theta^F(\cdot)$ is a *consistently optimal dynamic structure* with respect to $F(\cdot)$ if, and only if, $\theta^F(\cdot)$ satisfies

$$W(k) = F[k, \theta^F(k)] + \alpha W[\theta^F(k)]$$

$$= \max_{k' \in \mathcal{K}} \{ F(k, k') + \alpha W[k'] \}. \qquad (18.30)$$

The trajectory

$$k_{t+1} = \theta^F(k_t)$$

is consistently optimal with respect to F.

The fundamental existence theorem defined for a consistently optimal dynamic structure is the following.[11]

THEOREM 18.1   *Suppose*

(i) the time preference parameter $0 < \alpha < 1$;

(ii) the set $\mathcal{T}$ is bounded and convex;

(iii) the function $F(\cdot)$ is bounded, continuous, and concave on $\mathcal{T}$;

(iv) for each $k', F(\cdot, k')$ is strictly increasing in k;

(v) for each $k, F(k, k')$ is strictly concave and strictly decreasing in k'.

Then there exists a consistently optimal (continuous, single-valued) dynamic structure with respect to F.

18.3.2   Existence of Consistently Optimal Consumption Strategies for the One-Sector Growth Model

In what follows later it is important to notice that Theorem 18.1 is stated in terms of the value function $F(\cdot)$ and the convex sets $\mathcal{T}$ and $\mathcal{K}$. The utility and production functions that motivated the construction of $F(\cdot)$ and $\mathcal{T}$ in equations (18.27) and (18.28) do not appear. Consequently, this theorem as stated *does not establish existence of a consistently optimal dynamic consumption strategy* $h^{co}(\cdot)$ *and dynamic structure* $\theta^{co}(\cdot)$. To do so, it must be shown that the set $\mathcal{T}$ defined in (18.28) is indeed convex and that the value function defined in (18.27) satisfies the properties of (iii)–(v) of the theorem. This can be done when $f(\cdot)$ satisfies the properties Lemma 16.1 and $u(\cdot)$ satisfies (18.19). This result, which is proved elsewhere,[12] is:

THEOREM 18.2   *Suppose the production function $f(\cdot)$ satisfies the properties given in Lemma 16.1, the generational utility function $u(\cdot)$ satisfies the properties following (18.19), the value function $F(\cdot)$ is defined by (18.27), and the set $\mathcal{T}$ is defined by (18.28). Then*

(i) the optimal consumption/wealth strategy, $h^{co}(\cdot)$, exists for each k;

(ii) the function $h^{co}(\cdot)$ is continuously differentiable;

(iii) the indirect utility function, $V(k)$, is continuously differentiable;

(iv) for all k, such that $h(k) < Bf(k)$,

$$u'(c)\Big|_{c=h^{co}(k)} = \frac{\alpha}{1+n} V'(k')\Big|_{k'=\theta^{co}(k)} \tag{18.31}$$

where

$$\theta^{co}(k) = \frac{1}{1+n}[(1-\delta)k + Bf(k) - h^{co}(k)] \tag{18.32}$$

is the optimal dynamic structure with respect to $u(\cdot)$ and $f(\cdot)$;

(v) $\theta^{co}(\cdot) \equiv \theta^F(\cdot)$ and $W(k) \equiv V(k)$.

Thus, given (18.27) and (18.28), the solutions of (18.23) and (18.30) are equivalent.

18.4   The Dynamics of Intertemporally Consistent Optimal Capital Accumulation

18.4.1   Balanced Growth and Asymptotic Stability

What are the qualitative properties of the dynamical system of consistently optimal capital accumulation, and what kinds of "theoretical histories" do they imply? The answer to this question requires the following:

PROPOSITION 18.3   *Given the assumptions of Theorem 18.2,*

(i) there exists a unique, positive steady state, $\tilde{k}^{co}$, that solves

$$\tilde{r}^{co} = Bf'(\tilde{k}^{co}) = \frac{1+n}{\alpha} - (1 - \delta); \tag{18.33}$$

(ii) $\tilde{k}^{co}$ is globally asymptotically stable, that is, for all $k \in \mathcal{K} := [0, k^m]$,
$$\theta^t(k) \to \tilde{k}^{co} \quad as \quad t \to \infty,$$

and all trajectories are monotonic.

To establish this result, we need the following preliminary:

LEMMA 18.1   *The indirect utility function, $V(\cdot)$, is strictly increasing and strictly concave.*

Proof   First, consider Bellman's equation (18.25). Because $V(\cdot)$ is continuously differentiable,

$$V'(k) = u'[h(k)]h'(k) + \alpha V'[\theta(k)] \cdot \theta'(k) \tag{18.34}$$

where

$$\theta'(k) = \frac{1}{1+n}[1 - \delta + Bf'(k) - h'(k)]. \tag{18.35}$$

From (18.31),

$$u'[h(k)] = \frac{\alpha}{1+n} V'[\theta(k)]. \tag{18.36}$$

Using (18.34), we get

$$V'(k) = \frac{\alpha}{1+n} V'[\theta(k)](1 - \delta + Bf'(k)). \tag{18.37}$$

Or, using (18.36) again,

$$V'(k) = u'[h(k)](Bf'(k) + 1 - \delta).$$ (18.38)

From this it follows that

$$V'(k) > 0 \quad \text{and} \quad V''(k) < 0.$$ (18.39)

∎

Now let us establish the:

Proof of Proposition 18.3

(i) Consider $Bf'(k)$ for $k \in \mathcal{K}$. This function is monotonically decreasing from ∞ at $k = 0$ and approaches 0 as $k \to \infty$. But, as $\alpha < 1$ and $\delta < 1$, $(1 + n)/\alpha > (1 - \delta)$, so the right side of (18.32) is positive. Consequently, there exists a unique $\tilde{k}$ satisfying (18.32). Now substitute this value in (18.36). We find that (18.32) implies that $V'(\tilde{k}) = V'[\theta(\tilde{k})]$, so $k = \theta(\tilde{k})$. Therefore, $\tilde{k}$ is indeed the unique stationary state.

To consider stability, use the fact that $V(\cdot)$ is strictly concave. This implies that

$$V'[\theta(k)] < V'(k) \quad \text{if} \quad \theta(k) > k$$

and

$$V'[\theta(k)] > V'(k) \quad \text{if} \quad \theta(k) < k.$$

Together these expressions imply that

$$[V'[\theta(k)] - V'(k)] \cdot [k - \theta(k)] \geq 0.$$ (18.40)

Using (18.36) and (18.37), we get

$$[V'[\theta(k)] - V'(k)] = u'[h(k)]\left[r + (1 - \delta) - \frac{1 + n}{\alpha}\right].$$ (18.41)

At a stationary state, $\theta(\tilde{k}) = (\tilde{k})$ so that this equation implies (18.33).

(ii) Given that $u'(c) > 0$ for all $c > 0$, (18.40) and (18.41) imply that

$$\left[r + (1 - \delta) - \frac{1 + n}{\alpha}\right][k - \theta(k)] \geq 0.$$

That is,

$$\text{sgn}\left[r + (1 - \delta) - \frac{1 + n}{\alpha}\right] = \text{sgn}[k - \theta(k)]. \qquad (18.42)$$

Since $\tilde{r} = \frac{1+n}{\alpha} - (1 - \delta)$ and r is a decreasing function of k,

$$\text{sgn}\left[r + (1 - \delta) - \frac{1 + n}{\alpha}\right] = \text{sgn}[\tilde{k} - k].$$

With (18.42) this implies that

$$\text{sgn}[\tilde{k} - k] = \text{sgn}[\theta(k) - k].$$

That is, $k < \tilde{k}$ implies and is implied by $\theta(k) > k$, and $k > \tilde{k}$ implies and is implied by $\theta(k) < k$. But this means that

$$\theta^t(k) < \tilde{k} \quad \text{all} \quad k < \tilde{k} \quad \text{and} \quad \theta^t(k) > \tilde{k} \quad \text{all} \quad k > \tilde{k}.$$

Consequently, $\tilde{k}$ is the least upper bound for $\theta^t(k)$ for all $k < \tilde{k}$ and the greatest lower bound for $\theta^t(k)$ for all $k > \tilde{k}$. Consequently,

$$\lim_{t \to \infty} \theta^t(k) \to \tilde{k} \quad \text{all} \quad k \in \mathcal{K}.$$

This completes the proof of Proposition 18.3.   ∎

18.4.2   On the Asymptotic Optimality of Adaptive Economizing

Recall the adaptive economizing model of chapter 17. For such an economy it was seen that a unique, positive steady state exists, let us call it $\tilde{k}^{ae}$, and that the adaptive economizing, steady state, marginal product of capital

$$\tilde{r}^{ae} = Bf'(\tilde{k}^{ae}) = n + \delta + \frac{1 + n}{\psi}$$

where $\psi = \alpha/(1 - \alpha)$. From Proposition 18.3,

$$\tilde{r}^{co} = \frac{1 + n}{\alpha} - (1 - \delta).$$

Substituting for ψ in $\tilde{r}^{ae}$, we get

$$\tilde{r}^{ae} = n + \delta + \frac{(1-\alpha)}{\alpha}(1+n)$$

$$= \frac{1+n}{\alpha} - (1-\delta)$$

$$= \tilde{r}^{co}.$$

Thus, *the adaptive economizing steady state is consistently optimal in the sense of solving the intertemporal optimization problem of* §18.2.

However, the former is not always asymptotically stable. Indeed, it is both generically asymptotically stable and generically unstable. In the former case adaptive economizing trajectories converge to consistent, intertemporally optimal strategies, but not in the latter case when, instead, they fluctuate around the steady state. In particular, adaptive economizing trajectories become unstable as $\psi \to \infty$ or as $\alpha \to 1$.

To summarize, we have:

PROPOSITION 18.4 *Assume the conditions of Proposition 18.3; then*

(i) the balanced growth path determined by $\tilde{k}^{ae}$ for the adaptive economizing model is a consistent intertemporally optimal trajectory;

(ii) for all $k \neq \tilde{k}^{ae}$, the adaptive economizing trajectories are inconsistent (i.e., $c_t^1 \neq c_{t+1}$), but for all small enough ψ they are asymptotically consistently optimal (i.e., $c_t^1 \to c_{t+1}$ as $t \to \infty$);

(iii) for all sufficiently large ψ, adaptive economizing paths fluctuate around the consistent intertemporally optimal balanced growth path.

18.4.3 Convergence of Optimal Growth to the Golden Rule

As $\alpha \to 1$, $\tilde{r}^{co} \to n + \delta = \tilde{r}^{gr}$, so all consistently optimal growth paths are asymptotically stable. It follows that consistently optimal growth paths converge to the Golden Rule trajectory as $\alpha \to 1$. The solution to the infinite horizon optimal growth model, however, does not exist for $\alpha = 1$ (because the utility function is unbounded). Therefore, it cannot be said that the Golden Rule trajectory is consistently optimal in the sense of Bellman's equation. In effect, therefore, *the Golden Rule means not discounting the future.* That is, all generations should receive equal weight. Nonetheless, we have:

PROPOSITION 18.5 *As α approaches unity, consistently optimal capital/ labor ratio trajectories approach the Golden Rule steady state, and the* *corresponding capital and output trajectories approach the Golden Rule balanced growth path.*

18.5 Rationalizing Capital Accumulation Paths

18.5.1 The Dynamic Rationalization Theorem

A concept of considerable vintage in economics is the idea that actions may reveal preferences.[13] In the context of growth theory this translates into the following question. Suppose a growth path is generated by a given dynamical system. For what set of preferences, that is, for what utility function, is this trajectory consistently optimal?

The following *Dynamic Rationalization Theorem* was proved by Boldrin and Montrucchio.

THEOREM 18.3 (Boldrin and Montrucchio (1988)) *Let $\theta(\cdot)$ be any twice differentiable map from the interval $\mathcal{K} := [0, k^m] \to \mathcal{K}$ where k^m is as defined in equation (18.23). Then for some $\alpha^* \in (0, 1)$ and for every $\alpha \in [0, \alpha^*]$ there exists a map $F_{\alpha, \theta} := \mathcal{K} \times \mathcal{K} \to \mathbb{R}$, depending on α and $\theta(\cdot)$, satisfying properties (iii)–(v) of Theorem 18.1, such that $\theta(\cdot)$ is the consistently optimal dynamic structure with respect to $F_{\alpha, \theta}$.*

When Theorem 18.3 applies, we shall say that $F_{\alpha, \theta}(\cdot)$ is a *rationalization* of $\theta(\cdot)$ and that $\theta(\cdot)$ can be *rationalized* with respect to $F(\cdot)$.

The potential significance of this theorem rests on the fact, illustrated in many different economic contexts throughout this book, that the trajectories of a given dynamical system based on a map $\theta(\cdot)$ can be complex if $\theta(\cdot)$ is "sufficiently nonlinear." According to this theorem, such complex trajectories can be rationalized in principle, that is, a value function mathematically exists (and can be constructed) for which the given map $\theta(\cdot)$ satisfies the principle of intertemporal optimality in the form (18.30) and is, therefore, the consistently optimal structure for the dynamic programming problem (18.29).

18.5.2 Rationalizing Capital Accumulation Paths

Now consider the one-sector process of capital accumulation

$$k_{t+1} = \theta(k_t) := \frac{1}{1+n}[(1-\delta)k_t + Bf(k_t) - h(k_t)] \tag{18.43}$$

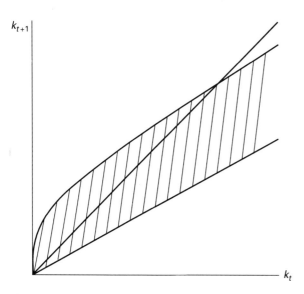

Figure 18.2
Feasible capital trajectories

with δ, B, f, and h given as in §18.2. If the consumption/wealth function $h(\cdot)$ and the production function $f(\cdot)$ are twice differentiable and satisfy

$$h(k) \le Bf(k) \quad \text{all} \quad k \in \mathcal{K}, \tag{18.44}$$

then $\theta(k)$ is twice differentiable. Let

$$M(k) := \frac{1}{1+n}[(1-\delta)k + Bf(k)] \tag{18.45}$$

and assume that

$$f'(k) > 0, \; f''(k) < 0 \quad \text{all} \quad k \in \mathcal{K}. \tag{18.46}$$

Then

$$\mathcal{T} = \left\{ (k,k') \mid k \in \mathcal{K}, k' \in \left[\left(\frac{1-\delta}{1+n} \right) k, M(k) \right] \right\}$$

is a convex set and has the appearance shown in figure 18.2.

According to the Dynamic Rationalization Theorem 18.3 we have:

PROPOSITION 18.6   *Assume that $f(\cdot)$ and $h(\cdot)$ are twice differentiable and assume (18.43)–(18.46). Then there exists a value function $F_{\alpha,\theta}(k,k')$—depending on α and $\theta(\cdot)$—that is a rationalization of $\theta(\cdot)$.*

This means that a fairly large class of capital accumulation models can be rationalized in the sense of Theorem 18.3, *including ones with complex dynamics.* However, the smoothness (differentiability) requirements are restrictive. The consumption/wealth strategy $h(k)$ has a kink at the capital stock k^s for which $h(k^s) = Bf(k^s)$. If $k^M = \max \theta(x) \le k^s$, then no problem arises because all trajectories beginning in $[0, k^s]$ remain there, so we can restrict $\mathcal{K}$ to this interval. This means the rationalization theorem applies to models whose trapping sets have the appearance shown in figure 16.5, Case II. If, however, $k^M > k^s$, the differentiability requirement is violated. For such models the trapping set will appear as in figure 16.5, Cases I or III.

18.5.3   Examples

The adaptive economizing growth model of chapter 17 provides an example where it is assumed that $f(k) = k^\beta$ and $u(c) = A + a \log c$. These are analytic functions whose derivatives exist everywhere except at $k = 0$ and $c = 0$. If the functions are confined to the set $\mathcal{K}^s$, Lemma 17.1 insures that

$$\theta(k) = \frac{1}{1+n}\left\{(1-\delta)k + Bk^\beta - \frac{1}{1+\psi}\left[1 + \frac{1+n}{\beta Bk^{\beta-1} - (n+\delta)}\right]\right.$$

$$\left. \cdot \left[Bk^\beta - (n+\delta)k\right]\right\}$$

$$\le M(k).$$

If $k^M \le k^s$, the theorem is satisfied and the adaptive economizing behavior of agents who only consider a single future generation can be rationalized. *That is, they behave as if they were maximizing some kind of infinite horizon utility function, even if their adaptive economizing behavior, which only looks ahead to a single future generation, leads to chaotic paths of capital accumulation.*

18.5.4   Rationalization and Optimality

How is a rationalization, $F_{\alpha,\theta}(\cdot)$, related to the structure of *optimal* capital accumulation? To answer this, we note from (18.27) that for $F(\cdot)$ to be consistent with the model of optimal capital accumulation, there must exist a utility function, say $u_\theta(\cdot)$, such that

$$F_{\alpha,\theta}(k,k') = u_\theta[(1-\delta)k + Bf(k) - (1+n)k']. \tag{18.47}$$

This suggests the following alternative definition of a rationalization. Suppose $F_{\alpha,\theta}$ is a rationalization with respect to (α,θ). If $u_\theta(\cdot)$ is a utility function satisfying (18.47) and $\theta(\cdot)$ satisfies (18.43)–(18.46), we say that $u_\theta(\cdot)$ rationalizes $\theta(\cdot)$.

Now consider the profile of $F_{\alpha,\theta}(\cdot)$, given in (18.47). Noting from (18.43) that the argument of $u_\theta(\cdot)$ is $h(k)$, consider

$$\frac{\partial F}{\partial k} = u_\theta'[h(k)][1 - \delta + Bf'(k)],$$

$$\frac{\partial F}{\partial k'} = -(1+n)u_\theta'[h(k)],$$

$$\frac{\partial^2 F}{\partial k'^2} = (1+n)^2 u_\theta''[h(k)].$$

From these expressions and recalling condition (iv) of Theorem 18.1, it is clear that $F_{\alpha,\theta}$ in (18.47) satisfies the requirements of the rationalization theorem if, and only if, $u_\theta(\cdot)$ is strictly increasing and concave. But from Proposition 18.3 *this implies that capital accumulation converges asymptotically to the balanced growth path.* This in turn implies the following fact:

PROPOSITION 18.7   *A one-sector model of capital accumulation satisfying (18.43)–(18.46) can be rationalized by a concave, monotonically increasing utility function $u_\theta(c)$ if, and only if, it is asymptotically stable.*

Thus, the value function that rationalizes a given model of capital accumulation *may not be consistent with the structural components of that model,* in particular with its underlying utility function. In general the rationalizing value function $F_{\alpha,\theta}(\cdot)$ depends on all the constituents of the model of capital accumulation, including the production function, the depreciation rate, and the rate of population growth. Returning to the adaptive economizing model of §18.5.3, it can be rationalized by a concave increasing utility function of consumption *only when it is asymptotically stable.* In general, it cannot be rationalized by an independent utility function—even though it can be rationalized by some kind of a value function dependent on technology.[14]

18.5.5 Constant Savings Rates

Perhaps the rationalization paradox can best be seen by considering simple trajectories.

Recall the basic growth model of §16.2 with a constant savings rate μ. The equation of capital accumulation is (16.9). It is easy to see that the conditions of Proposition 18.7 are satisfied. Therefore, there exist a value function $F_{\alpha,\theta}(\cdot)$, a utility function u_θ, and a time preference parameter α_θ such that $F_{\alpha,\theta}(\cdot)$ and u_θ, α_θ rationalize

$$\theta(k) = (1 - \delta)k + \mu B f(k). \tag{18.48}$$

Remember that the $F_{\alpha,\theta}$ rationalization depends on θ, that is, on all its constituents, so u_θ does also.

To see the significance of this fact, consider the Cobb-Douglas production function and take any fixed savings ratio $0 < \mu < 1$. We know from (18.33) that

$$r^{co} = \frac{1+n}{\alpha} - (1 - \delta).$$

From (16.16) it can be seen that

$$\tilde{r}^\mu = \frac{\beta}{\mu}(n + \delta).$$

Setting these equal and solving for α yields

$$\alpha_\theta = \frac{(1 + n)\mu}{\beta(n + \delta) + \mu(1 - \delta)}. \tag{18.49}$$

For the intertemporal optimizing problem to be well defined, it must be that $0 < \alpha_\theta < 1$. This requires the savings rate μ to be less than the elasticity of production, i.e., $\mu < \beta$.

Suppose, however, that $\mu = \beta$. Then no trajectory of (16.9) can be consistently optimal because this is the Golden Rule savings ratio, which implies that $\alpha_\theta = 1$. However, choose constants $n_\theta \leq n$, $\delta_\theta \leq \delta$ with $n_\theta + \delta_\theta < n + \delta$, and solve $\mathscr{F}^{gr} = \mathscr{F}^{co}$ to get

$$\alpha_\theta = \frac{1 + n_\theta}{1 + n + (\delta - \delta_\theta)}. \tag{18.50}$$

Then there exist a value rationalization $F_{\alpha_\theta \theta_n}$ and a utility rationalization u_θ of (18.48) satisfying (18.47). However, the time preference parameter α_θ is based on the biased constants n_θ and δ_θ.

What is going on here? In effect the rationalization must be based on a "fictional" or "perturbed" model of capital accumulation by choosing artificial population growth and capital depreciation rates n_θ and δ_θ. The Golden Rule trajectory for these perturbed rates would be quite different from the one obtained for the original n and δ. But if we discount the future and optimize with respect to the artificially low n_θ and δ_θ, the savings rate will be just the one that yields the Golden Rule trajectory for the *true* parameters n and δ. It is like cognitive dissonance: if we want to believe that the Golden Rule path is consistently optimal in the Bellman sense, then we must deceive ourselves.

Turning this argument around, suppose growth is determined by a consistently optimal path on the basis of parameters α, n, δ, β. The steady state to which this converges could be rationalized as a Golden Rule path for any parameter values n_{gr}, δ_{gr} that satisfied

$$n_{gr} + \delta_{gr} = \frac{1 + n}{\alpha} - (1 - \delta).$$

For example, if $n_{gr} = n$, then

$$\delta_{gr} = (1 + n)\frac{(1 - \alpha)}{\alpha} + \delta$$

would give a perturbed depreciation rate that would rationalize behavior actually based on discounting the utility of future generations by appealing to one based instead on the Golden Rule.

The implication of all this is that there are actions that can be rationalized from quite different preferences than those generating the action, thus raising the possibility that "revealed preferences" may be quite different from "true preferences.[15] In other words, rationalizing is not the same thing as optimizing. This distinction turns out to be just as important in pure theory as it is in common parlance.

18.6 Summary of Part V

The aggregate model of savings and capital accumulation captures an important stylized fact: the real world trend in output and productivity of the past two centuries. Incorporating wealth saturation adds possibilities of endogenous growth fluctuations around a growth trend. When an explicit tradeoff between present consumption and the potential future standard of living is introduced, similar complications occur. When the current generation alternatively underestimates and overestimates the rate of return on savings, fluctuations in optimism and pessimism are positively correlated with alternating expansions and contractions in the growth rate, much like the fluctuations observed in reality.

When optimal growth is considered within the simplest capital accumulation framework, intertemporally optimal growth trajectories converge to balanced growth paths. Cyclic or chaotic paths—*in this special setting*—cannot be optimal. Adaptive economizing paths will converge to a consistently optimal path when the future weight is not too large. When the future weight is big enough, they fluctuate around a balanced growth path and this balanced growth path converges to the Golden Rule path or to an intertemporally optimal growth path.

When each generation's weight on the bequest given the next generation increases, given any trajectory of the type generated by an adaptive economizing model, including cyclic and chaotic growth paths, there may exist an optimal growth model based on some utility function for which that trajectory is intertemporally optimal. In other words, a very large class of growth paths can be rationalized. But that rationalization cannot be consistent with the assumptions of the adaptive economizing framework. The implication is profound: the ability to construct an explanation that what has happened, or will happen, is the best that can happen is not the same thing as figuring out the best thing to do. In theory, as in practice, rationalization allows one to live in a fool's paradise.

VI ECONOMIC DEVELOPMENT

... expansion
collapse
renewal
turbulence
transition
a new age ...

19 Population, Productivity, and Generational Welfare

The restraints to population are in some degree loosened; and after a short period, the same retrograde and progressive movements ... are repeated ... in irregular manner.
—Thomas Malthus, *An Essay on the Principle of Population*

I came to suspect ... a self-generating mechanism, by which low fertility in one twenty year period led to high fertility in the next, and vice-versa.
—Richard A. Easterlin, *Birth and Fortune*

"Development" is a flexible word in the English language, having a variety of meanings with subtle distinctions depending on context. Among these are "to evolve the possibilities of" and "to go through a process of growth, differentiation, or evolution by successive changes." When considering economic processes, it implies both growth and structural change. Even more, it implies a progression of socioeconomic morphologies of advancing complexity. We are now going to reconsider macroeconomic growth from this evolutionary perspective, using the tools of complex economic dynamics.

The theory is extended in a series of steps. This chapter takes the first. Setting aside capital accumulation for simplicity, it introduces population as an endogenous variable that interacts with output and welfare. In this classical setting both population and welfare converge. Then a minimal income threshold for survival is introduced. With this simple but obviously relevant modification chaotic fluctuations can occur.

In chapter 20 household preferences are introduced as a reflection of cultural and economic factors. Then infrastructure is accommodated. It implies a kind of economy of scale that has a crucial role to play in the development story. The internal absolute diseconomy that occurs when population expands within a given system is also introduced, a factor that exaggerates the tendency for instability. These two chapters give an exhaustive account of the complex dynamics that arises in the interaction of population, productivity, and welfare when family preferences, social infrastructure, and absolute diseconomies matter.

Chapter 21 introduces multiple technological regimes, regime switching, and learning by doing. The implications include "growth, differentiation, and evolution through successive changes." These possibilities considerably expand the range of historical experience that can be explained by the interplay of population, productivity, and welfare.

In chapter 22 several additional growth mechanisms are introduced. First is *replication*—the process by which a group with given production and administrative technologies reproduces itself; and its obverse, *merging*—the coalescing of people from several groups with the same system to form a smaller number of groups with the same system as before. A distinction is made between *internal diseconomies* of population growth within a given economy and *external diseconomies* that arise from the total human population within a more or less closed region or in the world as a whole. We thus arrive at the concept of a *culture*, which in this context is a society made up of one or more economies, each with the same socioeconomic system. It is used to show how growth can occur by means of replication of economies with similar systems but bounded by environmental capacity.

The second growth mechanism is *integration*, the unification of several groups with a given system to form a single group with a more "advanced" culture; and its obverse, *disintegration*—the forming of several groups with less "advanced" systems out of a larger group with a more "advanced" system. All these mechanisms are combined to obtain a "grand dynamics" model of economic development. It is used to generate a numerical tale of economic growth in the very long run. Implications of the theory, both for the future and the immediate present, are considered.

Even though the various ingredients of the theory have been incorporated at a macroeconomic level and in the simplest possible way, the analysis of the existence and character of potential trajectories is greatly complicated. For this reason, and in contrast to the preceding parts of the book, that task is deferred to two separate chapters. Drawing on concepts introduced in chapters 6 and 9 of volume I, chapter 23 presents a self-contained development of the fundamental concepts required for the multiple-phase analysis. These concepts provide the basis for the existence analysis in chapter 24 of macroeconomic evolution when all the mechanisms mentioned above are put together.

The main payoff from these investigations is an improved understanding of why human history has not been one of steady growth and uniform improvement, as it has usually been portrayed in economic growth theory until now; why it has instead been a turbulent process of evolution involving periods of more or less stable growth interspersed with transitions to fundamentally different economic and social forms and structures.

Before we can entertain these vast issues, however, we have first to see how complex dynamics enters the classical picture.

19.1 The Classical Growth Theory

19.1.1 Background

An interest in economic growth—why it did or did not occur—was the motivating force behind the early economic writers. Adam Smith, and in more precise terms Thomas Malthus and David Ricardo, explained how output, population, and welfare were related to productivity and net birth rates. They concluded that, in the absence of technological advance, declining productivity would reduce per capita incomes, which, when low enough, would depress birth rates until further growth was arrested. Malthus went further in posing his remarkable conjecture, quoted at the head of this chapter, that population would eventually oscillate and that these oscillations would be irregular. This classical growth framework is the subject of this chapter.[1]

19.1.2 Population Growth

To set the stage, think of population as consisting of households, each with two adults and their children. The number of households shall be denoted by x_t. Under the assumption that the number of females and males is the same, let b_t give the average number of children of either sex per family. Then the average number of children per household is $2b_t$. Each household is assumed to supply one adult equivalent to household work, child-rearing, and leisure and one adult equivalent to outside work in society. Consequently, x_t gives the size of the "outside" work force. The time unit shall be considered to be a generation (say the classical twenty-five years). Children live a generation, then become adults who live a generation during which their own children are born and raised. The parents of each generation are the surviving children of the preceding period. The end-of-period death rate for adults is one, and for surviving children zero. In this way we greatly simplify the complicated demographic structure of actual population but retain an essential character of the human condition.[2]

Given these assumptions, the number of households in each succeeding generation is given by

$$x_{t+1} = b_t x_t.$$ (19.1)

The total population consisting of adults and children during any generation is

$$P_t = 2(1 + b_t)x_t.$$ (19.2)

For convenience in what follows, when we speak of a given population we shall have in mind the number of families, x_t, and not the number of people, P_t, unless explicitly indicated.

Malthus observed that when the necessities of life were in abundance, population tended to grow at a maximal biological rate, say n, which Ricardo called the "natural rate of growth"; when these necessities were scarce, he assumed that the net population birth rate was the maximum attainable given the output level, Y_t, and given a culturally determined standard of living, say σ, which Malthus called the "subsistence wage" and Ricardo called the "natural wage." I shall call it the *zero population growth* or ZPG income level. It is the standard of living at which society just reproduces itself generation after generation; it is a culturally determined parameter and not necessarily a biological subsistence level. In the next chapter this parameter will be derived from a representation of household preferences and the cost of raising children to adulthood.

Malthus hypothesized two regimes, one that we shall call the "natural growth" or n-phase in which population is governed by the equation

$$x_{t+1} = (1 + n)x_t \quad (n\text{-phase})$$

and one that we shall call the "subsistence" or s-phase in which population is governed by the equation

$$x_{t+1} = Y_t/\sigma \quad (s\text{-phase}).$$

The minimum of these two expressions is what governs population at any one time; that is,

$$x_{t+1} = \min\{(1 + n)x_t, Y_t/\sigma\}.$$ (19.3)

Combining (19.1) with (19.3), a *family function* can be defined which is given by

$$b(y) := \min\{1 + n, y/\sigma\}, \quad y \geq 0$$ (19.4)

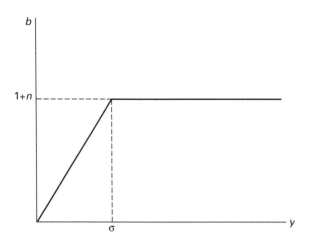

Figure 19.1
The family function

where $y = Y/x$ is per-family welfare in terms of average aggregate output per family. For each level of average welfare, y, $b(y)$ gives the number of children *who survive to adulthood*, as illustrated in figure 19.1.[3]

19.1.3 Production and Welfare

We recall that Adam Smith began his treatise on the welfare of nations with the observation that all the goods and necessities of life that a nation can enjoy depend on its population, which provides both the quantity and quality of labor on which production depends. This is perhaps the first explicit statement of an aggregate production function which, in the language that has evolved since, is expressed by $Y = BF(L)$ where L measures the number of adults in the labor force and where B is a positive parameter that represents the *technology level*.

Assume that the entire work force, which by our assumption is equal to the number of families, is employed in production of goods. Thus, $L = x$ so

$$Y = BF(x). \tag{19.5}$$

It shall be assumed that F is twice differentiable and that

$$F(0) = 0 \quad \text{and,} \quad \text{for all} \quad x > 0, \ F'(x) > 0, \ F''(x) < 0, \tag{19.6}$$

$$\lim_{L \to 0} F'(L) = \infty \quad \text{and} \quad \lim_{L \to \infty} F'(L) = 0. \tag{19.7}$$

This production function is monotonically increasing, strictly concave, and exhibits declining marginal productivity as shown in figure 19.2a.[4]

Average family welfare, Y/x, is given by

$$y := \omega(x) = B\frac{F(x)}{x}. \tag{19.8}$$

For future reference call $\omega(\cdot)$ the *average welfare or average product function*. The function $BF'(x)$ is the *marginal product function*.

Certain technical properties of the function $F(\cdot)$ play a crucial role in the dynamic analysis. These properties are derived below in Lemma 19.3. They imply that the marginal product and average welfare functions have the following properties.

LEMMA 19.1 (Properties of Average and Marginal Welfare Functions) *Assumptions (19.6)–(19.7) imply that for all $x > 0$,*

(i) $BF'(x) < \omega(x)$

(ii) $\omega'(x) < 0$

(iii) $\lim_{x \to 0} \omega(x) = \infty$

(iv) $\lim_{x \to \infty} \omega(x) = 0.$

Properties (i) and (ii) are illustrated in figure 19.2b.

19.1.4 The Dynamics of Population

The *demoeconomic function* gives the surviving number of children in terms of the number of families,

$$b[\omega(x)] = \min\{1 + n, \omega(x)/\sigma\}. \tag{19.9}$$

The relationships among the population, average welfare, the family function, and the demoeconomic function are illustrated in figure 19.3.

Since $\omega(x)$ declines continuously from $+\infty$ to 0 as x increases from 0 to ∞, as shown in Lemma 19.1, there exists a unique point x^s such that

$$\omega(x^s)/\sigma = 1 + n.$$

Define

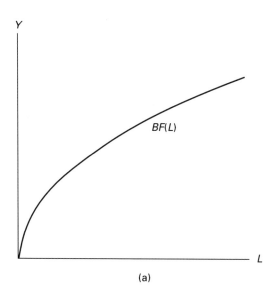

(a)

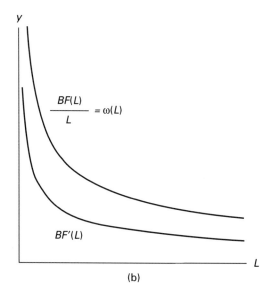

(b)

Figure 19.2
Production and welfare. (a) The classical production function. (b) Average and marginal welfare functions.

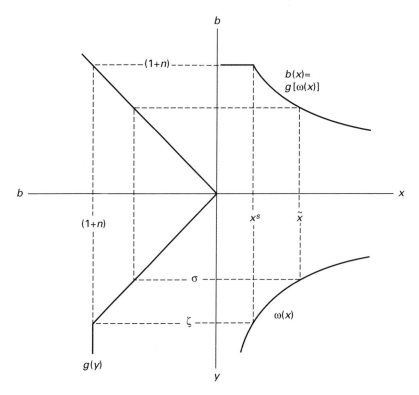

Figure 19.3
Population, welfare, and the demoeconomic function

$$\mathscr{D}^n := (0, x^s), \quad \mathscr{D}^s := [x^s, \infty).$$

Then

$$b[\omega(x)] = \begin{cases} 1 + n, & x \in \mathscr{D}^n \\ \omega(x)/\sigma, & x \in \mathscr{D}^s. \end{cases}$$

Substitute this expression into (19.1) to get the multiple-phase system,

$$x_{t+1} = \theta(x_t) = \begin{cases} \theta_n(x_t) := (1+n)x_t, & x_t \in \mathscr{D}^n := (0, x^s) \\ \theta_s(x_t) := (B/\sigma)F(x_t), & x_t \in \mathscr{D}^s := [x^s, \infty]. \end{cases} \tag{19.10}$$

The sets $\mathscr{D}^n$ and $\mathscr{D}^s$ are the *n-phase* and *s-phase zones*, respectively, and the maps $\theta_n(\cdot)$ and $\theta_s(\cdot)$ are the corresponding *n-*and *s-phase structures.*

The map $\theta(\cdot)$ is a two-piece continuous map. It is differentiable every-where except at x^s. However, the second piece $\theta_s(x) = \frac{B}{\sigma}F(x)$ is differ-entiable on $(0, \infty)$ and, as x^s is positive, the left and right derivatives of $\theta(\cdot)$ at x^s are, respectively, $(1 + n)$ and $\frac{B}{\sigma}F'(x)$. Consequently,

$$\theta'(x) \begin{cases} = 1 + n & \text{for} \quad x < x^s \\ < 1 + n & \text{for} \quad x > x^s. \end{cases}$$

This implies that, in the n-phase, population grows at its maximum potential rate governed by the natural rate of growth. Average welfare is above the ZPG level. At such a rate of growth, population eventually outstrips the available supply of goods. Diminishing returns imply that progress in this regime must eventually end, and a switch to the subsistence phase then takes place.

This fact implies in turn that a positive stationary state, $\tilde{x}$, if it exists, must occur in $\mathscr{D}^s$. Given the properties of $\omega(x)$, there exists a unique $\tilde{x}$ such that $\omega(\tilde{x}) = \sigma$, which implies that $\tilde{x} = (B/\sigma)F(\tilde{x})$. As $\omega(x)$ is mono-tonically declining, it follows that $\theta(x) > x$ for all $x < \tilde{x}$; $\theta(x) < x$ for all $x > \tilde{x}$. This means that every trajectory that begins below $\tilde{x}$ increases monotonically but is bounded above by $\tilde{x}$, while every trajectory that begins above $\tilde{x}$ decreases monotonically but is bounded below by $\tilde{x}$. It follows that $x_t \to \tilde{x}$, $Y_t = F(x_t) \to \tilde{Y}$, and $y_t \to \tilde{Y}/\tilde{x} = \sigma$. This can be summarized as:

PROPOSITION 19.1   *The classical demoeconomic model has a unique posi-tive, asymptotically stable stationary state, $\tilde{x}$. For small enough initial conditions, trajectories exhibit exponential growth in which income is above the ZPG level. Trajectories inevitably switch to a diminishing rate of growth. For all initial conditions, population and per capita income con-verge monotonically to their ZPG levels.*

This result is illustrated in figure 19.4.

19.1.5   Example

The standard *power production function*

$$Y = BF(x) = Bx^\beta, \quad x \geq 0, B > 0, \quad 0 < \beta < 1 \tag{19.11}$$

was used to obtain the graphs in figure 19.2.[5] It can easily be shown that it satisfies the conditions given in (19.6)–(19.7) and that it has a unique

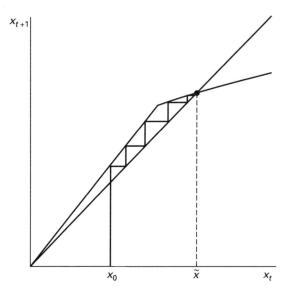

Figure 19.4
The two-phase classical growth model

stationary state

$$\tilde{x} = \left(\frac{B}{\sigma}\right)^{\frac{1}{1-\beta}}.$$

It follows that $0 < \theta'(\tilde{x}) = \beta < 1$ is the condition for asymptotic stability (Theorem 5.7).

19.1.6   Technological Change

Technological change can affect the outcome and delay convergence to a stationary state. If, for example, the production function shifts upward by an increase in B, the unique positive stationary state shifts upward. As long as shifts continue, growth continues.

Suppose that B increases according to the equation

$$B_{t+1} = (1 + \tau)B_t \tag{19.12}$$

where τ is a constant rate of technological advance. It is clear that x_t is moving toward $\tilde{x}$ but that $\tilde{x}$ depends on B_t. That is, population x_t is moving toward a moving equilibrium and will come to be dominated by the exogenous rate of productivity improvement τ.

PROPOSITION 19.2 *If an exponential advance in the level of technology, B_t, is introduced into the classical demoeconomic growth model, population growth will converge to an exponential trend.*

Convergence to a stationary state at the ZPG income level, therefore, is contingent on the suspension of technological advance, and this explains the classical attention to the social, political, and economic conditions that would enhance technology.

19.2 The Classical Model with Welfare Threshold

Malthus attributed fluctuations to an overshoot in the sustainable population level which leads to a fall in welfare and a subsequent drop in the birth rate followed eventually by an increase in the average output, and so on. Based on the empirical evidence adduced in support of the theory, he added the effects of extreme weather, epidemics, wars, natural calamities such as earthquakes, and other irregular outside influences. All of these things do play a role in demographic changes, of course, but it is the intrinsic causes that seem so intriguing to us now. Malthus's own explanation, quoted at the head of this chapter, was cryptic, but he clearly understood that there was far more in the growth story than stationary state and its reprieve through technological change.[6]

Given the monotonically convergent growth process derived in the preceding discussion, however, intrinsic fluctuations could occur in the classical theory only if its basic ingredients were changed: either the assumptions about the family function or technology. In this chapter we shall consider the former possibility.

Specifically, we shall reconsider the classical theory in the presence of a family welfare threshold. This threshold is based on the fact that the number of children who can survive to become adults must fall to zero for a low enough family income, for health reasons alone. As a further consideration, especially in the modern era, some couples wish to attain a minimum standard of living prior to raising a family. Such behavior implies an absolute preference for allocating income exclusively to adult consumption at relatively low levels of income. On either ground the survival of children to adulthood does not occur until a certain level of income is attained. Call it the Easterlinian or *welfare threshold* and denote it by η.[7]

19.2.1 The Demoeconomic Function and the Switch Points of Demoeconomic Behavior

Introducing the welfare threshold in the manner just described, we get, instead of (19.4), the family function

$$b(y) := \begin{cases} 0, & y \leq \eta \\ (y - \eta)/\gamma, & \eta < y < \zeta \\ 1 + n, & y > \zeta \end{cases} \tag{19.13}$$

where $\gamma, \eta > 0$ and where

$$\zeta = \eta + \gamma(1 + n)$$

is the income level at which the rising part of the function meets the bound given by $1 + n$.

The reciprocal of γ gives the rate of response of net births to increases in income *once income surpasses the birth threshold*. Think of η and γ as independent parameters. Setting $b(y) = 1$, the ZPG income level is determined by these two parameters:

$$\sigma = \gamma + \eta.$$

The family function now has the appearance shown in figure 19.5. In the next chapter it is shown that η and γ can be thought of as characteristics of household preferences and the cost of childrearing.

From (19.13) it is clear that the revised demoeconomic function, $b[\omega(x)]$, has the properties

$$\omega(x) < \eta \Rightarrow b[\omega(x)] = 0$$

$$\eta < \omega(x) < \zeta \Rightarrow b[\omega(x)] = (y - \eta)/\gamma$$

$$\zeta < \omega(x) \qquad \Rightarrow b[\omega(x)] = 1 + n.$$

Since $\omega(x)$ declines monotonically from $+\infty$ to 0 as x increases from 0, we can derive the following.

LEMMA 19.2 (Properties of the Phase Zone Switch Points)   *Given the properties of the average welfare function Lemma 19.1, there exist unique switch points x^s and x^u with $x^s < x^u$ such that*

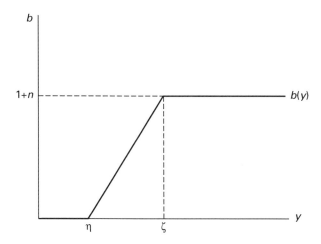

Figure 19.5
The family function with welfare threshold

(i) $\omega(x) \leq \eta$ *for all* $x \geq x^u$

(ii) $\omega(x^u) = \eta$

(iii) $\eta < \omega(x) < \zeta$ *for all* $x^s < x < x^u$

(iv) $\omega(x^s) = \zeta$

(v) $\zeta < \omega(x)$ *for all* $x < x^s$.

A proof of this lemma is given in §19.7.

The modified relationships among population, welfare, the family function, and the demoeconomic function are shown in figure 19.6. As can be seen by comparing the upper right quadrant with the corresponding diagram in figure 19.3, the positive birth threshold introduces a significant change in the demoeconomic function. There now exists a positive population level, say x^u, above which welfare is reduced below η so that $b[\omega(x)] = 0$ for all $x > x^u$. That is, given the fixed distributional assumption of this model, no children survive to adulthood if a given generation exceeds x^u; the per capita income is too low.[8]

19.2.2   The Multiple-Phase Dynamics

Substituting $y_t = \omega(x_t)$ into (19.4), the population dynamics can be expressed by

$$x_{t+1} = b[\omega(x_t)]x_t. \tag{19.14}$$

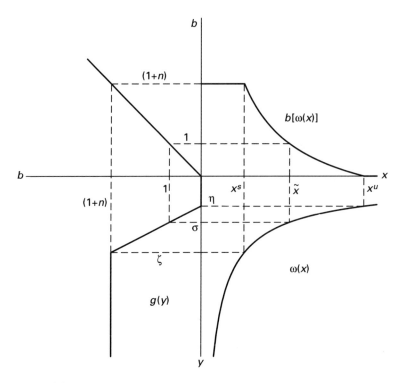

Figure 19.6
Population, welfare, and the demoeconomic function with positive birth threshold

Using (19.14), define the sets

$$\mathscr{D}^0 := (-\infty, 0] \cup [x^u, \infty)$$

$$\mathscr{D}^n := (0, x^s) \tag{19.15}$$

$$\mathscr{D}^s := [x^s, x^u)$$

and reexpress the demoeconomic function as

$$b[\omega(x)] = \begin{cases} (1+n), & x \in \mathscr{D}^n \\ [\omega(x) - \eta]/\gamma, & x \in \mathscr{D}^s \\ 0, & x \in \mathscr{D}^0. \end{cases} \tag{19.16}$$

Substituting into (19.14), we get the multiple-phase dynamic system that describes the behavior of population over time,

$$x_{t+1} = \theta(x_t) := \begin{cases} \theta_n(x_t) := (1+n)x_t, & x_t \in \mathcal{D}^n \\ \theta_s(x_t) := \frac{1}{\gamma}[BF(x_t) - \eta x_t], & x_t \in \mathcal{D}^s \\ \theta_0(x_t) := 0, & x_t \in \mathcal{D}^0. \end{cases} \tag{19.17}$$

Analogously to the basic Malthusian model, we call $(\theta_n(\cdot), \mathcal{D}^n)$ the *n-regime*, $(\theta_s(\cdot), \mathcal{D}^s)$ the *s-regime*, and $(\theta_0(\cdot), \mathcal{D}^0)$ the *null regime*. $\mathcal{D} := (0, x^u)$ is the *admissible zone*.

19.3 Qualitative Behavior

19.3.1 Stationary States

When $\eta = 0$ then $\gamma = \sigma$, and the model reduces to the classical model for which (in the absence of technological change) monotonic growth occurs, converging to the unique positive stationary state $\tilde{x}$. When $\eta > 0$, behavior can be very different. Indeed, it is remarkable that such a simple and realistic change can introduce a plethora of possibilities.

Note first that $x = 0$ is still a stationary state in the null phase zone. As $\theta'(0) = 1 + n$, any trajectory that begins above 0 and below x^s must grow exponentially at the rate n until it escapes the n-phase zone and enters the s-phase zone.

To see what can happen in this zone, we have first to find out what goes on near a positive stationary state. Such a state satisfies $\tilde{x} = \theta_s(\tilde{x})$ or, equivalently, $\tilde{y} = \omega(\tilde{x}) = \eta + \gamma$. From figure 19.6, the following is intuitively obvious.

PROPOSITION 19.3 (Existence and Properties of Positive Stationary States) *For each positive B, η, and γ there exists a unique positive stationary state, $\tilde{x}$, which depends continuously on $(\eta + \gamma)/B$ and which for all positive B, η, γ satisfies*

(i) $x^s < \tilde{x} < x^u$;

(ii) $\dfrac{\partial \tilde{x}}{\partial B} > 0$, $\dfrac{\partial \tilde{x}}{\partial \eta} < 0$, $\dfrac{\partial \tilde{x}}{\partial \gamma} < 0$;

(iii) $\lim_{\gamma \to 0} \tilde{x} = \lim_{\gamma \to 0} x^s = x^u$.

A proof is given in §19.7.

19.3.2 Asymptotic Stability, Fluctuations, and Expansiveness

We want to consider the local stability properties for all possible parameter values. To do so, we have to determine how

$$\theta_s'(\tilde{x}) = \frac{1}{\gamma}[BF'(\tilde{x}) - \eta]$$

changes as $\tilde{x}$ varies with B, η and γ. We also want to see if there exist parameter combinations such that $\theta(\cdot)$ is expansive. Let $\pi := (\eta, \gamma, n, B)$ and assume that $\pi \in (\mathbb{R}^{++})^4$. Define the parameter sets

$$\mathscr{P}^1 := \{\pi \,|\, \eta/B \leq F'(\tilde{x}) < (\eta + \gamma)/B\}$$

$$\mathscr{P}^2 := \{\pi \,|\, (\eta - \gamma)/B \leq F'(\tilde{x}) < \eta/B\}$$

$$\mathscr{P}^3 := \{\pi \,|\, F'(\tilde{x}) < (\eta - \gamma)/B\}$$

$$\mathscr{P}^4 := \{\pi \,|\, F'(x) < (\eta - \gamma)/B, x \in D^s\}.$$

The inequalities defining these sets are associated, respectively, with monotoinic convergence, dampening fluctuations, expanding fluctuations near $\tilde{x}$, and expansiveness of $\theta(\cdot)$ on D.

We can show that these sets are nonempty generically. Indeed, we can show that for all positive B, η, there exist constants γ^0, γ^1, with $\gamma^1 < \gamma^0$ such that

$$\mathscr{P}^1 = \{\pi \,|\, 0 < \gamma^0(B, \eta) < \gamma\}$$

$$\mathscr{P}^2 = \{\pi \,|\, 0 < \gamma^1(B, \eta) < \gamma < \gamma^0(B, \eta)\}$$

$$\mathscr{P}^3 = \{\pi \,|\, 0 < \gamma < \gamma'(B, \eta)\},$$

and that for all positive β, η, γ in $\mathscr{P}^3$ there exists a constant, say n^e, depending on β, η, γ such that

$$\mathscr{P}^4 = \{\pi \in \mathscr{P}^3 \,|\, 0 < n < n^e(B, \eta, \gamma).\}$$

To see this, consider figure 19.7. It is clear that the intervals defining $\mathscr{P}^1$ and $\mathscr{P}^2$ are symmetric around η. If η increases, these intervals shift upward and $\tilde{x}$ shifts to the left, and conversely. Where B increases or γ decreases, $\tilde{x}$ shifts to the right and the intervals narrow, which restricts the zones of asymptotic convergence and widens the instablility zone, and conversely. Clearly, these zones are nonempty, open sets, as in $\mathscr{P}^3$.

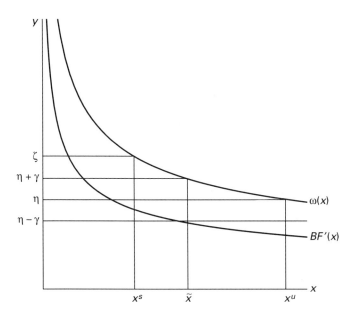

Figure 19.7
The conditions for generic asymptotic stability and instability near the stationary state

Consider $\mathscr{P}^4$. This set belongs to $\mathscr{P}^3$. By taking n small enough, we can guarantee that $x^s = x^{**}$ where $\theta(x^{**}) = \max_{x \in \mathscr{D}} \theta(x)$. Let n^e be such a point. Obviously, $\theta'(n) = 1 + n > 1$ for all $x \in \mathscr{D}^n$. By construction and the concavity of $\theta(\cdot)$, $\theta'(x^s) < -1$ for all $0 < n < n^e$. Consequently, for all $0 < n < n^e$, $\theta'(x) < -1$ for all $x \in \mathscr{D}^s$. Thus, $\mathscr{P}^4$ is a nonempty open set.

Figure 19.7 shows the relationship between the marginal product, average product, and the thresholds determined by η and γ. The parameters shown fall in $\mathscr{P}^4$. To summarize, we have:

PROPOSITION 19.4 (Asymptotic Stability, Fluctuations, and Expansiveness)

(i) For all $\pi \in \mathscr{P}^1$, trajectories converge monotonically to the unique positive stationary state $\tilde{x}$;

(ii) for all $\pi \in \mathscr{P}^2$, almost all trajectories that enter a small enough neighborhood of the unique positive stationary state, $\tilde{x}$, exhibit dampening fluctuations and converge;

(iii) for all $\pi \in \mathscr{P}^3$*, almost all trajectories that enter a small enough neighborhood of the stationary state,* $\tilde{x}$*, exhibit expanding fluctuations and escape from that neighborhood;*

(iv) for all $\pi \in \mathscr{P}^4$ *the map* θ *is expansive on* $\mathscr{D}$*;*

(v) the critical value n^e *is a decreasing function of* γ *(and an increasing function of* $\frac{1}{\gamma}$*).*

A picture of the zones $\mathscr{P}^1, \ldots, \mathscr{P}^4$ is shown in figure 19.8. Details of the proof are given in §19.7.

19.3.3 Viability and Escape

When fluctuations occur, some trajectories could escape. To obtain complete global results, therefore, we have to consider viability.

Viability requires that $\theta(x) \in \mathscr{D}$ for each $x \in \mathscr{D}$. If this is so, then by recursion $\theta^t(x) \in \mathscr{D}$ for all $t \geq 0$. Since for each positive B, η the feasible upper bound for population, $x^u(B, \eta)$, is positive, a necessary and sufficient condition for viability is that the maximum value of $\theta(x)$ on $\mathscr{D}$ be less than x^u. If the maximum value $\theta(x)$ takes on values that exceed x^u, then all trajectories that map into these points escape the viability domain. Let

$$\mathscr{F} := \{\pi \in (\mathbb{R}^{++})^4 \mid \theta(x) < x^4(B, \eta) \quad \text{all } x \in 0, x^u(B, \eta)\}.$$

Then the model is viable for all $\pi \in F$ and inviable for all $\pi \in \mathscr{F}^u$ where

$$\mathscr{F}^u := \backslash \mathscr{F}.$$

The maximum of $\theta_s(x)$ occurs at the maximizer x_s^{**} which satisfies $BF'(x_s^{**}) = \eta$. But $x_s^M = \theta_s(x_s^{**}) = \frac{1}{\gamma}[BF(x_s^{**}) - \eta x_s^{**}]$ increases as γ decreases. For some small enough value of γ, $x_s^M > x^u$. At some value of γ (given B and η), say γ^u, $x_s^M = x^u$. For still smaller values of γ, $x_s^M > x^u$. By constructing the backward iterates of the set of x such that $\theta_s(x) > x^u$, we get all the initial conditions whose trajectories must escape into the null domain—if n is big enough. If $x_s^M > x^u$ but n is small enough, then the maximum of $\theta(x)$ occurs at the switch point x^s and at a level less than x_s^M, so trajectories cannot escape. Thus, let n^u and x^s be the unique value such that $(1 + n^u)x^s = \theta(x^s) = x^u$; then for all $n < n^u$, $\theta(x) < x^u$. It is easy to see that as γ gets larger, the value of n^u gets larger until, for all

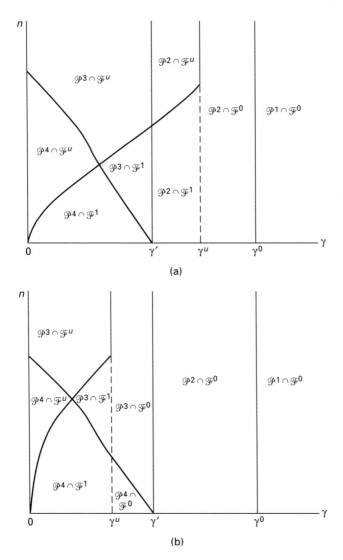

Figure 19.8
Parameter zones of qualitative dynamic behavior. (a) $\gamma' < \gamma^u$. (b) $\gamma^u < \gamma'$.

$\gamma \geq \gamma^u$, n^u is no longer defined, because then $x^M < x^u$ regardless of the value of n.

Define

$$\mathscr{F}^0 := \{\pi, \,|\, \gamma > \gamma^u(B, \eta), n > 0\}$$
$$\mathscr{F}^1 := \{\pi, \,|\, 0 < \gamma < \gamma^u(B, \eta), 0 < n < n^u(B, \eta, \gamma)\}.$$

Then

$$\mathscr{F}^u := \backslash (\mathscr{F}^0 \cup \mathscr{F}^1).$$

We still don't have everything we need to determine what happens in all cases. We know that for some parameter values some trajectories can escape and some do not. How many do one or the other? None, some, or almost all? An answer can be given if we know when $\theta(\cdot)$ is expansive. But this was done in Proposition 19.4(iv). We thus arrive at the following.

PROPOSITION 19.5 (Viability and Escape) *For each positive B, η there exists a unique value of γ, say γ^u, which depends on B and η, such that $\mathscr{F}^0$ is a nonempty open set. For each $\gamma < \gamma^u$ there exists a unique value of n, say n^u, which depends on B, η, and γ such that $\mathscr{F}^1$ is a nonempty open set.*

(i) For all $\pi \in \mathscr{F}^0 \cup \mathscr{F}^1$, the model is viable;

(ii) for all $\pi \in \mathscr{F}^u$, escape occurs in finite time for trajectories that begin in a set of positive Lebesgue measure;

(iii) for all $\pi \in \mathscr{F}^u \cap \mathscr{P}^4$ escape occurs almost surely.

Details of the proof are given in §19.7.

19.3.4 Generic, Qualitative Behavior

A complete characterization of the possible qualitative patterns of behavior can now be given for the classical model with positive birth threshold. Indeed, combining Propositions 19.4–5, our findings can now be summarized as follows:

PROPOSITION 19.6 (Generic Qualitative Behavior) *Given the classical demoeconomic model with birth threshold,*

(i) all trajectories that begin in $\mathscr{D}^n$ grow for a finite time and enter $\mathscr{D}^s$;

(ii) for all $\pi \in \mathscr{P}^1$, the system is viable and all trajectories converge monotonically to a unique positive stationary state;

(iii) for all $\pi \in \mathscr{P}^2 \cap (\mathscr{F}^0 \cup \mathscr{F}^1)$, the system is viable and almost all trajectories (except those that hit $\tilde{x}$ in finite time) eventually exhibit dampening fluctuations that converge to a unique stationary state;

(iv) for all $\pi \in \mathscr{P}^2 \cap \mathscr{F}^u$, both escape and dampening fluctuations eventually occur with positive Lebesgue measure;

(v) for all $\pi \in \mathscr{P}^3 \cap (\mathscr{F}^0 \cup \mathscr{F}^1)$, the system is viable and almost all trajectories (except those that hit $\tilde{x}$ in finite time) eventually exhibit persistent fluctuations that may be cyclic or chaotic;

(vi) for all $\pi \in \mathscr{P}^3 \cap \mathscr{F}^u$, fluctuations can occur and escape occurs with positive measure;

(vii) for all $\pi \in \mathscr{P}^4 \cap \mathscr{F}^1$, the system is viable and strongly ergodic; that is, relative frequencies of population, output, or welfare values converge to absolutely continuous, invariant ergodic measures;

(viii) for all $\pi \in \mathscr{P}^4 \cap \mathscr{F}^u$, escape occurs almost surely.

The parameter zones are illustrated in figure 19.8. Notice how the two cases depend on the relative magnitudes of γ' and γ^u.

Figure 19.9 illustrates how examples satisfying the alternative situation described in this proposition can be constructed. Panel (a) displays the map $\theta(\cdot)$ for three different values of γ. Let us denote them by γ', γ'', and γ'''. Curve 2 is constructed so that the maximum value of the phase structure $\theta_s(\cdot)$, which is given by $x_s^{M_2}$, exactly equals x^u where $\theta(x^u) = 0$. Because $\theta_s(\cdot)$ is a stretchable function, the maximizer x^{**} is the same for each value of γ. Obviously, $(n, \gamma') \in \mathscr{F}^0 \cap \mathscr{P}^1$. Moreover, for all $n > 0$ and for all $\gamma \in (\gamma'', \gamma')$, it is clear that $(n, \gamma) \in \mathscr{F}^0 \cap \mathscr{P}^1$. Given the value of n shown, $(n, \gamma''') \in \mathscr{F}^u \cap \mathscr{P}^3$. Indeed, for all $\gamma < \gamma''$, $(n, \gamma) \in \mathscr{F}^u \cap \mathscr{P}^3$.

Panel (b) shows a case where $(n, \gamma) \in \mathscr{P}^4 \cap \mathscr{F}^1$. Note that $n < n^u < n^e$. This example yields strongly ergodic trajectories. However, if $n > n^u$, then escape occurs, and as $n^u < n^e$, escape occurs almost surely. In panel (c), $n > n^u > n^e$ and escape occurs with positive measure. That is, $(n, \gamma) \in \mathscr{P}^3 \cap \mathscr{F}^u$. However, given γ, if $n < n^u$, escape could not occur. Then $(n, \gamma) \in \mathscr{P}^3 \cap \mathscr{F}^1$. And, if $n < n^e$, then $(n, \gamma) \in \mathscr{P}^4 \cap \mathscr{F}^1$ and behavior is strongly ergodic.

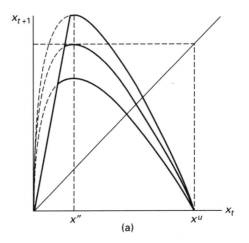

(a)

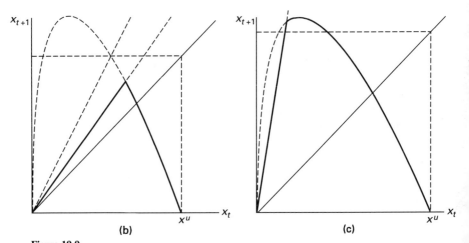

(b)   (c)

Figure 19.9
Constructing alternative qualitative dynamics. (a) The map $\theta_s(\cdot)$ is stretchable. (b) Strongly ergodic behavior. (c) Escape with positive measure.

19.4 An Example

It can be shown that the power production function

$$Y = Bx^\beta, \quad x \geq 0, \quad B > 0, \quad 0 < \beta < 1$$

satisfies (19.6), (19.7), and Lemma 19.1. We can also readily verify the findings of Lemma 19.2 and Proposition 19.3, and that

$$\theta'(\tilde{x}) = \beta - (1 - \beta)(\eta/\gamma).$$

It follows that conditions defining $\mathscr{P}^1$, $\mathscr{P}^2$, and $\mathscr{P}^3$ can be expressed as

$$\eta/\gamma < \beta/(1-\beta) \Rightarrow 0 < \theta'(\tilde{x}) < 1;$$

$$\beta/(1-\beta) < (\eta/\gamma) < (1+\beta)/(1-\beta) \Rightarrow -1 < \theta'(\tilde{x}) < 0;$$

$$(1+\beta)/(1-\beta) < (\eta/\gamma) \Rightarrow \theta'(\tilde{x}) < -1.$$

The parameter β replaces the unspecified function $F(\cdot)$, and the level of technology, B, does not appear. The latter property tells us that *in this special case technological change in terms of the parameter B will not alter the qualitative behavior of trajectories.*

The lines demarking the parameter regions for the qualitative types of local stability and instability are given by the set of parameters satisfying

$$(A) \quad \frac{\eta}{\gamma} = \frac{\beta}{1-\beta}$$

and

$$(B) \quad \frac{\eta}{\gamma} = \frac{1+\beta}{1-\beta}.$$

The parameter zones associated with asymptotic stability, instability, and expansiveness are respectively

$$\mathscr{P}^1 := \{\pi > 0 \mid \eta/\gamma < \beta/(1-\beta)\}$$

$$\mathscr{P}^2 := \{\pi > 0 \mid \beta/(1-\beta) < \eta/\gamma < (1+\beta)/(1-\beta)\} \tag{19.18}$$

$$\mathscr{P}^3 := \{\pi > 0 \mid (1+\beta)/(1-\beta) < \eta/\gamma\}.$$

$$\mathscr{P}^4 := \left\{ \pi > 0 \, \middle| \, \frac{1}{1-\beta} + \frac{\beta}{1-\beta}(1+n) < \eta/\gamma \right\}. \tag{19.19}$$

The line in parameter space separating expansive from nonexpansiveness given fixed n is therefore

$$(C) \quad \frac{1}{1-\beta} + \frac{\beta}{1-\beta}(1+n) = \frac{\eta}{\gamma}.$$

It can be shown that on the line (C), γ is a convex function of n.

Now consider viability and escape. We can show that for all

$$\pi \in \mathscr{F}^0 := \left\{ \pi > 0 \, \middle| \, \frac{\eta}{\gamma} < \frac{\beta}{1-\beta} \left(\frac{1}{\beta}\right)^{\frac{1}{1-\beta}} \right\}, \tag{19.20}$$

the system is viable. Note that $(\frac{1}{\beta})^{\frac{1}{1-\beta}} > 1$, so

$$\frac{\beta}{1-\beta} < \left(\frac{1}{\beta}\right)^{\frac{1}{1-\beta}} \cdot \frac{\beta}{1-\beta}.$$

This implies that $\mathscr{P}^1 \subset \mathscr{F}^0$; that is, when $\tilde{x}$ is asymptotically stable *and* trajectories are monotonic, the system is viable.

If $\pi \in \backslash \mathscr{F}^0$, then $x_s^M > x^u$, so if n is big enough, there must exist trajectories that escape. The boundary of $\mathscr{F}^0$ is given by

$$(D) \quad \frac{\eta}{\gamma} = \frac{\beta}{1-\beta} \cdot \left(\frac{1}{\beta}\right)^{\frac{1}{1-\beta}}.$$

Because $\theta_s(\cdot)$ is single-valued and single-peaked on $[0, x^u]$, there must exist two points, x', x'', with $x' < x''$ such that $\theta_s(x') = \theta_s(x'') = x^u$. Set

$$n^u = x^u/x'' - 1.$$

Then n^u satisfies the equation

$$\theta_s(x') = (1+n^u)x'' = x^u.$$

Now $x'' > x_s^\#$, so $\theta_s(\cdot)$ is declining for $x > x''$. Defining the switch point x^s as usual by the unique positive point satisfying $(1+n)x^s = \theta(x^s)$, it follows that $x^M = (1+n^u)x^s = \theta(x^s) = x^u$ for all $n < n^u$. Substituting for x^s and x^u, we get

$$(1+n)\left(\frac{B}{\eta + (1+n)\gamma}\right)^{\frac{1}{1-\beta}} = \left(\frac{B}{\eta}\right)^{\frac{1}{1-\beta}}.$$

Therefore, the line separating admissible from inadmissible parameter values is

$$(1+n^u)^{1-\beta} = 1 + (1+n^u)\frac{\gamma}{\eta}.$$

Moreover, it can be shown that γ is a convex function of n. Rearranging terms, it is clear that a sufficient condition for viability is that the η/γ ratio lie above the line given by

$$(E) \quad \frac{\eta}{\gamma} = \frac{1+n}{(1+n)^{1-\beta} - 1}.$$

Thus, for all

$$\pi \in \mathcal{F}^1 := \left\{\pi > 0 \ \middle| \ \frac{\beta}{1-\beta}\left(\frac{1}{\beta}\right)^{\frac{1}{1-\beta}} < \frac{\eta}{\gamma} < \frac{1+n}{(1+n)^{1-\beta} - 1}\right\}, \tag{19.21}$$

the system will be viable. Let $\mathcal{F}^u := \setminus(\mathcal{F}^0 \cup \mathcal{F}^1)$. Then for all $\pi \in \mathcal{F}^u$, except those falling on the boundary separating $\mathcal{F}^u$ and $\mathcal{F}^0 \cup \mathcal{F}^1$, escape can occur.

Given the definitions of the parameter zones $\mathcal{P}^1, \ldots, \mathcal{P}^4$ and $\mathcal{F}^0, \mathcal{F}^1$ as in (19.18)–(19.21), the classical demoeconomic model with birth threshold and power production function exhibits all the properties described in Proposition 19.6.

Figure 19.10 gives the zones of qualitative behavior in terms of η/γ and n for fixed β. In this diagram $\mathcal{F}^u$ lies above (E); $\mathcal{F}^1$ lies between (D) and (E); $\mathcal{F}^0$ lies below (D); $\mathcal{P}^1$ lies below (A); $\mathcal{P}^2$ lies between (A) and (B); $\mathcal{P}^3$ lies above (B); and $\mathcal{P}^4$ lies between (C) and (E).

Figure 19.11 illustrates a population trajectory for parameters chosen in the strongly ergodic domain when the "natural rate of growth," n, is very small and the η/γ ratio relatively large, as may have been the case early in human prehistory. In terms of generations, population expands for $2\frac{1}{2}$ centuries, then from time to time drops sharply. These "famines" occur at irregular intervals, from every other generation to once every century or so.[9]

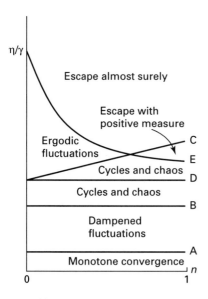

Figure 19.10
Regions of qualitative behavior in terms of η/γ and n given $\beta = .5$

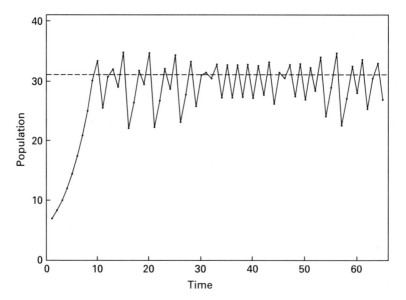

Figure 19.11
A population trajectory. Source: Day and Min (1996).

19.5   Technological Change

In the original classical growth model, a productivity growth factor that increased the coefficient B exponentially over time converted the qualitative performance from that of convergence to a stationary state to that of convergence to an exponential trend determined by the rate of productivity improvement. In the presence of a birth threshold we would also expect the qualitative dynamics to be modified. Without placing further restrictions on the production function, $F(\cdot)$, however, we cannot say exactly what will happen. Of course, the stationary state and the phase zone switch points depend on B, as shown in §19.7 and Proposition 19.3. Indeed, they all increase with B. This implies that exponential growth at the natural rate can be prolonged by a steady increase in the technological level parameter B. Moreover, if initial conditions place the economy in a zone of persistent fluctuation for fixed B, then a rising level of B will increase the amplitude of the fluctuations, which will occur around a rising trend, at least for a time.

If the power function characterizes production as in (19.11), it was learned from the analysis in §19.4 that the parameter zones of qualitative behavior are independent of B. Consequently, the latter result, that is, the increasing amplitude of persistent fluctuation, will also persist indefinitely.

19.6   Summary and Conclusions

To summarize the results of this chapter, growth converging to a stationary state, growth converging to a cyclic pattern of any periodicity, or growth evolving into nonperiodic fluctuations can occur in the classical model of demoeconomic growth when a birth threshold is present. When the technological level B increases exponentially, these patterns occur about an exponentially rising trend. However, viability cannot be taken for granted.

19.7   Technical Discussion

A more formal derivation of the results obtained in this chapter may be of interest to some readers. We begin with a lemma concerning properties of the function $F(\cdot)$.

Given assumptions (19.5)–(19.7), we have:

LEMMA 19.3 (Properties of the Production Function)

(i) For all $x > 0$, $xF'(x) < F(x)$ and $\frac{d}{dx}[F(x)/x] < 0$;

(ii) $\lim_{x \to 0} F(x)/x = \infty$; $\lim_{x \to \infty} F(x)/x = 0$;

(iii) for each $\kappa > 0$ there exists a unique positive value of u such that

$F(u) = \kappa u$;

(iv) for each $\kappa > 0$ there exists a unique point v and a function $T(\kappa)$ such that

$$T(\kappa) = F(v) - \kappa v = \max_{x>0} [F(x) - \kappa x]$$

and such that

$F'(v) = \kappa$;

(v) $u(\cdot)$, $v(\cdot)$, and $T(\cdot)$ are decreasing functions of κ;

(vi) for all $\kappa > 0$, $v(\kappa) < u(\kappa)$;

(vii) $\lim_{\kappa \to 0} u(\kappa) = \lim_{\kappa \to 0} v(\kappa) = \infty$; $\lim_{\kappa \to \infty} u(\kappa) = \lim_{\kappa \to \infty} v(\kappa) = 0$.

Proof

(i) By the Mean Value Theorem, there exists a value $\xi \in (0, x)$ such that $F(x) - F(0) = F'(\xi)x$, but $F'(\cdot)$ is a decreasing function, so $F'(x) < F'(\xi)$. Since $F(0) = 0$, the first inequality follows. It implies that $F'(x) < F(x)/x$. Consequently, $\frac{d}{dx}[F(x)/x] = \frac{1}{x}(F'(x) - F(x)/x) < 0$.

(ii) From (19.7) we have $\lim_{x \to 0} F'(x) = \infty$, so, using the first inequality in (i), it follows that $\lim_{x \to 0} F(x)/x = \infty$. By L'Hospital's Rule, $\lim_{x \to \infty} F(x)/x = \lim_{x \to \infty} F'(x) = 0$.

(iii) From (i)–(ii) $F(x)/x$ is a continuous, monotonically decreasing function from ∞ to 0 as x goes from 0 to ∞. It therefore takes on all intermediate values, so there exists a unique u such that $F(u)/u = \kappa$ and u varies continuously with κ.

(iv) Since $F'(x)$ is a continuous, monotonically decreasing function ranging over $(0, \infty)$, for each κ there exists a unique v with $F'(v) = \kappa$. Let $G(x) = F(x) - \kappa x$. Since $F'(\cdot)$ is continuous monotonically for all $x \in (0, v)$, there exits a ζ such that

$$\frac{G(v) - G(x)}{v - x} = G'(\zeta) = F'(\zeta) - \kappa > F'(v) - \kappa = 0,$$

so $G(x) < G(v)$. A similar application of the Intermediate Value Theorem shows that for all $x > v$, $G(x) < G(v)$. Consequently, $G(v) > G(x)$ for all $x \neq v$. Since v is a continuous function of κ, $T(\kappa) := F[v(\kappa)] - \kappa v(\kappa)$ is a continuous function of κ also.

(v) $u(\kappa)$ satisfies $F(u) = \kappa u$. Taking differentials, we get $F'(u)du = \kappa du + u d\kappa$. Since $F'(u) < F(u)/u = \kappa$,

$$\frac{du}{d\kappa} = \frac{u}{F'(u) - \kappa} < 0.$$

From (iv),

$$\frac{dv}{d\kappa} = \frac{1}{F'(v)} < 0.$$

From (iv) also,

$$T'(\kappa) = F'v'(\kappa) - \kappa v'(\kappa) - v(\kappa)$$

$$= [F'(v(\kappa)) - \kappa]v'(\kappa) - v(\kappa)$$

$$= -v(\kappa) < 0.$$

(vi) By (iii) and (iv), for each κ there exist u, v such that

$$F(v) - \kappa v > F(u) - \kappa u = 0 \Rightarrow F(v)/v > \kappa.$$

But $F(u)/u = \kappa \Rightarrow F(v)/v > F(u)/u$. Since $F(x)/x$ is a declining function, this implies that $v < u$.

(vii) Follows from (19.6) and (ii).   ∎

The properties of the marginal product and welfare functions given in Lemma 19.1 can easily be derived from Lemma 19.3.

Proof of Lemma 19.2   The phase zone boundaries x^s and x^u are continuous functions, say $x^s(\zeta/B)$ and $x^u(\eta/B)$, of the parameters (B, n, η, γ) and (B, η), respectively, that satisfy

$$\frac{\partial x^s}{\partial B} > 0, \quad \frac{\partial x^s}{\partial n} < 0, \quad \frac{\partial x^s}{\partial \eta} < 0, \quad \frac{\partial x^s}{\partial \gamma} < 0; \quad \text{(a)}$$

$$\frac{\partial x^u}{\partial B} > 0, \quad \frac{\partial x^u}{\partial \eta} < 0; \tag{b}$$

$$\lim_{\gamma \to 0} x^s = x^u. \tag{c}$$

To prove the inequalities in (a)–(b), use $F(u) = \kappa u$ from Lemma 19.3(iii). Take the total differential to get

$$\frac{\partial u}{\partial \kappa} = \frac{u}{F'(u) - \kappa}.$$

From Lemma 19.1,

$$F'(u) < \omega(u)/u = \kappa$$

which implies that

$$\frac{\partial u}{\partial \kappa} < 0.$$

Now set $u = x^v$ and $\kappa = \eta/B$ or ζ/B and use the chain rule. For example,

$$\frac{\partial x^r}{\partial B} = \frac{\partial x^r}{\partial \kappa} \frac{\partial \kappa}{\partial B} = -\frac{\zeta}{B^2} \frac{\partial x^r}{\partial \kappa} > 0.$$

To prove (c), note that since $\zeta = \eta + (1 + n)\gamma$, $\omega(x^s) \to \eta = \omega(x^u)$ as $\gamma \to 0$. The result follows from the continuity of $\omega(\cdot)$. ∎

Proof of Proposition 19.3 Set $\kappa = (\eta + \gamma)/B$ and use Lemma 19.3(iii) to get the existence of $\tilde{x}$ for each κ. The inequalities in (i) derive from Lemma 19.1(ii) and the fact that $\eta < \eta + \gamma < \zeta = \eta + (1 + n)\gamma$. From Lemma 19.3(v), $\tilde{x}(\cdot)$ is a decreasing function of $\kappa = (\eta + \gamma)/B$, i.e., $x'(\kappa) < 0$. The inequalities follow using the chain rule. (iii) Follows from the facts that $\omega(x)$ is continuous and $\eta + \gamma \to \eta$ as $\gamma \to 0$. ∎

Proof of Proposition 19.4   (i) Using Lemma 19.3(i), $F'(\tilde{x}) < F(\tilde{x})/\tilde{x} = (\eta + \gamma)/B$, which gives the righthand inequality in $\mathscr{P}^1$. Let $\kappa = \eta/B$ and use Lemma 19.3(iv) to get a value x^0 such that $F'(x^0) = \eta/B$. From (19.17) there is a unique γ^0 such that $\tilde{x}^0[(\eta + \gamma^0)/B] = x^0$ is a stationary state. Because $F'(\cdot)$ is a decreasing function,

$\eta/B < F'(\tilde{x}[(\eta+\gamma)/B])$ for all $\gamma > \gamma^0$.

This gives the lefthand inequality for $\mathscr{P}^1$, which implies $0 < \theta'(\tilde{x}) < 1$.

To get the global picture, all admissible initial conditions—not just those close enough to $\tilde{x}$—must be considered.

First, consider all $x \in (x^s, \tilde{x})$. (We already know that all trajectories in $(0, x^s)$ must enter this set.) Since $\omega(x)$ is a monotonically decreasing function for all $x < \tilde{x}$,

$BF(x)/x > BF(\tilde{x})/\tilde{x} = \eta + \gamma,$

from which it follows that $\theta(x) = \frac{1}{\gamma}[BF(x) - \eta x] > x$. Consequently, $\theta^t(x)$, $t = 0, 1, \ldots$ forms an increasing sequence. By our well-worked Mean Value Theorem, for all $x \in (x^s, \tilde{x})$ there exists $v \in (x, \tilde{x})$ such that

$$\frac{\theta(\tilde{x}) - \theta(x)}{\tilde{x} - x} = \theta'v = \frac{1}{\gamma}[BF'(v) - \eta] > \frac{1}{\gamma}[BF'(\tilde{x}) - \eta] = 0,$$

which implies that $\theta(x) < \theta(\tilde{x}) = \tilde{x}$. Consequently, the sequence $\theta^t(x)$, $t = 0, 1, \ldots$ is bounded above by $\tilde{x}$. Using the continuity of $\theta(\cdot)$, this is the least upper bound, so *all* trajectories that begin below $\tilde{x}$ converge monotonically to it.

Next, consider $x > \tilde{x}$. As $\theta'(\tilde{x}) > 0$, the function θ is increasing for x close enough to $\tilde{x}$. But $\theta''(x) = (B/\gamma)F''(x) < 0$ for all x, so $\theta'(\cdot)$ is a decreasing function that falls from a positive value at $\tilde{x}$ to 0 at a unique point, say x^{**}, and becomes negative thereafter. $\theta(x)$ assumes its maximum value, say $x^M = \theta(x^{**})$, at this point. For $x \in (\tilde{x}, x^{**})$, $BF(x)/x = \omega(x) < \omega(\tilde{x}) = \eta + \gamma \Rightarrow \theta(x) < x$, so $\theta^t(x)$ is a decreasing sequence converging monotonically to $\tilde{x}$. Since $\theta(\cdot)$ is single-peaked, there is a unique preimage, x', of $\tilde{x}$ with $x' > x^{**}$ such that $\theta(x') = \tilde{x}$. For all $x \in (x^{**}, x')$, $\theta(x) < x$, so $\theta(x) \in (\tilde{x}, x^{**})$ and trajectories converge as before. For all $x \in (x', x^u)$, $\theta(x) \in (0, \tilde{x})$, so trajectories decline one period and then increase monotonically after $t = 1$ and converge asymptotically.

(ii) For all $\gamma < \gamma^0$, obviously $F'(\tilde{x}) < \eta/B$, which implies that $\theta'_s(\tilde{x}) < 0$. Proposition 19.3(iii) implies that $\tilde{x} \to x^u$ as $\gamma \to 0$. This fact, together with the continuity of $\theta'_s(\cdot)$, implies that $\theta'_s(x^u) \to -\infty$ as $\gamma \to 0$. As $\theta'_s(\cdot)$ is continuous, it decreases from a positive number monotonically as γ decreases, becomes negative, and decreases without lower bound as $\gamma \to 0$. By the Intermediate Value Theorem, for each B, η there exists a constant, say γ^1, such that

$$\theta_s'[\tilde{x}(B,\eta,\gamma^1)] = -1 \quad \text{or} \quad BF'(\tilde{x}) = \eta - \gamma^1.$$

The inequality expression (19.19) follows, which implies local convergence. Again, to obtain global results, observe that $\theta(\cdot)$ is a single-humped, concave map on $\mathcal{D}$. Condition (19.19) now implies that $x^{**} < \tilde{x}$. Moreover, there exists a unique preimage of $\tilde{x}$, say x', with $\theta(x') = \tilde{x}$ such that $x' < x^{**}$. Since $\theta(x) > x$ for all $x \in (0, \tilde{x})$, all trajectories with initial conditions in $(0, x')$ grow and enter the interval $(x', \tilde{x})$. For any value in $x \in (x', \tilde{x})$, $\theta(x) > \tilde{x}$, so all trajectories (that do not hit $\tilde{x}$ exactly or that do not escape) must eventually overshoot the stationary state. However, for all $x > \tilde{x}$, $\theta(x) > \tilde{x}$, so such trajectories oscillate.

For all $(B, \eta, \gamma) \in \mathcal{P}^2$, condition (19.19) implies that there exists a neighborhood of $\tilde{x}$ (depending on π), say $\mathcal{N}$, such that for any $x, y \in \mathcal{N}$ there exists a z such that

$$-1 < \theta_s'(z) = \frac{\theta(y) - \theta(x)}{y - x} < 0.$$

This expression also implies that $\theta(\cdot)$ is locally contractive and, by Theorem 5.7, trajectories that enter $\mathcal{N}$ converge to $\tilde{x}$. The set of all initial conditions in $(0, x^u)$ whose trajectories eventually enter $\mathcal{N}$ is

$$\mathcal{C} = \bigcup_{n=0}^{\infty} \theta^{-n}(\mathcal{N}).$$

All these trajectories converge. Since $\mathcal{N}$ is an interval, $\mathcal{C}$ has positive Lebesgue measure.

(iii) Condition (19.20) implies that for all $\gamma < \gamma^1$ there must exist a point x' with $x^s \le x' < \tilde{x}$ such that $\theta_s'(x) < -1$ for all $x \in \mathcal{M} := (x', x^u)$. For all $x, y \in \mathcal{M}$ there exists (by the Mean Value Theorem) a point z with $x < z < y$ such that

$$\theta_s'(z) = \frac{\theta(y) - \theta(x)}{y - x} \le -1.$$

This implies that

$$\theta(y) - \theta(x) < -(y - x),$$

which implies that trajectories oscillate in $\mathcal{M}$. By the same reasoning, if $\theta(y), \theta(x) \in \mathcal{M}$, then

$$\theta^2(y) - \theta^2(x) < -(\theta(y) - \theta(x)).$$

Set $y = \tilde{x}$. Then

$$\tilde{x} - \theta^2(x) < -\tilde{x} + \theta(x)$$

$$\tilde{x} - \theta(x) < -\tilde{x} + x.$$

Combining these two expressions, we find that for all $x > \tilde{x}$ such that $\theta(x) \in \mathcal{M}$,

$$\theta^2(x) > x.$$

By recursion, we get $\theta^{2n}(x) > \theta^n(x)$ for all $\theta^n(x) \in (x', \tilde{x})$ and $\theta^{2(n+1)}(x) < \theta^{n+1}(x)$ for all $\theta^{n+1}(x) \in (\tilde{x}, x_s^{\#})$. Except for $x = \tilde{x}$, all such trajectories oscillate and move away from $\tilde{x}$ and escape $\mathcal{M}$. In a manner analogous to the construction of $\mathscr{C}$ in (ii), we can construct a set S with positive Lebesgue measure such that trajectories with initial conditions in S will enter $\mathcal{M}$.

(iv) Certainly, for each $\gamma < \gamma^1$ there exists a unique point x^e such that $F'(x^e) = (\eta - \gamma)/B$. Define n^e by

$$(1 + n^e)x^e = \frac{1}{\gamma}[BF(x^e) - \eta(x^e)]$$

or equivalently by $(1 + n^e)\gamma + \eta = \omega(x^e)$.

Since F' is downward sloping for each $x \ge x^e$, $F'(x) < F'(x^e) = \eta - \gamma$. From this it is obvious that for each $n < n^e$ the corresponding switch point $x^e < x^s$. Therefore, $\theta_s(x) < -1$ for all $x \in \mathscr{D}^s$.

(v) Both x^s and n^e depend on γ. Taking total differentials using (19.31), we find that

$$\frac{\partial x^e}{\partial \gamma} = \frac{-1}{BF''(x)} > 0.$$

Similarly, we find that

$$\frac{\partial n^e}{\partial \gamma} = -\left[\frac{1+n}{\gamma} + \frac{2+n}{x^s}\right]\frac{\partial x^e}{\partial \gamma} < 0 = \frac{\partial n^e}{\partial(1/\gamma)} > 0. \qquad \blacksquare$$

Proof of Proposition 19.5

(i) First consider the set of parameter values defined by $\mathscr{F}^0$. From Lemma 19.3(iv), for each κ there exists $v(\kappa)$ that gives

$$T(\kappa) = F[v(\kappa)] - \kappa v(\kappa) = \max_{x \in \mathscr{D}} [F(x) - \kappa x]$$

and satisfies $F'[v(\kappa)] = \kappa$. Let $\kappa = \eta/B$. Then $v(\kappa)$ also maximizes $\theta_s(x)$ on $\mathscr{D}$, so v is independent of γ. It follows that, for each B, η there exists a unique γ, say γ^u, such that

$$x^u(\eta/B) = x^M = \frac{B}{\gamma^u} T(\eta/B) = \frac{1}{\gamma^u} [BFx(\kappa) - \kappa v(\kappa)] = \max_{x \in \mathscr{D}} \theta_s(x).$$

Consequently,

$$\frac{1}{\gamma} BT(\eta/B) < \frac{1}{\gamma^u} BT(\eta/B) \quad \text{for all} \quad \gamma > \gamma^u,$$

so no matter what value n takes, $\theta(x) < x^u(\eta/B)$ for all $x \in \mathscr{D}$. This establishes viability for $\pi \in \mathscr{F}^0$.

(ii) Note that for $\gamma = \gamma^u(B, \eta)$ the model is viable for almost all $x \in \mathscr{D}$. In this case, $x^M(B, \eta, \gamma^u) = x^u(B, \eta)$ so $\theta^2[v(\eta/B)] = 0$. The maximizer, $v(\eta/B)$, has two preimages, each of which has two preimages, and so on. The set of all these preimages is the union $A = \bigcup_{s=1}^{\infty} \theta^{-s}(v(B, \eta))$. For any $x \in A$ there is an s such that $\theta^{s+2}(x) = 0$. This set has Lebesgue measure zero. For almost all $x \in D$, $\theta^t(x) < x^M$.

Next, consider the set of parameters not in $\mathscr{F}^0$. There exist exactly two values of x, say x', x'', with $0 < x' < v < x'' < x^u$, such that $\theta(x') = \theta(x'') = x^u$. Let $n^u = (x^u - x_s^{\#})/x_s^{\#}$. Then $(1 + n)x < \theta(x)$ for all $x \leq x_s^{\#}$ and for all $n < n^u$. Consequently, for all $x \in \mathscr{D}$, $\theta(x) = \min\{(1 + n)x, \theta_s(x)\} < x^u < x_s^M$. This gives the set $\mathscr{F}^1$ and completes the proof of (i).

Now consider the parameters not in $\mathscr{F}^u$. For each $\gamma < \gamma^u$ and each $n > n^u$ there exists a nonempty interval, which depends on B, η, γ,

$$E = E(B, \eta, \gamma) := \{x \in \mathscr{D} | \theta_s(x) > x^u(B, \eta)\},$$

such that $\theta^2(x) = 0$ for all $x \in E$. If we let

$$U = \bigcup_{n=1}^{\infty} \theta^{-n}(E),$$

then for all $x \in U$ there exists a t' such that $\theta^{t'+2}(x) = 0$. Since U is the union of nonintersecting intervals in $\mathscr{D}$, its Lebesgue measure is positive. This proves (ii).

(iii) Finally, consider the functions $\gamma^u(\cdot)$ and $n^u(\cdot)$. For all $\gamma > \gamma^u$, $(1 + n^u)x^s = \frac{1}{\gamma}(BF(x^s) - \eta x^s)$. Both x^s and n^u change with γ. Recall that $\theta(x_s^\#) = x^u$ and that $n^u = (x^u - x_s^\#)/x_s^\#$. Taking the total differential with respect to n^u and $x_s^\#$, we get

$$\frac{dn^u}{d\gamma} = -x_s^\# \frac{\frac{\partial x^u}{\partial \gamma} - x^u \frac{\partial x_s^\#}{\partial \gamma}}{(x_s^\#)^2},$$

but $\frac{\partial x^u}{\partial \gamma} = 0$, so

$$\frac{dn^u}{d\gamma} = \frac{x^u}{x_s^\#} \frac{\partial x_s^\#}{\partial \gamma}.$$

To determine the sign of this term, take the total differential of

$$\theta_s(x_s^\#) = x^u$$

with respect to γ and $x_s^\#$. This gives

$$(BF'(x_s^\#) - \eta) \frac{\partial x_s^\#}{\partial \gamma} = x^u.$$

We know that $\theta(\cdot)$ is declining at $x_s^\#$, so $BF'(x_s^\#) < 0$. This implies that the term in brackets is negative, which implies that

$$\frac{\partial x_s^\#}{\partial \gamma} < 0.$$

Combining this with (19.39) and observing that both x^u and $x_s^\#$ are positive, we get

$$\frac{\partial n^u}{\partial \gamma} > 0;$$

that is, $n(B, \eta, \gamma)$ is an upward-sloping function of γ. It is convenient to get this relationship in terms of $\frac{1}{\gamma}$, the response of family size to income. Thus,

$$\frac{\partial n^u}{\partial (\frac{1}{\gamma})} < 0.$$

As $\gamma \to 0$, $\frac{1}{\gamma} \to \infty$, so $n^u \to 0$; and as $\gamma \to \gamma^u$, $x^M \to x^u$, so $n^u \to (x^u - x^\#)/x^u$. ∎

20 Household Preferences, Social Infrastructure, and Production Diseconomies

The demand for children ... depends on household tastes, income and child cost considerations. The supply depends on natural fertility and the chances of survival.
—Richard A. Easterlin, "Relative Economic Status and the American Fertility Swing"

The performance of an economy is dependent on its organizational structure.
—Douglass North, *Structure and Change in Economic History.*

The next step is to ask whether it is feasible to draw up the approximate limits for the population size which permits or prevents the use of "population linked" technologies.
—Ester Boserup, *Population and Technological Change*

We now take into account household preferences, social infrastructure, and production diseconomies. This will pave the way for the discussion in chapter 21 of macroeconomic evolution in terms of fundamental structural change.

Let us review these concepts in general terms before taking up the technicalities.

20.1 Background

20.1.1 Household Preferences

The practice in classical times of infant exposure, in which newborn children were abandoned in the wild, or of the ingestion of contraceptive herbs, and, during later periods, the promotion of celibacy in various cultures suggest that population control has been practiced in one way or another for thousands of years.[1] Moreover, abortion and birth control have been practiced on a very wide scale in modern times. Thus, average family size is influenced by individual adult preferences which depend in turn on the general culture and its social values and institutions. It is of interest, therefore, to reconsider the growth theory when preferences for family formation are explicitly introduced into the analysis.[2]

20.1.2 Infrastructure

Another factor of great importance at any time and place is the division of effort between social infrastructure and "work." The former produces the social cohesion, coordination, and technical knowledge upon which the productivity of labor is based. *Given that effort*, the work force can effectively process materials and fabricate goods.[3]

In the simplest social groups this infrastructure may be created by many or even all individuals part of the time. In the family, for example, a part of the energy of the adults is expended on activity that develops cohesiveness in the "nuclear unit" and educates and socializes the gradually maturing children. Generally, both adults participate in at least some of these activities, and at least one of the two may specialize in them while the other works "outside" either in production in the usual sense, or in external organizations that make up the social infrastructure.

The simpler forms of human society were governed by councils of elders who met from time to time to adjudicate disputes and make decisions concerning timing of the hunt and other activities involving the group as a whole. Religious guidance was in the hands of a shaman and considerable energy was expended in religious rites and "nonproductive" social activity of various kinds. At the other extreme, advanced civilization involves an elaborate specialization of infrastructure with distinct judicial systems, governmental administrations, educational and religious institutions, research and development centers, political parties, military services, police departments, and a vast array of other social and political units. They contribute to society in one way or another but usually do not produce goods that are exchanged through the economic system of firms and markets.

Effective work and production of goods that *are* exchanged through the economic system of firms and markets may not require all of these institutions. Indeed, many of them, as individual components, may not be necessary at all. Yet, *as a whole* they provide an essential prerequisite for the elaborate coordination and cooperation that makes productive work possible. The knowledge upon which this coordinative function is based is called the *administrative technology*. For the purpose of reference, the people who work in the social infrastructure will be called the *infrastructural or administrative work force*; those who work in production of goods and services per se will be referred to as the *production work force* or *labor force*.[4]

In addition to the necessary allocation of people to the social infrastructure, an economy must also construct a complementary capital stock. Each of the human infrastructural components described above must have its complement of buildings, equipment, and other material goods. For example, a modern technology of any complexity requires a science and education system to produce, store, and disseminate the information required to use the technology effectively. Such a system requires in turn material support in terms of school buildings, libraries, laboratories, etc. One could think of these things as intermediate products used as inputs for the production of final commodities, but the economic calculations of productivity, profit, and loss cannot generally be made with any precision. Yet they are essential to the socioeconomic system as a whole.[5]

For the purpose of explaining changes in broad aggregates of population, production, productivity, and welfare, it is not possible to incorporate the individual types of human and material capital that make up the infrastructure. Rather, we shall simply divide the population into two component parts, one that is devoted to infrastructure services and one that is devoted to the direct production of goods. In the present book explicit account is taken of the infrastructure in terms of population. The allocation of capital to infrastructure is taken up elsewhere.[6]

20.1.3 Social Space and Diseconomies of Population Size

It has long been recognized that, *given a fixed technology*, the marginal productivity of labor declines as production expands due to the scarcity of land, water, and other resources. Moreover, as resource stocks decline, the cost of extracting and refining them grows. Further diseconomies are caused by the declining capacity of the atmosphere, rivers, and oceans to transport, dissipate, and recycle human and industrial waste. The scarcity of material resources and environmental limitations, however, are not the only causes of diseconomy in the production process. Another source is the increasing complexity of planning, communicating, and coordinating as output expands, and the increasing difficulty of managing the social goods and services required for productive work.[7]

From the macroeconomic perspective these considerations together imply that a given technology and social infrastructure possess a bounded capacity or "space" which is reduced as population and productive activity grow, and that there may eventually be not only diminishing marginal returns but also diminishing absolute returns to the work force or population size. Such a decline in absolute returns can be termed *overpopulation*. In the presence of this effect it can be said that as population increases, the environment becomes tighter or the *social slack* is reduced.

It is often argued that people would never reproduce to such an extent as to depress absolute production. But individuals seldom take into account the aggregate effects of reproductive decisions. Overpopulation *within the context of a given technology or given stage of development* seems to have occurred in the past and may be occurring in a number of places now.

All those diseconomies that accrue as the result of expansion within a single economic system using given production and administrative technologies are *internal diseconomies*. Those that occur as the result of total productive activity among all economic systems are *external diseconomies*. The distinction between the two is not used in this chapter but is crucial in the next.

20.1.4 Technological Change

The production technology describes how commodities can be produced using various factors of production, given that the appropriate prerequisite infrastructure is in place. As a first approximation, it may be presumed to be a fixed feature of a given economic system. Within this system, however, more or less steady increases in productivity can accrue with the gradual improvement in technique and operating skill through a process of learning and imitation. This kind of technological change is a very important part of any explanation of growth. In this chapter the effect of shifts in productivity is briefly considered. Chapter 21 will consider continuous learning by doing within a given system of technology and discrete changes in technology or "development blocks," which involve essentially new production/administration systems. The point not to be missed here is that technologies are "population-linked."[8]

20.2 The Adaptive Economizing Demoeconomic Growth Model

The classical demoeconomic growth model of chapter 19 is our jumping off point. First, the family function is derived from a specification of household preferences.

20.2.1 The Model

The family function $b(y)$ with welfare threshold (19.13) is

$$
b(y) := \begin{cases} 0, & y \leq \eta \\ (y - \eta)/\gamma, & \eta \leq y \leq \zeta \\ 1 + n, & y \geq \zeta \end{cases} \tag{20.1}
$$

where $\zeta = \eta + \gamma(1+n)$, $b(\zeta) = 1+n$, and $b(\sigma) = 1$. Recall that the model reduces to the convergent, Iron Law of Wages case when $\eta = 0$.

Suppose that each generation of parents determines its number of children, $2b$, in a tradeoff between the cost of childrearing and other forms of expenditure in accordance with family preferences. This choice is subject to an income constraint

$$c + qb \leq y \tag{20.2}$$

where y is family income, c is family consumption (including "high quality" or "high status" goods and services for children and adults), and q is the real cost to the parent of raising two children to adulthood. (Remember, we assume half the children are boys and half are girls, so b is the number of children of either sex.)

The choice of family size is also subject to a survival constraint

$$b \leq s(y) \tag{20.3}$$

where $s(y)$ is the maximum number of children *of a given sex* that can survive to adulthood. It is a function equal to zero when y is below some very low level, say y^0, and is bounded above by some number, say $\bar{b}$. In prehistoric times this number was only slightly above the ZPG level of 1.[9] Later the number increased. In any case, within this constraint the desire for rearing children to adulthood can operate. Given these definitions, the set of feasible consumption/family size pairs is

$$\Gamma(y) := \left\{ (c,b) \middle| \begin{array}{c} c + qb \leq y \\ b \leq s(y) \\ c, b \geq 0 \end{array} \right\}. \tag{20.4}$$

Each household makes a choice by adapting to the conditions of its own time as it understands them. Its members do not directly take into account preferences of their unborn children or of future generations. Instead, in a tradeoff between adult consumption and childrearing they decide how many children they want themselves. This choice is represented by

$$V(y) = \max_{(c,b) \in \Gamma(y)} u(c,b) \tag{20.5}$$

where the preferences of adult couples are represented by the utility function, $u(c,b)$. We do not assume that a given generation knows what future generations may want to do or what technological structures may eventually be available. This does not mean that families are myopic, however, because the utility of rearing children rests in some measure on the families' anticipated contribution to the future existence of society and the continuation of the parents' genes.

Under certain regularity conditions, it can be said that there is a continuous *consumption function*, $c = c(y)$, and a continuous *family function*, $b = b(y)$, giving the number of surviving children per household such that $(c(y), b(y)) \in \Gamma(y)$ and $u(c(y), b(y)) = V(y)$. The functions $V(\cdot)$, $c(\cdot)$, and $b(\cdot)$ all depend continuously on y.[10]

The household choice lies on the boundaries of the budget set, that is, either at the intersection of the maximal family size and budget constraints or along the budget constraint alone. There are, therefore, two potential regimes, defined by which constraints are "tight." In the *natural growth* regime family size is equal to the maximum number $s(y)$. This is analogous to the Malthusian biological regime (*n*-phase). In the *scarcity* regime the budget constraint limits both births and consumption. This is analogous to the subsistence regime (*s*-phase). Denote by $g(y)$ the family function obtained by maximizing utility subject to the income constraint *but ignoring the survival constraint*. Then

$$b(y) = \min\{s(y), g(y)\}. \tag{20.6}$$

Given the production function $Y = BF(x)$ and average per family income function $y = \omega(x) = BF(x)/x$, and recalling from (19.1) that $x_{t+1} = b(y_t)x_t$, we get the difference equation

$$x_{t+1} = \theta(x_t) := x_t \min\{s[\omega(x_t)], g[\omega(x_t)]\}. \tag{20.7}$$

20.2.2   Relationship to the Classical Theory

In the classical theory we recall from (19.4) that $b(y) = \min\{1 + n, y/\sigma\}$, which suggests setting

$$s(y) \equiv \bar{b} := 1 + n \quad \text{and} \quad g(y) = y/\sigma. \tag{20.8}$$

Could these forms reflect a reasonable specification of household preferences?

Consider the power utility function

$$u(c, b) := c^{1-\alpha}b^{\alpha}. \tag{20.9}$$

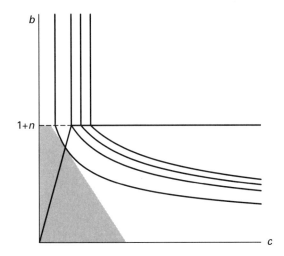

Figure 20.1
Deriving the "classical" family function. The dark piecewise linear line is the demoeconomic expansion path. The shaded triangular area is the "budget set" for a given income. The curved lines are indifference curves.

Let us call α the *family preference* parameter with $0 < \alpha < 1$. Using this in (20.5) and solving the choice problem, we get the demand for children in the scarcity regime,

$$g(y) = \frac{\alpha}{q} y. \tag{20.10}$$

Assuming that $s(y) \equiv 1 + n$ and setting $\sigma = q/\alpha$, we get (19.4). Thus, the Malthusian "subsistence" or ZPG income level can be derived from the real cost of childrearing and from the willingness of people, represented by the family preference parameter, α, to sacrifice consumption in order to raise children.

If we use the classical specification of technology (19.5)–(19.7), we get the Malthusian population equation (19.10). From this equivalence the results of Propositions 19.1–19.2 follow directly. The remarks concerning technological change in §19.5 obviously apply with equal force here.

Figure 20.1 shows how a birth function like the classical one of figure 19.1 can arise from a representation of the household tradeoff between consumption and family size.

20.2.3 The Birth Rate Threshold

When a birth rate threshold η is introduced in the classical model, equation (19.13) suggests setting

$$s(y) \equiv 1 + n \quad \text{and} \quad g(y) = \max\{0, (y - \eta)/\gamma\}. \tag{20.11}$$

For a function like $g(\cdot)$ to follow from an economizing choice, there must be an absolute preference for not raising children with an income below η, but with a desire for a family manifesting itself above this threshold. Such preferences can be represented by a utility function of the form

$$u(c,b) := \begin{cases} K_1 c^k, & 0 \le c \le \eta \\ K_1 \eta^k + K_2 (c - \eta)^{1-\alpha} b^\alpha, & c \ge \eta \end{cases} \tag{20.12}$$

with $0 < \alpha < 1$ as before. Given the budget constraint, $g(y)$ must be 0 for y below η. Utility is maximized then by setting $c = y$ until y exceeds η. Then utility maximization leads to

$$g(y) = \begin{cases} 0, & y \le \eta \\ \frac{\alpha}{q}(y - \eta), & y > \eta. \end{cases} \tag{20.13}$$

Consequently, the family function $b(y)$ is exactly the form given in (19.13) with $\gamma = q/\alpha$, as illustrated in figure 20.2.

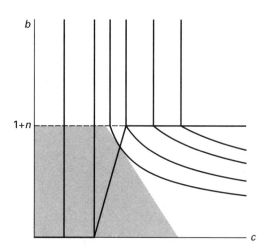

Figure 20.2
Deriving the family function based on Easterlinian preferences

An alternative way of deriving the same family function is to assume that preferences are like that given in (20.12) except that if $b > \lambda$, households gain no additional satisfaction from increasing family size without increasing consumption. Formally,

$$
u(c,b) = \begin{cases} K_1 c^\kappa, & 0 \le c \le \eta \\ K_1 \eta^\kappa + K_2 (c - \eta)^{1-\alpha} b^\alpha, & c \ge \eta \text{ and } b \le \lambda \\ K_1 \eta^\kappa + K_2 (c - \eta)^{1-\alpha} \lambda^\alpha, & c \ge \eta \text{ and } b \ge \lambda. \end{cases}
$$

From this we derive a natural rate $n = \lambda - 1$. Given these changes, we would get

$$
g(y) = \min \left\{ \max \left\{ 0, \frac{\alpha}{q}(y - \eta) \right\}, 1 + n \right\}.
$$

This formulation also implies (20.1). Note that ZPG income is $\sigma = \eta + q/\alpha$ and the point where $s(y) = g(y)$ is $\zeta = \eta + (1 + n)q/\alpha$. It would appear that λ also changes. Especially in the developed industrialized countries, it would seem to have declined drastically in the last century.

20.2.4   The Complete Qualitative Dynamics

Given the behavioral equivalence of this adaptive economizing theory to that of the classical theory with welfare threshold, the complete qualitative dynamic possibilities follow immediately. Thus, we have:

PROPOSITION 20.1   *The adaptive economizing demoeconomic growth model with threshold preferences $\eta > 0$ and classical production function is equivalent to the classical demoeconomic model with birth rate threshold (19.13), and Proposition 19.6 holds with $\gamma = q/\alpha$. If $\eta = 0$, then the model is equivalent to the classical model (19.10). The results of Propositions 19.1 and 19.2 follow with $\sigma = q/\alpha$.*[11]

20.2.5   Example

Substitute q/α for γ in (19.13)–(19.17). Then the assertions of Proposition 19.6 hold. These assertions can be interpreted as follows.

- Given a fixed technological parameter, β, and natural growth rate, n:

  the greater the family preference (α), and/or

  the greater the birth threshold (η), and/or

  the smaller the cost of childrearing (q),

the less likely asymptotic stability, the more likely instability, the more likely "escape."

- Given n:

    the greater the birth threshold (η), and/or

    the greater the family preference (α), and/or

    the smaller the cost of childrearing (q),

    the larger the labor elasticity of production, β, must be to achieve viability and asymptotic stability.

The remarks concerning technological change in §19.5 hold with equal force here.

In the remainder of this book the family function will be represented by (20.1) with positive η and $\gamma = q/\alpha$.

20.3   The Classical Model with Infrastructure Social Slack and Production Diseconomies

Infrastructure and social slack are now introduced into the picture.

20.3.1   Production and Welfare

I shall continue to assume that each household utilizes one adult equivalent of effort in household production, childrearing, and leisure, and one adult equivalent of effort to society. The former could be thought of as the *private infrastructure*. The latter is divided into two parts: L, the number of adult equivalents allocated to the labor force, and M, the number of adult equivalents allocated to the administrative workforce that manages the infrastructure outside the family. In a decentralized economy much of this will be part of the private sector. A large part will also be part of the public sector. Both are necessary for a productive labor force. Given this, the number of households is

$$x = M + L. \tag{20.14}$$

Let S be the *social slack* variable. If S increases, the effect on productivity is positive; if it decreases, the effect on productivity is negative. When $S \leq 0$, society cannot function. Let N be the *social space*, which defines the maximum number of households compatible with an effective socioeconomic order and with the feasible operation of the society's production process. The social slack is $S = N - x$.

Assume that the production function,

$$Y = BG(L, S), \quad L \geq 0, \quad S \geq 0, \tag{20.15}$$

is continuous in the arguments L and S, strictly concave, and satisfying

$$G(0, S) = G(L, 0) = 0 \quad \text{for all} \quad L, S \tag{a}$$

$$\lim_{L \to 0} \frac{\partial G}{\partial L} = \lim_{S \to 0} \frac{\partial G}{\partial S} = \infty. \tag{b}$$

(20.16)

These assumptions imply that both labor and social slack are necessary for positive production and that both labor and social slack contribute positive but declining marginal productivities. The parameter B is, as usual, the technology "level."

Substituting for L and S, the production function can be written as

$$H(x) := \begin{cases} 0, & x \in \backslash (M, N) \\ BG(x - M, N - x), & x \in (M, N). \end{cases} \tag{20.17}$$

In words, output depends on the technology level, labor effect, and slack effect. The parameters M and N are the limits for population size that permit or prevent the use of population-linked technologies. Equation (20.16b) implies that

$$\lim_{x \to M} H'(x) = \infty \tag{a}$$

$$\lim_{x \to N} H'(x) = -\infty, \tag{b}$$

(20.18)

and that for all $x \in (M, N)$, $H''(x) < 0$, so that $H(\cdot)$ is strictly concave on $[M, N]$. The production function therefore has the appearance shown in figure 20.3a, which is quite different from figure 19.2a where neither infrastructure nor social slack play a role.

The average product or average welfare function is

$$\omega(x) := \begin{cases} 0, & x \in \backslash [M, N] \\ \frac{H(x)}{x}, & x \in [M, N). \end{cases} \tag{20.19}$$

Average welfare is 0 for $0 \leq x \leq M$. As x passes M it rises, reaches a maximum, and then declines monotonically until it falls to 0 at N. It is a single-peaked continuous (pseudo-concave and strictly quasi-concave) function.[12] Compare figure 20.3b with figure 19.2b.

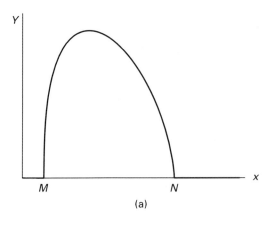

(a)

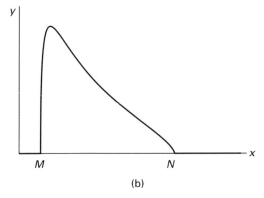

(b)

Figure 20.3
Production and welfare with infrastructure and social slack. (a) The production function. (b)
Its average welfare function.

The existence of a positive infrastructure, M, implies a type of increasing returns to scale, because average welfare increases from 0 when the
population size increases above M even though labor exhibits declining
marginal productivity. The existence of finite social space N implies that
absolute decreasing returns to scale eventually takes over as social slack
is used up. The relationships among population, welfare, and the demoeconomic function are shown in figure 20.4, which may be compared to
figure 19.6. Now *too small* as well as too large a population reduces welfare below the positive birth threshold.

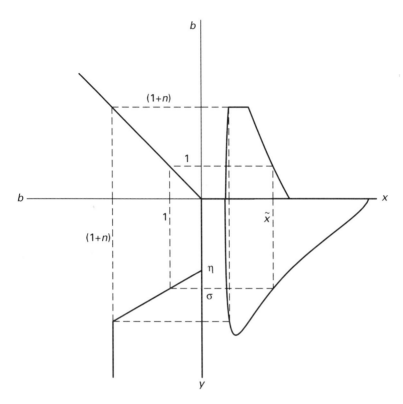

Figure 20.4
Population, welfare, and the demoeconomic function with infrastructure and social slack.

20.3.2   The Switch Points of Demoeconomic Behavior

It was seen in figure 19.7 that the branches of $b(\cdot)$ that govern family size depend on where y falls relative to the points η and $\zeta = \eta + (1+n)q/\alpha$. But the average welfare function is quite different now that infrastructure and social slack have been incorporated. The implication is that several additional switch points may exist.

LEMMA 20.1 (Properties of the Phase Zone Switch Points)

(i) If $y^M > \eta$, then there exist exactly two switch points, x^ℓ, x^u say, with $x^\ell < x^\# < x^u$ such that

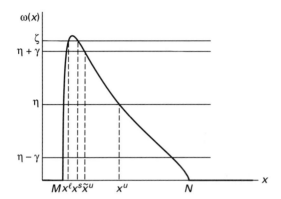

Figure 20.5
The phase zone switch points. Note that x^ℓ is close to M.

$$\omega(x) \begin{cases} > \eta, & x \in (x^\ell, x^u) \\ = \eta, & x = x^\ell \text{ or } x = x^u \\ < \eta, & x \in (M, x^\ell) \cup (x^u, N) \\ = 0, & x \in (0, M) \cup (N, \infty). \end{cases}$$

(ii) If $y^M > \zeta > \eta$, then there exist exactly two distinct switch points, x^r, x^s say, with $x^\ell < x^r < x^\# < x^s < x^u$ such that

$$\omega(x) > \zeta, \quad x \in (x^r, x^s)$$

$$\omega(x) = \zeta, \quad x = x^r \text{ or } x = x^s$$

$$\eta < \omega(x) < \zeta, \quad x \in (x^\ell, x^r) \cup (x^s, x^u).$$

The complete story is easily derived from figure 20.5.[13]
     Define the sets

$$\mathscr{D}^0 := (-\infty, x^\ell] \cup [x^u, \infty)$$

$$\mathscr{D}^s := (x^\ell, x^r) \cup (x^s, x^u) \tag{20.20}$$

$$\mathscr{D}^n := [x^r, x^s].$$

Reexpressing the family function in terms of x gives the demoeconomic function[14]

$$b[\omega(x)] = \begin{cases} 1 + n, & x \in \mathscr{D}^n \\ \frac{\alpha}{q}[H(x)/x - \eta], & x \in \mathscr{D}^s \\ 0, & x \in \mathscr{D}^0. \end{cases} \qquad (20.21)$$

20.3.3 The Multiple-Phase Dynamics

Substituting (20.21) into the equation of population dynamics

$$x_{t+1} = b[\omega(x_t)]x_t \qquad (20.22)$$

yields the multiple-phase system

$$x_{t+1} = \theta(x_t) := \begin{cases} \theta_s(x_t) := \frac{1}{\gamma}[H(x_t) - \eta x_t], & x_t \in \mathscr{D}^s \\ \theta_n(x_t) := (1 + n)x_t, & x_t \in \mathscr{D}^n \\ \theta_0(x_t) := 0, & x_t \in \mathscr{D}^0. \end{cases} \qquad (20.23)$$

20.4 Qualitative Behavior when Infrastructure and Social Slack Matter

20.4.1 Stationary States

It should already be obvious that introducing the parameters M and N modifies the qualitative dynamics in several ways. As before, $x = 0$ is a stationary state, but now one that is stable because for all $0 < x < M$, no production is possible. That is, the initial population must be big enough to support the infrastructure required by the given technology before growth is possible.

Any positive stationary state must therefore exceed M. Because exponential growth occurs in $\mathscr{D}^n$, this set is unstable, so any trajectory that enters it escapes. Therefore, stationary states, if they exist, must occur in $\mathscr{D}^s$ and satisfy the equation

$$\omega(x) = (\eta + \gamma). \qquad (20.24)$$

For such points to exist, y^M must exceed $\eta + \gamma$. (Remember, $\gamma = q/\alpha$.) Notice that for all η such that $y^M > \eta$, there exists $\gamma > 0$ such that $y^M > \eta + \gamma$. Moreover, one easily shows that the maximizer of $\omega(x)$, $x^{\#}$, is independent of B. Hence, for any positive M, N, η, α, and q there exists a B, say B^0, such that $y^M > \eta + \gamma$ for all $B > B^0$. Likewise, for any $B > 0$

there exists an M, say M^0, depending on B, η, and γ, such that $y^M > \eta + \gamma$ for all $M < M^0$. By reasoning in this manner, we establish that the parameter zones

$$\mathscr{P}^0 := \{\pi \mid y^M > \eta + q/\alpha, n > 0\}$$

and

$$\mathscr{P}^{00} := \{\pi \mid y^M > \zeta = \eta + (1+n)q/\alpha, n > 0\}$$

are nonempty, open sets where

$$x^\ell < \tilde{x}^\ell < x^r < x^s < \tilde{x}^u < x^u.$$

Using the method of chapter 19, the following can be derived.

PROPOSITION 20.2 (Existence and Properties of Positive Stationary States)

(i) For all positive parameter values, $x = 0$ is a stationary state in the null domain;

(ii) for all $\pi \in \mathscr{P}^0$ there exist two stationary states $\tilde{x}^\ell$ and $\tilde{x}^u$ in the s-domain that satisfy

$$H(\tilde{x}^\ell) = \eta + \gamma = H(\tilde{x}^u)$$

such that

$$x^\ell < \tilde{x}^\ell < x^\# < \tilde{x}^u < x^u;$$

(iii) for all $\pi \in \mathscr{P}^{00}$ two switch points x^r, x^s exist which satisfy

$$\frac{H(x^r)}{x^r} = \zeta = \frac{H(x^s)}{x^s}$$

with

$$x^\ell < \tilde{x}^\ell < x^r < x^\# < x^s < \tilde{x}^u < x^u.$$

The relationship of the stationary states to the several switch points defining the three regimes can be seen in figure 20.5.[15]

20.4.2 Asymptotic Stability and Fluctuations

The analysis of asymptotic stability, dampening, fluctuations, instability, and expansiveness requires a consideration of $\theta'(x) = \frac{\alpha}{q}[BH'(x) - \eta]$.

Consider the smaller of the two stationary states, $\tilde{x}^{\ell}$. From Proposition 20.2, $\tilde{x}^{\ell} < x^{\#}$, which implies (because $H(\cdot)$ is strictly concave) that $H'(\tilde{x}^{\ell}) > H(\tilde{x}^{\ell})/\tilde{x}^{\ell} = (\eta + \gamma)$. Rearranging this implies that

$$\theta'(\tilde{x}^{\ell}) = \frac{\alpha}{q}[H'(\tilde{x}^{\ell}) - \eta] > 1$$

which tells us that $\tilde{x}^{\ell}$ is unstable: for initial conditions close enough to but above $\tilde{x}^{l}$ population will grow because $\theta(x) > x$. For initial conditions below $\tilde{x}^{l}$, population must decline because $\theta(x) < x$; the system becomes inviable in finite time.

Let $\pi := (\eta, \alpha, q, n, B, M, N)$. Remembering that $H(x) = BG(x - M, N - x)$, define the parameter zones

$$\mathcal{P}^1 := \{\pi \mid \eta < H'(\tilde{x}^u) < (\eta + \gamma)\}$$

$$\mathcal{P}^2 := \{\pi \mid (\eta - \gamma) < H'(\tilde{x}^u) < \eta\}$$

$$\mathcal{P}^3 := \{\pi \mid H'(\tilde{x}^u) < (\eta - \gamma)\}.$$

There are just the sets defining parameter values for which the upper stationary state is locally monotonic and asymptotically stable, asymptotically stable with locally dampening fluctuations, and unstable, respectively.

The ratios defining the intervals in these sets determine the existence and position of the upper stationary state and the stability properties. Notice that the intervals in $\mathcal{P}^1$ and $\mathcal{P}^2$ are symmetric around η. If B becomes large or γ becomes small, these intervals become narrower with the effect that $\tilde{x}^u$ becomes larger and $H'(\tilde{x}^u)$ smaller. Thus, for large enough B or small enough γ instability occurs. Conversely, if B becomes smaller or γ larger, instability does not occur. These results follow from the pseudo-concavity of $\omega(x)$. Clearly, these parameter zones are nonempty, open sets.

Now consider

$$\mathcal{P}^4 := \{\pi \mid \theta'(x) < -1 \text{ for all } x \in \mathcal{D}^s\}.$$

By taking n small enough, the switch point x^s will move close to $\tilde{x}^u$. By continuity of $\omega(\cdot)$ there must exist a value of n, say n^e, depending on all the other parameters such that $\omega'(x^s) = -1$. Then for all $n < n^e$, $\omega'(x) < -1$, so $\mathcal{P}^4$ is a nonempty, open set.

We summarize these findings as:

PROPOSITION 20.3 (Asymptotic Stability, Fluctuations, and Expansiveness) *The sets $\mathscr{P}^i, i = 0, 1, 2, 3, 4$ are nonempty. Note that $\mathscr{P}^i \subset \mathscr{P}^0$, $i = 1, 2, 3$, and $\mathscr{P}^4 \subset \mathscr{P}^{00}$.*

(i) For all positive parameter values, the stationary state $\tilde{x} = 0$ in the null domain is stable;

(ii) for all $\pi \in \mathscr{P}^0$, $\tilde{x}^\ell$ exists and is unstable;

(iii) for all $\pi \in \mathscr{P}^1$, $\tilde{x}^u$ is asymptotically stable and all trajectories near $\tilde{x}^u$ converge monotonically;

(iv) for all $\pi \in \mathscr{P}^2$, $\tilde{x}^u$ is asymptotically stable and all trajectories near $\tilde{x}^u$ exhibit dampening fluctuations converging to $\tilde{x}^u$;

(v) for all $\pi \in \mathscr{P}^3$, $\tilde{x}^u$ is unstable and all trajectories near $\tilde{x}^u$ exhibit expanding fluctuations for a finite interval of time;

(vi) for all $\pi \in \mathscr{P}^4$, the map θ is expansive on $\mathscr{D}$.

A proof of this lemma is given in §20.6.

The parameter zones of asymptotic stability, instability, and expansiveness appear very much as they did in figure 19.8. The local dynamics are the same, but with positive M the global dynamics are changed. To pin down the differences, viability has to be considered.

20.4.3 Viability and Escape

Significant implications for infrastructure come from the possible existence of *two* positive stationary states and the possible nonexistence of a positive stationary state. This expands the possibilities for inviability. Let

$$V := [\tilde{x}^\ell, x^{00}] \quad \text{where} \quad \theta(x^{00}) = \tilde{x}^\ell.$$

Clearly, V depends on π and is nonempty for all $\pi \in \mathscr{P}^0$ and empty for all $\pi \in \backslash \mathscr{P}^0$. The map $\theta(x)$ is concave so for all $x \in \backslash V$, $\theta(x) < x$, which implies that any trajectories with these initial conditions escape in finite time. Also, for all $\pi \in \backslash \mathscr{P}^0$, V is empty, which implies that $\theta(x) < x$ for all $x \in \mathscr{D}$ so that *all* trajectories escape in finite time.

In a manner analogous to the discussion in §19.3.3, there exists a nonempty, open parameter set $\mathscr{F}^0$ in $\mathscr{P}^0$ such that $x^M < x^{00}$ for all $\pi \in \mathscr{F}^0$ and such that x^M does not depend on n. Likewise, a set $\mathscr{F}^1 \subset \mathscr{P}^0$ exists such that, for all $\pi \in \mathscr{P}^0$ such that $x^M > x^{00}$, there exists a finite range of values of n such that $x^M = \theta(x^s) < x^{00}$. Thus, define

$$\mathscr{F}^0 = \{\pi \in \mathscr{P}^0 \,|\, x^s < x^M < x^{00}\}$$

$$\mathscr{F}^1 = \{\pi \in \mathscr{P}^0 \,|\, \theta(x^s) = x^M < x^{00}\}.$$

This set is obviously empty if $\pi \in \backslash\mathscr{P}^0$ and nonempty if $\pi \in \mathscr{P}^0$. Clearly, $\theta(x) < x$ for all $x < \tilde{x}^\ell$ and for all $x > x^{00}$. Thus we have:

PROPOSITION 20.4 (Viability and Escape)

(i) For all $\pi \in \backslash\mathscr{P}^0$, all trajectories that begin in $\mathscr{D}$ escape in finite time;

(ii) for all $\pi \in \mathscr{P}^0$ and for all initial conditions not in V, trajectories escape in finite time;

(iii) for each $\pi \in \mathscr{F}^0 \cup \mathscr{F}$, for all initial conditions $x \in V$, trajectories remain in V;

(iv) let $\mathscr{F}^u := \backslash(\mathscr{F}^0 \cup \mathscr{F}^1)$. Then

for all $\pi \in \mathscr{F}^u$, trajectories in V escape with positive measure;

for all $\pi \in \mathscr{F}^u \cap \mathscr{P}^4$ trajectories in V escape almost surely.

20.4.4 Generic Qualitative Behavior

Together, Propositions 20.3 and 20.4 give a complete global characterization of the dynamics, which we summarize in:

PROPOSITION 20.5 (Generic Qualitative Behavior When Infrastructure Matters) *Given the adaptive economizing demoeconomic model with threshold preferences and positive infrastructure,*

(i) for all $\pi \in \mathscr{F}^0 \cap \mathscr{P}^1$, all trajectories in V are viable, locally monotonic, and converge asymptotically to $\tilde{x}^u$;

(ii) for all $\pi \in \mathscr{F}^0 \cap \mathscr{P}^2$, almost all trajectories in V are viable, eventually exhibit dampening fluctuations, and converge asymptotically to $\tilde{x}^u$;

(iii) for all $\pi \in \mathscr{F}^u \cap \mathscr{P}^2$ and trajectories in V, escape and dampening fluctuations converging to $\tilde{x}^u$ each occur on sets of initial conditions with positive measure in V;

(iv) for all $\pi \in \mathscr{F}^u \cap \mathscr{P}^3$ and trajectories in V, unstable (expanding) fluctuations occur near $\tilde{x}^u$ and escape occurs with positive measure;

(v) for all $\pi \in \mathscr{F}^1 \cap \mathscr{P}^3$, all trajectories in V are viable and almost all eventually exhibit persistent fluctuations;

(vi) for all $\pi \in \mathscr{F}^1 \cap \mathscr{P}^4$, all trajectories in V are viable, and almost all fluctuate and are strongly ergodic;

(vii) for all $\pi \in \mathscr{F}^u \cap \mathscr{P}^4$, trajectories in V escape almost surely;

(viii) for all $\pi \in \backslash \mathscr{P}^0$, all trajectories escape surely in finite time;

(ix) for all $\pi \in \mathscr{P}^0$, all trajectories not in V escape surely in finite time.

To put it in a nutshell, *given the adaptive economizing demoeconomic model with threshold preferences, infrastructure, and social slack, all the qualitative types of simple and complex dynamics occur generically.*

It is clear that, given B, η, γ, the effect of the slack variable $S = N - x$ is to increase the tendency toward instability and expansiveness compared to the model of chapter 19.

20.4.5 Example

For the production function use $G(L, S) = BL^\beta S^\gamma$, which yields

$$Y = \begin{cases} 0, & x \le M, x \ge N \\ B(x - M)^\beta (N - x)^{1-\beta}, & x \in (M, N). \end{cases} \tag{20.25}$$

Then the dynamic process (20.11) becomes

$$x_{t+1} = \begin{cases} 0, & x_t \in \mathscr{P}^0 \\ \frac{\alpha}{q}[B(x_t - M)^\beta (N - x_t)^{1-\beta} - \eta x_t], & x_t \in \mathscr{P}^\sigma \\ (1 + n)x_t, & x_t \in \mathscr{P}^n. \end{cases} \tag{20.26}$$

The possible trajectories are essentially like those described in chapter 19, except that inviability for all x can occur as shown in figure 20.6a. Note that $0 \le M < N$ is sufficient (given large enough B) for fluctuations to occur even if the thresholds η and M are zero.

20.5 Continuous Technological Change

As in the previous versions of the theory, the critical population levels that give the phase zone switch points depend on the technological level B. If this parameter is small enough, then growth cannot occur, all trajectories "escape," and the model is inviable. For large enough but not too large values of B, the model is viable for an interval of initial population levels. However, for relatively large values of B for which viability occurs, the stationary state will be unstable so that it is overshot and fluctuations must occur. When B is still larger, the instability can become so great that escape will occur with positive measure. Thus, if B

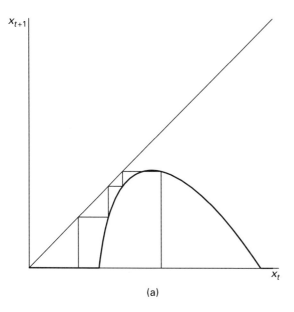

(a)

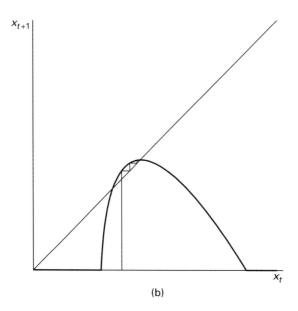

(b)

Figure 20.6
Inviability, asymptotic stability, and strong ergodicity (a–c).

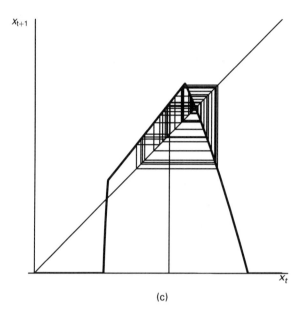

(c)

Figure 20.6 (continued)

increases exponentially from a relatively low level, the prospects for viability may be increased, with growth approaching an increasing stationary
state, but one that eventually becomes unstable so that fluctuations occur.
Eventually, such great population levels can be achieved as to enter the
inviability zone where, in spite of the improvement in technology, the
infrastructural needs of society can no longer be met.

Of course, such inferences are based on the *ceteris paribus* assumpion,
including that the social space N does not increase with B. Our presump-
tion here is that the social space depends on the qualitative character of
the system as a whole and cannot be expanded without fundamental
structural change. The latter possibility is taken up in the next chapter.

20.6   Technical Discussion

The following lemma allows us to derive the results of this chapter.

LEMMA 20.2 (Properties of the Classical Production Function with Infrastructure)   *For all M, N such that $0 < M < N$,*

(i) there exists a unique point $x^{\#}$ which depends on M and N such that

$$H(x^{\#})/x^{\#} = \max_{x \in (M,N)}[H(x)/x]$$

and satisfies

$$H(x^{\#})/x^{\#} = H'(x^{\#});$$

(ii)

$$H'(x) - H(x)/x \begin{cases} > 0, & x \in (M, x^{\#}) \\ = 0, & x = x^{\#} \\ < 0, & x \in (M, N); \end{cases}$$

(iii) let κ^M satisfy $H(x^{\#}) = \kappa^M x^{\#}$. Then

$$\frac{dx^{\#}}{dM} > 0, \quad \frac{d\kappa^M}{dM} < 0;$$

(iv) for each $0 < \kappa < \kappa^M$ there exist exactly three points, u, v, w, depending on κ, M, and N with

$$u < x^{\#} < v < w$$

such that

$$H'(v) = \kappa, \quad H(u) = \kappa u, \quad H(w) = \kappa w;$$

(v)

$$\frac{\partial u}{\partial \kappa} > 0, \quad \frac{\partial u}{\partial M} > 0, \quad \frac{\partial u}{\partial N} > 0$$

$$\frac{\partial v}{\partial \kappa} < 0, \quad \frac{\partial v}{\partial M} > 0, \quad \frac{\partial v}{\partial N} > 0$$

$$\frac{\partial w}{\partial \kappa} < 0, \quad \frac{\partial w}{\partial M} < 0, \quad \frac{\partial w}{\partial N} < 0.$$

Proof

(i) Define

$$T(\kappa) := H(v) - \kappa v = \max_{x \in (M,N)}[H(x) - \kappa x].$$

It is easy to see that $T(\kappa)$ is a decreasing function of κ and that there exists a unique κ, say κ^M, such that $T(\kappa^M) = 0$. Moreover, v must satisfy the first-order condition $H'(v) = \kappa$ uniquely. These two results imply that

$$H(v) - H'(v)v = 0.$$

Setting $v = x^{\#}$, we get the first-order conditions in (i). Also, for all $x \geq M$, $0 = T(\kappa^M) = H(x^{\#}) - \kappa^M x^{\#} > H(x) - \kappa^M x$. This implies that for all x, $H(x^{\#})/x^{\#} = \kappa^M > H(x)/x$ so that $x^{\#}$ is the unique maximizer of $H(x)/x$.

(ii) Use the Intermediate Value Theorem.

(iii) Using the first-order conditions in (i) and taking the total differential, we get

$$\frac{dx^{\#}}{dM} = \frac{x^{\#} H^{\#}(x^{\#}) - H'(x^{\#})}{x^{\#} H^{\#}(x)} > 0.$$

From the left side of (20.7),

$$\frac{d\kappa^M}{dM} = \frac{1}{x^{\#}}\left(H'(x^{\#}) - \frac{H(\#)}{x^{\#}}\right)\frac{dx}{dM} - \frac{1}{x^{\#}}H'(x^{\#})$$

$$= -\kappa^M/x^{\#} < 0.$$

(iv) Use the Intermediate Value Theorem to get a unique v satisfying $\kappa = H'(v)$. Then use the Mean Value Theorem to show that v maximizes $H(x) - \kappa x$. An argument similar to (i) yields u and v.

(v) These inequalities are obtained by taking total differentials with respect to κ, M, and N. For example, consider $H(u)/u = \kappa$. We get

$$\frac{\partial u}{\partial M} = \frac{1}{H'(u) - \kappa}.$$

The denominator is positive because of (ii) above. This gives the first expression in (v). The other inequalities are derived in a similar way. ∎

Proof of Proposition 20.3   Set $\psi'' = \eta$ and use Lemma 20.2(iv) to get a unique $z(\psi'')$ such that $H'[z(\psi'')] = \eta$. Let γ'' be the value of γ such that

$$H[z(\psi'')]/z(\psi'') = (\eta + \gamma'').$$

Define γ^M by the equation

$$(\eta + \gamma^M) = \kappa^M. \tag{20.27}$$

Note that $\gamma^M = \kappa^M - \eta = y^M - \eta$. Then for all $\gamma'' < \gamma < \gamma^M$,

$$\eta < H'(\tilde{x}^u - M) < H(\tilde{x}^u)/\tilde{x}^u = (\eta + \gamma).$$

Of course, $v < \tilde{x}^u z(\psi'')$ where $H'(v) = H(v)/v$. This gives us the inequalities defining $\mathcal{P}^1$.

In a like manner, to get the inequalities defining $\mathcal{P}^2$, set $\psi' = (\eta - \gamma^0)$ and use Lemma 20.2(iv) to get a unique $z(\psi')$ such that

$$H'[z(\psi')] = \psi'.$$

Let γ' then be the value of γ such that

$$H[z'(\psi')]/z'(\psi') = (\eta + \gamma');$$

then, since $\tilde{x}^u$ is a decreasing function of γ, for all $\gamma' < \gamma < \gamma''$,

$$(\eta - \gamma) < H'(\tilde{x}^u) < \eta.$$

Obviously, for all $0 < \gamma < \gamma'$,

$$H'(\tilde{x}^u) < (\eta - \gamma),$$

which gives the inequalities required to get $\mathcal{P}^3$.   ∎

21 Macroeconomic Evolution

The impact of technological innovation upon the economic process consists . . . of both an industrial rearrangement and . . . often of a structural change in society.
—Nicholas Georgescu-Roegen[1]

The demoeconomic growth model with infrastructure and social space can be thought of as defining a socioeconomic system. Suppose now that there are a number of alternative systems, each with distinct production and administrative technologies, each with characteristic infrastructural prerequisites, and each limited by its social space. A society in effect "chooses" among these alternatives, growing within a particular one, then, as it becomes uneconomic, abandoning it and switching to another. In this way the society evolves through epochs of distinctly differing character. In addition to such discrete changes of technology, productivity can improve more or less continuously as experience accumulates within a given system but without changing the system's fundamental structure. The dynamics of development with these mechanisms of regime switching and learning by doing is modeled and illustrated with numerical examples in this chapter.

Chapter 22 introduces replication or merging of economies and the integration or disintegration of cultures. The theory yields insights about the entire span of human development from the earliest hunting and food-collecting societies up to the present period, when a new world economic system is unfolding through the integration and disintegration of national economies. The technical existence questions concerning this multiple-phase theory of macroeconomic evolution are taken up in chapter 23. Sufficient conditions for the existence of various development scenarios are derived for a class of "regular mountainous" systems. The results are then applied in chapter 24 to show how various scenarios can occur in the model of chapters 21–22.

21.1 Background

We begin with a nontechnical discussion of alternative systems, regime switching, and continuous productivity development.

21.1.1 Alternative Systems

We assume the existence of alternative systems, each fundamentally different in technology or social structure, yet each potentially available for adoption. The relevance of this general conception of technology becomes evident when we recognize that when a wholly new form of consumption, production, management, or social organization is created, a discrete shift in production and/or administrative technology is possible. Examples come readily to mind: the development of the wheel, the domestication of plants and animals, the internal combustion engine, double-entry book-keeping, the corporate form of business, the electronic processing and transmission of information. Some of these breakthroughs have an impact so great that they are best thought of—at least for the purposes of macroeconomic theory—as distinct events that shift society's production function in one large jump. Once they take place, more or less steady improvements in production efficiency can be achieved through learning and imitation. For this reason, the discrete shifts have been called "development blocs."[2]

Discrete changes in the overall socioeconomic organization or infrastructure of society are not so simply described as the dramatic breakthroughs in the production of things. They occur, however, when a society adopts a drastically differentiated political system, a new religion, or a novel way of organizing management. Changes in political systems might involve the introduction of private property and special courts to resolve economic conflict, a new system of popular representation that engages the willing participation of formerly dissident members of society, or a change in the organization of public sector administrations that overcomes problems of graft and corruption. A new religion might introduce a new set of values, or spiritual exercises that enhance the sense of social cohesion in a people. New managerial systems could involve different modes of supervision, new communications media among people in an enterprise, different sequencing or spacing of the several tasks that make up a production process, or a new incentive scheme.

New production and managerial techniques and new forms of social organization can all enhance productivity by promoting individual effort and group cooperation. In order to be carried out on a wide enough scale, such changes often involve an increase in the resources devoted to infrastructural activity or to its support. These resources, in effect, provide new environments within which ordinary work, learning, and imitation can take place. Thus, private property requires a system of courts, law schools, and a police force; the widespread use of accounting in business requires schools for training accountants and for training teachers to train accountants. Representative government requires meeting places, political parties, and so on.

The crucial point is that a satisfactory infrastructure is an essential requisite for an effective society, and the nature of that requisite infrastructure depends on both production and administrative technologies.[3]

21.1.2 Switching

The actual process by which a society generates alternative systems and selects one among them involves an intricate process of technical and organizational invention, innovation, learning, adoption and diffusion, social and political action, and so on. For purposes of pure macro theory, the basic effect on growth of such a complex process can be incorporated by assuming a formal switching criterion. One such criterion is that of maximum average welfare. This criterion implies that a given generation adopts the system that yields the maximum output for *its* population.[4]

One might think that this artifice is extreme, recognizing that in reality transitions need not occur even though they are possible and that actual production may fall short of what is theoretically feasible. However, a model production function need not be thought of as representing maximum potential output; it may instead characterize what is practicable within a given state of the art and can be improved more or less gradually with accumulating experience. This is the interpretation taken here. When coupled with the concepts of social and environmental space, it has interesting, perhaps startling, implications.

Given the existence of internal diseconomies of the kinds described in chapter 20, continued expansion within any given system with a more or less fixed infrastructure must eventually lead to a decline in output and average welfare, and possibly to fluctuations in production and welfare or even to a collapse. If an alternative system is available that can be adopted if society reorganizes itself to provide the appropriate infrastructure, it may be able to switch or jump to the new system and resume growth. Eventually, the expanding economy might converge to a stationary state, or, failing that, it might experience fluctuations when absolutely diminishing returns set in. It could collapse and revert to an earlier, simpler system. Or, if still another more productive system is available, another jump could occur and growth could resume once again.

After a jump to a new system, further growth is possible only if the internal diseconomies are greatly diminished by such a change. This suggests that, in reality, a primary feature of system evolution must be the discovery and implementation of production and administrative innovations that lower internal diseconomies of the human population. Given success in this endeavor, a much larger worldwide population becomes possible before diseconomies again become acute. Such a change in regime is unlikely to occur unless average productivity is enhanced by doing so. This does not mean that each successive technology is uniformly more productive than its predecessor, but only that at a given total population *the switch to a new regime will enhance the standard of living of the current population.* In other words, *local efficiency* is sufficient to drive the selection process of technological regime switching.

21.1.3 Continuous Improvement, the Decay of Knowledge, and the Efficiency Gap

In contrast to discrete regime switching, continuous technological advance occurs within a given system when productivity is increased by improving competence in the use of the system's productive and administrative structures and when relatively small improvements are gradually made within the same basic social and technological framework. A key aspect of this form of technological change is the role of experience that comes with practice, or, to use the colloquial expression that formed the basis for Arrow's well-known explanation of the process, from "learning by doing."[5]

It is a part of the burden of each generation to pass on its technology and level of competence to the next. But this may not be accomplished in full, so that in effect the stock of knowledge or competence decays or depreciates just as does a capital stock. There are many reasons why this should be so. Among them are the difficulty of encoding, communicating, and preserving knowledge, and the great time and effort required to learn knowledge that has already been encoded and preserved. The greater the knowledge of a given generation, the more can potentially be inherited— and the more can be lost. If more is gained than lost, the level of knowledge accumulates. Its rate of growth may be attenuated by the difficulty of refining the components of a given system when there is a declining gap between a maximal potential level of technology and its current realized level. The closer the full potential is realized, the smaller this gap and the harder it is to improve still more. That is, the accumulation of technical knowledge tends to behave something like an epidemiological contagion.

I shall set this aspect of technological change aside initially, turning to its consideration after the more fundamental process of structural evolution has been examined.

21.2 Multiple Technologies

21.2.1 The Technology Menu

Let i be an index identifying a distinct socioeconomic system. The production function for a given economy with technology i is

$$H_i(x) := \begin{cases} 0, & x \in \backslash(M^i, N^i) \\ B^i G_i(x - M^i, N^i - x), & x \in (M^i, N^i) \end{cases} \tag{21.1}$$

where B^i is the productivity level, M^i is the infrastructural requiremeqnt, $x - M^i$ is the labor force, N^i is the social space in terms of the maximal population size, $N^i - x$ is the social slack, and $0 < M^i < N^i$. The function $G_i(x)$ is continuous, positive, homogeneous, and strictly concave on the feasible production set (M^i, N^i), as illustrated in figure 20.3. See §20.3.1. For later reference I refer to the parameters B^i, M^i, N^i, and any others that enter the function G_i as *technology parameters*.

The *technology menu* of the society is

$$\mathcal{M} := \{H_i(x); M^i, N^i, B^i, i \in \mathcal{T}\}.$$

where

$$\mathcal{T} := \{1, \ldots, \tau\}, \quad 1 < \tau \leq \infty.$$

Assume in what follows that the technology menu is *advancing*, in the sense that the technologies can be arranged so that

$$M^j > M^i \quad \text{and} \quad N^j > N^i \quad \text{for all} \quad j > i.$$

This gives precise meaning to the terms "higher" or "more advanced" and "lower" or "less advanced."

21.2.2 The Dominating Production Function

To characterize the switching criterion of local efficiency, define an index function $i = I(x)$ which gives for each population x the locally efficient regime with smallest index, that is,

$$I(x) := \min \arg \max_{j \in \mathcal{T}} H_j(x).$$

I shall call $I(\cdot)$ the *selection operator* and $H_{I(x)}(x)$ the *dominant technology* for population x. Locally efficient production—given the technological menu—therefore satisfies

$$H_{I(x)}(x) = \min_{k}\left\{ H_k(x) := \max_{j \in \mathscr{T}} H_j(x) \right\}.$$

Define the *dominant technology zone i*:

$$\mathscr{X}^i := \{x \mid I(x) = i \text{ and } H_i(x) > 0\}.$$

System i is *dominant* for population levels in $\mathscr{X}^i$. If $\mathscr{X}^i = \varnothing$, then system i is not dominant for any population level.

Let

$$\mathscr{T}^* := \{i \in \mathscr{T} \mid \mathscr{X}^i \neq \varnothing\} \quad \text{and} \quad \mathscr{X} = \bigcup_{i \in \mathscr{T}^*} \mathscr{X}^i.$$

$\mathscr{T}^*$ is the subset of dominant technology indexes and $\mathscr{X}$ is the set of populations for which there exists a dominant technology. Call $\mathscr{X}$ the *dominating production zone*. $\mathscr{M}^* = \{H_i, i \in \mathscr{T}^*\}$ is the *relevant menu*. If $\mathscr{T}^* = \mathscr{T}$, then $\mathscr{M}$ is *entirely relevant*.

Given the selection criterion, demoeconomic behavior at any one time depends on the locally efficient technology. Whether or not a given menu is relevant depends on all the parameters defining it. Thus, for one set of parameter values a given system could be relevant, but for some other set it might not be.

In particular, note that $H_i(x)$ is a stretchable function.[6] Given its strict concavity on (M^i, N^i), its maximum value increases monotonically and proportionately with the technology level parameter B^i. Consequently, for any fixed values for the parameters B^j, $j \neq i$, a large enough value of B^i will insure that $\mathscr{X}_i \neq \varnothing$. Thus we have:

PROPOSITION 21.1 (Relevant Technologies) *For fixed finite productivity levels B^j, $j \neq i$, technology i is relevant if B^i is a large enough finite value. If it is relevant for a given value, say $\bar{B}^i$, then it is relevant for all greater values, $B^i \geq \bar{B}^i$.*

To extend $H_{I(x)}(x)$ to the non-negative real domain, define the *null production zone*

$$\mathscr{X}^0 := \backslash \mathscr{X}.$$

Then set

$$I(x) \equiv 0 \quad \text{and} \quad H_0(x) \equiv 0 \quad \text{for all} \quad x \in \mathscr{X}^0.$$

$I(x)$ is now defined for all $x \in \mathbb{R}^+$. $H_0(\cdot)$ is the *null technology*; it dominates on $\mathscr{X}^0$. Refer to

$$H^*(x) := H_{I(x)}(x)$$

as the *dominating production function*. It is well defined for all possible population levels and is the envelope of the individual production functions in the menu.

The properties of the average welfare and marginal productivity functions for an individual technology are easily derived from Lemma 20.2. They are illustrated in figure 20.3. With multiple systems the *dominating welfare function* is

$$\omega^*(x) := H^*(x)/x.$$

The *dominating marginal welfare function* is

$$H^{*'}(x) = H'_{I(x)}(x) = H'_i(x), \quad x \in \mathscr{X}^i,$$

wherever the derivative is defined.

21.2.3 Example

To illustrate, we use the production function of chapter 20 given in equation (20.25) but with parameters identified by the system indexes

$$H_i(x) = \begin{cases} 0, & x \in \backslash (M^i, N^i) \\ B^i(x - M)^{\beta_i}(N - x)^{1-\beta_i}, & x \in (M^i, N^i), \quad i = 1, 2. \end{cases} \tag{21.2}$$

Two dominating production functions and their corresponding dominating welfare and marginal welfare functions are illustrated in figures 21.1 and 21.2, using the two different sets of parameters given in table 21.1.

The graphs of $H^*(\cdot)$, $\omega^*(x)$, and $H^{*'}(x)$ are illustrated by the heavy lines. Notice that the individual production functions in 21.1a are separated while those in 21.2a are overlapping. Notice also that the marginal welfare functions become negative. This reflects absolute, decreasing returns due to diseconomies of population with given infrastructures. (The "free disposal axiom" usually assumed in general equilibrium theory is specifically not adopted in this context.)

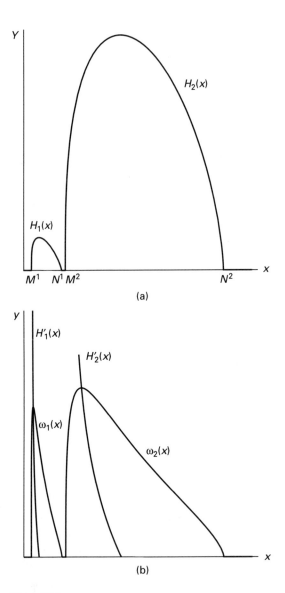

Figure 21.1
A separated technology menu: Case I. (a) Production function. (b) Average and marginal
welfare functions.

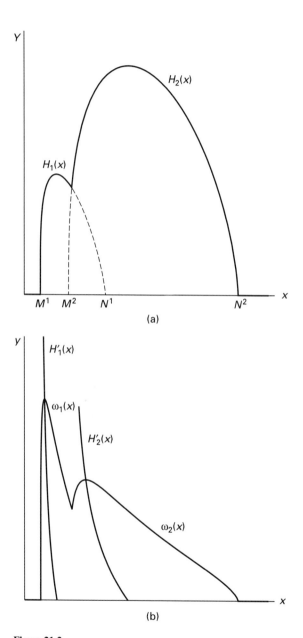

Figure 21.2
An overlapping technology menu: Case II. (a) Production function. (b) Average and marginal welfare functions.

Table 21.1
Technology Parameters

	Case I		Case II	
i	1	2	1	2
B	4	6	10	8
M	4	22	8	22
N	20	105	40	105
β	.25	.35	.25	.35

21.3   The Basic Macroevolutionary Model

21.3.1   Alternative Socioeconomic Systems

With each system is associated the birth function, as derived in §20.2, $b_i(\cdot)$, and the *social parameters* of demoeconomic behavior, η, α, q, and n. Supposing that these may differ from one system to another, we shall index them accordingly,

$$b_i(y) = \begin{cases} 0, & y < \eta^i \\ (\alpha^i/q^i)(y - \eta^i), & \eta^i < y < \zeta^i \\ 1 + n^i, & \zeta^i < y, \end{cases} \tag{21.3}$$

where η^i is the birth threshold, α^i is the preference parameter for children, q^i is the "real cost" of childrearing, n^i is the "natural" population rate of growth, and $\zeta^i = \eta^i + (q^i/\alpha^i)(1 + n^i)$ is the income level where the switch between the s-regime and n-regime takes place.

A given system can then be referred to by

$$\mathscr{S}^i := \{b_i(\cdot); \eta^i, \alpha^i, q^i, n^i, H_i(\cdot); M^i, N^i, B^i\}, \quad i \in \mathscr{T}. \tag{21.4}$$

For reference, when the term "society" is used in what follows, we shall have in mind the collection of potential systems,

$$\sum := \{\mathscr{S}^i, i \in \mathscr{T}\}. \tag{21.5}$$

21.3.2   The Switch Sets of Demoeconomic Behavior

To determine the switching sets of demoeconomic behavior, we must consider the restriction of $\omega^*(x)$ to each dominating technology set $\mathscr{X}^i$ with the corresponding switch points η^i and $\zeta^i = \eta^i + (q^i/\alpha^i)(1 + n^i)$.

Define the zones of demoeconomic behavior:

$$\mathscr{D}^{0i} := \{x \in \mathscr{X}^i \mid 0 < \omega_i(x) \le \eta^i\}$$

$$\mathscr{D}^{si} := \{x \in \mathscr{X}^i \mid \eta^i < \omega_i(x) \le \zeta^i\} \tag{21.6}$$

$$\mathscr{D}^{ni} := \{x \in \mathscr{X}^i \mid \zeta^i < \omega_i(x)\}.$$

Substituting $y = \omega^*(x)$ into the birth function (21.3) gives the demoeconomic function for each system,

$$b_i[\omega_i(x)] = \begin{cases} 0, & x \in \mathscr{D}^{0i} \\ (\alpha^i/q^i)[\omega_i(x) - \eta^i], & x \in \mathscr{D}^{si} \\ 1 + n^i, & x \in \mathscr{D}^{ni}. \end{cases}$$

It follows that

$$\mathscr{D}^{0i} = \{x \in \mathscr{X}^i \mid (\alpha^i/q^i)[H_i(x) - \eta^i x] \le 0\}$$

$$\mathscr{D}^{si} = \{x \in \mathscr{X}^i \mid 0 < (\alpha^i/q^i)[H_i(x) - \eta^i x] \le (1 + n^i)x\}$$

$$\mathscr{D}^{ni} = \{x \in \mathscr{X}^i \mid (1 + n^i)x < (\alpha^i/q^i)[H_i(x) - \eta^i x]\}.$$

21.3.3   The Dynamic Structure and the Governing Regime

Define the ith phase domain

$$\mathscr{D}^i := \mathscr{D}^{si} \cup \mathscr{D}^{ni}.$$

It is the set of populations with dominating technology i whose heirs survive to adulthood. The null domain is

$$\mathscr{D}^0 := \mathscr{X}^0 \bigcup_i \mathscr{D}^{0i}.$$

Extend the selection operator $I(\cdot)$ to all of $\mathscr{D}^0$ by defining $I(x) \equiv 0$ for all $x \in \mathscr{D}^{0i}$ for all $i \in \mathscr{T}$.

Define

$$\theta_i(x) := b_i[\omega_i(x)]x$$

$$\theta_0(x) := 0.$$

The map $\theta_i(\cdot)$ is the ith phase structure and the pair $(\theta_i, \mathscr{D}^i)$ is the ith regime. The pair $(\theta_0, \mathscr{D}^0)$ is the null regime. With these definitions, the population, dynamics $x_{t+1} = b_t x_t$ becomes the multiple-phase dynamic process

$$x_{t+1} = \theta(x_t) := \theta_{I(x_t)}(x_t) \tag{21.7}$$

where $I(x_t)$ can be called the *governing regime*.[7]

Using (21.3), the map $\theta_i(x)$ is defined by

$$\theta_{si}(x) := (\alpha^i/q^i)[H_i(x) - \eta^i x]$$

$$\theta_{ni}(x) := (1 + n^i)x.$$

I shall refer to θ_{si} and θ_{ni} as *subphase structures*, to $\mathscr{D}^{si}$ and $\mathscr{D}^{ni}$ as *subphase zones*, and to the pairs $(\theta_{si}, \mathscr{D}^{si})$ and $(\theta_{ni}, \mathscr{D}^{ni})$ as *subregimes* for all $x \in \mathscr{D}^0$.

The explicit dynamics in the governing regime is

$$x_{t+1} = \begin{cases} \theta_0(x_t) = 0, & x_t \in \mathscr{D}^0 \\ \theta_{si}(x_t) = (\alpha^i/q^i)[H_i(x_t) - \eta^i x_t], & x_t \in \mathscr{D}^{si} \\ \theta_{ni}(x_t) = (1 + n^i)x_t, & x_t \in \mathscr{D}^{ni}. \end{cases} \tag{21.8}$$

Define $\mathscr{T}^{**} := \{j \in \mathscr{T}^*, \mathscr{D}^j \neq \varnothing\}$. Call $\mathscr{D} := \bigcup_{i \in \mathscr{T}^{**}} \mathscr{D}^j$ the *admissible population zone*. That is, populations can exist at least temporarily for systems with indexes in $\mathscr{T}^{**}$. Obviously, the admissible population zone belongs to (and is strictly contained in) the dominating production zone, that is, $\mathscr{D} \subset \subset \mathscr{X}$. For convenience we refer to $\sum^{**} := \{\mathscr{S}^i, i \in \mathscr{T}^{**}\}$ as an *admissible society*.

21.3.4 Example

To illustrate the derivation of phase zones and phase structures, use the production function given in (21.2) with parameter values. The subphase structures for the two possible regimes are

$$\theta_{si}(x) = (\alpha^i/q^i)[B^i(x - M^i)^{\beta^i}(N^i - x)^{1-\beta^i} - \eta^i x]$$
$$\theta_{ni}(x) = (1 + n^i)x \tag{21.9}$$

for all $i \in \mathscr{T}$.

Assume that the technology parameters are those given in table 21.1. Assume the social parameters that enter the demoeconomic function are the same for each system and have the values given in table 21.2.

Table 21.2
Social Parameters

α	.67
q	.67
η	1.0
n	.2

Table 21.3
Critical Income Switch Points

η	1.0
$\eta + \gamma$	2.0
ζ	2.2

The critical values for determining the subphase zones can be obtained from (21.6). They are η^i and $\zeta^i = \eta^i + (1 + n^i)(q^i/\alpha^i)$. Using the values in table 21.3, we get the same switch points for each system. These values are indicated on figure 21.3, from which one can readily construct the phase zones and subphase zones for the two cases.

In figure 21.4, graphs of the map $\theta(\cdot)$ are given for each of the cases. As before, these graphs are the envelopes of the graphs of the individual phase structures.

21.3.5 Epochal Evolutions

To characterize the trajectories generated by (21.8), we employ the nomenclature of chapters 7 and 9. If $\tau(x) = \{\theta^t(x)\}_{t=1}^{\infty}$ is the trajectory of a society when x is the initial condition, then the sequence $I(\theta^t(x))$, $t = 0, 1, 2, \ldots$ gives the history of that society in terms of the sequence of regimes through which it passes.

If $I(x_{t+1}) = I(x_t)$, then there is no structural change, just growth, fluctuation, or decline within the given regime, as the case may be. If $I(x_{t+1}) \neq I(x_t)$, *then there is a phase change or a switch in regime* from generation t to $t + 1$. Thus, as time passes, a sequence of episodes emerges, each governed by a distinct economic system and entered into on account of conditions prevailing in the preceding episode. An *episode* is a sequence of periods during which a given socioeconomic system or regime governs the dynamics. If s_k is the period in which regime p_k is entered, then $[s_k, s_{k+1})$ is the kth episode, and $d_k = s_{k+1} - s_k$ its duration. Thus, a trajectory can

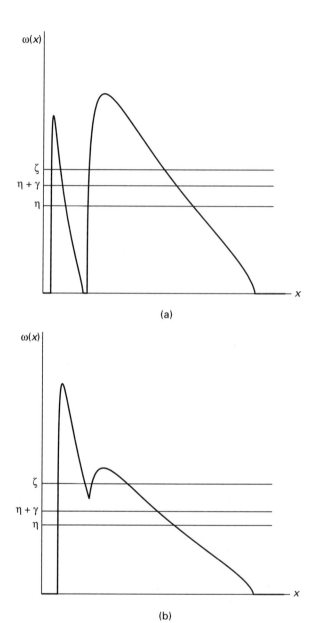

Figure 21.3
Derivation of the admissible population zones. (a) Case I. (b) Case II.

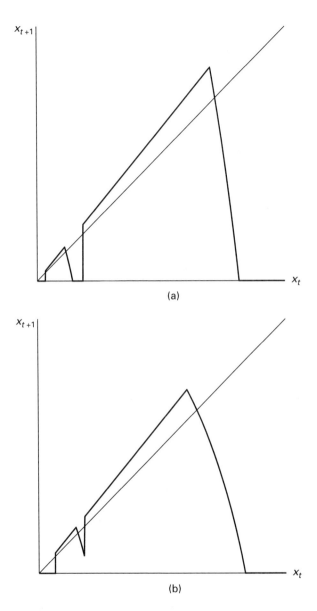

Figure 21.4
Multiple-phase structures. (a) Case I. (b) Case II.

be decomposed into an *epochal evolution*, $\mathscr{E}$, which is a denumerable
sequence $k = 1, \ldots$ of episodes, each governed by a specific regime:

$$\mathscr{E} := \{\mathscr{D}^{p_1}, \mathscr{D}^{p_2}, \ldots, \mathscr{D}^{p_k}, \ldots\}$$

where

$$p_k = I(x_t) \quad \text{for all} \quad t \in [s_k, s_{k+1}), \quad k = 1, \ldots.$$

If a given trajectory can be characterized by the epochal evolution $\mathscr{E}$, we
shall say it *passes through* $\mathscr{E}$ or $\tau(x) \sim \mathscr{E}$.

Given an initial population, $x_0 = x$, such a trajectory yields the following description of an economic development path, period after period,
$t = 1, 2, 3, \ldots$ indefinitely, or until the null regime is entered:

the number of households	x_t
aggregate production	Y_t
average product per family	y_t
average family size	$2[1 + b(y_t)]$
the dominant system	$p_k = I(x_t))$
the time of entry into each episode	s_k
the sojourn of each episode	$[s_k, s_{k+1})$
the duration of each episode	$d_k = s_{k+1} - s_k$
size of the social infrastructure	M^{p_k}
size of the labor force	$L_t = x_t - M^{p_k}$
the amount of social slack	$S_t = N^{p_k} - x_t$

Note that p_k and s_k are functions of the initial population, x, and the
number of periods, t, since the initial date.

If x belongs to the admissible set, then $\theta(x) > 0$, so there must be at
least one episode with a non-null regime and duration $d_1 \geq 1$. If the null
regime is never entered, that is, if $I(x_t) > 0$ for all t, then $p_k(x) > 0$ for all
k and the system is *viable* for x.

If for all $x \in \mathscr{D}^{**} \subset \mathscr{D}$ the system is viable, then $\mathscr{D}^{**}$ is a *viability domain*. If, instead, the null regime is entered at some time, say after the kth
non-null episode at time $s_{k+1}(x)$, then $p_{k+1}(x) = 0$ and $x_t \in \mathscr{D}^0$ for all $t \geq$
$s_{k+1}(x)$. In this case, the system is inviable for x: the trajectory has a *finite
history*, that is, x_t is admissible for all $t \in [0, s_{k+1}(x))$ but inadmissible
thereafter. The set of initial conditions, for which the system is inviable, is

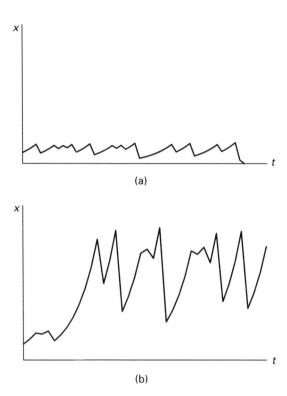

Figure 21.5
Simulated trajectories for Cases I and II in tables 21.1–21.3.

the complement of $\mathscr{D}^{**}$. Obviously, the null domain belongs to this set, i.e., $\mathscr{D}^0 \subset \backslash \mathscr{D}^{**}$. (Notice that a trajectory is well defined for inviable systems because if $\mathscr{D}^0$ is the last episode in a finite sequence $\mathscr{E}$ that is entered at time s_n, say, then $\theta^t(x) = \theta^s(x) = 0$ for all $t \geq s_n$.)

No assumption has been made about the order of the regimes $\{p_k, \ldots\}$. As shall be seen in chapter 24, these can take on many different permutations and combinations of indexes in $\mathscr{T}$. The permutation and combination making up any given epochal evolution depends both on the initial condition and on the parameter values of all the available systems.

21.3.6 Simulated Trajectories

Two trajectories are shown in figure 21.5 using the technology parameters given in table 21.1 and the social parameters given in table 21.2.

For the Case I example shown in figure 21.5a, a transition from the first to the second system could not take place because the maximum population reachable within the first regime does not exceed the phase switch point. Growth takes place initially, but fluctuations emerge, followed eventually by collapse.

For Case II in panel (b), monotonic growth also occurs, fluctuations break out, but a transition to and growth within the next system is achieved. However, with no opportunities for further switching, fluctuations again emerge.

21.4   Structural Change with Continuous Productivity Improvement

Now introduce continuous productivity improvement so that any given technology becomes more productive when it is being used.

21.4.1   Learning by Doing

Think of the positive parameter $\hat{B}$ as the *maximum heritable technology level* and let B_t be the actual technology level achieved by the adult generation of period t. Taking account of the decay factor, the technology level that can be inculcated to the next generation is κB_t where κ is a parameter of *enculturation* with $0 < \kappa < 1$. The *efficiency gap* is $\hat{B} - \kappa B_t$, or in proportional terms,

$$(\hat{B} - \kappa B_t)/\hat{B}.$$

(The system superscript is omitted for the time being.)

The change in knowledge from one generation to the next depends on the efficiency gap and can be represented by

$$\frac{B_{t+1} - B_t}{B_t} = \rho \frac{(\hat{B} - \kappa B_t)}{\hat{B}}$$

where ρ is the *learning parameter*. Dividing both numerator and denominator on the right by κ, we get the quadratic difference equation

$$B_{t+1} = B_t + \rho B_t[1 - B_t/\tilde{B}]$$

where $\tilde{B} = \hat{B}/\kappa$ is the unique positive stationary state. The process is asymptotically monotonically stable if

$$0 < \rho \leq 1.$$

We can think of $\tilde{B}$ as the *technology potential* for a given system. The maximum heritable level $\hat{B}$ is less than $\tilde{B}$ as a consequence of the loss of knowledge in the transmission from one generation to the next. However, in a steady state each generation's learning exactly makes up for this loss. Given this interpretation, we can think of ρ and $\tilde{B}$ as the two fundamental parameters.

The value of the technology parameter when a given regime is entered for the first time will be called the *innovating technology level*, denoted by the parameter B_0 and assumed to satisfy $0 < B_0 < \tilde{B}$. Then productivity will grow. The larger the potential and the smaller the innovating level, the larger is the technology gap; and the larger this gap, the more rapid the initial rate of growth. However, as the stock of practical knowledge accumulates, the rate of accumulation eventually declines, and the technology level approaches its potential asymptotically.

Now suppose that the type of learning-by-doing process we have in mind takes place within a given system *only when it is the one governing behavior* (for only then can practical knowledge based on experience accumulate). If i is the system index identifying the governing regime, then

$$B_{t+1}^i = (1 + \rho^i)B_t^i - \rho^i(B_t^i)^2/\tilde{B}^i$$

$$B_{t+1}^j = B_t^j, \quad j \neq i.$$

(21.10)

21.4.2 Example

The process of continuous productivity improvement is illustrated for several values of ρ in figure 21.6. In this diagram the process is given in terms of the relative productivity index, $z_t = B_t/\tilde{B}$.[8]

21.4.3 The Switch Points of Demoeconomic Behavior

To incorporate this contagion process into the multiple-phase theory of development, the several parameters must be given their appropriate system indexes. Thus, we have $\tilde{B}^i$ for the technology supremum and ρ^i for the contagion parameter, $i \in \mathcal{T}$.

A system is now designated by

$$\mathcal{S}^i = \{b^i(\cdot); \eta^i, \alpha^i, q^i, n^i, \rho^i, H^i(\cdot); M^i, N^i, B_0^i, \tilde{B}^i\}, \quad i \in \mathcal{T}. \quad (21.11)$$

The production function (21.1) and phase structure (21.8) must be modified to recognize the role of the productivity levels as endogenous

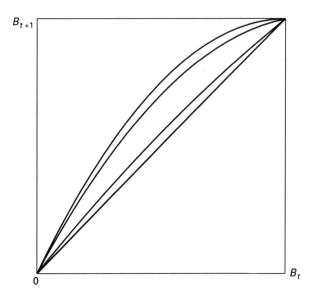

Figure 21.6
Learning by doing

state variables. For this purpose let us modify the definition of the function $H(\cdot)$ given in (21.1) and define $H_i(x, B^i) := B^i G_i(x - M^i, N^i - x)$. Then

$$Y = \begin{cases} 0, & x \in \backslash (M^i, N^i) \\ H_i(x, B^i), & x \in (M^i, N^i) \end{cases} \tag{21.12}$$

and

$$H_i(x, B^i) = \begin{cases} 0, & x \in \backslash (M, N) \\ B^i G_i(x - M^i, N^i - x), & x \in (M, N). \end{cases} \tag{21.13}$$

The switching criterion of local efficiency that governs the "choice" of systems must also be defined in terms of productivity state variables B_t^i, $i \in \mathcal{T}$, as well as in terms of population. Let $B := (B^i)_{i \in \mathcal{T}}$. The selection operator is defined by

$$i = I(x, B) := \min \left\{ \arg \max_{j \in \mathcal{T}} H_j(x, B^j) \right\}.$$

The dominant technology for any population x now satisfies

$$H^*(x, B) = H_{I(x, B)}(x, B^{I(x,B)}) = \min_k \left\{ H_k(x, B^k) := \min_{p \in \mathscr{T}} H_p(x, B^j) \right\};$$

the dominant technology zone i is

$$\mathscr{X}^i := \{x \mid I(x, B) = i, H_i(x, B^i) > 0\}$$

with $\mathscr{T}^*$, $\mathscr{X}$, and $\mathscr{X}^0$ defined as before. The dominating welfare function is

$$\omega^*(x, B) := H^*(x, B)/x = H_i(x, B)/x, \quad x \in \mathscr{X}^i,$$

and the dominating marginal welfare function at any given time is

$$\frac{\partial H^*(x, B)}{\partial x} = B^i H_i'(x, B^i), \quad x \in \mathscr{X}^i,$$

wherever the derivative is defined.

Note that now the B^i and the dominating production zeros are functions of time. Consequently, the phase zeros are also. They are defined just as before (21.6):

$$\mathscr{D}^{0i} = \{x \mid (\alpha^i/q^i)[H_i(x, B^i) - \eta^i x] \le 0\}$$

$$\mathscr{D}^{si} = \{x \mid 0 < (\alpha^i/q^i)[H_i(x, B^i) - \eta^i x] \le (1 + n)x\} \qquad (2.14)$$

$$\mathscr{D}^{ni} = \{x \mid (1 + n^i)x < (\alpha^i/q^i)[H_i(x, B^i) - \eta^i x]\}.$$

21.4.4 The Dynamic Structure and the Governing Regime

Define

$$\theta_i(x, B) := b_i[\omega_i(x, B)]x$$

$$\theta_0(x, B) := 0$$

and extend $I(\cdot, \cdot)$ to $\mathscr{D}^0$ by defining $I(x, B) = 0$ for all $x \in \mathscr{D}^0$. With these definitions, the population dynamics $x_{t+1} = b_t x_t$ is determined by

$$x_{t+1} = \theta(x_t, B_t) := \theta_{I(x_t, B_t)}(x_t, B_t) \qquad (21.15)$$

where $I(x_t, B_t)$ gives the governing regime.

In terms of the subregimes, the multiple-phase dynamical system with continuous technological change now consists of

$$i = I(x_t, B_t), \qquad (21.16)$$

$$
x_{t+1} = \begin{cases} \theta_0(x_t) & = 0, & x_t \in \mathscr{D}^0 \\ \theta_{si}(x_t, B_t^i) = (\alpha^i/q^i)[H_i(x_t, B_t^i) - \eta^i x_t], & x_t \in \mathscr{D}^{si} \\ \theta_{ni}(x_t) & = (1 + n^i)x_t, & x_t \in \mathscr{D}^{ni}, \end{cases} \qquad (21.17)
$$

$$
B_{t+1}^i = (1 + \rho^i)B_t^i - \rho^i(B_t^i)^2/\tilde{B}^i
$$

$$
B_{t+1}^j = B_t^j, \quad j \neq i, \qquad (21.18)
$$

with initial conditions

$$
x_0 = x \quad \text{and} \quad B_0^i, \quad i \in \mathscr{T}. \qquad (21.19)
$$

21.4.5   Epochal Evolution

Given that $\rho^i > 0$, a model trajectory yields all of the information obtained before in §21.3.5 but with the variables now dependent on both population and the productivity level variables, which it also traces out.

Of course, if $\rho^i = 0$, then continuous productivity improvement cannot occur, so the parameter B^i is fixed at the innovating productivity level B_0^i. When ρ^i is positive, however, the complete model has the additional productivity state variables and the corresponding difference equations that govern their change over time.

21.4.6   The Effect on Qualitative Behavior

How does the introduction of the technology contagion equations influence the dynamics of the system? The present model takes us beyond the single structural equation format to which the preceding chapters are limited. Given the form of the contagion process, however, and the character of the production function, we can use a knowledge of the dynamics when the productivity levels are fixed to determine what happens when they vary. This will be done in chapter 24.

It should be evident, however, from the analysis of chapter 20, that the introduction of continuous neutral technological improvement that raises the level of productivity once a given regime has been adopted, but which does not modify the other parameters of the system, not only can accelerate growth but can destabilize a given system by leading eventually to a nonempty escape zone. With a single regime the result of escape is demise. In the present context escape may permit a transition to a more advanced regime, a transition that might not be possible without this form of cumulative productivity improvement. Indeed, given the class of production functions considered here, it can be shown that any regime that possesses the capacity for continuous neutral technological change ($\rho^i > 0$), that has a high enough population growth rate n, and that has a large enough technological potential ($\bar{B}^i$) will be destabilized in finite time, guaranteeing the possibility of both fluctuations and phase transitions.

If the technological menu is bounded, that is, if $\sup_i\{\bar{x}^i\} \leq \bar{x} < \infty$, then the possibility emerges that a society may eventually overshoot the region of viability, which may lead to population declines and reversion to less advanced regimes—or to a collapse sufficient to bring about the demise of society altogether.

If, on the other hand, the technological menu is both unlimited and unbounded and if the technology suprema are large enough, then the existence of continuous learning virtually guarantees structural evolution indefinitely.

These and other technical aspects of existence are discussed in chapters 23 and 24.

21.4.7   Numerical Simulations

In order to illustrate the theory when continuous productivity improvement takes place within a given system, use the production function (21.2). The subphase structures are the same as (21.9) except that the vector of technology levels $B = (B^1, \ldots, B^\tau)$ is endogenous:

$$\theta_{si}(x_t, B_t^i) = (\alpha^i/q^i)[B_t^i(x_t - M^i)^{\beta^i}(N^i - x_t)^{1-\beta^i} - \eta^i, x_t]$$
$$\theta_{ni}(x_t) = (1 + n^i)x_t. \tag{21.20}$$

Given the innovating productivity levels shown in table 21.1, and if continuous productivity improvement could not occur ($\rho_i = 0$), the phase diagram for the reduced model would appear as shown in figure 21.5a. Recall that there can be no escape interval in the first phase zone because the maximum reachable population, x^{M_1}, is below the boundary level separating the two phase zones $\mathscr{D}^1$ and $\mathscr{D}^2$. Consequently, a switch in systems cannot occur.

Now assume that continuous productivity improvement does take place with ρ^i taking on the values shown in table 21.4. As B_t^1 increases from period to period when $I(x_t) = 1$, the part of the phase diagram for the first regime must shift upward due to the contagion process. Fluctuations can still occur, but their (average) amplitude must increase until an escape

Table 21.4
Continuous Productivity Improvement for Case I Parameter Values

	Case I	
i	1.00	2.00
η^i	2.00	2.00
α^i	.25	.25
q^i	.50	.50
n^i	.20	.20
B_0^i	4.00	5.00
$\tilde{B}^i$	8.00	10.00
ρ^i	.03	.03
β^i	.25	.35
M^i	4.00	22.00
N^i	20.00	105.00

interval emerges. It can be shown that a switch must then take place sooner or later almost surely, leading to a switch to the second regime where growth resumes, as it did in the illustration of Case II (figure 21.4b). But now the average amplitude of the fluctuations will increase as the productivity level of this technology improves. Sooner or later an escape interval will emerge in this regime also, but, as there are no "more advanced" technologies available, it will be associated with a reversion to the first regime or a collapse into the null regime. In the former event, growth and fluctuation within the first regime could occur again, but a switch to the more advanced regime would take place, again, almost surely. A structural fluctuation between the two regimes could continue over quite a few episodes. Eventually, however, given the inability to expand the social space, an escape interval opens up wide enough to permit a collapse from the second regime to the null domain. The society self-destructs almost surely. This story is illustrated in figure 21.7.

21.5 Summary

With the introduction of a number of empirically important features into the classical theory, a framework for describing growth and structural change has been constructed that is flexible enough to generate many different potential development patterns. It would seem to offer insight into at least some of the possible reasons why human societies have grown

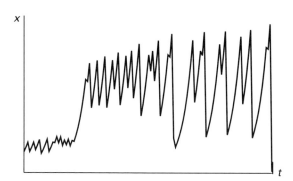

Figure 21.7
Simulated trajectories with technological contagion

and flourished, sometimes passing through turbulent periods at the transition, eventually progressing to more advanced levels of socioeconomic technology and organization with productivity continually increasing, and have succumbed in the end to what might be called a crisis of over-development.

22 A Grand Dynamics of Economic Development

Flaubert noted ... the perpetual evolution of humanity and therefore the evolution of social forms.
—Julien Barnes, *Flaubert's Parrot*

This chapter combines regime switching, replication/merging, and integration/disintegration to obtain a general model of macroeconomic development. The model is used to simulate economic history in its broadest terms as it has traversed six broad macro cultures: the hunting band, village agriculture, city-states, trading empires, the industrial nation-state, and the global information economy. The simulation represents a new kind of "qualitative econometrics" which involves determining parameter values that enable the model to fit known qualitative features of factual history.

Baumol used the term "magnificent dynamics" for the classical works of Smith, Malthus, Ricardo, Marx, and Schumpeter, who had attempted "to analyze growth and development of entire economies over relatively long periods of time—decades or even centuries."[1] I use the term "grand dynamics" as a synonym for the application of complex economic dynamics to explain crucial aspects of development over the very long run, that is, over millennia. Obviously, mathematical theories do not and cannot incorporate the full range of psychological, social, and environmental forces involved in human history, for which all the social and historical sciences must be marshaled. But, in building on and incorporating knowledge from various disciplines, they can nonetheless be grand in scope, as, it seems to me, is demonstrated in the pages that follow.

22.1 Background

As before, we begin with a nontechnical description of the new concepts involved.

22.1.1 Replication and Merging

Consider the processes of replication and merging. Very early human societies were built around such small groups that families themselves and councils of elders could provide the required infrastructure without the need for elaborate organizations. The hunting and gathering band thus takes its place early in the process of economic development. Archaeologists have traced its diffusion throughout the world. The mechanism that mediated this diffusion is that of *fission*. As a band grew, it would eventually deplete the animal and plant foods in its neighborhood. The cost of search increased and the productivity of search decreased. Even with no significant change in the basic system of technology and organization, a given band could split to form two smaller, more or less independent bands that, moving apart, could greatly increase the total area supplying food, reduce the cost of search, and increase productivity. This process of growth and replication could continue until there was no vacant terrain left. By these means, the Western Hemisphere was probably populated within a few centuries. It is at this point that overshoot and fluctuation, as described in chapters 19 and 20, might be expected to occur.[2]

One need not go back into prehistory to find this process at work. Indeed, the splitting up of societies into parts that become more or less independent is described already by Herodotus in his famous account of the division of Lydia's population. It has now been established to have been a common colonization process by which city-states spread throughout the Mediterranean world.[3]

Such a process is easily explained by the presence of internal diseconomies due to declining marginal productivity of labor, the productivity-diminishing effect of decreasing social space, and the requirements of infrastructure which, of course, play a much enlarged role in urban society. At some point in the expansion of a given economy, the population may reach a level at which average productivity has fallen enough that a new society with a newly constituted infrastructure can be split off in such a way as to increase welfare, just as Herodotus describes.

The process of growth through fission, even in the absence of external diseconomies, need not be monotonic. Indeed, a reduction in output could occur large enough to force more or less autonomous economies to recombine or *fuse* into a smaller number of economies, each with the same system as before but each newly constituted economy with an enhanced number of people in the workplace, in effect economizing on social overhead.

An alternative to the process of fission and fusion is that of shedding and assimilation. Some individuals from each of several economies could leave to form an additional group. Obviously, a new economy can form only if enough people leave the old ones to meet the infrastructural prerequisites for a new one. Conversely, if productivity were to decline sufficiently at some point during a process of expansion, a given economy might be disbanded, with individuals dividing themselves up among and assimilating into the remaining groups.

Under some conditions, replication or merging in this way may be less likely than through the mechanisms of fission or fusion of entire economies, because shedding requires individuals who have been living in different groups to assimilate, while fission enables half the members of a group to continue their association.

In the real world there are crucial differences between these two processes that involve differences in organizational costs. These costs have not been included here. In reality both processes have occurred, and sometimes at the same time. For our purposes we shall not look at the conditions under which one or the other or both would take place, but simply compare the development possibilities for each process.

Technically, the process of growth through replication involves the emergence over time of multiple aggregate production functions, each based on the same administrative and production technologies and each forming the basis for a more or less autonomous economy. If, in this process, sufficient contractions in output and population occur to force merging, not only population but the number of autonomous economies will fluctuate over time.

22.1.2 Environmental Capacity and External Diseconomies

Replication—whether that of hunting and food-collecting bands or that of city-states—could continue until the known world is full of such units. To see what is meant by the term "full," besides the *internal* diseconomies that operate within a given socioeconomic unit, we must take account of the *external* ones that derive from the total population of all the economies together. These are, for example, caused by the exhaustion of the environment's waste-absorbing capacity. For hunting and food-collecting or agricultural systems, this capacity can be stated in terms of the space available, which in turn depends on the population density. In more advanced systems, the cost of extracting and refining grows as resources become scarce. There may eventually be diminishing absolute returns to the work force.

In general, the human population develops within a physical and biological context that provides the *environmental capacity* for human economic activity. As this capacity becomes filled, the effect on productivity can be drastic. The internal diseconomies can be overcome by replication; the external ones cannot. *Once the world is full in the sense that the aggregate population diseconomies become important, the replication of the same basic structures must come to an end.* This is as true of the city-state as it is of the hunting and gathering band. It must be true of all the more advanced systems as well.[4]

22.1.3 Overcoming External Diseconomies through Integration

To overcome external diseconomies and their dire consequences, innovations must lead to technical and administrative technologies that expand the environmental capacity, in effect raising the bound on potential population size. Such innovation could involve new knowledge that transforms some material aspect of the environment into a new potential resource for economic exploitation; it could involve discovering a new means of disposing of waste or of transforming it into benign or useful forms; or, it could involve a new form of social organization that makes possible the coexistence and cooperation of people in much greater numbers than before.

Thus, each new system offers a potential new development bloc. Each is structurally distinct, depending on production and administrative technologies with very different infrastructural requirements. And each successive system requires a greater overhead of human capital as a prerequisite for production. Growth through replication within a culture can proceed as described in the previous chapter, but if the total size of the economy becomes large enough to "afford" the infrastructure of a more advanced system, a switch could occur if existing economies combined. Thus, the integration of less advanced economies can become the basis for jumping to a more advanced system.

But this may not always be possible. A relatively advanced system may present such imposing requirements that even a world full of economies with an existing system would not have the aggregate resources to permit a switch to it. For example, it would not have been possible for a Greek city-state of the first millennium B.C. to switch to the industrial or atomic age, even had its philosophers known about steam and electricity and even were its theories of matter as advanced as our own. It did not have the educational, engineering, and scientific infrastructure to support such a change. Systems intermediate between the city-state and the industrial nation-state had to be passed through first.

When such intermediate systems can be achieved by reorganizing and integrating individual economies, a jump to a new development bloc can offer a potential means for surmounting the existing limits to growth, even though no preexisting individual economy could attain the new system on its own. Such a process is known to have occurred when the villages scattered across the plains of Attica rather abruptly coalesced to form the Athenian city-state.[5] A similar process enabled "the village-centered agrarian population in Galilee to form an integrated urban-centered economy in the Second Temple period."[6] Closer to the modern era, the unification of the separate American colonies in the late eighteenth century provides an example, as does the establishment of the Union of Soviet Socialist Republics after World War I and, more recently, the efforts at European integration. The integration of economies to form larger ones with more elaborate infrastructures must surely be recognized as an important aspect of economic development.

22.1.4 Disintegration

If in the course of expansion by means of growth and replication a given system's potential limits are approached, a drastic drop in productivity must occur. Then, instead of a switch to a more advanced system and a resurgence of growth, a decline might take place. This could come about in one of three ways. The simplest would be a reduction in output and population in the several economies with no change in the existing techno-infrastructure. This would be the result if the productivity drop were relatively minor. If the productivity drop were quite major and followed by such a substantial contraction in output that none of the economies could afford their infrastructure, then the tendency would be for some economies to merge. With higher productivity, growth could resume. Or, finally, in the face of a sufficiently drastic collapse in productivity, the several economies in existence might disintegrate into a larger number of simpler systems which in the aggregate required a smaller commitment of resources to the infrastructure. Thus, productivity decline could bring about (i) a contraction of existing economies; (ii) a merging of existing economies to form a smaller number but with the same production and administrative technologies as before; or (iii) a disintegration of the given systems into a larger number of economies each with less elaborate techno-infrastructures.

The record of early development in Mesopotamia and Egypt provides many examples of integration, disintegration, and reintegration.[7] The emergence of complex "precivilized" city-states from more or less independent village economies, their pattern of growth, subsequent collapse, and reversion, followed by a resumption of growth and integration to form a complex system again, has been described as a fluctuating process that continued for hundreds of years in parts of East Africa and Polynesia.[8] Examples in the classical era are the disintegration of Alexander's and the Roman empires; and similarly the vicissitudes of the great pre-Columbian American civilizations. The present disintegration of the Eastern European bloc and that of some of its constituent political units (Yugoslavia, the Soviet Union) would appear to provide contemporary examples. Chinese and Indian histories offer perhaps the most striking cases, which are told in terms of successions of dynastic integrations and disintegrations.[9]

22.1.5 Structural Change through Macroeconomic Evolution

From the point of view of the present theory, then, economic history in the very long run can be interpreted in the following vein. Once a given culture is established, growth within it can occur for a time within a given set of economic units until the limits on population are approached and productivity falls. Even with no new development blocs, by reorganizing resources through replication, new infrastructures create viable new economies and growth can continue. In the presence of external diseconomies, however, this process must be bounded.

At various critical periods the inherent limits to growth in a given socioeconomic system may be overcome by the emergence of and transition to a drastically different system, one that requires a considerably enlarged infrastructure but that is reachable by the integration and reorganization of existing economic units and that, by doing so, can greatly expand the bounds on population so that growth can resume both within the new much larger economy and eventually through replication of this much larger entity. Eventually, as the greater bounds are approached, diseconomies again begin to impinge, setting the stage for another potential transition to a still more complex system. In this way, a given society may progress through one culture after another.

Though a given society may not disappear, its culture might. During such critical junctures an enlarged system may not emerge, or if it does it may fail to take hold. Instead of an advance, a collapse might occur that causes a reversion to a smaller number of economies with the given system or to a larger number of economies with less advanced regimes. In the former case, some economies are essentially abandoned and their population absorbed in those remaining. In the latter, the relatively advanced economy splits into less advanced ones with smaller infrastructural requirements. In either case, productivity increases, growth resumes, and the process of evolution with jumps and reversions continues.

In theory, as well as in fact, the development path need not be smooth or even monotonic. It can be characterized by changes in output, population, and standards of living and also by the numbers and qualitative character of the economies making up the process as a whole. It is in this sense that a more grand dynamics than conceived by the classical economists is involved, one that seems to mimic the growth and vicissitudes of human economic activity through its many historical forms.[10]

Of course, the actual course of human socioeconomic evolution is the resultant of innumerable psychological, social, and physical forces that interact on a micro level. The theory propounded here only captures a part of this vast and variegated drama. But it is a crucial part, because our fortunes and our prospects do depend on our productivity, which depends on how many of us there are and how we are organized. How many of us there can be depends in turn on how productive we are. It is within this macroeconomic, evolutionary context that political, social, psychological, and microeconomic movements unfold.

22.2 Replication and Merging Processes

22.2.1 Cultures and the Cultural Production Function

Consider a society made up of a *collection of several more or less independent economies with the same socioeconomic system*. As each has the same production and administrative technologies and the same parameters of preference for consumption and childrearing, the term *culture* for the collection is not inappropriate.

Let $\mathscr{K}$ be the set of allowable numbers of economies and assume that it is a subsequence of the positive integers

$$\mathscr{K} := \{k_j \in \mathbb{N}^{++}, k_{j+1} > k_j, \ j = 1, 2, 3, \ldots\}.$$

(For the time being, assume that the number of allowable economies is unbounded.) I shall refer to each pair $\{\mathscr{S}, \mathscr{K}\}$ as a *culture*.

In the interest of simplicity, *assume that any given population is divided equally among its economic units*. Given this assumption, the production function for each economy is $Y = kH(x/k)$, $k \in \mathscr{K}$ where $H(\cdot)$ is defined in (21.1) except that for the time being the system index is omitted. That is, output in the culture with population x is just k times the output that could be obtained by a single economy with population x/k. Its infrastructure and social space are k times those of the individual economies considered separately, so its feasibility domain is $k(M, N) = (kM, kN)$. Since $H(x/k)$ is positive for $x/k \in (M, N)$, $kH(x/k)$ is positive for $x \in (kM, kN)$. Otherwise, output will be impossible because population within each individual economy is too large or too small. Therefore,

$$Y = kH(x/k) = \begin{cases} 0, & x \in \backslash k(M, N) \\ kBG(x/k - M, N - x/k), & x \in k(M, N). \end{cases} \tag{22.1}$$

Note that for all $k \in \mathscr{N}$ there is an index $j \in \mathbb{N}^{++}$ such that $k = k_j$. Therefore, we can substitute k_j for k in this expression. If $G(\cdot)$ is homogeneous of degree one, then (21.1) takes on the equivalent form

$$Y = kH(x/k) = \begin{cases} 0, & x \in \backslash (kM, kN) \\ BG(x - kM, kN - x), & x \in (kM, kN). \end{cases} \tag{22.2}$$

Assume the same selection criterion as in the case of technological regime switching, that of reorganizing society whenever total or average productivity at the current population can be increased by doing so. To characterize this criterion, define the index function $j = J(x)$ which identifies the locally efficient number k_j of economies in the culture for a population of size x, that is,

$$j = J(x) := \arg \max_{l \in \mathbb{N}^{++}} k_l H(x/k_l).$$

The *cultural production function* $K_j(x)$ for population x with k_j autonomous economies is defined by

$$K_j(x) = K_{J(x)}(x).$$

The *dominating production zone* for a culture with k_j autonomous economies is given by

$\mathscr{X}^j := \{x \,|\, J(x) = j \text{ and } K_j(x) > 0\}.$

Let $\mathscr{X} := \cup_{j \in \mathscr{N}} \mathscr{X}^j$ and define $\mathscr{X}^0 := \backslash \mathscr{X}$. Define $J(x) \equiv 0$ and $K_0(x) \equiv 0$ for all $x \in \mathscr{X}^0$. Then we can define the *cultural production function* by

$$K_*(x) := K_{J(x)}(x) \quad \text{for all} \quad x \in \mathbb{R}^+$$

$$= k_j H(x/k_j), \qquad x \in \mathscr{X}^j. \tag{22.3}$$

By definition,

$$K_*(x) \begin{cases} = 0, & x \in \mathscr{X}^0 \\ > 0, & x \in \mathscr{X}. \end{cases}$$

The set

$$\mathscr{N} := \{kH(x/k), \, k \in \mathscr{K}\}$$

is analogous to the technological menu $\mathscr{M}$ of §21.2.1, and the nomenclature developed there applies to it. Indeed, $\mathscr{N}$ is *advancing* in the sense that $k_{j+1}M > k_j M$, $k_{j+1}N > k_j N$.

The *cultural welfare function* is

$$\omega_*(x) = K_*(x)/x$$

$$= \frac{k_j H(x/k_j)}{x} = \frac{H(x/k_j)}{(x/k_j)}, \quad x \in \mathscr{X}^j.$$

The *marginal cultural product function* is

$$K_*'(x) = K_j'(x) = H'(x/k_j), \quad x \in \mathscr{X}^j$$

wherever the derivative is defined.

22.2.2   The Fission/Fusion Process

It was observed above that if the population of a given economy is big enough to supply the resources not only for its own infrastructure but for that of a second economy, it can divide, each of the new economies possessing its own infrastructure, and each yielding an average welfare higher than before the split. On the other hand, if productivity declines but a split is not feasible, it may increase productivity for several individual economies to fuse, in effect reallocating resources from infrastructure to production. These dual possibilities are referred to as the *fission/fusion (F/F) process*.

Begin with a single initial economic unit. An initial split produces separate economies of equal size. As economic conditions are identical in these, the conditions favoring fission or fusion will be the same for each. This implies that the number of economies in a culture, after fission has occurred j times, satisfies the equation

$$k_{j+1} = 2k_j \quad \text{with} \quad k_1 = 1,$$

so

$$k_j = 2^{j-1}, \quad j \in \mathbb{N}^{++},$$

and

$$\mathscr{K}^{F/F} = \{1, 2, 4, 8, \ldots\}.$$

22.2.3 The Shedding/Assimilation Process

If shedding and assimilating is also allowed, then any discrete number of economies can form. Families could emigrate from existing economies and form a new one. Alternatively, one or more groups could disband, their individual members scattering among and being assimilated into the remaining economies. This process of reorganization is denoted the *shedding/assimilation (S/A) process*. In this case,

$$k_j = j \in \mathbb{N}^{++} \quad \text{so} \quad \mathscr{K} \equiv \mathscr{K}^{S/A} = \{1, 2, 3, \ldots\}.$$

The distinction between this and the F/F process has some interesting implications. For example, in the fission/fusion process each preexisting economy must give up more than M families to form the new units. (It takes M just to get the requisite infrastructure for each economy.) After several fissions, total population must become very large to permit further fissions. Contrastingly, suppose the shedding/assimilation process is possible after j' fissions have occurred. From that period on, the infrastructural resources required to form an additional economy is just M, which can be acquired by assimilating a mere M/j individual families from each preexisting economy.

Assume that the cultural production function is based on the system production function used throughout this chapter, that is,

$$Y = B(x - M)^{\beta}(N - x)^{1-\beta}.$$

For the F/F process,

$$K_{J(x)}(x) = 2^{j-1}B(x/2^{j-1} - M)^{\beta}(N - x/2^{j-1})^{1-\beta}$$

$$= B(x - 2^{j-1}M)^{\beta}(2^{j-1}N - x)^{1-\beta}, \quad J(x) = j. \tag{22.4}$$

For the S/A process,[11]

$$K_{J(x)}(x) = jB(x/j - M)^{\beta}(N - x/j)^{1-\beta}$$

$$= B(x - jM)^{\beta}(jN - x)^{1-\beta}. \tag{22.5}$$

Notice that replication expands a given system's social space so that neighboring systems will intersect when, in the absence of replication, they would be separated.

22.2.4 Production and Environmental Capacity

The social slack $S = (N - x/k)$ that appears in each individual production function accounts for the internal diseconomies within a given unit economy as its population grows and the social "space" is "used up." But now that economies can split, the process of growth is no longer bounded by internal diseconomies. What must stop it is *external* diseconomies caused by the total population of all the economies operating together within a given culture in a bounded environment. Such a limit can exist if—given a fixed technology—the absorbing capacity of the environment must be reached and this absorbing capacity cannot be expanded by forming new groups with the same technology.

Like social slack, *environmental slack*, E, has a productivity-enhancing effect. Represent this by the *slack function* $g(E)$ and assume that

$$g(E) \begin{cases} = 0, & E = 0 \\ > 0, & E \in (0, \bar{x}] \\ = 1, & E \geq \bar{x} \end{cases} \tag{22.6}$$

and

$$g'(E) \geq 0, \quad E \in (0, \bar{x}), \quad \lim_{E \to \bar{x}} g'(E) = 0, \quad \text{and} \quad \lim_{E \to 0} g'(E) = \infty$$

where $\bar{x}$ is the *environmental capacity*.

Suppose that the maximum potential population in a given isolated region (island, continent, or planet) is bounded by a limit that depends on the techno-infrastructure and defines the environmental capacity $\bar{x}$. Then the environmental slack can be measured in terms of population using

$$E := \bar{x} - x.$$

The slack effect now becomes a *damage function* of x with

$$g(\bar{x} - x) = \begin{cases} = 1, & x = 0 \\ > 0, & x \in (0, \bar{x}) \\ = 0, & x = \bar{x} \end{cases} \tag{22.7}$$

where for all $x \in [0, \bar{x}]$,

$$\frac{dg}{dx} \leq 0, \quad \lim_{x \to 0} \frac{dg}{dx} = 0, \quad \text{and} \quad \lim_{x \to \bar{x}} \frac{dg}{dx} = -\infty.$$

22.2.5 The Constrained Cultural Production Function

The description of a system must be augmented to include $g(\cdot)$ and $\bar{x}$,

$$\mathscr{S} = \{\eta, \alpha, q, n, B, G(\cdot), M, N, g(\cdot), \bar{x}\}, \tag{22.8}$$

where for the time being the system index is omitted and the continuous productivity improvement rate is assumed to be zero. Both factors will be reintroduced in the next chapter. A constrained culture is a pair $\{\bar{S}, k\}$. The set of possible constrained cultures is $\mathscr{C} = \{\mathscr{S}, \mathscr{K}\}$. Define the dominating production zone index by

$$k_{\bar{j}} = \bar{J}(x) = \arg\max_{l \in \mathbb{N}^{++}} k_l H(x/k_l) g(\bar{x} - x)$$

where $k_l = 2^{l-1}$ is the variable number of economies and $l - 1$ the variable number of fissions.

The dominating production zone $\overline{\mathcal{X}}^{\bar{j}}$ for a culture with $k_{\bar{j}}$ autonomous economies and the dominating cultural production function are given by

$$\overline{X}^{\bar{j}} := \{x \mid \bar{J}(x) = k_j \quad \text{and} \quad \bar{K}_j(x) > 0\},$$

$$\overline{X} = \bigcup_{j \in \mathscr{N}} \overline{X}^{\bar{j}}, \quad \overline{X}^0 = \backslash \overline{X}, \quad \text{and for all} \quad x \in X^0, \bar{J}(x) \equiv 0, \bar{K}_0(x) \equiv 0.$$

Then the *constrained cultural production function* is

$$\bar{K}_*(x) := \bar{K}_{\bar{J}(x)}(x), \qquad\qquad x \in \mathbb{R}^+$$

$$= k_{\bar{j}} H(x/k_{\bar{j}}) g(\bar{x} - x), \quad x \in \bar{X}^{\bar{j}}. \qquad\qquad (22.9)$$

By definition,

$$\bar{K}_*(x) := \begin{cases} = 0, & x \in \bar{X}^0 \\ > 0, & x \in \bar{X}. \end{cases}$$

The cultural constrained welfare function is

$$\bar{\omega}_*(x) := \frac{H(x/k_j) g(\bar{x} - x)}{x/k_j}, \qquad x \in \bar{X}^j = \bar{K}_*(x)/x,$$

and the marginal cultural constrained welfare function is

$$\bar{K}'_*(x) := K'_j(x) g(\bar{x} - x) - K_j(x) g'(\bar{x} - x)$$

$$= H'(x/k_j) g(\bar{x} - x) - H(x/k_j) g'(\bar{x} - x),$$

wherever the derivative is defined in $\bar{X}^j$.

22.2.6   The Limits to Growth through Replication

The effect of a limited environmental capacity is to place a limit on growth through replication when the system is fixed. The maximum number of economies, $\bar{k}$, with admissible populations and that are compatible with environmental capacity, $\bar{x}$, is

$$\bar{k} := k_{\bar{j}} \quad \text{where} \quad \bar{j} = \arg \max_{l \in \mathcal{N}} \{k_l | k_l M < \bar{x}\}.$$

For the F/F mechanisms, the upper bound on the number of economies is, therefore,

$$\bar{k} = 2^{\bar{j} - 1}.$$

For the S/A process it is

$$\bar{k} = \bar{j}.$$

Above this number and given the replication process, population cannot reach the level required to populate more infrastructures without exceeding the environmental capacity. This implies that

$$\bar{X}^j = \emptyset \quad \text{for all} \quad j > \bar{j} \quad \text{and} \quad \bar{X}^0 \supset [0, M] \cup [\bar{k}M, \infty).$$

To illustrate the preceding concepts, use as the slack function

$$g(E) := (E/\bar{x})^\delta \quad \text{where} \quad 0 < \delta < 1,$$

so the damage function is

$$g(\bar{x} - x) = (1 - x/\bar{x})^\delta. \tag{22.10}$$

Using the functional form (22.4) for the F/F process, the dominating cultural production function is made up of pieces given by

$$\bar{K}_j(x) = B(x - 2^{j-1}M)^\beta (2^{j-1}N - x)^{1-\beta} (1 - x/\bar{x})^\delta, \quad x \in \bar{X}^j. \tag{22.11}$$

22.3   A "General" Model of Macroeconomic Evolution

We now integrate the various mechanisms described in this chapter and in chapter 21.

22.3.1   Multiple Cultures

In order to completely define a system, the environmental space and damage function must be taken into account. With these components, each system is denoted by

$$\mathscr{S}^i = \{\eta^i, \alpha^i, q^i, n^i, B_0^i, \tilde{B}^i, \rho^i, H_i(\cdot), M^i, N^i, g(\cdot), \bar{x}^i\}, \quad i \in \mathscr{T}. \tag{22.12}$$

I shall assume that the set of potential numbers of economies is generated by the fission/fusion process and is the same for each system,

$$\mathscr{K} \equiv \mathscr{K}^i = \{2^{j-1}, j \in \mathbb{N}^{++}\}.$$

Recall that a culture is identified by its system and its potential numbers of economies. Therefore, each *culture* is denoted by

$$\mathscr{C}^i = \{\mathscr{S}^i, \mathscr{K}\}, \quad i \in \mathscr{T}.$$

A *society* is now described as the collection of cultures it can potentially adopt,

$$\sum = \{\mathscr{C}^i, i \in \mathscr{T}\}.$$

Assume that all economies in a given culture (that is, all economies with the same system) improve productivity in the same way; and assume that if economies change in number through replication or merging, the level of productivity achieved by the previous economies in the culture is inherited by each of the new economies. This process will increase the maximum possible output, possibly speeding up the process of growth but destabilizing the society as the environmental capacity is filled.

22.3.2 Selection and the Dominant Production Function

The selection mechanisms among possible regimes must now allow for the choice of socioeconomic systems with their varied production and administrative technologies, the number of autonomous economies within the culture, and the fact that the productivity levels B^i, $i \in \mathcal{T}$ are state variables along with the population x. As before, let $B = \{B^i, i \in \mathcal{T}\}$.

The switching criterion must now be based on efficiency with respect to the processes of replication/merging, integration/disintegration, and regime jumping. The pair (i,j) represents the efficient system and the efficient number of fissions, j (or equivalently the efficient number of economies, k^j, with system i), and is defined by

$$(i,j) = IJ(x, B) := \min\left\{\arg\max_{p \in \mathcal{T}} \max_{l \in \mathbb{N}^{++}} k_l B^p H_p(x/k^l) g_p(\bar{x}^p - x)\right\}.$$

That is, $k^{ij} = 2^{j-1}$ is the efficient number of economies when the efficient system has index i.

The dominating production zone $\overline{X}^{ij}$ for a culture with $k_j \in \mathcal{K}$ autonomous economies, each with the system i, is given by

$$\overline{X}^{ij} := \{x \mid IJ(x) = (i,j) \text{ and } \overline{K}_{ij}(x, B^i) > 0\}$$

with the feasible and null regimes

$$\overline{X} = \bigcup_{i \in \mathcal{T}} \bigcup_{j \in \mathcal{N}^i} \overline{X}^{ij}, \quad \overline{X}^{00} = \backslash\overline{X}.$$

Setting $IJ(x) = (0,0)$ and $\overline{K}_{00}(x) \equiv 0$ for all $x \in \overline{X}^0$, the dominating production function for the society is

$$\bar{K}_*^*(x, B) := \bar{K}_{IJ(x)}(x, B)$$

$$= \max_{p \in \mathcal{J}} \max_{l \in \mathbb{N}^{++}} k_l B^p H_p(x/k^l) g_p(\bar{x}^p - x)$$

or equivalently

$$\bar{K}_{ij}(x, B^i) = k_j B^i H_i(x/k_j) g^l(\bar{x}^i - x), \quad x \in \bar{X}^{ij}.$$

It gives the maximum production a population can achieve by reorganizing itself into the number of economies that for the current population take best advantage of the available alternative systems. By definition,

$$\bar{K}_*^*(x, B) \begin{cases} > 0, & x \in \bar{X} \\ = 0, & x \in \bar{X}^{00}. \end{cases}$$

The constrained cultural welfare function, taking account of the multiple regimes, is now

$$\bar{\omega}_*^*(x, B) := \bar{K}_*^*(x, B)/x, \quad x \in \bar{X}$$

or

$$\bar{\omega}_{ij}(x, B) = \bar{K}_{ij}(x, B^i)/x, \quad x \in \bar{X}^{ij}.$$

The marginal product function for $x \in \bar{X}^{ij}$ is

$$\bar{K}_*^{*\prime}(x, B) = \bar{K}_{ij}'(x, B^i)/x$$

$$= k_j[B^i H_i'(x/k_j) g_i(\bar{x}^i - x) - B^i H_i(x/k_j)]g_i'(\bar{x}^i - x)], \quad x \in \bar{X}^{ij}.$$

wherever the derivative is defined.

22.3.3 The Switch Points of Demoeconomic Behavior

Since productivity levels are now endogenous, *the production, welfare, and marginal welfare functions all shift over time.* The subphase zones of demoeconomic behavior are analogous to those obtained in the previous versions of the theory, but because of the last observation, *these phase zones themselves shift over time.*

Define

$$\bar{\mathcal{D}}^{oij} := \{x \in \bar{X}^{ij} \mid 0 < \bar{\omega}_{ij}(x, B^i) \le \eta^i\}$$

$$\bar{\mathcal{D}}^{sij} := \{x \in \bar{X}^{ij} \mid \eta^i < \bar{\omega}_{ij}(x, B^i) \le \zeta^i\}$$

$$\bar{\mathscr{D}}^{nij} := \{x \in \bar{X}^{ij} \mid \zeta^i < \bar{\omega}_{ij}(x, B^i)\}.$$

Certainly,

$$\bar{X}^{ij} = \bar{\mathscr{D}}^{oij} \cup \bar{\mathscr{D}}^{sij} \cup \bar{\mathscr{D}}^{nij}.$$

Now

$$b(y) = b[\bar{\omega}_*^*(x, B^i)] = \begin{cases} 0, & x \in \bar{\mathscr{D}}^{oij} \\ (\alpha^i/q^i)[\bar{\omega}_{ij}(x, B^i) - \eta^i], & x \in \bar{\mathscr{D}}^{sij} \\ 1 + n^i, & x \in \bar{\mathscr{D}}^{nij}. \end{cases}$$

Therefore,

$$\begin{aligned} \bar{\mathscr{D}}^{oij} &= \{x \in \mathscr{X}^{ij} \mid (\alpha^i/q^i)[\bar{K}_{ij}(x, B^i) - \eta^i x] \le 0\} \\ \bar{\mathscr{D}}^{iuj} &= \{x \in \mathscr{X}^{ij} \mid 0 < (\alpha^i/q^i)\bar{K}_{ij}(x, B^i) - \eta^i x] \le (1 + n^i)x\} \qquad (22.13) \\ \bar{\mathscr{D}}^{nij} &= \{x \in \mathscr{X}^{ij} \mid (1 + n^i)x < (\alpha^i/q^i)[\bar{K}_{ij}(x_{ij}, B^i) - \eta^i x]\}. \end{aligned}$$

22.3.4 The Dynamic Structure and the Governing Regime

Define the $(ij)^{\text{th}}$ phase zone

$$\bar{\mathscr{D}}^{ij} := \bar{\mathscr{D}}^{sij} \cup \bar{\mathscr{D}}^{nij}.$$

It is the set of families in the ith culture with 2^{j-1} autonomous economies whose heirs will survive to adulthood. The null domain is

$$\mathscr{D}^{00} := X^0 \bigcup_{ij} \bar{\mathscr{D}}^{0ij} = \Big\backslash \bigcup_{ij} \bar{\mathscr{D}}^{ij}.$$

Define

$$\theta_{ij}(x) := b_i[\bar{\omega}_{ij}(x)]x$$

$$\theta_{00}(x) := 0.$$

The map $\theta_{ij}(\cdot)$ is the $(ij)^{\text{th}}$ phase structure, and the pair $(\theta_{ij}, \mathscr{D}^{ij})$ is the $(ij)^{\text{th}}$ regime. Also, extend the selection operator $IJ(\cdot, \cdot)$ to all of $\mathscr{D}^{00}$ by setting $IJ(x, B) = 0$ for all $x \in \mathscr{D}^{00}$.

With these definitions, the population dynamics $x_{t+1} = b_t x_t$ is given by the process

$$x_{t+1} = \theta_*^*(x_t, B_t) = \theta_{IJ(x_t, B_t)}(x, B_t), \quad x_t \in \mathbb{R} \qquad (22.14)$$

where $IJ(x_t, B_t)$ is the governing regime with 2^{j-1} autonomous economies all with system i.

The map $\theta_{ij}(\cdot, \cdot)$ is defined by the subregimes

$$\theta_{sij}(x, B^i) := (\alpha^i/q^i)[\bar{K}_{ij}(x, B^i) - \eta^i x]$$

$$\theta_{nij}(x, B^i) := (1 + n^i)x.$$

The state variables include the population x_t in terms of the number of "families," and the productivity levels $B_t = (B_t^i)_{i \in \mathscr{T}}$. The complete multiple-phase dynamics is described by

$$(i,j)_t = IJ(x_t, B_t), \tag{22.15}$$

$$\begin{aligned} B_{t+1}^i &= B_t^i + \rho^i B_t^i(1 - B_t^i/\tilde{B}^i) \\ B_{t+1}^p &= B_t^p, \quad p \neq i, \end{aligned} \tag{22.16}$$

and

$$x_{t+1} = \begin{cases} \bar{\theta}_{(0,0)_t}(x_t, B_t) = 0, & x_t \in \mathscr{D}^{00} \\ \bar{\theta}_{s(i,j)_t}(x_t, B_t) = (\alpha^i/q^i)[\bar{K}_{ij}(x_t, B_t^i) - \eta^i x_t], & x_t \in \mathscr{D}^{sij} \\ \bar{\theta}_{n(i,j)_t}(x_t, B_t) = (1+n)^i x_t, & x_t \in \mathscr{D}^{nij}. \end{cases} \tag{22.17}$$

22.3.5 Epochal Evolutions

Given initial conditions $x_0 = x, B_0 = (B_0^i)_{i \in \mathscr{T}}$, the theory describes economic history in terms of a sequence of episodes characterized by the system $\mathscr{S}^i$ and the number of autonomous economies that is locally efficient. Thus, we have:

The Characterization of Macroeconomic Development with Multiple Systems, Replication, and Technology Contagion:

number of households	x_t
aggregate production	Y_t
average welfare per family	y_t
number of children who survive to adulthood	$2b_t$
average family size	$2[1 + b_t]$
the technology levels	B_t
the time of entry into each episode	s_k
the sojourn of each episode	$[s_k, s_{k+1})$

the duration of each episode	$d_k = s_{k+1} - s_k$
the governing regime	$(i, j)_t = I(x_t, B_t)$
the dominant system in episode k	$p_k = i$
the governing number of economies	k_j
the size of the aggregate infrastructure	$k_j M^i$
the size of the labor force	$L_t = x_t - k_j M^i$
the social slack	$S_t = k_j N^i - x_t$
the environmental slack	$\bar{x}^i - x_t.$

22.4 A Mathematical World History

We are now going to see how the theory can be used to portray a few salient features of a very-long-run picture of human history.

Archaeologists, aided by modern methods of dating materials, have extended backward in time the picture of economic development already obtained by the economic historians, giving a proximate but coherent chronology of major developments on a worldwide basis that stretches back to the earliest evidence of a human presence. To social scientists accustomed to the extensive data resources of "advanced" economies, the archaeological record, no doubt, appears sketchy and essentially qualitative. For purposes of understanding socioeconomic evolution, however, there is a certain advantage in the very-long-run perspective it affords: salient features of the process stand out in bold relief.

Briefly, the great variety of human societies can be grouped into a relatively small number of forms based on production technology and social infrastructure. Any such grouping is somewhat arbitrary, and, by taking account of more and more details, a progressively finer array of types can be identified. In order to describe the major developments throughout the entire span of our species and to take advantage of the known archaeological information, at least the following should be considered: hunting and gathering, quasi-settled agriculture and herding, settled agriculture, complex societies, the city-state, trading empires, industrial economies, and the emerging information economy that is now integrating the entire world into a single, vast interconnected communications-oriented system.

Various geographical areas traversed these stages at very different times, and did not always proceed uniformly from lower to higher.

Rather, progress, especially in earlier times, was interrupted by reversions to lower stages. Moreover, there have typically been fluctuations in income, population, and capital. The overall picture is one of growth at fluctuating rates with sometimes smooth, sometimes turbulent transitions when jumps and reversions occurred until a higher stage became firmly established. It is this overall moving picture that we aim to represent.

22.4.1 The Macro Cultures

For the following illustrative purpose, I shall aggregate the eight systems just mentioned into (1) hunting and food collecting; (2) village agriculture (herding, quasi-settled and settled agriculture); (3) the city-state (complex societies and urban civilization); (4) trading empires; (5) the nation-state (the industrial revolution); and (6) the information economy.[12] First, let us outline the essential features of these several macro systems.

1. The Hunting Band Modern people (*Homo sapiens sapiens*) are thought to have emerged at least 100,000 years ago and eventually began replacing their Neanderthal predecessors (*Homo sapiens neanderthalensis*). Like their predecessors, they were hunting and food-collecting people but with improved social organization and technology. Their bands were probably twice the size of the earlier groups; their hunting-gathering technology involved an expanded ensemble of specialized stone implements of consummately skilled manufacture for various tasks of killing game, processing food, and fabricating clothing and habitations. This great advance was apparently made possible by an improved brain and vocal organs that yielded a distinct advantage in communication, hence in social interaction. The new linguistic capacity may also have been intimately related to a superior creative capacity that made possible the striking improvement in technology and adaptation to virtually every region and environment of the globe—a process that came to an end some 10,000 years ago when the world was essentially filled with representatives of the hunting and gathering culture.

Examples have been identified in the archaeological record of fluctuations in the populations of such people, especially those inhabiting relatively isolated areas. Vicissitudes of climate and other noneconomic factors no doubt played an important part, as they have throughout human history. But endogenous demoeconomic forces provide an additional explanation, and that is the aspect of development that is explicitly considered here. The fluctuations could have involved increases and decreases both in the number of people in given bands and in the number of bands, through fission, as described earlier in this chapter.

2. Village Agriculture About ten millennia ago three roughly coincident developments occurred: the megafaunal prey species disappeared, villages emerged, and plants and animals were domesticated. The subsequent agricultural and herding societies based on horticulture and animal husbandry marked the transition to a new epoch, one that occurred eventually throughout a very large part of the world. The new culture involved tribal organizations and a completely different technology that could support greater population densities. As this new culture spread, and it seems to have done so quite steadily, human numbers exhibited a worldwide surge. Earlier people were displaced, adopted the new culture themselves, or fused into larger and more productive groups than before. Here, too, evidence indicates that population fluctuated at various times and places. We know that reversions to the earlier hunting and food-collecting culture also occurred, a possibility that our theory can explain endogenously. Of course, external factors also played an important role. Nonetheless, hunting cultures gradually faded into remote areas relatively unsuited for agricultural activity. For purposes of illustrating the general model, we will not distinguish between the earlier quasi-settled (slash and burn) and settled agriculture.

3. Complex Societies and Urban Civilization (The City-State) About 3,000–5,000 years ago agricultural villages began to coalesce into centrally controlled, bureaucratically administered city-states that used writing and accounting to monitor and control economic transactions. At least in some parts of the world these early civilizations were preceded by intermediate, complex societies that possessed roads, schools, police, standing armies, and bureaucracies but not written language. Prominent examples of such societies persisted in Africa and Polynesia until the European commercial expansion.

It is known that in both cases reversions occurred. Indeed, it is here that structural fluctuations in the evolutionary sense played an especially important part. Obviously, the resources devoted to infrastructure played a much expanded role, and it is not unlikely that a very large fraction of a given economy's population would be involved in the political/military/religious/social activities that have more to do with producing cooperation and maintaining order than with the direct production of goods for consumption. Once complex societies adopt arithmetic and written language, the resulting civilization can pass on knowledge from one generation to the next more completely and with less deterioration. In spite of this improved ability to preserve culture, there is evidence of societies apparently abandoning written language and, from the retrospective point of view, passing through a kind of "dark age," as in the case of the Greek peoples toward the end of the second millennium B.C.[13]

4. Trading Empires   The emergence of empires about 500 B.C., based on widespread trading networks, made possible a great increase in specialization and a pronounced expansion again in productivity. Another surge in population followed. Development through the subsequent three millennia was turbulent, with various empires rising and falling, reverting to smaller agglomerations, only to be reorganized into different, yet in many ways essentially similar trading empires. In the West one thinks of Persia, Greece under Macedonian rule, Rome, and the Byzantine Empire. In China and India this rise and fall and rise again of empires played such a prominent role that it is given a fundamental place in their concepts of history and culture.

Social, cultural, and scientific progress of various kinds occurred throughout this age, leading after the Renaissance to a new commercial age when nation-states and trading empires spread civilization throughout much of the world.

5. The Industrial Revolution   The use of power technology beginning in the eighteenth century, based on improved metallurgy, steam, electricity, and large-scale production of consumer goods, distinguishes the industrial revolution. More advanced methods of business management (double-entry accounting) became widespread, banking institutions developed, legal institutions associated with the development of private property were established, and various new methods of political and educational organization emerged. Productivity quickly rose above that of earlier systems that were based to a much greater extent on rural production, and, compared to previous rates, a truly explosive growth in population took place. People emigrated from rural areas, creating populous, urban concentrations. This, too, has been a turbulent epoch, with many reorganizations of the basic economic units but with the culture as a whole experiencing a growth trend for some two centuries.

Table 22.1
The Macro Systems in Word History

Index	Description	Duration (years)	Duration (generations)	Initial Entry (generations ago)
1	Hunting band	100,000–8000 BC	3680	4080
2	Village agriculture	8000–3500 BC	180	400
3	City-state	3500–500 BC	120	220
4	Trading empires	500 BC–1750 AD	90	100
5	Industrial societies	1750–1975 AD	9	10
6	Global information economy	1975–present AD	1	1

6. The Information Economy Toward the end of the twentieth century a worldwide infrastructure of political institutions, electronic communications, and cultural transmissions has been in the process of development, involving even more vast infrastructural allocations of human and physical capital. The population explosion that began with the industrial revolution continued, then began to decelerate in some regions of the world. Nonetheless, at the time of this writing the growth rate for the world as a whole is still very high.

Summary A rough time line for the macro systems we are considering is given in table 22.1. We can summarize the essential characteristics as follows:

1. The several systems form an advancing sequence of increasing infrastructures and social spaces.

2. Demoeconomic conditions are a part of the prerequisites for the advance from one system to another. Thus, for example, hunting and food-collecting people did not adopt agriculture until the declining productivity of their own culture made a switch desirable. They integrated to form more or less settled tribal societies when the economic conditions became relatively favorable for agriculture.

3. Disintegrations followed by eventual reintegrations have occurred at least from the second through the fourth stages, and seemingly also through the fifth and sixth states. Viewing our history as a whole, we would say that it can be described in the language of chapter 9 as a conditional structural evolution involving structural fluctuations.

4. There have been more or less continuous improvements of productivity within each epoch, and the rates of improvement seem to have increased successively.

5. Although population fluctuation is an important aspect of the story, the long-run trend is strongly positive, and, viewed over a hundred thousand years of modern human evolution, appears to be explosive.

6. The bounds within which the entire human population could live as hunting and food-collecting peoples have been exceeded manyfold. Likewise, the number of people existing today could not have lived in any epoch prior to the industrial revolution. A reversion to an earlier system could only occur if it were accompanied by a drastic fall in population.

Of course, historical development through these stages has taken place in fits and starts, and at different times at different places. This is partly because the world is very heterogeneous in terms of topography and resource endowment, which means that similar technologies can have different productivities, and partly because many societies were more or less isolated from one another, which, in combination with even tiny perturbations in technology and/or social parameters, can—as we learned in the previous chapter—make huge differences in the sequencing and timing of the major transitions.

We will ignore all these details and assume that *all the economies of a given culture are homogeneous and that all economies start with the same initial conditions.*

22.4.2   Functional Forms and Parameter Values

To represent the technology, we assume the fission/fusion process of replication and use the production function (22.11) for each of the six socioeconomic systems but with different parameter values for each. Crude "guestimates" for the various parameters for each of the six macro systems are provided in table 22.2. It would be interesting to base these estimates on a careful survey of all the available evidence. That, however, would be a major undertaking in itself and is surely not necessary for the purpose at hand, which is not to mimic detailed quantitative properties of economic development in the very long run but rather to establish the theory's ability to explain some of the most prominent qualitative features of the process.

Table 22.2
Parameter Values in the Model (K = 1,000)

Parameter	System 1 Hunting	System 2 Village	System 3 City-state	System 4 Trading	System 5 Industrial	System 6 Information economy
η	0.5	0.5	0.45	0.63	0.7	0.4
α	0.6	0.6	1	1	1	1
q	1	0.9	1.5	2	2.2	1.1
n	0.01	0.018	0.053	0.045	0.3	0.25
B	2.97	2	2.5	2	0.4	1.75
$\tilde{B}$	7	10	12	8	30	30
ρ	0.0003	0.02	0.12	0.2	0.4	0.45
β	0.9	0.6	0.6	0.6	0.6	0.5
M	5	250	250K	$2.5K^2$	$5K^2$	$500K^2$
N	30	2000	$1K^2$	$10K^2$	$500K^2$	$2K^3$
δ	0.1	0.1	0.1	0.1	0.1	0.1
$\bar{x}$	$1.6K^2$	$25K^2$	$250K^2$	$1K^3$	$6K^3$	$24K^3$

22.5 A Numerical Simulation of World Development

22.5.1 What Should We Expect?

What can be expected from a simulation of the complete model? We should want to display an advance through the several systems, but with structural fluctuations between hunting and food-collecting and village agriculture systems, between village agriculture and city-state systems, and between city-state and trading empire systems. We should want to observe examples of fission, integration, and disintegration; we might expect to see endogenously induced population fluctuations in at least some of the regimes until the industrial revolution is reached.

Because the model does not account for many of the relevant details of technology and culture that influence actual events, we should not expect it to produce quantitative data that would match the empirical history of any special region or of any particular stretch of time, nor should we expect the number, duration, and timing of individual episodes to match actual events even if we knew such data exactly.

22.5.2 Macroeconomic Evolution to the Present

With these caveats, let us see what the model can do. A simulation was begun with an initial population of 100 families ($x_0 = 100$) and was con-

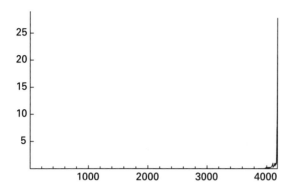

Figure 22.1
A simulated population history. Time is measured in "generations" of 25 years; population in billions of families.

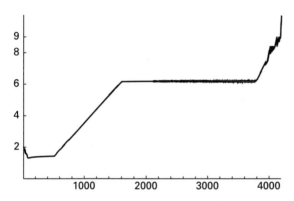

Figure 22.2
Logarithm of simulated population (to the base 10)

tinued for 4,185 periods or generations, a span of a little over 100,000 years. Figure 22.1 shows the graph of population for this run—virtually a vertical line over the present, caused by explosive growth after a takeoff a few centuries ago. Very close to the present, fluctuations can be observed, but, in terms of sheer numbers, human population—relative to the present—appears utterly insignificant until the most recent centuries.

This picture, however, is quite misleading, as can be seen by transforming family numbers to logarithms as in figure 22.2, which, in effect, gives a heavy weight to small populations. It reveals some prominent features that are disguised within the thickness of the horizontal axis in figure 22.1.

Thus, at the beginning of the run population is seen to fall, then increase very slowly. Next, it undergoes a considerable span of pronounced growth, reaches a kind of plateau, then enters an era of very rapid growth interspersed with fluctuations. Finally, the explosive growth of the recent past emerges as an almost vertical spike.

When the data are plotted for shorter time spans, using an expanded scale, still more detail in the behavior of population emerges. This is shown in figure 22.3. Panel (a) plots population for system 1 in millions of families. We see that rapid growth appeared only after some 25 millennia. Then irregular fluctuations of increasing magnitude appear. Panel (b) plots population for systems 2, 3 and 4, also in millions of families for some 300 generations. Prominent fluctuations are featured, no doubt an exaggeration of reality. Panel (c) plots population in billions of families for systems 4, 5, and 6 and brings the story up to the end of the twentieth century.

Turning to the underlying economic forces, we find much more going on in terms of structural evolution. This can be seen in figure 22.4, which displays the dominant system index at each time. The initial population in our simulation adopted the first system and remained with it for well over 3,000 generations. Growth during this long epoch thus occurred by means of the fission process.

A more detailed presentation of this epochal evolution is presented in figure 22.5. Panel (a) gives the system indexes from late in the system 1 epoch through to the "permanent" switch to system 4. Early in this evolution, temporary jump to system 2 occurs. It involves the integration of the very large number of hunting bands into a considerably smaller number of agricultural economies. They disintegrate, however, within a generation back into the original number of system 1 groups. Then structural fluctuation occurs, involving successive integrations and disintegrations, until the society locks into system 2 in period 3,784 or about 8050 B.C. Growth then continues within this village agriculture system by replication for 182 generations or 4,550 years. A similar sequence of structural fluctuations occurs between systems 2 and 3 and systems 3 and 4, with corresponding fluctuations in the number of economies as integrations and disintegrations bring about system jumps and reversions.

In panel (b) the story is continued. The switch to system 4 shown in panel (a) is indeed not permanent. A reversion occurs to system 3, followed by reintegration; also integration and disintegration between 4 and 5. The run terminates with a jump to system 6 (the global information

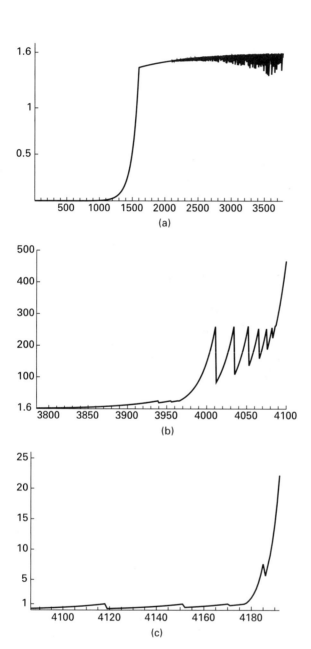

Figure 22.3
Details of the population dynamics. (a) System 1, population in millions of families. (b)
Systems 2, 3, and 4, population in millions of families. (c) Systems 4, 5, and 6, population in
billions of families. Note the changing time scale from (a) to (c).

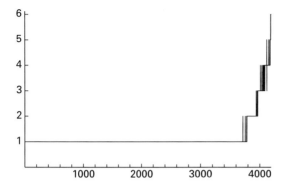

Figure 22.4
Simulated history of structural change in terms of the dominant systems index

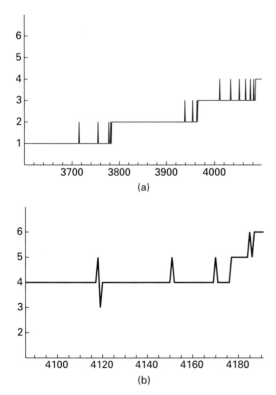

Figure 22.5
The evolution of socioeconomic systems. (a) Systems 1, 2, 3, and 4. (b) Systems 4, 5, and 6.
Note that structural fluctuations occur between 1 and 2, 2 and 3, and 3, and 4 and 5.

economy), which takes place through an integration of industrial economies, then a reversion followed by another jump. Note that the time scales used in diagrams (a) and (b) are different and obscure the fact that the great instabilities in a structural sense are compressed into the 10,000 years, since the advent of agriculture.

These outcomes approximate similar changes that are known to have occurred in reality and are briefly described at the beginning of this chapter. The parameters used and the crucial events taking place in this epochal evolution are summarized in table 22.2.

22.5.3 Two Conditional Scenarios

Using as initial conditions the variable levels reached at the end of the first simulation, two additional runs of the model were produced, carrying it forward into the future. The first retains all the model structure and parameters as in the base simulation just described. In a second simulation, which also begins where the base simulation terminated, all the parameters are retained except the natural growth rate n, which is reduced for system 6 from .25 to .05. The results in terms of population and structural change are shown in figures 22.6 and 22.7.

In the extended stories, population continues to grow within several "global information systems" until the environmental space becomes so crowded that productivity is drastically lowered and the model economy experiences a disastrous fall in population. Using our modeling language, when $n = .25$, the society self-destructs in some 5 generations, or about 2125 A.D.; when $n = .05$, growth is slower but a similar catastrophe occurs after 126 generations, or about 3 millennia.

These computations are not a forecast of what will happen. Rather, they are conjectures about what *could* happen if no fundamental changes in technology or social parameters take place, except, in the second case, for a very large reduction in the birth and survival rate.

22.5.4 Implications

In these model-generated histories, all of the structural features play a role. They depend on the functional forms, parameter values, and initial conditions. Perturbations in any of these, either once and for all or at intervals (fixed or random), must—almost surely—lead to different epochal evolutions and qualitative histories. This fact suggests that this very model, calibrated to represent the special conditions of various parts of

Table 22.3
Crucial Events in the Structural Evolution

	System 1 Hunting	System 2 Village	System 3 City-state	System 4 Trading	System 5 Industrial	System 6 Information economy
First switch to the system		3715	3939	4011	4118	4185
Period of locking into the system		3784	3966	4086	4177	4185
Year	102650 B.C.	8050 B.C.	3500 B.C.	500 B.C.	1775 A.D.	1975 A.D.
Duration in experiment (since locked)	3784	182	120	91	8	1

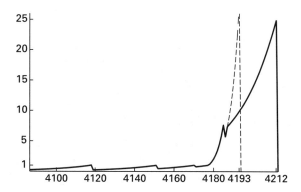

Figure 22.6
Conditional scenarios: population dynamics. The dashed line assumes $n = .25$ for system 6; the solid line assumes $n = .05$. Population is in billions.

the world that developed more or less independently for long periods of time, such as China, Polynesia, Europe, Africa, pre-Columbian America, and smaller more or less isolated areas within these great regions, could describe epochal evolutions and qualitative histories more accurately in a qualitative sense than when the model is used to represent the general trend in the world as a whole. The selection mechanisms, combined with the homogeneity of population and of technologies within cultures, in effect aggregates the entire world population into an undifferentiated culture at any one time, with the entire population switching regimes within the same generation. Such is manifestly not the case in reality. So it is not surprising that the progressions as shown in the graphs are only a coarse reflection of actual world history. In reality, there was and there is considerable overlapping of regimes, with vestiges of the first and second systems continuing through to the present century.

The theory does not explain *how* new systems appear in the menu of society's possible systems. The theory in general and the quantitative models that embody it neither explain the process of innovation that yields new systems nor incorporate the *process* of transition from one regime to another.

Even in its present form, however, various insights of considerable interest would seem to follow from the simulations. First, *model parameters that can be modified by factors not included in the model, but which work in reality, can have a potential impact on qualitative as well as quantitative*

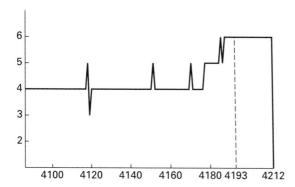

Figure 22.7
Conditional scenarios: epochal evolution. The dashed line is for $n = .25$ in system 6; the solid line is for $n = .05$.

model histories. This leaves plenty of room for forces in addition to the fundamental endogenous demoeconomic relationships; in particular, for aspects of human psychological and social character such as the effect of a great man who precipitates a transformation in the cooperative spirit of a people so as to permit a more effective infrastructure to emerge.

Second, instability is an essential aspect of evolution. If a regime is globally stable, then once it has been adopted, switching to another regime cannot occur. Only if a regime is unstable can a structural change take place. *Evolution is not the cause of instability, rather instability is a necessary condition for evolution.*

Third, technical advance in the form of learning by doing that raises average productivity within a regime while leaving the social and environmental spaces unchanged, enhances instability both in the sense of accelerating growth but also of triggering more frequent regime switching. As will be demonstrated in chapter 24, such continuous productivity improvement *must* under well-defined conditions eventually destabilize any regime. This suggests that as world population grows, more and more attention needs to be focused on expanding the social and environmental space so as to diminish the effects of internal and external diseconomies of population.

Fourth, if the environmental space is ultimately bounded, and if continuous productivity improvement within existing regimes takes place, then (again as will be shown in chapter 24) a catastrophic collapse must take place.[14] This suggests that the only alternative to expanding the social and environmental spaces is to modify the parameters of human reproduction, by lowering the preference for or increasing the cost of raising children to adulthood, or by developing voluntary or coercive bounds on the average number of children per family. Moreover, as the conditional scenarios illustrated, for an ultimate collapse to be avoided, the population growth rate *must* fall to zero or below.

Of course, if there should be no ultimate environmental bound, and if human ingenuity can continue to invent systems that will expand social space and environmental capacity, then—in theory—human numbers could continue growing forever.

23 Existence of Evolutionary Scenarios

Many different development scenarios are possible within the framework of our assumptions, depending on the number of systems, on the parameters, and on the initial conditions. We would like to determine whether precise answers can be obtained to the following questions concerning existence:

(i) Under what conditions could a given sequence of qualitative events occur?

(ii) In particular, could evolution through an entire sequence of specified regimes occur surely, or almost surely, or at least with positive measure? Or, would such a path be improbable?

(iii) Under what conditions can a society exist indefinitely?

(iv) Under what conditions can a society eventually collapse with positive measure or almost surely?

   In this chapter these questions are answered for a special class of "regular mountainous" multiple-phase dynamical systems. The results are then used in chapter 24 to determine the existence of various scenarios in the models of macroeoconomic evolution described in chapters 21–22.[1]

23.1   Epochal Evolutions and Transitional Histories

We begin by recalling necessary nomenclature from chapters 6 and 9.

23.1.1   Multiple-Phase Dynamical Systems and Transition Histories

Let $\{\theta_i(\cdot), \mathscr{D}^i, i \in \mathscr{T} := \{1,\ldots,\tau\}\}$ be a multiple-phase dynamical system (MPDS) defined on the non-negative real domain $\mathbb{R}^+$ by

$$x_{t+1} = \theta_i(x_t), \quad x_t \in \mathscr{D}^i, \tag{23.1}$$

or, equivalently,

$$x_{t+1} = \theta(x_t) := \theta_{I(x_t)}(x_t), \tag{23.2}$$

$$I(x) := \sum_{j=0}^{\tau} j\chi_{\mathscr{D}^j}(x) \tag{23.3}$$

where χ is the indicator function and where $\mathscr{D} := \bigcup_{i \in \mathscr{T}} \mathscr{D}^i$, $\mathscr{D}^0 := \backslash\mathscr{D}$, $\theta_0(x) \equiv 0$, $x \in \mathscr{D}^0$.

A trajectory, $\tau(x)$, satisfying (23.1) can be characterized by the epochal evolution,

$$\mathscr{E} := \{\mathscr{D}^{p_1}, \mathscr{D}^{p_2}, \ldots, \mathscr{D}^{p_k}, \ldots\},$$

which is the sequence of regimes through which the trajectory passes. Then we write $\tau(x) \sim \mathscr{E}$. If $\mathscr{E}$ is a finite epochal evolution with n episodes, then

$$\mathscr{E} = \mathscr{E}_{p_1, p_n} = \{\mathscr{D}^{p_1}, \ldots, \mathscr{D}^{p_n}\}.$$

A finite sequence can also be thought of as the first n episodes of an evolution which is unspecified after the nth episode. Interpreted in this way, $\mathscr{E}_{p_1, p_n}$ is called a *conditional evolution*.

Transition events characterize the switch from one regime to another within a given epochal evolution. Suppose we are in episode k of an epochal evolution and the regime index $p_k = i$. The *escape set* E^i is the set of points in the phase zone $\mathscr{D}^i$ that escape in one period. The *switching set* E^{ij} is the set of points in E^i that enter phase zone $\mathscr{D}^j$; that is, if $x_t \in E^{ij}$, then $\theta(x_t) \in \mathscr{D}^j$ and $p_{k+1} = j$.

If $j > i$ when the trajectory enters $\mathscr{D}^j$, the switching set, E^{ij}, is called a *jump*; if $j < i$, it is called a *reversion*. The *transition event*

$$U^{ij} := \bigcup_{s=0}^{\infty} \theta_i^{-s}(E^{ij}), \quad j \neq i$$

is called a *jumping event* J^{ij} if $j > i$ and a *reverting event* R^{ij} if $j < i$.[2] If $E^i = \varnothing$, then trajectories that enter $\mathscr{D}^i$ are *trapped*. If $E^i \neq \varnothing$, some trajectories will escape but some may remain in $\mathscr{D}^i$. The *trapping event* is the set of points T^i in $\mathscr{D}^i$ that do not eventually jump or revert. All trajectories that enter $\mathscr{D}^i$ eventually jump, revert, or are trapped. If we let J^i be the set of points that eventually jump and R^i the set of points that eventually revert, then $J^i = \bigcup_j J^{ij}$, $R^i = \bigcup_j R^{ij}$, and the trapping event is

$$T^i = \mathscr{D}^i \backslash (J^i \cup R^i).$$

An epochal evolution can be characterized by its *transitional history*, that is, by the sequence of transition events,

$$\mathscr{H} := \{U^{p_1, p_2}, U^{p_2, p_3}, \ldots, U^{p_k, p_{k+1}}, \ldots\}.$$

If $\mathscr{H}$ is an infinite sequence, then regime switching continues indefinitely. If the number of regimes is finite, structural fluctuation among them must occur. This structural fluctuation could be periodic or nonperiodic. That is, the sequence of integers $\{I(\theta^t(x))\}_{t=0}^{\infty}$ could be periodic, nonperiodic, or random.

If $\mathcal{H}$ is a finite sequence, then regime switching ends with a trapping event $U^{p_n, p_n} = T^{p_n}$.

Associated with any finite or conditional evolution $\mathcal{E}_{p_1, p_n} = \{\mathcal{D}^{p_1}, \ldots, \mathcal{D}^{p_n}\}$ is a *finite* or *conditional transition history*

$$\mathcal{H}_{p_1, p_n} := \{U^{p_1, p_2}, \ldots, U^{p_{n-1}, p_n}, S^{p_n} \subset \mathcal{D}^{p_n}\}$$

where $S^{p_n} = T^{p_n}$ if $\mathcal{H}$ is finite.

Since each $U^{ij} \subset \mathcal{D}^i$, we can write $\mathcal{H} \subset \mathcal{E}$. Certainly, $p_{i+1} > p_i \Leftrightarrow U^{p_i, i+1} = J^{p_i, p_{i+1}}$, and $p_{i+1} < p_i \Leftrightarrow U^{p_i, i+1} = R^{p_i, p_{i+1}}$. Therefore,

$$\tau(x) \sim \mathcal{E}_{p_1, p_n} \Leftrightarrow \tau(x) \sim \mathcal{H}_{p_1, p_n}. \tag{23.4}$$

23.1.2 General Switching and Existence Conditions

Denote the range of $\theta_i(\cdot)$ on $\mathcal{D}^i$ by $\mathbb{R}^i := \theta_i(\mathcal{D}^i)$. Then $E^{ij} = \theta_i^{-1}(\mathbb{R}^i \cap \mathcal{D}^j)$, from which follows the *switching conditions*:

$$\mathbb{R}^i \subset \mathcal{D}^i \Leftrightarrow E^i = \varnothing \quad \text{and} \quad T^i = \mathcal{D}^i$$

$$\mathbb{R}^i \cap \mathcal{D}^j \neq \varnothing \Leftrightarrow E^{ij} \neq \varnothing \Rightarrow U^{ij} \neq \varnothing$$

$$\Rightarrow J^{ij} \neq \varnothing \quad \text{if } j > i \tag{23.5}$$

$$\Rightarrow R^{ij} \neq \varnothing \quad \text{if } j < i.$$

Let $S^{p_n} \subset \mathcal{D}^{p_n}$ and define

$$U^{p_{n-1}, \ldots, p_n} := \bigcup_{s=1}^{\infty} \theta_{p_{n-1}}^{-s}(\mathbb{R}^{p_{n-1}} \cap S^{p_n}). \tag{23.6}$$

This is the set of points in $\mathcal{D}^{p_{n-1}}$ that eventually escape and enter the set S^{p_n} in regime p_n. Now construct the recursion

$$U^{p_{n-i}, \ldots, p_n} := \bigcup_{s=1}^{\infty} \theta_{p_{n-i}}^{-s}(\mathbb{R}^{p_{n-i}} \cap U^{p_{n-i+1}, \ldots, p_n}), \tag{23.7}$$

$i = 2, \ldots, n - 1$. Any trajectory that enters this set will wend its way through the conditional history $\mathcal{H}_{p_{n-i}, p_n}$, ending up in the set S^{p_n}. I shall call a nonempty set $U^{p_1, \ldots, p_n}$ or U^{∞} an *evolutionary potential*. Note that $U^{p_{n-i}, \ldots, p_n} \subset U^{p_{n-i}, p_{n-i+1}}$. By construction we get:

PROPOSITION 23.1 (Evolutionary Potentials)

(i) Let $\mathcal{H}_{p_1, p_n}$ be any conditional or finite transitional history. If $U^{p_1,\ldots,p_n} \neq \varnothing$, then

$$x \in U^{p_1,\ldots,p_n} \Leftrightarrow \tau(x) \sim \mathcal{H}_{p_1, p_n}.$$

(ii) If $\mathcal{E}$ is an infinite epochal evolution, set $S^{p_n} = U^{p_n, p_{n+1}}$ and let $U^{\infty} := \bigcap_{n=2}^{\infty} U^{p_1,\ldots,p_n} \neq \varnothing$. Then

$$x \in U^{\infty} \Leftrightarrow \tau(x) \sim \mathcal{E}.$$

If the number of epochs is infinite and if the sequence of regimes is non-cyclic, we must, in effect, construct an infinite sequence of conditional histories. *The implication is that the existence condition for an infinite evolutionary potential can never be derived explicitly even though it may "exist."*

A sufficient condition for the existence of finite or conditional transitional histories can be given for the general class of multiple-phase dynamical systems under consideration so far.

PROPOSITION 23.2 (Sufficient Conditions for Existence)   *Assume $S^{p_n} \neq \varnothing$, $U^{p_i, p_{i+1}} \neq \varnothing$, $i = 1, \ldots, n-1$,*

$$\mathbb{R}^{p_{n-1}} \cap S^{p_n} \neq \varnothing \quad \text{and} \quad \mathbb{R}^{p_i} \cap U^{p_{i+1}, p_{i+2}} \neq \phi, \quad i = 1, \ldots, n-2.$$

Then $U^{p_1,\ldots,p_n} \neq \varnothing$.

Proof   From (23.6), $U^{p_{n-1},\ldots,p_n}$ must be nonempty. Certainly, $U^{p_{n-i},\ldots,p_n} \subset U^{p_{n-i}, p_{n-i+1}}$, $i = 1, \ldots, n-1$. From (23.7), $U^{p_{n-i},\ldots,p_n} \neq \varnothing$, $i = 1, \ldots, n-1$. ∎

Let $p(\cdot)$ be a probability measure (absolutely continuous with respect to Lebesgue measure) defined on $\mathcal{D}^{p_1}$. Then we can say that, for initial conditions chosen at random, the chance that a trajectory can follow a given transition history $\mathcal{H}_{p_1, p_n}$ is $p(U^{p_1,\ldots,p_n})$. Thus, we can write,

$$\text{Prob}\{\tau(x) \sim \mathcal{H}_{p_1, p_n}\} = p(U^{p_1,\ldots,p_n}). \tag{23.8}$$

In other words, if an evolutionary potential has positive measure, then its corresponding transitional history, $\mathcal{H}_{p_1, p_n}$, occurs with positive measure. If $p(U^{p_1,\ldots,p_n}) = 1$, $\mathcal{H}_{p_1, p_n}$ occurs almost surely.

23.1.3 Regular Mountainous Dynamical Systems

In the formal analysis, attention will be restricted to the following special case.

DEFINITION 23.1 (Regular Mountainous Systems) *The MPDS (23.1) is regular mountainous if the following conditions hold. For each $i \in \{1, \ldots, \tau\}, \tau > 1,$*

(i) the phase domain $\mathscr{D}^i$ is an open or semi-open interval with boundary points l^i, u^i with $l^1 \geq 0, l^i < u^i, i = 1, \ldots, \tau;$

(ii) the phase domains are advancing, that is,

$$l^i < l^{i+1}, \quad u^i < u^{i+1}, \quad i = 1, \ldots, \tau - 1;$$

(iii) if $l^{i+1} \geq u^i$, then $[u^i, l^{i+1}] \subset \mathscr{D}^0$. Let $\mathscr{N}^0 := \{i \,|\, l^{i+1} \geq u^i\}$. (Note that $\mathscr{N}^0$ can be empty.) The null domain is defined by

$$\mathscr{D}^0 := [0, l^1] \bigcup_{i \in \mathscr{N}^0} [u^i, l^{i+1}] \cup [u^\tau, \infty);$$

(iv) each map $\theta_i(\cdot), i \in \{1, \ldots, \tau\}$ can be extended to an interval $\bar{\mathscr{D}}^i := [\bar{l}^i, \bar{u}^i] \supset \mathscr{D}^i$ where $\theta_i(\bar{l}^i) = \theta_i(\bar{u}^i) = 0$. Denote this extension of $\theta_i(\cdot)$ by $\bar{\theta}_i(\cdot)$. Note that if $i \in \mathscr{N}^0$, then $l^i = \bar{l}^i$ and $u^i = \bar{u}^i$ so $\mathscr{D}^i = \text{int} \, \bar{\mathscr{D}}^i;$

(v) the map $\bar{\theta}_i(x)$ is positive continuous, differentiable, and pseudo-concave almost everywhere on $x \in \bar{\mathscr{D}}^i$ (in particular, at any fixpoint), $i = 1, \ldots, \tau.$[3]

If the MPDS is regular mountainous, the map $\theta(\cdot)$ is said to be regular mountainous. It is not assumed that $\theta(x)$ is continuous on $\mathbb{R}^+$.

The *maximum and minimum states* within a given regime determine the possibilities of jumping, reverting, or trapping. The extrema of the ith phase structure on its phase domain are

$$x^{M_i} = \sup_{x \in \mathscr{D}^i} \theta(x), \quad x^{m_i} = \inf_{x \in \mathscr{D}^i} \theta(x), \quad i \in \{1, \ldots, \tau\}.$$

Their existence is given in:

PROPOSITION 23.3 (Local Extrema of Regular Mountainous Maps) *Assume the MPDS is regular mountainous. Then for each $i \in \{1, \ldots, \tau\},$*

(i) a maximizer x^{**i} and a minimizer x^{*i} on the closure of $\mathscr{D}^i$ satisfy, respectively, $x^{M_i} = \theta_i(x^{**i}), x^{m_i} = \theta_i(x^{*i});$

(ii) the range $\mathbb{R}^i = \theta_i(\mathscr{D}^i)$ *is an interval with* $c\ell\,\mathbb{R}^i = [x^{m_i}, x^{M_i}]$;

(iii) the maximizer x^{**i} *is unique;*

(iv) the minimizer $x^{*i} \in \{l^i, u^i\}$ *and* $x^{m_i} = \min\{\theta_i(l^i), \theta_i(u^i)\}$;

(v) if $i \in \mathscr{N}^0$, *then* $x^{m_i} = x^{m_{i+1}} = 0$.

Proof (i) A continuous map takes on its maximum and minimum values on a closed set. Since $\mathscr{D}^i$ is not closed, the maximizer or minimizer could occur at a boundary point of $c\ell\,\mathscr{D}^i$. (ii) Follows from continuity. (iii) Follows from pseudo-concavity. (iv) Also follows from pseudo-concavity. (v) From Definition 23.1 (iii) it follows that $i \in \mathscr{N}^0 \Rightarrow \mathscr{D}^i \cap \mathscr{D}^{i+1} = \varnothing$, so $\theta_i(u^i) = \theta_{i+1}(l^{i+1}) = 0$.   ∎

From this we get:

PROPOSITION 23.4 (Existence of Transition Events)

(i) Assume the MPDS is regular mountainous. Let $i, j \in \{1, \ldots, \tau\}$ *with* $i < j$. *Then*

(a) $x^{M_i} > l^j$ *and* $x^{m_i} < u^j \Leftrightarrow J^{ij} \neq \varnothing$;

(b) $x^{m_j} < u^i$ *and* $x^{M_j} > l^i \Leftrightarrow R^{ji} \neq \varnothing$;

(c) a fixpoint or cycle in $\mathscr{D}^i \Leftrightarrow T^{ii} \neq \varnothing$;

(d) nonempty transition events J^{ij}, R^{ji}, *or* T^{ii} *are either intervals or denumerable sequences of disjoint intervals where the intervals for trapping events can be degenerate, that is, consist of a point or a denumerable set of points.*

(ii) Suppose $l^1 > 0$ *and for some* $k, 0 \leq x^{m_k} < l^1$. *Then* $R^{k,0} \neq \varnothing$.

(iii) Assume $i \in \mathscr{N}^0$. *Then*

(a) $[x^{m_k}, x^{M_k}] \cap [u^i, l^{i+1}] \neq \varnothing \Rightarrow R^{k,0} \neq \varnothing$;

(b) $x^{M_i} > u^i \Rightarrow R^{i,0} \neq \varnothing$;

(c) $x^{M_{i+1}} > u^i \Rightarrow R^{i+1,0} \neq \varnothing$.

Proof

(i(a)) The inequalities and the continuity of θ_i on $\mathscr{D}^i$ imply that $\mathbb{R}^i \cap \mathscr{D}^j \neq \varnothing$. Since $\theta_i(\cdot)$ is continuous and strictly quasi-concave, E^{ij} is a nonempty interval if $j > i$ and at most the union of two intervals if $j < i$. Consequently, $J^{ij} = \bigcup_{s=0}^{\infty} \theta^{-s}(E^{ij}) \neq \varnothing$.

(i(b)) In this case, E^{ij} consists of one or two nonempty intervals.

(i(c)) Any trajectory that hits a point in a finite orbit must be trapped. Continuity implies that a nonempty trapping set contains at least one fixpoint.

(i(d)) Since each $\theta_i(\cdot)$ is strictly quasi-concave, it is either strictly monotonic or strictly bitonic. Therefore, E^{ij} is an interval and $\theta_i^{-1}(E^{ij})$ is at most two disjoint intervals; $\theta_i^{-2}(E^{ij})$ consists of at most four disjoint intervals; in general $\theta_i^{-s}(E^{ij})$ consists of at most 2^s disjoint intervals. Therefore, J^{ij} is at least a nonempty interval and at most a denumerable sequence of disjoint intervals. It follows that if $E^{ij} \neq \varnothing$, then $J^i = \bigcup_{j>i} J^{ij} \neq \varnothing$. If E^{ij} can be the union of two disjoint intervals, then $\theta^{-1}(E^{ij})$ is at most the union of four disjoint intervals, and so on. Correspondingly, $E^{ji} \neq \varnothing \Rightarrow R^j = \bigcup_i R^{ji} \neq \varnothing$. Since $T^i = \mathscr{D}^i \backslash (J^i \cup R^i)$, the trapping zone is also at most a denumerable sequence of disjoint intervals.

(ii) $l^1 > 0 \Rightarrow [0, l^1] \subset \mathscr{D}^0 \neq \varnothing$; $\quad 0 \leq x^{m_k} < l^1 \Rightarrow \mathbb{R}^k \cap \mathscr{D}^0 \neq \varnothing \Rightarrow R^{k,0} \neq \varnothing$.

(iii) First, note that $i \in \mathcal{N}^0 \Rightarrow [u^i, l^{i+1}] \subset \mathscr{D}^0$ and $x^{m,i+1} = 0$:

(a) $\mathbb{R}^k \cap \mathscr{D}^0 \neq \varnothing \Rightarrow R^{k,0} \neq \varnothing$;

(b) $u^i < l^{i+1} \Rightarrow x^{m_i} = 0 = x^{m_{i+1}}$, so $\mathbb{R}^k = [0, x^{M_k}]$. Therefore, $x^{M_i} > u^i \Rightarrow R^i \cap [u^i, l^{i+1}] \neq \varnothing$;

(c) similarly, $u^i < l^{i+1} = x^{m_{i+1}} = 0$, so $\mathbb{R}^{i+1} = [0, x^{M_{k+1}}]$. Therefore, $x^{M_{i+1}} > u^i \Rightarrow \mathbb{R}^{i+1} \cap [u^i, l^{i+1}] = \varnothing$. ∎

The number of transaction events that can potentially occur in a given phase domain is extremely large. To keep the discussion within reasonable bounds, *this chapter restricts the discussion of existence to regular mountainous systems that are continuously admissible*, whose trajectories can collapse only if they enter the first or last regime, and which (except for the last regime) can jump or revert only to an adjacent regime. I call these *strongly regular mountainous systems*.

DEFINITION 23.2 (Strongly Regular Mountainous Systems)

(i) An MPDS is continuously admissible if there exist constants b^i, $i = 0, \ldots, \tau$ such that

$$\mathscr{D}^i = (b^{i-1}, b^i], \quad i = 1, \ldots, \tau - 1, \quad \mathscr{D}^n = (b^1, b^\tau).$$

(ii) A regular mountainous system is strongly regular if and only if

(a) it is continuously admissible;

(b) $x^{m_{i+1}} > b^i$, $i = 1, \ldots, \tau - 1$;

(c) $x^{M_i} < b^{i+1}$, $i = 1, \ldots, \tau - 1$;

(d) $\bar{\theta}_i(x)$ is concave on $(\bar{l}^i, x^{\#\#i})$ where $x^{\#\#i}$ is the maximizer of $\bar{\theta}_i(x)$ on $\bar{D}^i$ (recall the definition of $\bar{\theta}_i$ in (Definition 23.1 (iv)).

The conditions given in the preceding definition imply:

PROPOSITION 23.5   *Assume that the MPDS is strongly regular mountainous. Then*

(i) it possesses at most two positive stationary states in each phase domain;

(ii) (a) $U^{i,i-1} = R^i \equiv R^{i,i-1} \neq \emptyset$, $i = 2, \ldots, \tau$,

(b) $U^{i,i+1} \equiv J^i \equiv J^{i,i+1} \neq \emptyset$, $i = 1, \ldots, \tau - 1$, and

(c) $U^{\tau,\tau-i} \equiv R^{\tau,\tau-i} \neq \emptyset$, $i = 1, \ldots, \tau$.

Proof

(i) The assumptions of Proposition 23.4 imply that $\bar{\theta}_i(x)$ is strictly quasi-concave on $[\bar{l}^i, \bar{u}^i]$, which implies the existence of a unique interior maximizer $x^{\#\#i}$ of $\bar{\theta}_i(x)$ on $[\bar{l}^i, \bar{u}^i]$. Consider the set $X^i := \{(x, y) \mid y \leq \bar{\theta}_i(x), x \in [\bar{l}^i, x^{\#\#}]\}$. This is a convex set by virtue of Definition 23.12(ii)(d). Assume there exists an $x \in \bar{D}^i$ such that $\theta(x) > x$. Then the ray segment $\{(x, x) \mid x \in \bar{D}^i\}$ intersects the boundary of X^i at least at one and at most at two positive points. Suppose there are two. Denote them $\bar{x}^{li}, \bar{x}^{ui}$. Then $\theta(\bar{x}^{li}) = \bar{x}^{li}$ and $\theta(\bar{x}^{ui}) = \bar{x}^{ui}$, which implies that $\theta'(\bar{x}^{li}) > 1$ and $\theta'(\bar{x}^{ui}) < 1$, which implies that $\theta(x) < \theta(x^{\#\#}) < x^{\#\#}$ for all $x > x^{\#\#}$, that is, $x > x^{\#\#} \Rightarrow \theta(x) < x$. So there can be no more fixpoints in $\bar{\mathcal{D}}^i$.

Now suppose $\{(x, x) \mid x \in \bar{\mathcal{D}}^i\} \cap X^i$ is a unique point. This implies that $\theta(x) > x$ for all $x \in (\bar{x}^{li}, x^{\#\#})$. As $\theta_i(x)$ is pseudo-concave, it is falling monotonically, and as $\bar{\theta}_i(u^i) = 0$, there must exist a fixpoint $\bar{x}^{ui} \in (x^{\#\#i}, u^i)$. The existence of a third fixpoint would contradict the monotonicity of $\bar{\theta}^i(x)$ on $[x^{\#\#}, u^i]$. To conclude, if $\bar{x}^{li} \in (l^i, u^i)$, then $\tilde{x}^{li} = \bar{x}^{li}$ is a stationary state of $\theta^i(x)$ in $\mathcal{D}^i$. If $\bar{x}^{ui} \in (l^i, u^i)$, then $\tilde{x}^{ui} = \bar{x}^{ui}$ is a stationary state of $\theta^i(x)$ in $\mathcal{D}^i$.

(ii(a)) Conditions $(a), (b) \Rightarrow R^{i,j} = \emptyset$, $j < i - 1$.

(ii(b)) Conditions $(a), (c) \Rightarrow J^{i,j} = \emptyset$, $j > i + 1$.   ∎

PROPOSITION 23.6 (Existence of Transitional Histories) *Assume that the MPDS is strongly regular mountainous. Let $\mathscr{H}_{p_1,p_n}$ be a conditional or finite transitional history (in the latter case $S^{p_n} = T^{p_n}$). Assume $p(\cdot)$ is a measure defined on $\mathscr{D}^{p_1}$ that is absolutely continuous with respect to Lebesgue measure. Assume S^{p_n} is a denumerable collection of intervals in $\mathscr{D}^{p_n}$ and assume that*

(i) $x^{m_{p_{n-1}}} < (\text{inf or sup})\ S^{p_n} < x^{M_{p_{n-1}}},$

(ii) $x^{m_{p_{n-i}}} < (\text{inf or sup})\ U^{p_{n-i},\ldots,p_n} < x^{M_{p_{n-i}}},\ i = 2,\ldots,n.$

Then $p(U^{p_1,\ldots,p_n}) > 0.$

Proof $\mathbb{R}^{p_{n-1}}$ is an interval; therefore $\mathbb{R}^{p_{n-1}} \cap S^{p_n}$ and $U^{p_{n-1},\ldots,p_n}$, each comprised of a denumerable set of intervals, are also. Likewise, the $\mathbb{R}^{p_{n-i}}$, $i = 2,\ldots,n-1$ are nonempty intervals. By recursion, $\theta_{p_{n-i}}^{-1} \times (\mathbb{R}^{p_{n-i}} \cap U^{p_{n-i+1},\ldots,p_n})$ is a set of nonempty intervals; therefore $U^{p_{n-i},\ldots,p_n}$ is also for $i = 2,\ldots,\ldots,n-1$. ∎

23.2 Scenarios

Let us refer to a specific finite or conditional transitional history as a *scenario*. Even if only a few phases are present, the number of possible scenarios can be extremely large. It is possible, however, to show how the existence of any arbitrary scenario can in principle be determined. We do this by focusing on three special conditional histories from which virtually any scenario can be constructed. These are *structural growth, structural decline, and structural 2-cycles.* The existence analysis is then completed by considering two very general types of strongly regular mountainous systems called "cascading" and "ratcheting."

23.2.1 Structural Growth and Structural Decline

First, consider structural growth. Let $1 \le p_1 = i < k = p_n \le \tau$. (Note that $p_n = k = i + n - 1$ and $p_1 = k - n + 1$.) Assume that $U^{p_j,p_{j+1}} = J^{i+j-1}$, $j = 1,\ldots,n-1$. The structural growth scenario can be designated by

$$\mathscr{H}_{p_1,p_n} = (J^i, J^{i+1},\ldots,J^{k-1}, S^k \subset \mathscr{D}^k). \qquad (23.9)$$

Set $J^{i,\ldots,k} := U^{p_1,\ldots,p_n}$. Then existence is given by the following.

PROPOSITION 23.7 (Structural Growth with Positive Measure)

(i)

(a) Assume that S^k is the union of a denumerable set of nondegenerate intervals and

$$x^{m_{k-1}} < \inf S^k < x^{M_{k-1}}.$$

(b) Assume the smaller fixpoint, $\bar{x}^{l_i}$, of $\theta_i(\cdot)$ on $(\bar{l}_i, \bar{u}_i)$, if it exists, and assume that

$$b^{k-j+1} > x^{M_{k-j}} > \max\{b^{k-j}, \bar{x}^{l_{k-j+1}}\} > x^{m_{k-j}}, \quad j = 2, \dots, n-1.$$

   Then $p(J^{i,\dots,k}) > 0$.

(ii) Assume (i)(a)–(b) and assume either

(c) $\theta(b^j) > b^j, j = 1, \dots, k$, or

(d) $\theta(b^{k-j}) > b^{k-j-1}$ and $|\theta'(x)| > 1$ for all $x \in (b^{k-j-1}, b^{k-j}) \backslash E^{i+j}$, $j = 2, \dots, n-1$.

Then $p(J^{i,\dots,k}) = 1$.

Proof

(i) Obviously, (a) $\Rightarrow \mathbb{R}^{k-1} \cap S^k \neq \varnothing$. Since $\mathbb{R}^{k-1}$ is an interval, $\mathbb{R}^{k-1} \cap S^k$ is a denumerable set of intervals. Let $J^{k-1,\dots,k} := \bigcup_{s=1}^{\infty} \theta^{-s}(\mathbb{R}^{k-1} \cap S^k)$. This set is also a denumerable set of intervals. Any trajectory that enters it arrives in S^k in finite time. Recall from (23.6)–(23.7) the recursive construction of $U^{i,\dots,k}$, i.e.,

$$J^{k-j,\dots,k} := \bigcup_{s=1}^{\infty} \theta^{-s}(\mathbb{R}^{k-j} \cap J^{k-j+1,\dots,k}),$$

$j = 2, \dots, n-1$. Each is nonempty in turn and, since each $\mathbb{R}^{k-j}$ is an interval, each $J^{k-j,\dots,k}$ is composed in turn of a denumerable sequence of intervals. Clearly, (b) $\Rightarrow \inf J^{k-j} = \max\{b^{k-j}, \bar{x}^{l_{k-j+1}}\}, j = 1, \dots, n$. Let $p(\cdot)$ be a probability measure on $\mathscr{D}^i$ absolutely continuous with respect to Lebesgue measure and assume supp $p = (b^i, b^i + \varepsilon)$ for some $\varepsilon > 0$. Then supp $p \cap J^{k-j} \neq \varnothing$. Therefore, $p(J^{i,\dots,k}) > 0$.

(ii) Conditions (b) and (c) $\Rightarrow \theta(x) > x$ for all $x \in (b^i, b^k)$ so all trajectories increase monotonically until they enter S^k.

(ii) Conditions (b) and (d) imply that in any regime $i, \ldots, k$ almost all trajectories escape. The first expression in (d) $\Rightarrow E^j := E^{j,j+1} \neq \emptyset$ and $E^{j,j-1} = \emptyset$. Therefore, almost all trajectories in one regime must jump into the next one in sequence. ∎

Turning to structural decline, assume

$$\tau > p_1 = k > i = p_n \geq 1.$$

Set $p_j = k - j + 1, j = 1, \ldots, n$. Note that $p_1 = k = i + n - 1$ and $p_n = i = k - n + 1$. Assume that $U^{p_j, p_{j+1}} = R^{k-j+1}, j = 1, \ldots, n - 1$. Then the structural decline scenario can be designated by

$$\mathcal{H}_{p_1, p_2} := (R^k, R^{k-1}, \ldots, R^{k-n+2}, S^{k-n+1}). \tag{23.10}$$

By an argument analogous to Proposition 23.7, existence is then given by the following.

PROPOSITION 23.8 (Structural Decline with Positive Measure) *Assume*

(a) $x^{m_{k-j+1}} < b^{k-j}, j = 1, \ldots, n - 1$;

(b) S^i *is the union of a denumerable set of nondegenerate intervals;*

(c) $\sup R^{k-j} < x^{M_{k-j+1}} < b^{k-j+1}, j = 1, \ldots, n - 2$;

(d) $\theta_{k-j+1}(b^{k-j+1}) < x^{M_{k-j+1}} < b^{k-j+1}, j = 1, \ldots, n - 2$;

(e) *either* $\theta_{k-j+1}(x) < x$ *for all* $x \in (b^{k-j}, b^{k-j+1})$

(f) *or* $|\theta'_{k-j+1}(x)| > 1$ *for all* $x \in (b^{k-j}, b^{k-j+1}) \backslash E^{k-j+1}$.

Then

(i) (a)–(c) $\Rightarrow p(R^{k, \ldots, i}) > 0$;

(ii) (a)–(f) $\Rightarrow p(R^{k, \ldots, i}) = 1$.

23.2.2 Structural Fluctuations and Cascading Scenarios

Another class of scenarios involve transition histories that can be described as *structural fluctuations*. These are sequences of jumping and reversion transitions in which, except for the last transition, any series of jumps is followed by a reversion, and any series of reversions is followed by a jump.

It was observed in §22.4.1 that structural fluctuations had occurred between the complex societies and village agriculture, and between city-states, nation-states, and trading empires. In order to derive existence conditions for such scenarios, we define a *structural 2-cycle*: a sequence of two alternating regimes. Let

$$U^{p_j, p_{j+1}} = \begin{cases} J^i & \text{for } j \text{ odd} \\ R^{i+1} & \text{for } j \text{ even}, \end{cases} \quad j = 1, \ldots, n-1.$$

Let $S^{p_n} \subset \mathscr{D}^{i+1}$ for n even and $S^{p_n} \subset \mathscr{D}^i$ for n odd, where S^{p_n} is an interval or set of nondegenerate intervals. Then

$$\mathscr{H}_{p_1, p_n} = (U^{p_1, p_2}, \ldots, U^{p_{n-1}, p_n}, S^{p_n})$$

$$= (J^i, R^{i+1}, J^i, R^{i+1}, \ldots, S^{p_n})$$

is a structural 2-cycle.

Let us call any finite scenario composed of sequences of structural growth, structural fluctuations, and structural decline a *cascading scenario*.

DEFINITION 23.3 (Cascading Systems)   *A cascading system is a strongly regular mountainous MPDS such that*

(a) for each $i \in \mathscr{T}$, $\theta_i(b^i) < b^i$, $\theta_i(b^{i-1}) < b^{i-1}$, and there exists a $y \in \mathscr{D}^i$ such that $\theta_i(y) > y$;

(b) $x^{M_i} > \tilde{x}^{l,i+1}$ for each $i \in \{1, \ldots, \tau - 1\}$ and $x^{M_i} > b^\tau$;

(c) $\theta_i(b^i) < \tilde{x}^{l_i}$ for each $i \in \mathscr{T}$;

(d) $|\theta_i'(x)| > 1$ for all $x \in \mathscr{D}^i \backslash E^i$ for each $i \in \mathscr{T}$.

PROPOSITION 23.9 (Existence of Structural 2-Cycles)   *Assume we are dealing with a cascading system. Then*

(i) for every $i \in \{1, \ldots, \tau - 1\}$ there exists an uncountable set $S^i \subset \mathscr{D}^i$ such that every trajectory entering S^i is periodic or chaotic and can be characterized by an infinite structural 2-cycle between $\mathscr{D}^i$ and $\mathscr{D}^{i+1}$;

(ii) for every $i \in \{1, \ldots, \tau - 1\}$ there exist finite structural 2-cycles ending in $\mathscr{D}^{i-1}$ for every odd n and ending in $\mathscr{D}^{i+1}$ above $\tilde{x}^{l,i+1}$ for every even n; structural 2-cycles are finite almost surely.

Proof

(i) The conditions in Proposition 23.15 (i) imply that each phase domain i possesses exactly two stationary states, $\tilde{x}^{l_i}, \tilde{x}^{u_i}$. Inequalities (i)–(iii) of that proposition imply that there exist points c', c'', d', d'', and e, all in $\mathcal{D}^i$, and a point f in $\mathcal{D}^{i+1}$ such that $\theta_i(c') = \theta_i(c'') = b^i$, $\theta_i(d') = \theta_i(d'') = \tilde{x}^{l,i+1}$ and $\theta_i(e) = \theta_{i+1}(f) = \tilde{x}^{l,i}$. Let $K := [\tilde{x}^{l,i}, \tilde{x}^{l,i+1}]$ and define a map $G(x)$ on K by

$$
G(x) := \begin{cases} \theta(x), & x \in K \setminus ([d',d''] \cup [e,f]) \\ \tilde{x}^{l,i}, & x \in [e,f] \\ \tilde{x}^{l,i+1}, & x \in [d',d'']. \end{cases}
$$

Then $G(\cdot)$ is a continuous map from K into K. Let $A := (c',c'')$ and $B := (b^i, \tilde{x}^{l,i+1})$. By construction, $G(A) = B$ and $G(B) \supset A \cup B$. From theorems 5.3 and 7.1 there exist admissible periodic itineraries where every A is followed by at least one B. Each such itinerary contains an admissible trajectory. Let $S \subset A$ be the set of initial conditions generating these trajectories. Now $A \subset \mathcal{D}^i$ and $B \subset \mathcal{D}^{i+1}$. Moreover, A and B are in the interior of K, so for all $x \in S$, $\theta^t(x)$ belongs to A or B and can therefore be characterized by an infinite structural 2-cycle.

(ii) Consider the restriction of $\theta(\cdot)$ to the set K (defined above). This map is strongly expansive on K in the sense of Definition 8.7. The set $E := [d',d''] \cup (e,f)$ is an escape set in K. Therefore, by Theorem 8.10 there exists an absolutely continuous measure μ conditionally invariant on K. Following Definition 8.7 there exists an α, $0 < \alpha < 1$, such that $\mu(\theta^{-1}(S)) = \alpha\mu(S)$ for all measurable $S \subset K$. Let $S = (e,f)$; then

$$\mu(\theta^{-1}(e,f)) = \alpha\mu(e,f)$$

$$\mu(\theta^{-2}(e,f)) = \alpha\mu(\theta^{-1}(e,f))$$

$$= \alpha^2\mu(e,f)$$

$$\mu(\theta^{-n}(e,f)) = \alpha^n\mu(e,f).$$

Therefore, escape from K into $\mathcal{D}^{i-1}$ occurs with positive measure $\frac{1}{1-\alpha}\mu(e,f)$. Likewise, escape from K into $[\tilde{x}^{l,i}, b^{i+1}]$ occurs with positive measure $\frac{1}{1-\alpha}\mu[d',d'']$.

Escape through either route occurs with measure $\frac{1}{1-\alpha}\mu(E)$. Consider the possibility of trapping in an infinite 2-cycle in K. The kickout time $n_\theta(x) = \max\{n \mid \theta^k(x) \in K, k = 1, \dots, n\}$. Therefore, $\mu\{x \mid n_\theta(x) \geq k\} = \alpha^k\mu(E)$ gives the measure of trajectories that remain in K for at least k periods.

Certainly,

$$\lim_{k \to \infty} \mu\{x \mid n_\theta(x) > k\} = 0.$$

That is, infinite structural cycles occur with zero measure; or, putting it the other way around, we have (ii). ∎

Remember that for strongly regular mountainous systems, any jumps or reversions in a cascading scenario can only occur between neighboring regimes, except for the τth regime, which cannot jump but can revert to any preceding regime or to the null regime. Notice also that all of the jumping and reverting qualitative events described in §S23.2 are non-empty.

THEOREM 23.1 (Existence of Growth, Decline, or Cascading Scenarios)

(i) Assume the MPDS is a cascading system, that $\mathcal{H}_{p_1,p_n}$ is any growth, decline, or cascading scenario with $p_1 = 1$, and that S^{p_n} is composed of a denumerable set of intervals. Then $p(U^{p_1,\dots,p_n}) > 0$.

(ii) If S^{p_n} consists of a cycle or stationary state, then $p(U^{p_1,\dots,p_n}) = 0$.

Proof

(i) Conditions (a)–(c) of Definition 23.3 satisfy Proposition 23.4, so $J^i \neq \varnothing$ for all $i \in (1, \tau - 1)$, $R^i \neq \varnothing$ for all $i \in (0, \tau)$, and all such events are composed of denumerable sets of intervals; and given τ finite, $R^{\tau,i} \neq \varnothing$ for all $i = 0, \dots, \tau - 1$. Therefore, any qualitative history terminating with $R^{\tau,i}$ can occur.

(ii) Any trajectory that hits a periodic point in $\mathcal{D}^{p_n}$ must be of finite length. Moreover, the sets $U^{p_1,\dots,p_n}$ must consist of denumerable sets of *points* with zero Lebesgue measure. ∎

Evidently, we get in particular:

COROLLARY 23.1   *Let $\mathcal{H}_{p_1,p_n}$ be any decline or cascading scenario with $p_{n-1} = j \in \{1, \tau\}$ and $p_n = 0$. Then $p(U^{p_1,\dots,p_n}) > 0$.*

These results imply that virtually any transitional history is possible in a cascading system. Those that get stuck in infinite cycles or stationary states occur with zero measure, but those that collapse occur with positive measure.

23.2.3   Ratcheting Progressions

As we were reminded above, world history as a whole seems to have experienced reversions and structural fluctuations, at the end of which more advanced systems (with larger infrastructures and greater population limits) have so far always been attained. These facts motivate the consideration of *structural progressions*: finite sequences of transitions in which any regime in a given scenario (except the last) is eventually followed by a jump to a regime with higher indexes.

Such scenarios are special cases of cascading scenarios, so we know that given the condition of Theorem 23.1, they exist with positive measure. As shall be seen in the next chapter, a still narrower class of cascading scenarios is of interest, *ratcheting progressions*: structural progressions in which, once a given regime i has been entered, no regime less than $i - 1$ can be attained unless $i = \tau$. That is, $p_{i-1} < p_{i+1}$, $i = 2, \ldots, \tau - 1$.

A ratcheting scenario can contain finite sequences of structural 2-cycles, but once a trajectory passes a "ratchet" in the more advanced of the two regimes, say $i + 1$, further structural 2-cycles can occur only between two neighboring regimes with indexes higher than i. Structural cycles need not occur between every two neighboring regimes or even between any of them, but structural and ratcheting progressions containing one or more finite structural 2-cycles can occur with positive measure. Then define:

DEFINITION 23.4 (Ratcheting Systems) *Ratcheting systems are strongly regular mountainous systems that possess the following properties:*

(a) for each $i = 1, \ldots, \tau, \theta_i(b^i) < b^i$ and there exists a $y \in \mathscr{D}^i$ with $\theta_i(y) > y$.
 Let

$$r^i = \begin{cases} b^{i-1} & \text{if } \theta_i(b^{i-1}) \geq b^{i-1} \\ \tilde{x}^{l,i} & \text{if } \theta_i(b^{i-1}) < b^{i-1}. \end{cases}$$

Then

(b) for each $i = 1, \ldots, \tau - 1, x^{M_i} > r^{i+1}, x^{M_\tau} > a^\tau$;

(c) $\theta_i(b_i) > r^i$;

(d) $|\theta_i'(x)| > 1$ for all $x \in \mathscr{D}^i \backslash E^i$.

Let $P^i := (r^i, b^i], i = 1, \ldots, n - 1$. Then, given (a)–(d), P^i is called the ratcheting zone and r^i the ith ratchet.

The existence of ratcheting progressions follows directly as a corollary of Theorem 23.1:

COROLLARY 23.2 (Existence of Ratcheting Progressions) *Assume the MPDS is a cascading system.*

(i) Let $\mathcal{H}_{p_1,p_n}$ be any ratcheting progression with $p_1 = 1$ and $p_n = \tau$. Then $p(U^{p_1,\dots,p_n}) = 1$.

(ii) If $\mathcal{H}_{p_1,p_n}$ is a ratcheting system, then every cascading scenario can be decomposed into a sequence of m ratcheting progressions, say

$$\mathcal{H}_{p_{n_i},p_n}, \quad i = 1,\dots,m$$

such that for each $i \in 1/2,\dots,m-1$ there exists a $j \in \{1,\dots,\tau-1\}$ such that $p_{n_i} = j$ and $p_{n_i} - 1 = \tau$.

The first statement says that *evolution occurs almost surely in the sense of a progression through all the regimes.* The second says that once the regime τ has been reached, a reversion to any earlier regime could occur, followed by another ratcheting progression that will again arrive at the last regime almost surely. It also implies that a sequence of ratcheting progressions that ends with $p_n = 0$ occurs with positive measure.

23.3   Appendix: Qualitative Histories

The qualitative behavior of trajectories during episodes goerned by individual regimes may be of considerable interest. Nonstationary behavior may involve three modes: *monotonic growth, G, monotonic decline, D, or fluctuation, F (nonmonotonic change).*

All three modes may be possible within a given phase domain, depending on the "profile" of the dynamic structure for that regime and the initial state of entry. After a period of growth, decay, or fluctuation within a given transition set, a jump to a higher or a reversion to a lower regime may take place. Another episode occurs, again characterized by growth, fluctuation, or decline, as the case may be. Or, a trajectory exhibiting one of these modes may become trapped, either converging to a stationary state or fluctuating in a cyclic or nonperiodic manner.

23.3.1   Qualitative Events and Qualitative Histories

The combination of a behavior mode with a transition event is a *qualitative event.* Nine possibilities are shown in table 23.1. To these possibilities must be added a tenth event in which a trajectory entering a given regime

Table 23.1
Qualitative Events

Transition Event	Behavior Mode		
	Grow G	Fluctuate F	Decline D
Jump J^{ij}	$G_{J^{ij}}$	$F_{J^{ij}}$	$D_{J^{ij}}$
Revert R^{ij}	$G_{R^{ij}}$	$F_{R^{ij}}$	$D_{R^{ij}}$
Trap T^{ii}	$G_{T^{ii}}$	$F_{T^{ii}}$	$D_{T^{ij}}$

"sticks" at a stationary state or cyclic orbit after a finite number of periods. This shall be referred to as a *sticking event* and will be denoted by the symbol $S_{T^{ii}}$.

We recall conventions from chapters 6 and 9. The qualitative event symbols arc used to denote the subset of state values where the given qualitative events occur. These subsets are also called *qualitative events*. Let $\mathscr{Z}$ be the collection of ten possible qualitative events. Let $Z^{ij} \in \mathscr{Z}$. Then a *qualitative history* is a denumerable sequence

$$\mathscr{Q} := \{Z^{p_1, p_2}, \ldots, Z^{p_{n-i}, p_n}, \ldots\}$$

where each $Z^{p_i, p_{i+1}} \in \mathscr{Z}$ gives the mode of behavior in episode i and the index of the subsequent regime in the sequence. A finite sequence,

$$\mathscr{Q}_{p_1, p_n} := \{Z^{p_1, p_2}, \ldots, Z^{p_{n-1}, p_n}, S^{p_n} \subset \mathscr{D}^{p_n}\},$$

is a *conditional qualitative history*. If $S^{p_n} = Z^{p_n, p_n}$ where $Z^{p_n, p_n} \in \{G_{T^{p_n, p_u}}, F_{T^{p_n, p_u}}, D_{T^{p_n, p_u}}, S_{T^{p_n, p_n}}\}$, it is a *finite qualitative history*.

If a trajectory $\tau(x)$ passes through an epochal evolution $\mathscr{E}$ it can be described by the qualitative history $\mathscr{Q}$, and we write $\tau(x) \sim \mathscr{Q}$. As each set $Z^{p_i, p_{i+1}}$ is a subset of $U^{p_i, p_{i+1}}$, it is clear that $\mathscr{Q} \subset \mathscr{H}$. That is, a qualitative history is a more detailed or "finer" qualitative description of a trajectory than is a transition history. This means that there may be several (indeed many) distinct qualitative histories, say $\mathscr{Q}_i$, such that $\mathscr{Q}_i \subset \mathscr{H}$ for each i.

The existence of qualitative histories can be characterized in a manner analogous to the existence of transition histories. Define

$$Z^{p_{n-1}, \ldots, p_n} := \bigcup_{s=1}^{\infty} \theta_{p_{n-1}}^{-s} (\theta_{p_{n-1}} (Z^{p_{n-1}, p_n}) \cap S^{p_n})$$

and the recursion

$$Z^{p_{n-i},\ldots,p_n} := \bigcup_{s=1}^{\infty} \theta_{p_{n-i}}^{-s}\left(\theta_{p_{n-i}}\left(Z^{p_i,p_{n-i+1}}\right) \cap Z^{p_{n-i+1},\ldots,p_n}\right),$$

$i = 2,\ldots,n-1$. Notice that $Z^{p_{n-1},\ldots,p_n} \subset Z^{p_{n-1},p_n}$. Any trajectory that enters this set will follow the conditional qualitative history $\mathcal{Q}_{p_{n-i},p_n} = \{Z^{p_{n-1},p_n}, S^{p_n}\}$. We then have by construction the following.

PROPOSITION 23.10 (Potential Qualitative Histories)

(i) Let $\mathcal{Q}_{p_1,p_n}$ be a conditional or finite qualitative history. In the latter case set $S^{p_n} = T^{p_n}$. If $Z^{p_1,\ldots,p_n} \neq \emptyset$, then $\tau(x) \sim \mathcal{Q}_{p_1,p_n} \Leftrightarrow x \in Z^{p_1,\ldots,p_n}$.

(ii) Assume $\mathcal{Q}$ is an infinite qualitative history and $S^{p_n} = Z^{p_n,p_{n+1}}$, $n = 2$, $3,\ldots$. If $Z^{\infty} := \bigcap_{n=1}^{\infty} Z^{p_1,\ldots,p_n} \neq \emptyset$, then $\tau(x) \sim \mathcal{Q} \Leftrightarrow x \in \mathcal{Z}$.

I shall call $Z^{p_1,\ldots,p_n}$ a *qualitative evolutionary potential* if it is nonempty. In a manner analogous to Proposition 23.6, we find the following:

PROPOSITION 23.11 (Existence of qualitative evolutionary potentials) *Let $\mathcal{Q}_{p_1,p_n}$ be a finite unconditional qualitative history. Assume $S^{p_n} \subset \mathcal{D}^{p_n}$ is an interval or a collections of intervals, and assume*

(i) $x^{m_{p_{n-1}}} < (\text{inf or sup})\ S^{p_n} < x^{M_{p_{n-1}}}$,

(ii) $x^{m_{p_{n-i}}} < (\text{inf or sup})\ Z^{p_{n-i+1},\ldots,p_n} < x^{M_{p_{n-1}}}$, $p = 2,\ldots,n$.

Then $Z^{p_1,\ldots,p_n} \neq \emptyset$.

In a manner analogous to (23.8), we can write

$$\text{Prob}\{\tau(x) \sim \mathcal{Q}_{p_1,p_n}\} = p(Z^{p_1,\ldots,p_n}) \tag{23.11}$$

where $p(\cdot)$ is a probability measure defined on $\mathcal{D}^{p_1}$.

23.3.2 Existence of Qualitative Events

Determining the conditions for which the various qualitative events can occur is equivalent to determining when the corresponding qualitative event sets are nonempty. There are a large number of possibilities depending on the positions of the boundaries separating the regimes, on the maxima and minima of the regimes, and on the local asymptotic and global stability/instability condition. In order to reduce the number of cases, I shall formally consider only strongly regular mountainous systems and *only those trajectories that occur for initial conditions in sets of positive Lebesgue measure.*

Let $p_i(\cdot)$ be a conditional probability measure defined on $\mathcal{D}^i$. Given that a trajectory enters the ith phase zone $\mathcal{D}^i$, we say that $0 < p_i(Z^{ij}) \le 1$ implies event Z^{ij} "occurs" with positive measure and that $p_i(Z^{ij}) = 1$ implies event Z^{ij} "occurs" almost surely. The discrete set of points not formally discussed are those that stick at a stationary state or hit a cyclic orbit in a finite number of periods, the endpoints of the phase domain, and points that map onto endpoints of phase domains.

The following results are easily established and are stated without proof, except for the most complicated case in which both jumps and reversions can occur within the same regime. At one extreme of simplicity are the situations in which all trajectories that enter a given regime are trapped. That case is given first.

PROPOSITION 23.12 (All Trajectories Are Trapped)   *Assume* $l^i < x^{m_i}$, x^{M_i} $< u^i$. *Then*

(i) all trajectories are trapped and $p_i(T^{ii}) = 1$;

(ii) there exists a unique stationary state, $\tilde{x}^{ui} \in \mathcal{D}^i$, *where one of the following holds:*

(a) (monotonic convergence)

$$0 \le \theta'(\tilde{x}^{ui}) < 1 \quad and \quad \theta(u^i) \ge \tilde{x}^{ui} \Rightarrow p(G_{T^{ii}}) > 0, \quad p(D_{T^{ii}}) > 0;$$

(b) (monotonic convergence from below)

$$0 \le \theta'(\tilde{x}^{ui}) < 1 \quad and \quad \theta(u^i) < \tilde{x}^{ui} \Rightarrow p(G_{T^{ii}}) > 0, \quad p(F_{T^{ii}}) > 0;$$

(c) (local dampening fluctuations occur with positive measure)

$$-1 < \theta'(\tilde{x}^{ui}) < 0 \Rightarrow p(F_{T^{ii}}) = 1;$$

(d) (locally expanding, bounded fluctuations persist almost surely)

$$\theta'(\tilde{x}^{ui}) \le -1 \Rightarrow p(F_{T^{ii}}) = 1;$$

(e) (fluctuations are strongly chaotic in $\mathcal{D}^i$)

$$|\theta_i'(x)| \ge \delta > 1 \quad for \ all \quad x \in \mathcal{D}^i \Rightarrow$$

there exists an absolutely continuous, invariant measure on $\mathcal{D}^i$ *and chaotic fluctuations occur almost surely.*

At another extreme of simplicity are cases where there is no stationary state in $\mathcal{D}^i$. Two cases arise. In one you have decline and reversion. In the other you have growth and jumping. In both cases the regime is globally unstable, that is, all trajectories that enter must escape, so we don't need the distinction about "almost surely." We state the following without proof.

PROPOSITION 23.13 (All Trajectories Escape)

(i) Assume $\theta(x) < x$ for all $x \in \mathscr{D}^i$:

(a) if $1 \le i \le \tau - 1$ and if $\lim_{x \to l^i} \theta_i(x) < l^i$, then all trajectories that enter $\mathscr{D}^i$ decline and revert to the preceding regime, i.e.,

$$D_{R^{i,i-1}} \equiv \mathscr{D}^i;$$

in particular, all trajectories that enter $\mathscr{D}^1$ decline and collapse;

(b) if $i = \tau$, then there exists a partition of $\mathscr{D}^\tau$, say $\{\mathscr{D}_0^\tau, \ldots, \mathscr{D}_{\tau-1}^\tau\}$, such that all trajectories that enter $\mathscr{D}_p^\tau$ decline and revert to regime $\tau - p$, $p = 1, \ldots, \tau$.

(ii) Assume $1 < i < \tau, \theta_i(l^i) > l^i$, and $\theta_i(u^i) > u^i$; then all trajectories grow and jump to the succeeding regime, i.e., $G_{J^{i,i+1}} = \mathscr{D}^i$. (Note that the inequality conditions cannot hold for $i = 1$ or τ.)

In between these extreme cases are those where trajectories escape or are trapped with positive measure.

PROPOSITION 23.14 (Jumping with Positive Measure)   Assume $\theta(l^i) > l^i$, $l^i < \theta(u^i) < u^i$, and $x^{M_i} > u^i$. Then growth and jumping occurs with positive measure,

$$p(G_{J^{i,i+1}}) > 0;$$

and

(a) (locally dampening fluctuations with positive measure with fluctuations and jumping possible)

$$-1 < \theta'(\tilde{x}^{u^i}) < 0 \Rightarrow p(F_{T^{ii}}) > 0, p(F_{J^{i,i+1}}) \ge 0;$$

(b) (locally expanding fluctuations within both trapping and jumping possible)

$$\theta'(\tilde{x}^{u^i}) < -1 \Rightarrow p(F_{T^{ii}}) \ge 0, \quad p(F_{J^{i,i+1}}) \ge 0, \quad and$$

$$p(F_{T^{ii}}) + p(F_{J^{i,i+1}}) > 1;$$

(c) (growth and fluctuations with jumping almost surely)

$\theta'(x) < -1$ *for all* $x \in \mathcal{D}^i \Rightarrow p(F_{Ji,i+1}) > 0$ *and*

$p(J^i) = p(G_{Ji,i+1}) + p(F_{Ji,i+1}) = 1.$

PROPOSITION 23.15 (Revert with Positive Measure (I))   *Assume* $\theta(u^i) < l^i < \theta(l^i)$ *and* $x^{M_i} < u^i$. *Then*

$p_i(D_{R^{i,i+1}}) > 0;$

and

(i) $0 \le \theta'_i(\tilde{x}^{ui}) < 1 \Rightarrow p(G_{T^{ii}}) > 0,\ p(D_{T^{ii}}) > 0,\ p(F_{T^{ii}}) > 0;$

(ii) $-1 < \theta'_i(\tilde{x}^{ui}) < 0 \Rightarrow p(G_{R^{i,i-1}}) \ge 0,\ p(F_{T^{ii}}) > 0,\ p(F_{R^{i,i-1}}) \ge 0;$

(iii) $\theta'_i(\tilde{x}^{ui}) > -1 \Rightarrow p(G_{R^{i,i-1}}) \ge 0,\ p(F_{T^{ii}}) \ge 0,\ p(F_{R^{i,i-1}}) \ge 0$ *with*

$p(G_{R^{i,i-1}}) + p(F_{T^{ii}}) + p(F_{R^{i,i-1}}) > 0;$

(iv) $\theta'_i(x) < -1$ *for all* $x \in \mathcal{D}^i \backslash D_{R^{i,i-1}} \Rightarrow p(G_{R^{i,i-1}}) > 0,\ p(F_{R^{i,i-1}}) > 0$ *with*

$p(D_{R^{i,i-1}}) + p(G_{R^{i,i-1}}) + p(F_{R^{i,i-1}}) = 1.$

PROPOSITION 23.16 (Revert with Positive Measure (II))   *Assume that* $\theta_i(l^i) < l^i,\ \theta(u^i) < u^i$, *and* $x^{M_i} < u^i$. *Assume also that there exists an* $x \in \mathcal{D}^i$ *such that* $\theta(x) > x$. *Then*

$p(D_{R^{i,i-1}}) > 0.$

(i) Assume also that $\theta_i(x^{M_i}) \ge \tilde{x}^{li}$; *then* $p(G_{T^{ii}}) \ge 0,\ p(D_{T^{ii}}) \ge 0,$ $p(F_{T^{ii}}) \ge 0$, *and* $p(G_{T^{ii}}) + p(D_{T^{ii}}) + p(F_{T^{ii}}) > 0$; *and*

(a) $0 \le \theta'(\tilde{x}^{ui}) < 1 \Rightarrow p(G_{T^{ii}}) > 0,\ p(D_{T^{ii}}) > 0;$

(b) $\theta'(\tilde{x}^{ui}) < 0 \Rightarrow p(F_{T^{ii}}) > 0.$

(ii) Alternatively, assume that $\theta_i(x^{M_i}) < \tilde{x}^{li}$; *then* $p(F_{R^{i,i-1}}) > 0$ *and*

(a) $0 \le \theta'_i(\tilde{x}^{ui}) < 1 \Rightarrow p(G_{T^{ii}}) > 0,\ p(D_{T^{ii}}) > 0,\ p(F_{T^{ii}}) > 0;$

(b) $-1 \le \theta'_i(\tilde{x}^{ui}) < 0 \Rightarrow p(F_{T^{ii}}) > 0;$

(c) $\theta'_i(\tilde{x}^{ui}) < -1 \Rightarrow p(F_{T^{ii}}) \ge 0;$

(d) there exists a set E such that if $\theta'(x) > x$ *for all* $x \in \mathcal{D}^i \backslash E$, *then* $p(F_{R^{i,i-1}}) = 1$ *(fluctuate and revert almost surely).*

Finally, the most complicated cases occur where both jumping and reverting can occur with positive measure.

PROPOSITION 23.17 (Jump and Revert with Positive Measure)

(i) Assume $\theta(l^i) < l^i, \theta(u^i) > u^i$. Then

$$p(D_{R^{i,i-1}}) > 0, \quad p(G_{J^{i,i+1}}) > 0, \quad and \quad p(D_{R^{i,i-1}}) + p(G_{J^{i,i+1}}) = 1.$$

(ii) Assume $\theta(l^i) > l^i, \theta(u^i) < l^i$, and $x^{M_i} > u^i$. Then

$$p(G_{J^{i,i+1}}) > 0, \quad p(F_{J^{i,i+1}}) > 0, \quad p(D_{R^{i,i-1}}) > 0, \quad p(F_{R^{i,i-1}}) > 0; \quad and$$

(a) $-1 \le \theta'(\tilde{x}^{ui}) < 0 \Rightarrow p(F_{T^{i,i-1}}) > 0;$

(b) $|\theta'(x)| > 1$ for all $x \in \mathscr{D}^i \backslash E^i$ where E^i is the escape set $\Rightarrow p(G_{J^{i,i+1}}) + p(F_{J^{i,i+1}}) + p(D_{R^{i,i-1}}) + p(F_{R^{i,i-1}}) = 1.$

(iii) Assume $\theta(l^i) < l^i, \theta(u^i) < u^i$, and $x^{M_i} > u^i$. Then

$$p(D_{R^{i,i-1}}) > 0, \quad p(G_{J^{i,i+1}}) > 0; \quad and$$

(a) $-1 < \theta'(\tilde{x}^{ui}) < 0 \Rightarrow p(F_{T^{ii}}) > 0;$

(b) $\theta(u^i) < \max K^i$ (where K^i is the escape and jump interval) $\Rightarrow p_i(F_{J^{i,i+1}}) > 0;$

(c) $\theta(u^i) < \tilde{x}^{li} \Rightarrow p(F_{R^{i,i-1}}) > 0;$

(d) $|\theta'(x)| > 1$ for all $x \in \mathscr{D}^i \backslash E^i \Rightarrow p(G_J \cup F_J \cup F_R \cup D_R) = 1.$

Proof

(i) The conditions imply the existence of a stationary state, $\tilde{x}^{li}$ with $\theta'(\tilde{x}^{li}) > 1$, and that $\theta(x) < x$ for all $x < \tilde{x}^{li}$, $\theta(x) > x$ for all $x > \tilde{x}^{li}$.

(ii) The conditions insure a single upper stationary state. By pseudo-concavity $x^{m_i} = u^i$, so $x^{m_i} < l^i$. Consequently, the escape set consists of two intervals, one yielding reversions and one yielding jumps. These intervals are constricted as follows. Clearly, $x^{m_i} = \theta(u^i) < l^i$. By continuity there exists a unique point $y < u^i$ such that $\theta_i(y) = l^i$. Then $D_{R^{i,i-1}} = (y, u^i)$ and is composed of the backward iterates of $D_{R^{i,i-1}}$. Likewise, by continuity and pseudo-concavity there exist two points, say b, c, such that $\bar{l}^i < b < x^{\#\#} < c < y$ such that $\theta_i(b) = \theta_i(c) = u^i$. Let $K^1 = (\max\{l^i, b\}, c)$. This is the set of points that jump in one period. The backward iterates include those that wind around $\tilde{x}^{ui}$. These give $F_{K^{i,i+1}}$ which, consisting of a sequence of intervals, has positive Lebesgue measure. If $b > l^i$, then $K^1 = (b, c)$ and the backward iterates of K^1 include a finite sequence of intervals, say $K^s, \ldots, K^p$, such that if $x \in K^s$, then

$\theta_i(x) \in K^{s-1}$ and $\theta_i(x) > x$, so for all $x \in K^p, \theta_i^{p-1}(x) \in K^1$ and $\theta_i^p(x) \in \mathscr{D}^{i+1}$. Therefore, $G_{K^{i,i+1}} = \bigcup_{s=1}^p K^s$.

(a) The derivative condition gives a neighborhood of $\tilde{x}^{ui}$ with dampening fluctuations.

(b) We know that there must exist points a,d such that $\bar{l}^i < a < b < c < d$ and such that $\theta_i(a) = \theta_i(d) = l^i$ and where b,c were defined above. By constriction, $D_{R^{i,i-1}} = (y, u^i)$. Let $R^2 = (\max\{\bar{l}^i, a\}, \min\{\bar{l}^i, b\}) \cup (c, d)$. Then for all $x \in R^2, \theta(x) \in D_{R^{i,i-1}}$. Thus, all points in the interval $E^i = (\max\{\bar{l}^i, a\}, d)$ escape $\mathscr{D}^i$. The derivative condition then gives the existence of a conditionally invariant measure, yielding escape in finite time almost surely.

(iii) The results here follow more or less from arguments analogous to those in (ii). ∎

Given these existence conditions, existence for any particular qualitative evolutionary histories for regular mountainous and cascading MPDSs can be derived in a manner analogous to the argument of §23.2.

24 Generic Behavior in Macroeconomic Development

The purpose of this chapter is to show how the analysis of chapter 23 can be used to establish the existence of relevant scenarios of macroeconomic evolution. Our goal is to trace the existence conditions back to the structural features of each model: first for the basic evolutionary model, then for the grand dynamic model.

24.1 The Basic Evolutionary Model (BEM)

We are concerned with a society $\sum = \{\mathscr{S}^i, i \in \mathscr{T}\}$ where $\mathscr{S}^i = \{b^i(\cdot); (\alpha^i, q^i, \eta^i, n^i), H_i(\cdot); B^i, M^i, N^i\}$.

24.1.1 Properties of Production

Recall the production function defined in equation (21.1) which is repeated here for reference:

$$H_i(x) := \begin{cases} 0, & x \in \backslash (M^i, N^i) \\ B^i G_i(x - M^i, N^i - x), & x \in (M^i, N^i) \end{cases} \tag{24.1}$$

Recall the description of the technology menu $\mathscr{M}$ in §21.2. The technology menu is *advancing* if

$$M^{i+1} > M^i \quad \text{and} \quad N^{i+1} > N^i, \quad i \in \mathscr{T}. \tag{24.2}$$

An advancing technology i is *isolated* if $N^{i-1} < M^i$ and $N^i < M^{i+1}$. Then $(M^i, N^i) \cap (M^j, N^j) = \varnothing$ for all $j \neq i$. If a technology is not isolated, then it *intersects*. Advancing technologies are *overlapping* if the feasible sets of neighboring technologies i and $i + 1$ intersect, that is, if

$$M^{i+1} < N^i. \tag{24.3}$$

A sequence of advancing, overlapping technologies is *sequentially overlapping* if neighbors overlap but non-neighbors are separated, that is, if

$$N^i < M^{i+2} \quad \text{for all} \quad i \in [1, \tau - 2]. \tag{24.4}$$

The examples shown in figure 21.1 illustrate intersecting, overlapping, and sequentially overlapping technologies.

Each dominant technology zone belongs to the corresponding feasible production set, that is, $\mathscr{X}^i \subset (M^i, N^i)$. If i, j are dominating technologies, then $\mathscr{X}^i \cap \mathscr{X}^j = \varnothing$. If an advancing technology menu is *overlapping* and *each* dominating technology zone, $\mathscr{X}^i$, *is an interval*, then we shall say that it is *connected*.

If all technologies in a given menu satisfy one of the above conditions, then we shall say that the menu is, respectively, isolated or intersecting, overlapping or sequentially overlapping, connected, or sequentially connected. On the other hand, if some of the technologies are isolated while others possess one of the above properties, then we shall say that the menu is *piecewise intersecting, piecewise overlapping, piecewise connected*, as the case may be. Taking account of the strict concavity of the production function on the feasibility regime, the following can be derived.

PROPOSITION 24.1 (Properties of Production)

(i) Assume that the technology menu $\mathcal{M}$ is finite and piecewise intersecting. Then

(a) the dominating technology zone of each isolated technology is the open interval $\mathcal{X}^i = (M^i, N^i)$;

(b) the dominating technology zone of each intersecting technology is the union of a finite number of closed, open, or half-open intervals;

(c) the restriction of the dominating production function $H^*(x)$ to each constituent interval of each dominating technology zone is continuous, positive, and strictly concave;

(d) the dominating welfare function $\omega^*(x)$ is well defined and continuous on $\mathbb{R}^+$, and single-peaked (pseudo-concave and strictly quasi-concave) on each interval piece of $\mathcal{X}^i$, $i \in \mathcal{T}^*$; the marginal productivity function is well defined, continuous, and monotonically decreasing on each interval in each dominating production zone.

(ii) Assume $\mathcal{M}$ is overlapping. Let $a^i = \arg\min_y \{H_i(y) = H_{i+1}(y)\}$ and assume

$$H_{i+1}(x) > H_i(x) \quad for \ all \quad x \in (a^i, N^{i+1}), \tag{24.5}$$

$i = 1, \ldots, \tau - 1$. Let $a^0 = M^1$ and $a^\tau = N^\tau$. Then

(a) M is connected and

$$\mathcal{X}^i = (a^{i-1}, a^i], \quad i = 1, \ldots, \tau - 1$$

$$\mathcal{X}^\tau = (a^{\tau-1}, a^\tau)$$

$$\mathcal{X} = (a^0, a^\tau)$$

$$\mathcal{X}^0 = (0, M^1] \cup [N^\tau, \infty);$$

(b) the production function of $H_i(\cdot)$ is continuous, positive, and strictly concave on $\mathcal{X}^i$ for each $i = 1, 2, 3, \ldots, \tau$;

(c) the dominating welfare function $\omega^*(x)$ is single-peaked (pseudo-concave and strictly quasi-concave) on each interval of $\mathcal{X}^i$ and the function $H^{*\prime}(x)$ is well defined, continuous almost everywhere, and monotonically decreasing almost everywhere (except at the boundaries of the dominating production zones).

It is easy to construct examples that show that if the technologies are overlapping but are not sequentially connected, then one technology could switch to another if population increased and then switch back after population increased still more. Connectedness that depends on (24.5) means *this* kind of reswitching cannot occur.

24.1.2   Properties of the Dynamic Structure

Recall the definitions of §21.3.1–21.3.3 which lead to the dynamic structure (21.8) or (21.9). The phase zones of the dynamical system under consideration belong to the dominating technology zones, i.e., $\mathcal{D}^i \subset \mathcal{X}^i \subset (M^i, N^i)$. Since the production function $H_i(x)$ is strictly concave on the feasible set (M^i, N^i), we get the following.

PROPOSITION 24.2 (Properties of the Regimes $(\theta_i, \mathcal{D}^i)$)

(i) The phase zone $\mathcal{D}^i \neq \varnothing$ if and only if $\mathcal{X}^i \neq \varnothing$ and $y^{M_i} > \eta^i$. If $y^{M_i} \leq \eta^i$, then $\mathcal{D}^{i0} = \mathcal{X}^i$.

(ii) If $y^{M_i} > \eta^i$ and technology i is isolated, then

(a) there exist constants l_i, u_i with $M^i < l_i < u_i < N^i$ such that

$$\mathcal{D}^i = (l_i, u_i) \quad and \quad \mathcal{D}^{i0} = (M^i, l_i] \cup [u_i, N^i);$$

(b) if, in addition, $y^{M_i} > \zeta^i$, there exist constants r_i, s_i with $l_i \leq r_i < s_i \leq u_i$ such that

$$\mathcal{D}^{si} = (l_i, r_i] \cup [s_i, u_i) \quad and \quad \mathcal{D}^{ni} = (r_i, s_i);$$

(c) $\theta_i(x)$ is concave on $\mathcal{D}^i$; the s-subphase structure $\theta_{si}(x)$ is strictly concave on $\mathcal{D}^{si}$ and the n-subphase structure $\theta_{ni}(x)$ is linear on $\mathcal{D}^{ni}$.

(iii) Assume the menu $\mathcal{M}$ is piecewise intersecting. Then

(a) each nonempty $\mathcal{D}^i$ is the union of a finite number of disjoint open, closed, half-open intervals;

(b) if $\mathcal{D}^i$ is nonempty, then $\theta_i(x)$ is concave on each interval piece of $\mathcal{D}^i$, linear on each nonempty interval piece of $\mathcal{D}^{ni}$, and strictly concave on each nonempty interval piece of $\mathcal{D}^{si}$.

We can now show that there exists an equivalent BEM that is regular mountainous.

PROPOSITION 24.3   *Let $\mathcal{M}$ be an advancing piecewise intersecting technology menu and $\sum = \{\theta_i(\cdot), i \in \mathcal{T}\}$ be the corresponding BEM. There exists an equivalent BEM, $\sum^u := \{\theta_k(\cdot), k \in \mathcal{S} := \{1, \dots, \sigma\}$ where $k = K(x)$ is the dominating index for $x \in \mathcal{D}^k$ such that*

$$\theta_{I(x)}(x) = \theta_{K(x)}(x) \quad \text{for all} \quad x \in \mathbb{R}^+$$

and such that $\sum^u$ is regular mountainous.

Proof   Using Proposition 24.2(iii), we can form a partition of each phase zone into the set of intervals it contains, labeling them consecutively in their natural order. Let n_i be the number of intervals in the ith phase zone and let $\{\mathcal{D}^{i,j}, j = 1, \dots, n_i\}$ give the decomposition of $\mathcal{D}^i$ into its constituent intervals. Then $\mathcal{D} = \bigcup_{i=1}^{\tau} \bigcup_{j=1}^{n_i} \mathcal{D}^{i,j}$. The natural ordering establishes a one-one map $k(i, j)$ such that for each $k = 1, \dots, \sigma = \sum_{j=1}^{\tau} n_j$ there is one and only one pair (i, j) such that $\mathcal{D}^k \equiv \mathcal{D}^{i,j}$ and $\theta_k^l(x) \equiv \theta_i(x)$ for all $x \in \mathcal{D}^k$. Let $\mathcal{K} := \{1, \dots, \sigma\}$. By construction, $x \in \mathcal{D}^k$, $y \in \mathcal{D}^l \Rightarrow x < y$ for any pair $1 \le k < l \le \sigma$. From Proposition 24.2(iii(b)), each $\mathcal{D}^k$ is an interval and $\theta_k(x)$ is concave on each $\mathcal{D}^k$.   ∎

The conditions for a BEM to be continuously admissible are given in the following.

PROPOSITION 24.4   (i) *A society $\sum = \{\mathcal{H}, \mathcal{M}\}$ is continuously admissible if, and only if,*

(a) the technology menu $\mathcal{M}$ is connected with dominant technology zones $\mathcal{X}^i = (a^{i-1}, a^i], i = 1, \dots, \tau - 1, \mathcal{X}^\tau = (a^{\tau-1}, a^\tau)$ where $a^0 = M^1$ and $a^\tau = N^\tau$;

(b) there exist constants $b^0 \in \mathcal{X}^1$, $b^\tau \in \mathcal{X}^\tau$ such that

$$\omega_1(b^0) = \eta^1 \quad \text{and} \quad \omega_\tau(b^\tau) = \eta^\tau;$$

(c) $\omega_i(a^i) > \eta^i, i = 1, \dots, \tau - 1.$

(ii) If the society is continuously admissible, let $b^i = a^i$, $i = 1, \ldots, \tau - 1$. Then

$$\mathscr{D}^i = (b^{i-1}, b^i], \quad \mathscr{D}^\tau = (b^{\tau-1}, b^\tau), \quad \mathscr{D} = (b^0, b^\tau),$$

and $\theta_i(x) > 0$ for all $x \in \mathscr{D}^i$.

$$\mathscr{D}^0 = [0, b^0] \cup [b^\tau, \infty).$$

Proof Exploit the pseudo-concavity of the welfare functions to show that $\omega_i(x) > \eta^i$ for all $x \in (a^{i-1}, a^i]$, $i = 2, \ldots, \tau - 1$; $\omega_1(x) > \eta^i$ for all $x \in (b^0, a^1)$; and $\omega_\tau(x) > \eta^i$ for all $x \in (a^{\tau-1}, b^\tau)$. ∎

Notice that $\theta(x)$ on $\mathscr{D}$ may not be continuous at the boundaries of the phase zones even though $\sum$ is continuously admissible because of parameter differences among the constituent systems. (You can see this by constructing graphical examples.)

24.1.3 Generic Dynamics

To show that cascading and ratcheting scenarios exist generically, we proceed constructively, taking advantage of the regularity properties of our assumed technology. First, recall that the function $B^i G(x - M^i, N^i - x)$ is stretchable, so its maximizer is constant but its maximum increases continuously (and proportionally) with the productivity level parameter B^i. Recall also that $G'_i(x) \to \infty$ as $x \to M^i+$ and $G'_i(x) \to -\infty$ as $x \to N^i-$.

Now consider

$$\theta_i(x) = \min\left\{ \frac{\alpha^0}{q^i} [B^i G_i(x - M^i, N^i - x) - \eta^i x], (1 + n^i)x \right\}. \tag{24.6}$$

From the properties of production just described and using Proposition 24.4, we get:

PROPOSITION 24.5 *Assume the technology menu is connected. For large enough $B^i, i \in \mathscr{T}$,*

(i) $\sum$ is continuously admissible;

(ii) $x^{M_i} = \max_{x \in \mathscr{D}^i} \theta_i(x) = (1 + n^i)x^{si} = \frac{\alpha^i}{q^i}[B^i G_i(x^{ai} - M^i, N^i - x^{si}) - \eta^i x^{si}]$;

(iii) $B^i \to \infty \Rightarrow x^{si} \to N^i$, $x^{M_i} \to (1 + n^i)N^i$, $b^1 = a^1 \to N^1$, and $\theta'_i(x^{si}) \to -\infty$.

We can now set forth the principal results of this section. We show that for any finite cascading or ratcheting scenario there exists a robust set of basic evolutionary models, each of which possesses a corresponding non-empty, evolutionary potential with positive measure.

THEOREM 24.1 *Cascading scenarios are generic in the basic evolutionary model.*

Proof To construct a cascading system, begin with $i = 1$ and choose M^1, N^1 so that $0 \leq M^1 < N^1$. From Proposition 24.4, for large enough B^1 there must exist two positive stationary states $\tilde{x}^{l_1}$, $\tilde{x}^{l_2}$ such that $\theta_1'(x^{si}) = -1$. Since θ_1 is strictly concave on (x^{s1}, b^1), it follows that $\theta_1(\cdot)$ is expansive on (b^0, b^1), and this can be done for any M^1, N^1. Let $\mathcal{B}^1$ be the set of technology parameters that satisfy these conditions. Choose any one set $(B^1, M^1, N^1) \in \mathcal{B}^1$, then choose M^2, N^2 so that $0 \leq M^1 < M^2 < N^1 < N^2$. In this case a^1 satisfies $B^1 G_1(a^1 - M^1, N^1 - a^1) = B^2 G_2(a^1 - M^2, N^2 - a^1)$ and is positive. By choosing M^2 close enough to N^1 but not too close and B^1 large enough, we can obtain $b^1 = a^1$ such that $\theta_1(b^1) < \tilde{x}^{l_1}$ and $x^{M_1} > b^1$. We have now satisfied Proposition 23.9 for $i = 1$ and have guaranteed that $D_{R^2} \neq \emptyset$. Therefore, structural 2-cycles between the two regimes can occur with positive measure.

Now increase B^2 until $\tilde{x}^{l,2}$, $\tilde{x}^{u,2}$ exist, $x^{M_1} > \tilde{x}^{l_2}$, and $\theta_2'(x^{s2}) = -1$. Then $\theta_2(\cdot)$ is expansive on (b^1, N^2). Let $\sum_2$ be the system with $\tau = 2$. Then $\sum_2$ is a cascading system. Because all the critical states change continuously with changes in the parameters, for any $(B^1, M^1, N^1) \in \mathcal{B}^1$ there exist a robust range of parameters B^2, M^2, N^2 depending on (B^1, M^1, N^1) for which $\sum_2$ is cascading. For convenience, let $\pi^1 = (B^1, M^1, N^1)$. Then $\pi^1 \in \mathcal{B}^1$. Let $\Pi^1 \equiv \mathcal{B}^1$ and define $\Pi^{1,2} := \{\pi^1, \pi^2 \,|\, \pi^2 \in \mathcal{B}^2(\pi^1)$ and $\pi^1 \in \mathcal{B}^1\}$. Let $\sum_2(\Pi^{1,2})$ be the set of systems for which $(\pi^1, \pi^2) \in \Pi^{1,2}$. By construction, all such systems are cascading.

To proceed, assume that $(B^1, M^1, N^1), \ldots, (B^{i-1}, M^{i-1}, N^{i-1})$ have been chosen recursively so that the family of maps $\theta_1(x), \ldots, \theta_{i-1}(x)$ satisfy the cascading conditions of Definition 23.3. Then exactly as was done for regime $i - 1$, B^i and M^i can be chosen so as to satisfy the cascading conditions for regime i, $i = 2, \ldots, \tau - 1$. In an analogous manner to the foregoing, let $^1\pi^i := (\pi^1, \ldots, \pi^i)$ and let $\Pi^{1,i} := \{^1\pi^i \,|\, \pi^i \subset \mathcal{B}(^1\pi^{i-1})$, $^1\pi^{i-1} \in \Pi^{1,i-1}\}$, $i = 3, \ldots, \tau$. Then for each i, $\sum_i(\Pi^{1,i})$ is a family of cascading systems, $i = 1, \ldots, \tau - 1$. Given $^1\pi^{\tau-1} \in \Pi^{1,\tau-1}$, $a^\tau = N^\tau$. Choose

(B^τ, M^τ, N^τ) with $\theta_\tau(b^\tau) = 0$ so that $x^{M_i} > b^\tau$ and $\theta'_i(x) < -1$ for all $x \in \mathcal{D}^\tau$. Find $b^\tau(B^\tau, M^\tau, N^\tau) \in \mathcal{B}^\tau({}^1\pi^{\tau-1})$ when ${}^1\pi^{\tau-1} \in \Pi^{1,\tau-1}$. The condition of Definition have been satisfied for all ${}^1\pi^\tau \in \Pi^{1,\tau}$. Notice that the family of parameters $\Pi^{1,\tau}$ depend on the demoeconomic parameters n^i, η^i. But such a family exists for any $(\alpha^i, q^i, n^i, \eta^i) \in \mathbb{R}^4_{++}$, $i = 1, \ldots, \tau$. ∎

This theorem, combined with Theorem 23.1, implies:

COROLLARY 24.1 *Finite scenarios of structural growth, decline, fluctuation, and progression with or without collapse are all generic in a BEM.*

24.2 The Basic Evolutionary Model with Learning by Doing (BEM-LD)

The basic model of macroeconomic evolution with continuous productivity improvement described in §21.4 treats the technology parameter, B^i, as a state variable governed by a monotonically increasing learning-by-doing or contagion process (21.10). The model incorporates two new parameters for each technology regime, the learning-by-doing or contagion parameter ρ^i and the technology potential $\tilde{B}^i$. In addition to the initial population x_0, for each regime an initial technological level B_0^i must be specified. The resulting dynamical system can be written

$$i_t = I(x_t, B_t) := \arg \max_{l \in \mathcal{T}} \{B^l B_l(x_t - M^l, N^l - x_t)\}, \tag{24.7}$$

$$x_{t+1} = \theta_t(x_t, B_t) := \max\{0, \{\min\{(\alpha^i/q^i)[BG_i(x_t - M^i, N^i - x_t)]$$
$$-\eta^i x_t, (1+n)x_t\}\}, \tag{24.8}$$

$$B_{t+1}^{i_t} := (1 + \rho^{i_t})B^{i_t} + \rho^{i_{t+1}}(B_t^{O_{t+2}}/\tilde{B}_t^{i_t}) \tag{a}$$

$$B_{t+1}^{j_t} := B_t^{j_t}, \quad j_t \neq i_t. \tag{b}$$
$$\tag{24.9}$$

Beginning with initial conditions

$$x_0, \quad B_0 = (B_0^1, \ldots, B_0^\tau), \quad i_0 = I(x_0, B_0), \tag{24.10}$$

a sequence (i_t, x_t, B_t), $t = 1, \ldots$, is generated.

THEOREM 24.2 *Let $\sum^{ld}$ be a BEM-LD such that the initial technology menu $\mathcal{M}(B_0)$ is overlapping. Then*

(i) there exist technology potentials $\tilde{B}$ such that $\sum(\tilde{B})$ is a ratcheting system;

(ii) the learning-by-doing process generates a sequence of models $\sum(B_t)$ such that for some s, $\sum(B_t)$ is a ratcheting system for all $t \geq s$;

(iii) for some $T \geq s$ there exists a scenario $\mathcal{H}_{p_1, p_T}$ such that $p_T = 0$ and $p(U^{p_1, \ldots, p_T}) = 1$.

Proof Since the technology levels are now endogenous variables, the resulting multiple-phase dynamical system lives in $\mathbb{R}_{++}^{1+\tau}$ state space with state variables $(x_t, B_t^1, \ldots, B_t^\tau)$. However, it is a reducible system, or "doubly recursive." Beginning with the initial conditions x_0, B_0, the index $i_1 = i_0$ is selected, then x_1 and B_1 are determined; given these, the index $i = i_1$ is obtained, then x_2 and B_2, and so on. At each stage the qualitative events that can occur, given the parameters $(M^i, N^i, \rho^i, \tilde{B}^i, \alpha^i, q^i, \eta^i, n^i)$ $i = 1, \ldots, \tau$, depend on the technology levels.

This implies that all the critical parameter values that determine the transition and qualitative event zones become functions of the technology levels also. Thus, the fixpoints of the extended map $\bar{\theta}_i(x, B_t^i)$ are functions of time, $\bar{x}_t^{li}, \bar{x}_t^{ui}$, as are the phase zone boundaries (l_t^i, u_t^i), the maximum and minimum potential populations, $x_t^{M_i}, x_t^{m_i}$, and so on.

Given the analysis of §24.1, it is evident that for positive social parameters $(\alpha^i, q^i, \eta^i, n^i)$, the parameter $(\tilde{B}^i, M^i, N^i)$, $i = 1, \ldots, \tau$, can be chosen so that the corresponding basic evolutionary model is a ratcheting system. (Remember that the technology potentials $\tilde{B}$ place an upper bound on productivity growth.)

Viewed in isolation, the learning-by-doing process (24.9) is asymptotically stable for any i fixed with B_t^i increasing monotonically as t increases and bounded above by the technology supremum $\tilde{B}^i$. Moreover, as long as the dominating regime does not switch, the behavior of (24.9(a)) is independent of x_t. With these observations we can characterize the trajectories of the complete model.

Begin with x_0, B_0 such that $i_0 = 1$ and consider the sequence $(x_t, B_t)_{t=1}^s$. Given the properties of the contagion process, B_t^1 increases until the jumping transition set opens up. Then, either $\theta_1(x_s, B_s^1) \in E^1$ and $x_{s+1} \in \mathscr{D}^2$ or the process continues with B_t^1 continuing to increase and E^1 widening. As a result, either escape occurs or the process continues in $\mathscr{D}^1$ and $\theta_1'(x_t, B_t^2)$ decreases until $\theta_1'(x_t^{s1}) < -1$, in which case $p_1(B_{J^1}) + p_1(F_{J^1}) = 1$. That is, a jump will occur in finite time almost surely. Let this occur at time $t = s_1$. Now $x_{t+1} \in \mathscr{D}^2$ and $B_{s_1}^2 = B_0^2$. As the economy develops in the second regime, B_t^2 will increase as long as $I(x_t, B_t) = 2$. If $x_{s+1} \in D_{R^2}$, then a 2-cycle $(J^1, R^1, J^1, R^1, \ldots, S^{p_n})$ will exist. During alternate epochs, B_t^1 and B_t^2 will continue to increase, the first regime will become increasingly unstable, and escape will occur sooner and sooner. Eventually, $\tilde{x}_t^{l,2}$ will exist and become a ratchet. Then the structural 2-cycle scenario $\mathscr{H}_{p_1, p_n}$ with $S^{p_n} = P^2$ will become inevitable with $p(U^{p_1, \ldots, p_n}) = 1$.

By repeating the argument recursively, escape to successively higher regimes must occur almost surely and every scenario will become a structural progression until regime τ is entered. Here the learning by doing destabilizes the regime until either a reversion to a lower regime or a collapse occurs. In the former event, learning continues in the regime entered until a jump occurs and another ratcheting progression occurs, inevitably reaching $\mathscr{D}^1$ again.

What we have shown is that for any $\sum$ with overlapping technology there exist technology suprema such that $\sum(\tilde{B})$ is a ratcheting system and that for large enough t, $\sum(B_t)$ becomes a ratcheting system almost surely. Thus, there exists a $\mathscr{H}_{p_1, p_n}$ with $p_n = 0$ such that after enough and long enough epochs in $\mathscr{D}^\tau$, $p(R^{\tau,0}) \to 1$ so that there exists p_n such that $p_n = 0$ almost surely, which implies that $p(U^{p_1, \ldots, p_n}) \to 1$. ∎

THEOREM 24.3 *Ratcheting systems are generic in the basic evolutionary model.*

Proof Let $\mathscr{M}$ be *any* overlapping technology menu and let $\mathscr{H}$ be *any* socioeconomic behavior menu. Given M^1, N^1 there exists a $\bar{B}^1$ such that for all $B^1 \geq \bar{B}^1$, $\tilde{x}^{l,1}$ exists and is a ratchet. Then there exists a $\bar{B}^2$ so that $\tilde{r}^2$ exists. Next, there exists $\bar{\bar{B}}^1$ such that for all $B > \bar{\bar{B}}^1$, $M^{M_1} > \tilde{r}^2$. And so on. The same story pertains. Notice that as B^3 increases, b^2 and $\tilde{x}^{l,3}$ decrease, so when the ratchet $\tilde{r}^3$ emerges, $\tilde{r}^2$ is still a ratchet.

By recursion, a sequence of $B^1, \ldots, \bar{\bar{B}}^\tau$ can be obtained such that for any $B^i > \bar{\bar{B}}^i$, $\sum$ is a ratcheting system. ∎

When combined with Theorem 23.1 and its corollary, the preceding two theorems imply the following.

COROLLARY 24.2 *(i) Finite structural growth, decline, fluctuation, progressions, and ratcheting progressions are all generic in the basic evolutionary model with learning by doing.*

(ii) For any finite τ, after a long enough period of time, collapse occurs almost surely.

24.3 The Replication and Merging Model (RAM)

A process of economic growth (or decline) through replication (or merging) with a given sociotechnical regime was described as a multiple-phase dynamical process. It leads to a system very much like the basic model of macroeconomic evolution, but with special properties that are important for considering existence in the grand economic dynamics of chapter 22. To determine exactly what these properties are, we must take a close look at the production function and at the process of replication.

24.3.1 Properties of Production

Recall from §22.2.1 that for any given techno-social system (and suppressing the system index i), the cultural production function is

$$K_j(x) = k_j H(x/k_j) > 0 \quad \text{for all} \quad x/k_j \in (M, N), \quad k_j \in \mathcal{K},$$

$k_1 = 1$ and $k_{j+1} > k_j$, $j = 1, \ldots$. This implies that the technology menu is advancing. Recall also that the dominating production index is

$$j = J(x) := \arg \max_{l \in \mathbb{N}_{++}} K_l(x), \quad x \geq 0$$

where

$$K_l(x) = k_l H(x/k_l)$$
$$= k_l BG(x - k_l M, k_l N - N),$$

and the dominating production sets are $\mathcal{X}^j := \{x \mid J(x) = j\}, j = 1, \ldots, \tau.$

PROPOSITION 24.6

(i) If the feasible production sets are overlapping then there exists a unique sequence $a^j \in (k_j N, k_{j+1} M)$, $j \in \mathbb{N}^{++}$ where $a^0 = M$ and $a^j = k_j a$, $j \in \mathbb{N}_{++}$ where a satisfies $H(a) = k_2 H(a/k_2)$, such that

$$\mathcal{X}^1 = (a^0, a^1), \quad \mathcal{X}^j = (a^{j-1}, a^j) = (k^{j-1}a, k^j a], \quad j > 2.$$

(ii) The dominating production function

$$K_*(x) := k_{J(x)}H(x/k_{J(x)})$$

$$= k_j B^G(x/k_j - M, N - x/k_j)$$

$$= BG(x - k_j M, k_j N - x) := K_j(x) \quad \text{for all} \quad x \in \mathscr{X}^j$$

is continuous and its restriction $K_j(x)$ to $\mathscr{X}^j$ is strictly pseudo-concave.
(iii) The dominating welfare function

$$\omega_*(x) = K_*(x)/x$$

is positive, continuous on $\mathbb{R}^+$, and pseudo-concave on each $\mathscr{X}^j$, $j \in \mathbb{N}^{++}$.
(iv) The dominating marginal welfare function

$$\omega_*'(x) = BG'(x/k_j - M, N - x/k_j)$$

is monotonically decreasing on each dominating production zone $\mathscr{X}^j$ and continuous on the interior of the $\mathscr{X}^j$.

Proof For each j, define

$$Z_j(x) := k_j H(x/k_j) - k_{j+1} H(x/k_{j+1}).$$

Then

$$Z_j(x) = \begin{cases} k_j H(x/k_j) > 0, & x \in (k_j M_j, k_{j+1} M) \\ -k_{j+1}H(x/k_{j+1}) < 0, & x \in (k_j N, k_{j+1} N). \end{cases}$$

Clearly, $Z_j(x)$ is continuous on the interval $(k_{j+1}M, k_j N)$ and changes sign from positive to negative as x increases on this interval. Therefore, there exists an a^j satisfying $Z_j(a^j) = 0$. But

$$Z_j'(x) = H'(x/k_j) - H'(x/k_{j+1})$$

and, as $k_{j+1} > k_j$, $Z_j'(x) < 0$ on the interval $k_{j+1}M, k_j N$, so $Z_j(x)$ changes sign only once. Therefore, a^j is unique. Since $H(\cdot)$ is strictly concave on (M, N) and $k_j H(a^j/k_j) = k_{j+1}H(a^{j+1}/k_{j+1})$, it follows that $k_j H(x/k_j) > k_i H(x/k_i)$ for all $x \in (a^{j-1}, a^j]$ for all $i \neq j$. Therefore, $\mathscr{X}^i = (a^{j-1}, a^j]$, $j = 1, \ldots$.

Assume that $K_{j+1}(k_j a) = K_j(k_j a)$. Then

$$K_{j+1}(k_j a) = k_{j+1}H(k_j a/k_j) = k_{j+1}H(a/k_{j+1}/k_j)$$

$$K_j(k_j a) = k_j H(k_j a/k_j) = k_j H(a).$$

Therefore, $k_{j+1}H(a/k_{j+1}/k_j) = k_j H(a)$, and $a^j = k_j a$ satisfies $K_{j+1}(a^j) = K_j(a^j)$, $j = 1, \ldots, \tau - 1$. But we found above that the a^j must be unique.   ∎

24.3.2 Examples

For the fission and fusion (F/F) process $k_j = 2^{j-1}$, $j \in [\phi, \tau]$. It is easy to see that the inequality

$$2M \leq N \tag{24.11}$$

is a necessary and sufficient condition for the technology menu generated by such a process to be overlapping. Thus,

$$2M < N \Leftrightarrow 2^j M < 2^{j-1}N \Rightarrow M^{j+1} < N^j, \quad j \in [1, \tau - 1],$$

which is the inequality (24.3). Likewise the inequalities (24.11) and

$$N \leq 4M \tag{24.12}$$

are necessary conditions for the menu to be sequentially overlapping, since (24.12) is easily shown to imply inequality (24.4).

For the shedding and assimilation (S/A) process $k^j = j$, so inequality (24.3) becomes $(j+1)M < jN$. Since $M < N$ by hypothesis, $(j-1)M < (j-1)N$, $j \in [z, \tau]$. Combining this expression with (24.11), we get

$$2M < N \Leftrightarrow (j+1)M < jN \Rightarrow M^{j+1} < N^j,$$

$j \in [1, \tau - 1]$. Consequently (24.11) in a necessary and sufficient condition for the technology menu generated by the S/A process to be overlapping.

On the contrary let r be any fraction in $[0, 1]$ and consider the inequality

$$M < rN. \tag{24.13}$$

For the S/A process, inequality (24.4) becomes $iN < (i+2)M$, $i \in [1, \tau - 2]$. Combining this fact with (24.13) we get

$$\frac{i}{i+2} < \frac{M}{N} < r.$$

The leftmost fraction approaches 1 for i large enough, so that for some integer, say i',

$$\frac{i}{i+2} > r \quad \text{for all} \quad i \geq i'.$$

Consequently, the menu cannot be sequentially overlapping because for any r inequality (24.4) will be violated for some large enough i. For example if $r = \frac{1}{2}$ then (24.12) is satisfied but i' is only equal to 2.

24.3.3 Constrained Replication: Properties of Production

The concept of environmental "space" was introduced in §22.1.2 to account for the external restrictions on the number of economies that can be generated by replication. The effect on productivity was given by the damage function (22.7). From (22.9) the constrained cultural production function was given by

$$\bar{K}_*(x) = \bar{K}_j(x)$$

$$= k_j H(x/k_j) g(\bar{x} - x), \quad x \in \bar{X}^j, \quad j = 1, \ldots, \bar{j}$$

where

$$j = J(x) := \arg \max_{l \in \mathbb{N}_{++}} \bar{K}_l(x)$$

$$= \arg \max_{l \in \mathbb{N}_{++}} k_l \bar{H}(x/k_l), \quad x \geq 0,$$

where $\bar{H}(x/k_j) = k_l BG(x/k_l - M, N - x/k_l)$, $x/k_l \in k_l(M, N)$, and where $\bar{X}^j := \{x \mid J(x) = j\}$ when $\bar{X} = \bigcup_{j=1}^{J} \bar{X}^j$ and $X^0 = \setminus\bar{X}$.

Using our familiar methods, we can derive:

PROPOSITION 24.7 (Properties of the Dominating Production Function with Constrained Replication) *Assume that the set of possible cultures $\mathscr{C} = \{\mathscr{S}, k \in \mathscr{N}\}$ based on any fixed system $\mathscr{S} \in \sum$ satisfies $k_{j+1}/k_j < N/M$ for all $j \in \mathbb{N}^{++}$. Then*

(i) $\bar{X}$ is connected and there exists a unique sequence $a^0, a^1, \ldots, a^{\bar{j}}$ such that

$$\bar{X}^j = (a^{j-1}, a^j], \quad j = 1, \ldots, \bar{j} - 1$$

$$\bar{X}^{\bar{j}} = (a^{\bar{j}-1}, a^{\bar{j}})$$

where a^0 satisfies $K_1(a^0) = 0$, where $a^j = k_j a$, $j = 1, \ldots, \bar{j} - 1$, where $\bar{j} = \arg \max_l \{k_l \mid k_l M < \bar{x}\}$, and where

$$a^{\bar{j}} = \min\{k^{\bar{j}} N, \bar{x}\};$$

(ii) the dominating constrained production function $K_*(x)$ is positive, continuous on $\overline{X}$, and its restrictions $K_j(x)$ are strictly pseudo-concave on each $\overline{X}^j$, $j = 1, \ldots, \bar{j}$;

(iii) the constrained cultural welfare function

$$\bar{\omega}^*(x) = \overline{K}_*(x)/x$$

is well defined and continuous on $\overline{X}_*$, pseudo-concave on each dominating production zone $\overline{X}^j$, $j = 1, \ldots, \bar{j}$, and

$$\bar{\omega}_*(x) \quad \text{for all} \quad x \in \overline{X};$$

(iv) the constrained dominating marginal welfare function

$$\overline{K}'_*(x) = H'(x/k^j)g(\bar{x} - x) - k^j H(x/k^j)g'(x - \bar{x}), \quad x \in \overline{X}^j$$

is monotonically decreasing on each dominating production zone $\overline{X}^j$ and continuous on the interior of the $\overline{X}^j$.

The difference between the constrained F/F and S/A replication processes is striking. If $k^{F/F}$ and $k^{S/A}$ are the maximum number of feasible economies for a given culture with the F/F and S/A processes, respectively, then

$$k^{\bar{j}^{F/F}} M \le \bar{x} < 2k^{\bar{j}^{F/F}} + 1)M \quad \text{and} \qquad \text{(a)}$$
$$k^{S/A} M \le \bar{x} < (k^{S/A} + 1)M. \qquad \text{(b)}$$
$$\text{(24.14)}$$

These inequalities imply that

$$\log_2(\bar{x}/M) < k^{F/F} < 1 + \log_2(\bar{x}/M) \quad \text{and} \qquad \text{(a)}$$
$$\bar{x}/M < k^{S/A} \le 1 + \bar{x}/M. \qquad \text{(b)}$$
$$\text{(24.15)}$$

Clearly, the F/F process places a far more stringent limitation on the number of feasible autonomous economies than the S/A process.

It is also obvious that

$$\bar{\omega}^{F/F}_* < \bar{\omega}^{S/A}_*(x) \quad \text{for all} \quad x \in X^* \quad \text{for all} \quad j.$$

Note that while the function $\overline{K}_*(x)$ is continuous, it need not be smooth. Thus, if $2M$ is close enough to N, then, as the work force grows, the product will eventually fall absolutely before a split is feasible. The result is that $\overline{K}_*(\cdot)$ will have a kink for each population at which fission occurs, and over its full range will have a scalloped profile.

24.3.4 Properties of the Dynamic Structure

Assume that $k_{j+1}/k_j < N/M$ for all $j \in \mathbb{N}^{++}$. Then, leaving aside multiple regimes and learning by doing for the time being, the dynamics of replication/merging can be represented by the equations

$$j_t = J(x_t) = \arg \max_{l \in \mathbb{N}_{++}} K_l(x_t), \quad x_t \geq 0,$$

$$x_{t+1} = \theta(x_t) := \max\{0, \min\{(\alpha/q)BG(x_t - k_jM, k_jN - x_t)$$

$$- \eta x_t, (1+n)x_t\}\}, \quad x_t \in \mathcal{D}^j$$

$$= \theta_j(x_t) = \min\{(\alpha/q)[BG(x_t - k_jM, k_jN - x_t)$$

$$- \eta x_t(1+n)x_t\}, \quad x_t \in \mathcal{D}_j.$$

Given Proposition 24.7, the following can be derived:

PROPOSITION 24.8 *For a large enough technology level B,*

(i) a RAM model is regular mountainous and continuously admissible. There exists a unique sequence $(b^0, \ldots, b^{\bar{j}})$ such that $\mathcal{D}^1 = (b^0, b^1)$, $\mathcal{D}^j = (b^{j-1}, b^j) = \bar{X}^j$, $j = 2, \ldots, \bar{j} - 1$ $\mathcal{D}^{\bar{j}-1} = (b^{j-1}, b^{\bar{j}})$;
*(ii) $s^{M_j} = k_jx^{M_1} = x^{M_j} = \max_{x \in \mathcal{D}^j} \theta_j(x) = (1+n)$, k^jx^s where $(1+n)x^{s_1}$
$= (\alpha/q)[\bar{K}_j(x^{s_1}) - \eta]$;*
(iii) $x^{s_1} \to b^1$, $x^{M_1} \to (1+n)b^1$, and $\theta'_j(x^{si}) = \theta'_1(x^{s_1}) \to -\infty$ as $B \to \infty$.

24.3.5 Qualitative Dynamics

The properties obtained in Proposition 24.8 provide the basis for the analog of Theorem 24.1.

THEOREM 24.4 *Cascading and ratcheting scenarios are generic in the RAM model.*

COROLLARY 24.3 *(i) Finite structural growth, decline, fluctuation, and progression, as well as ratcheting progression, all with or without collapse, are all generic in an RAM.*
(ii) For a large enough technology level B, collapse occurs almost surely.

Clearly, this corollary would enable us to derive an analog of Theorems 24.3 and 24.4 for an RAM with learning by doing. Without writing down such an RAM-LD model, we can surmise that for sufficiently high technology potential, $\tilde{B}$, all the results obtained for the BEM-LD described in Theorem 24.3 and Corollary 24.1 would hold.

24.4   The Grand Dynamic Evolutionary Model (GEM)

In the model presented in chapter 22, multiple regimes and regime switching, continuous productivity improvement through learning by doing, the replication or merging of economies with the same technology, and the integration of several economies with a given technology to form one with a more advanced system, or the disintegration of an economy with a given system to form several economies with less advanced systems, are all incorporated. The character of trajectories generated by this more complicated "grand evolutionary" model is found to share common properties with the BEM and RAM models.

Let

$$\mathcal{K} := \{\mathcal{K}^i = \{k^i_j, j \in \mathbb{N}^{++}\}, i \in \mathcal{T}\}$$

$$\mathcal{M} := \{\mathcal{M}^i = \{\tilde{B}^i, \rho^i, B_i(\cdot), M^i, N^i, g_i(\cdot), \bar{x}^i\}, i \in \mathcal{T}\}$$

$$\mathcal{H} := \{\mathcal{H}^i = \{\alpha^i, q^i, \eta^i, n^i\}, i \in \mathcal{T}\}.$$

The ith culture is the set of economies with the same i^{th} system $\mathcal{S}^i = \{\mathcal{H}^i, \mathcal{M}^i\}$ denoted by

$$\mathcal{C}^i = \{\mathcal{S}^i, \mathcal{K}^i\}.$$

The GEM can be denoted

$$\sum\nolimits^{gem} := \{\mathcal{H}, \mathcal{M}, \mathcal{K}\}.$$

24.4.1   Properties of Production

Recall that the operator $IJ(\cdot, \cdot)$ that selects the culture at any given state (x, B), $B := (B^1, \dots, B^\tau)$, is given by

$$(i, j) = IJ(x, B)$$

$$:= \arg \max_{l \in \mathcal{T}} \left\{ \max_{p \in \mathbb{N}_{++}} \{\bar{K}_{l,p}(x, B)\} \right\}$$

where

$$\bar{K}_{l,p}(x, B) = \begin{cases} k_l \bar{H}_l(x/k_l) g(\bar{x}^l - x) \\ k_p^l B^l G_p(x/k_p^l) g_p(\bar{x}^l - x). \end{cases}$$

The dominant production function is

$$K_*^*(x) := \bar{K}_{IJ(x,B)}(x, B), \quad x \in \mathscr{X}^{IJ(x,B)}.$$

In line with the previous analyses of production, one can derive:

PROPOSITION 24.9 (Characteristics of the Dominating Production Function) *Assume*

(a) each culture $\mathscr{C}^i$ satisfies $k_{j+1}^i / k_j^i < N^i / M^i$, for each $j \in \mathscr{K}^i$;

(b) for each system $\mathscr{S}^i$, $\bar{x}^i > M^{i+1}$, $k_j^i N^i > M^{i+1}$ for each $j \in \mathscr{K}^i$.

(c) Let $\bar{j}_i = \arg \max_j \{ k_j^i \mid k_j^i M < \bar{x}^i \}$. For each B, let $\mathscr{X}^{i,j}(B) := \{ x \mid IJ(x, B) = i, j \}$. Then

(i) the $\mathscr{X}^{i,j}(B)$ are connected;

(ii) the dominating production function

$$K_*^*(x, B) = K_{i,j}(x), \quad x \in X^{i,j}, \quad j = 1, \dots, \bar{j}_i, \quad i = 1, \dots, \tau$$

is positive and continuous on $\mathscr{X}(B) = \bigcup_{i,j} \mathscr{X}^{i,j}(B)$ and strictly pseudo-concave on each $\mathscr{X}^{i,j}(B)$;

(iii) the dominating welfare function $\omega_*^*(x, B) := K_*^*(x, B)/x$ is positive and continuous on $\mathscr{X}(B)$ and strictly pseudo-concave on each $\mathscr{X}^{i,j}(B)$;

(iv) the dominating marginal welfare function $K_*^{*'}(x, B)$ is continuous and monotonically decreasing on the interior of each $\mathscr{X}^{i,j}(B)$;

(v) each $(\mathscr{M}(B), \mathscr{K}(B))$ is a connected technology menu with a total of $\sum_{i=1}^{\tau} \bar{j}_i$ dominating production zones.

24.4.2   The Dynamic Structure of GEM

The dynamic structure of a GEM can be represented by the following equations:

$$(i, j)_t = IJ(x_t, B_t)$$

$$= \arg \max_{p \in \mathscr{T}} \left\{ \max_{l \in \mathbb{N}_{++}} \{ \bar{K}_{l,p}(x, B) g_p(\bar{x}^p - x) \} \right\}, \tag{24.16}$$

$$x_{t+1} = \max\{0, \min[(\alpha^{i_t}/q^{i_t})\overline{K}_{(i,j)_t} - \eta^{i_t}x_t], (1 + n^{i_t})x_t\}, \qquad (24.17)$$

$$B_{t+1}^{i_t} = B_t^{i_t} + \rho^{i_t}B_t^{i_t}(1 - B_t^{i_t}/\tilde{B}^{i_t})$$

$$B_{t+1}^{l_t} = B_t^{l_t}, \quad l_t \neq i_t. \qquad (24.18)$$

For any $B = (B^1, \ldots, B^\tau)$ the pair $\{\mathscr{M}(B), \mathscr{K}(B)\}$ is an overlapping, connected technology menu and $\sum(B) = \{\mathscr{H}, \mathscr{M}(B), \mathscr{K}(B)\}$ is equivalent to a basic evolutionary model with $\sum_{i=1} \bar{j}_i$ regimes. Call it a BEM-RAM. Its trajectories are generated by equations (24.16)–(24.18). Proposition 24.9 enables us to derive the properties of a BEM-RAM in the same manner as for a BEM.

PROPOSITION 24.10   *Let* $\sum^{gem} = (\mathscr{H}, \mathscr{M}, \mathscr{K})$ *be a GEM system and let* $\sum(B) = (\mathscr{H}, \mathscr{M}(B), \mathscr{K}(B))$ *be the corresponding BEM-RAM for given B. Then for large enough B,*

(i) $\mathscr{M}(B)$ *is connected and* $\sum = (\mathscr{H}, \mathscr{M}(B), \mathscr{K}(B))$ *is continuously admissible;*

(ii) for large enough B, $x^{M_{i,j}} = \max_{x \in \mathscr{D}^{i,j}} \theta_{i,j}(x) = (1 + n^i)x^{s,i,j}$;

(iii) for each $i \in \mathscr{T}$, $B^i \to \infty \Rightarrow x^{M_{i,j}} \to (1 + n^i)x^{s,i,j}$ *and* $\theta'_{i,j}(x^{s,i,j}) \to -\infty$.

24.4.3   Generic Dynamics

Following the line of argument developed in chapter 23 and using Proposition 24.10, we can prove:

THEOREM 24.5   *Cascading and ratcheting systems are generic in the general evolutionary model.*

Proof By incorporating learning by doing, our BEM-RAM model becomes a GEM. Just as the BEM-LD model generates a sequence of BEM models, GEM trajectories generate a sequence of BEM-RAM models. At each period the technology level of the dominant technology increases until eventually switching occurs—as it must almost surely do. After generating growth, decline, or cascading scenarios long enough in duration, ratcheting scenarios and collapse become increasingly likely, and in the limit a ratcheting scenario with collapse occurs almost surely. ∎

COROLLARY 24.4

(i) Finite structural growth, decline, fluctuations, progressions, and ratcheting progressions with or without collapse occur generically in the general evolutionary model.

(ii) For large enough vector of technology potentials, collapse occurs almost surely.

24.5 Summary and Conclusions

Chapters 21–22 introduced salient features of long-run economic development into the classical demoeconomic growth theory. Historians and anthropologists may observe that our theory leaves out a host of important considerations, certainly a justifiable complaint. But a similar complaint holds for any theory. *This* theory, such as it is, does capture salient—and important—features of the development process, and that is all we demand of it. Macroeconomic growth theorists might complain that the model is far too complicated. However, some complications cannot be avoided if the minimal hypotheses of structural change—as we know them to be involved—are incorporated even in the simplest possible way, as has been done here. So we must admit the complications but deny that the theory is too complicated. Given my purpose, it is "as simple as possible—but not more so."

Our analysis leads to the following conclusions:

(i) Evolution *in this theory* is driven by an unstable, deterministic (intrinsic) process.

(ii) The "chance" or probabilities that various possible historical scenarios occur can (in principle) be derived in terms of the measure of sequences of qualitative "events."

(iii) If the technological potential of each technology is great enough, then evolution in terms of continued progression to the most advanced regime occurs almost surely.

(iv) *In the absence of technological learning by doing* and if the map $\theta(\cdot)$ is unstable and closed, history must involve endless fluctuations, eventually sticking within a given regime or cycling in a nonperiodic fashion through an endless sequence of regimes. If, by way of contrast, there is a reachable regime with a stable stationary state, world history could converge, possibly after many periods of local chaos, to a classical equilibrium.

(v) When learning by doing is explicitly incorporated, if the technological potentials and initial technological levels are high enough, then extremely complex sequences of jumps and reversions among cultures and among the number of economies within a given culture can eventually take place. Sequences of conditional ratcheting progressions separated by reversions subsequently emerge almost surely, with complete collapse more and more likely to occur as the society increasingly exhausts the environmental space of the "last" regime.

(vi) Therefore, the key to continuing socioeconomic evolution ultimately rests on the identification of entirely new regimes with expanded social and environmental spaces and on the reorganization of the society's existing resources to permit the transition to a new age. Improvements in productivity through learning by doing leave unchanged the techno-infrastructural thresholds and the environmental spaces. They can only accelerate progress through the several epochs and hasten the advent of socioeconomic catastrophe.

(vii) Changing social preferences that decrease the birth rate, that increase the birth threshold and the opportunity cost of raising children, can play a role in delaying a collapse but cannot prevent one unless a zero bound on the population growth rate is established at a low enough total population.

(viii) Ultimately, the moral of the theory would seem to be that the creative human faculty focused on the design for group living is the ultimate resource in a finite world.

VII DYNAMICAL ECONOMIC SCIENCE AND POLICY

25 Precursors and Ongoing Developments

Poincaré's criticism ... is aimed at the very idea that a quantitative model, accurate as it may be, can be used to predict the future.
—Ivar Ekeland, *Mathematics and the Unexpected*

The models presented in this book cover only a part of the territory of dynamic economics. This territory has been expanding at a rapid rate. It would be impossible to survey it all, but a brief summary of how the original ideas were developed, an outline of that part of the field related to the topics covered here, and a summary of the related work being actively pursued will provide a useful starting point for those who want to delve deeper into the subject. That is the purpose of this chapter. I present it with apologies to the many scholars whose important contributions have not been cited but with hopes that the reader will be stimulated to seek them out and give them the attention they deserve.

25.1 Nonlinear Dynamics

Let us begin with the underlying concepts.

The basic ideas of analytical dynamics must have arisen, at least intuitively, at a very early stage in the development of human culture. Many perceived relationships were no doubt the result of serendipity. Nonetheless, the basis of the hunting and food-collecting way of life that dominated human economy for many thousands of years had to rest not only on a vast empirical knowledge of nature but also on a clear understanding of cause and effect. Without such an understanding, serendipitous observations could not have been accumulated to form a systematic knowledge base for producing tools, weapons, storage containers, clothing, and shelter, for organizing hunts and for identifying, collecting, and processing edible seeds, fruits, and so forth.

Continued observation of earthly phenomena and the heavens led to the perception of empirical regularities and to the idea that these could be used to predict events of great importance for human survival and welfare. Even the erratic, seemingly random and arbitrary events that so often impinged on human fortunes were given causal explanations in terms of supernatural beings whose whims and purposeful actions caused natural events that had no other clear explanation—like storms, earthquakes, accidents, disease, the swirling turbulences of waters and winds, and the rise and fall of heroes.

Already during the classical age, the foundations were being developed for an analytical—in contrast to a mythological—explanation of experience. Eventually, Newton, building on millennia of observed regularities, and on the more precise measurements of astronomical phenomena that the telescope had made possible, could formulate a theory of persistent motion in time and space in abstract mathematical terms, in this way providing a rigorous format for conducting dynamic analysis.

The domain of observed regular behavior was large and expanded rapidly as the tools and methods of observation and experimentation developed. There was plenty of scope for modeling regular change. Moreover, the existence and local stability of stationary states and periodic motion could be investigated thoroughly using linear mathematics, which correspondingly dominated applied research for more than two centuries.[1]

Newtonian mechanics was, however, based on nonlinear interactions. Linear analysis could only approximate dynamics in the neighborhood of asymptotically stable stationary states or cycles. Such approximations were not useful for describing the behavior of matter in gaseous states, where motion appeared to be more or less random, or of liquids under various conditions when their flow was turbulent. The idea that processes involving large numbers of elements moving in strict accord with Newtonian equations could move more or less randomly occurred to Clausius, Boltzmann, and Maxwell, who used the term "chaos" to describe such motion.[2] They found a way to describe the properties of such systems with a generalized concept of the steady state in terms of distribution functions. Einstein's 1902 paper provides a clear statement of this general point of view, and about the same time Gibbs gave a comprehensive treatment of the approach (see Gibbs 1981). The ergodic theory of dynamical systems developed into a major branch of mathematics, a trenchant treatment of which is given in Dunford and Schwartz (1958, chapter VIII, especially sections 4 and 5). Sections 1–3 of that chapter give an abstract treatment of semidynamical systems based on semigroups of operators in continuous time. My treatment is likewise based on semigroups of operators composed of the iterated maps generated by dynamic structures operating in discrete time.

Toward the end of the nineteenth century, in a striking departure from the study of many interacting elements, Poincaré perceived the possibility that a Newtonian system with only three elements could behave in a complicated way. His classic study is the origin of a prominent line of studies of complex dynamics for continuous-time systems. An engaging account of these developments will be found in Ekeland (1988).

During the second half of the twentieth century there was a rapid acceleration of progress. The advent of electronic computers made possible numerical simulation studies of complicated systems whose behavior could not yet be described by available methods of pure mathematical analysis. A particularly influential advance was made by Eduard Lorenz (1963a, 1963b, 1964), who participated in an effort to develop meteorological theory on the basis of fluid dynamics, a field based on an extension of Newtonian mechanics to the explanation of material flows in the fluid state. Scientists had created an elaborate system of nonlinear differential equations to see if aspects of the weather (temperature, barometric pressure, wind velocity, etc.) could be explained and predicted. Numerical results often behaved in a highly irregular manner that seemed to mimic actual experience. Lorenz wanted to understand how such deterministic equations could generate trajectories that were so erratic that they bore a close resemblance to the kind of data associated with purely random processes. It led him to a series of model simplifications and analytical studies that demonstrated how nonperiodic changes could arise in very simple but sufficiently nonlinear dynamic equations. His system of three differential equations with quadratic terms is known as the Lorenz equations. A vast literature has been devoted to their study, a sample of which is contained in Sparrow (1982).

Also at midcentury, Ilya Prigogine and his collaborators reconsidered biochemical phenomena from the point of view of stability and nonlinearity, which led to his award of the Nobel Prize in chemistry in 1977. See Nicolis and Prigogine (1977) and Prigogine (1980, 1996). Prigogine subsequently devoted much of his energy to encouraging and supporting younger scholars through a widely varied program of multidisciplinary research and by fostering the international exchange of ideas in the field through various conferences held in Europe and America, to which many pioneering researchers contributed. Several proceedings were published, including Allen (1987) and Day and Chen (1993). At the time of this writing, Prigogine continues efforts to develop the subject, emphasizing the statistical character of dynamical systems. For examples, see Antoniou, Prigogine, and Tasaki (1996) or Antoniou and Gustafson (1997).

Lasota and Mackey (1985) tell us in their preface that the distinct line of work based on iterated maps began with a seminal paper of Borel (1908) and took its modern form in a much later contribution by Ulam and von Neuman (1947). This work showed that statistical concepts could be exploited not just in continuous time but also in discrete-time processes governed by a single difference equation. Continuing to follow his reductionist approach, Lorenz derived several examples of such systems. Much of the subsequent mathematical work was conducted in terms of iterated maps on the unit interval—the discrete-time dynamical system in a single state variable that forms the analytical foundation for the present study.

In spite of progress in the development of these ideas during the first half of the nineteenth century, most mathematicians, scientists, and engineers concentrated on the development of analytical dynamics using the methods of linear algebra that had also emerged at the close of the nineteenth century. These linear methods allowed for a very satisfactory theory of orderly behavior, one that could explain change in terms of periodic functions or of sequences of periodic functions, and linear analysis was used to study properties of local convergence. The second part of Samuelson's classic *Foundations of Economic Analysis*, first published in 1947, provided economists with a comprehensive introduction to the role of linear methods in the study of local dynamic behavior, including the behavior of nonlinear systems in the neighborhood of stationary states.

For my purposes, a breakthrough occurred in the 1970s with the work of James Yorke and his colleagues and students Lasota, Li, Misiurewicz, and Pianigiani. They derived the constructive, global conditions for the existence of chaos and ergodic behavior outlined in chapters 7–9 and used repeatedly throughout this study. Fundamental to some of their work is the much-cited paper of Šarkovskii (1964) on the existence of cycles of various orders. The tent map, the "baker's transformation," and the quadratic (logistic) map are frequently illustrated in these early papers. One of the contributions of the present study has been to construct and illustrate a variety of additional examples motivated by economic considerations.

Many books and articles have been written about these mathematical developments. Robert May, among others, in a series of engaging articles, explained the technical ideas and applied them to his own field of biological population dynamics. It is worth noting that Prigogine, Joseph Ford, and David Ruelle recognized very early that nonlinear dynamics and chaos might have some bearing on economics. In any case, there followed in rapid succession a host of theoretical and applied studies.

Those who want to master the mathematical details of the subject will find a pedagogically brilliant introduction in Strogatz (1994). The books by Collet and Eckmann (1980) and Lasota and Mackey (1985) have authoritative treatments on various aspects of the nonlinear difference equation; Devaney (1989) is also widely cited. The original papers cited in part II of this book are still excellent references.

The closely related subjects of chaos and statistical dynamics come together explicitly in the exploration of robustness of chaotic trajectories with respect to initial conditions. My discussion of robustness in §8.9 of volume I is based on discussions with Giulio Pianigiani. The many examples produced throughout this book would seem to remove any doubt about the relevance of chaos for economic theory.

Computational experiments have played an important role in this line of work. Gumowski and Mira (1980) published extensive examples. More recently, Nusse and Yorke (1995) have come out with beautifully illustrated numerical studies.

All the parts of this book have shown that multiple-phase dynamics is fundamental in economics. One does not find explicit treatments of the multiple-phase dynamics of such systems in standard mathematical works, but the idea has a central place in physics and engineering. The properties of physical systems are very different under various conditions, as in the basic states of matter or when alternative electrical circuits, machinery, or chemical processes are activated or deactivated by means of switches. Mathematical models representing such switching dynamics have been studied for a long time. The so-called Van der Pol equations constitute a classic example.

Throughout this book it has been shown that quite different economic forces or relationships govern behavior in differing situations of state. Multiple-phase dynamic models formalize this fact. In 1951 Georgescu-Roegen attributed to Le Corbeiller the idea that the theory of relaxation oscillations discussed earlier by Van der Pol could give multiple-regime explanations of business fluctuations. In the same year Richard Goodwin published his famous "Nonlinear Acceleration and the Persistence of Business Cycles," telling us of his inspiration from the same source. Goodwin focused on a nonlinear explanation of aggregate business cycles. Georgescu's contribution was an outgrowth of Leontief's dynamic (linear) multisector model, which was also based on the acceleration principle and which, likewise, led to the problem of multiple regimes.

This literature, together with Simon's (1951) insightful analysis of "trigger effects" in mathematical programming, was the inspiration for my own use of multiple-phase dynamics to model very general forms of structural change in microeconomic processes (Day, 1963, 1978) and in macroeconomic growth (Day and Walter, 1989). Elsewhere, I have described (Day, 1995) the approach in more general terms than done in this book. Haavelmo (1956) had already emphasized the inevitable intrusion of multiple regimes in the study of growth, and subsequently Malinvaud (1980) took the same approach in his macroeconomic reconsideration of unemployment. Despite these seminal contributions and despite the likelihood that many apparent anomalies can be explained in these terms, multiple-phase dynamics is conspicuous by its underrepresentation in the theoretical literature of economics.

At about the time Lorenz was investigating nonlinear dynamics in the context of meteorology and Prigogine in the context of biochemical processes, Steven Smale was investigating dynamical systems from a purely abstract mathematical point of view. Many of the techniques that have been used since were first presented in his work. Expositions include those by Ruelle (1980) and Moser (1973). This line of work is based on the class of "diffeomorphisms" which lead to groups of operators, but this is too restricted a class for nonlinear economic analysis in discrete time, which only generates semigroups of operators which are not time-"reversible."

One of the most fascinating findings that has emerged from the study of these systems is that of the *strange attractor*. These are abstract objects made up of sets of points to which the orbits of chaotic dynamic systems converge and which lack the regularity properties of usual geometric shapes. An example is the "Lorenz attractor" of the Lorenz equation mentioned earlier.

A closely related mathematical phenomenon is that of "self-replication," which appears in bifurcation diagrams of chaotic processes. These strange attractors and bifurcation diagrams form objects called fractals that have a self-replicating character. Economic models sometimes (probably often) generate fractal patterns. T. Y. Lin (1988) computed an example later incorporated into our joint paper (Day and Lin, 1992). Many authors have explored such possibilities in various economic settings. For recent examples, see Puu (1997), Hommes (1994), and Nusse and Yorke (1995).

Recent developments in mathematical ergodic theory have provided a deeper understanding of the relationship between deterministic chaos and axiomatically defined stochastic processes. Amy Radunskaya (1987) has shown that a large class of nonlinear models are observationally equivalent to a class of stochastic Markov processes. "Observationally equivalent" is meant in the sense of "observed with error." These developments have important implications for statistical hypothesis testing for nonlinearity using economic time series. For useful surveys of these latter methods, see Brock and Chamberlain (1984), Brock (1986), Chen (1993), and Barnett and Hinich (1993). This is a particularly active field of current research and is discussed further below.

25.2 Complex Economic Dynamics

I turn now to studies of complex dynamics in economic settings. First, literature related to the topics presented in parts III–VI of this book is discussed, then a sample of other economic work is included.

25.2.1 Market Mechanisms

The idea that competition in market processes involved a sequence of adjustments to imbalances in supply and demand over time is already inherent in the work of Adam Smith. It received its first formal, if primitive, treatment in Walras's *Elements of Pure Economics*. Walras outlined two mechanisms: that of consumer's tatonnement, which was studied above in chapters 10 and 11 of volume I, and that of producer's tatonnement, which was used for an introductory example in chapter 2. The first substantial analytical progress in the study of the former mechanism will be found in Samuelson's *Foundations* (1947, pp. 270–276). Within a decade and a half most of the prominent mathematical economists had contributed to its further elucidation, including Arrow, Block, and Hurwicz (1959), Arrow and Hurwicz (1962), Hahn (1973), Uzawa (1961), and Nikaido (1968). See also Morishima (1996). Local linear methods were used to obtain sufficient conditions for asymptotic stability. It was not yet possible to capture the turbulent dynamics Walras had described so vividly (*Elements*, pp. 380–381). But asymptotic dynamics in the neighborhood of an equilibrium was nailed down and definitively derived from the underlying economic primitives.

My application of the methods of this book to the topic was introduced in a lecture at a conference organized by Jean-Pierre Aubin at the Institut Henri Poincaré in Paris in the spring of 1981. It was first published in a paper coauthored with Giulio Pianigiani (1991). Saari and Simon (1978) had already demonstrated the implausibility of asymptotic convergence and hinted at the much more likely complexity of competitive market behavior, a finding given a pedagogical exposition in Saari (1991). Recently, many authors have contributed analyses of the process for a single market with nonadpative agents using various alternative qualitative assumptions about demand and supply and alternative functional forms, among whom are Bala and Majumdar (1992), Chichilnisky, Heal, and Lin (1995), Kaizouji (1994), Weddepohl (1995), and Goeree, Hommes, and Weddepohl (1997).

Many macro theorists ignore the out-of-equilibrium viability problem recognized by general equilibrium theorists such as Arrow and Hahn (1971) and discussed above in §10.5. Clower and Friedman (1986) introduced an approach toward solving it by formulating a price adjustment model in a pure exchange economy with trade specialists. They focused on asymptotic stability. In Day (1984), I show that markets require mediation mechanisms to maintain viability out of equilibrium, in general, whether or not they are asymptotically stable. By considering a single market in abstraction from intermarket dependencies, the present book provides an analysis of competitive market mediation in which both simple and complex dynamics are generic. This was done in chapter 11, which includes an application of tatonnement with mediation to stock exchange dynamics, yielding an endogenous theory of randomly switching "bear" and "bull" markets. Similar ideas are being developed more generally at the present time; see, for example, Kaas (1998).

The cobweb model of price/quantity fluctuations in markets with production lags, which I used to introduce chapter 12, originated in the work of Henry Moore and received extensive attention in the 1930s. Those studies appeared long before much was known about nonlinear dynamics, but Leontief's (1934) characteristically trenchant exposition was in effect based on the concept of an iterated map, perhaps the latter's first application in economics. The cobweb model is still the one most often used to introduce beginning students to dynamic economics, but interest in it waned until a number of authors reconsidered it using the new methods of chaos, among them Jensen and Urban (1984) and Hommes (1991).

Sune Carlsson (1939) introduced a financial budget constraint into the standard microeconomic model of the firm, but John Burr Williams (1967) was perhaps the first to consider the dynamic implications of working capital on production when market feedback is involved. Motivated by the objective of providing a theoretically tractable example of recursive programming, or, as I call it in this book, "adaptive economizing," I developed a mathematical version of Williams's theory. I carried out a bifurcation analysis in terms of the underlying parameters of demand and supply (Day, 1967b) and extended it to incorporate two commodities (1969), several regions (Day and Tinney, 1969), cost differentials among competing firms (1968), and capital accumulation in a paper coauthored with Morley and Smith (1974). Later, Kenneth Hanson and I reconsidered the model, obtaining generic chaos as the central result (Day and Hanson, 1991). With the exception of these studies, few economists have taken up this highly realistic aspect of microeconomic theory. Significant exceptions are Woodford (1988), Greenwald, Kohn, and Stiglitz (1990), and Huang (1995).

25.2.2 Business Cycles

As experience with market fluctuations accumulated through the nineteenth and twentieth centuries, economists began producing theoretical explanations—many of them. They are not all conflicting; many are complementary, each providing an aspect of what must be a complicated story, as described by Haberler (1937). Some authors focused on real factors brought about by production lags; others focused on information lags and forecast errors; while still others focused on speculative, monetary, and financial mechanisms. Formal models were introduced by Kaleki, Frisch, Harrod, and Kaldor. A charming summary of these early developments was given by Goodwin (1993b).

Keynes was the first, however, to show how the endogenous interaction of real and monetary activity could have a profound influence on an economy working out of equilibrium. To the extent that he couched his analysis in rigorous terms, he utilized the Marshallian comparative static method, but a broader, fully dynamic theory and its implications for understanding economic fluctuations was intended and summarized in the terse, often-quoted passage from *The General Theory* appearing at the beginning of chapter 13 above. Goodwin (1943) gave a cogent exegesis of it. Hicks, Modigliani, Samuelson, Tobin, Schinasi, Smyth, Rose, and many others extended it.

As pure theory, all of the models possessed deficiencies that did not plague the equilibrium approach. Unfortunately, many of these deficiencies have not been overcome and remain among the outstanding challenges for the discipline. In spite of these deficiencies, the basic principle of monetary/real interactions discovered by Keynes retains its central place in virtually all discussions of monetary and fiscal policy and its relation to the business cycle.

I had been exposed to a graphical analysis of the Keynesian model while still an undergraduate student in a version that I subsequently learned had been developed by Richard Goodwin as a pedagogical alternative to the IS-LM approach. It involves a kind of four-quadrant cobweb model that contains the fundamental Keynesian nonlinear demand for money. It was a natural for reconsideration from the point of view of complex economic dynamics. I developed various versions of the model, which in effect involved reconsidering the Modigliani (1944)/Samuelson (1947) version from the global, nonlinear, dynamic point of view. T. Y. Lin conducted simulations of these and Wayne Shafer joined in the study of the model's statistical properties. This work was described in a series of papers: Day and Shafer (1985), Day and Lin (1992), with a policy orientation in Day (1996). These studies are the basis for chapters 13–15.

Matti Pohjola produced a number of examples of chaotic fluctuations in his Ph.D. dissertation (1981b) and in subsequent publications, including a real Keynesian model in which the nonlinearity is induced by a progressive tax rate (1981b). At about this time, Rose-Anne Dana and Pierre Malgrange (1984) demonstrated chaos in the Kaldor business cycle model. Related studies were contributed by Lorenz (1993). Much of the current work is pushing on into multi–state variable models that enable explicit study of many more economic relationships and interactions than are possible in the Day-Lin-Shafer models of part IV. These include papers by Franke and Asada (1994), and Chiarella and Flaschel (1996). A major treatise of Keynesian dynamics in continuous time has appeared in Flaschel, Franke, and Semmler (1997).

25.2.3 Growth

The classical economists understood that capital accumulation and technological change were an essential aspect of continued growth that could delay indefinitely the onset of the "iron law." Perhaps because of the rapid increase in population at the onset of the industrial revolution, it was the simpler demoeconomic analysis that received the most attention. By the mid-twentieth century, trends in capital accumulation, technological improvement, and per capita output were so well established that theorists turned to an explanation of *these* stylized facts, treating the exponential trend in population as an exogenous event. Tinbergen (1958) addressed the problem in a little-known article first published in 1943, entitled "A Theory of the Trend." A more or less definitive analysis of a similar conception of the growth process was given in Solow (1956). A collection of classic papers describing the early development of growth theory is provided in Sen (1970). A useful text is Burmeister and Dobell (1970).

In my 1982 paper on "Irregular Growth Cycles," I reconsidered this model in a discrete time version that incorporated a variable savings rate and a behavioral growth or flexibility constraint. It was then an easy matter to derive chaotic growth fluctuations that produce a graphical appearance somewhat like aggregate data. Chapter 16 is an elaboration of this analysis.

In 1958 Leontief had published his own version of the growth theory, which incorporated the kind of sequential optimizing with feedback behavior that Cournot had used to describe duopolistic markets and which is also implicit in Walrasian tatonnement. I gave this a mathematical analysis which showed that in its reduced form, capital accumulation satisfied a nonlinear difference equation from which the conditions leading to fluctuations could be derived in terms of the time preference and production parameters. This work was eventually published in 1968. Later T. Y. Lin (1988) extended the analysis, and his work formed the basis of our later collaboration (Day and Lin, 1992) and of my own treatment of the model above in chapter 17.

The essence of these adaptive economizing models of growth is a boundedly rational representation of economic tradeoff. The implication is that, due to informational error, the resulting trajectories have only an intended and temporary optimality. The growth trajectories as a whole do not satisfy an equilibrium condition and are not intertemporally optimal *except* along a balanced growth path.

In the meantime, however, growth theorists had recast the theory of capital accumulation using the concepts of optimal control and eventually introducing the dynamic programming theory developed in the seminal works of Bellman (1957) and Karlin (1959). An early mathematical and philosophical appraisal will be found in Koopmans (1965). Subsequently, an enormous literature emerged and the subject held center stage among economic scholars well into the 1970s, with work continuing unabated to this day. A definitive exegesis of both the mathematical theory and its application to economic growth is in Stokey and Lucas (1989).

The early emphasis was on the sufficient conditions for the existence and asymptotic stability of optimal balanced growth paths. Chapter 18 considered the standard discrete-time, one-sector model of optimal capital accumulation which exhibits only monotonic trajectories. I drew heavily on the Stokey and Lucas version of that theory. The novelty of the chapter consists in showing how the behavioral (Solow), adaptive economizing (Leontief-Day-Lin), Golden Rule (Phelps), optimal growth (Cass-Koopmans), and inverse optimality (Boldrin-Montrucchio) approaches are related, and in exploring the implications of the inverse optimal approach.

Eventually, attention shifted, first to the exploration of cyclic growth paths and then to the possibility of chaos. Magill (1979) and Benhabib and Nishimura (1979) surmised the possibility of cyclic optimal growth paths. These works were followed by a host of studies extending and generalizing their results, including versions whose optimal trajectories are chaotic. Examples of this work include Deneckere and Pelikan (1986), Dawid and Kopel (1998), Mitra (1998), Nishimura and Yano (1995), and Majumdar and Mitra (1997). To obtain these more general results, the authors departed from the standard single-sector model, which I analyzed in chapter 18, by introducing modified utility and/or production functions, or by incorporating more than one sector.

25.2.4 Development

The Malthusian growth theory was also a natural for considering the possibility of chaos in an economic growth context. Early studies include

Stutzer (1980) and Day (1982). My discussion of it in chapters 19 and 20 served primarily to introduce long-run considerations that are involved subsequently in the multiple-phase theory of economic development outlined in chapters 21–24.

As experience with rapid economic growth accumulated during the nineteenth century, scholars began to recognize that the unfolding market system with power technology and industrial production had a character quite different from the preceding mercantile period of long-distance commerce and trade, and still more different from the earlier feudal system with its manorial economy and small-scale local manufacturing. Economic development involved more than population growth, the accumulation of capital, advancing technology, and improvements in productivity and welfare within a given set of economic structures. It was clear that over the long run human society had passed through various epochs or stages, each with a distinct political and economic character. Certainly, economic history had to be described not only in terms of growth, but in terms of stages of growth.

Distinct schemes were advanced by List, Fischer, Hildenbrand, Schmoller, Bücher, and Gräss. Each involved three or more individual stages arranged in a fixed sequence and defined by one or another criterion such as the mode of production or exchange. Limitations of the approach were eventually recognized. Indeed, Alexander Gerschenkron found that some societies experienced different stages, passed through them in an atypical order, exhibited several at the same time, or skipped some altogether.[3] Nonetheless, Rostow subsequently expounded still another example of the genre.

Certainly, the stage-makers piled up persuasive evidence for the relevance of distinct stages, evidence that has been reinforced by archaeological research, samples of which are cited in Day and Walter (1989) and in the references cited in the notes to chapters 21 and 22 of this book. But that evidence also reinforces Gerschenkron's criticisms and raises the questions of what causes the transition from one stage to another, and what determines the order in which the stages occur.

In the multiple-phase theory of macroeconomic evolution presented in chapters 21–24, the answer to the first question is the *instability of a given regime*. To escape a given regime, the society must possess an escape set, entry into which forces the system outside of its current stage and into some other one. The answer to the second question is found by determining the relationship between local growth maxima and minima and thresholds in more advanced or less advanced regimes. These thresholds occur at population levels that define the boundaries separating the regimes and that define the existence and number of stationary states. They are determined by all the parameters of all the regimes. Boserup captured the essence of these answers in literary terms in *The Conditions of Agricultural Growth* (1975) and subsequently in her classic *Population and Technological Change* (1981). She has sketched out her own stage concepts in a recent note (1996). The archaeological literature offers much related empirical and theoretical work, but I do not know of any in economics.

Others, however, have developed the theory of long-run economic development using nonlinear dynamics but without the explicit use of multiple regimes. A number of suggestive essays on the subject are contained in Batten, Casti, and Johansson (1987). Goodwin elaborated his ideas in a number of papers (e.g., 1990) culminating in what he called the Marx-Keynes-Schumpeter model of economic growth and fluctuation (1993a): Marx because it emphasizes the fluctuating nature of the growth process, Keynes because it incorporates output controlled by effective demand, and Schumpeter because it includes the swarming nature of innovation.

25.2.5 Overlapping-Generations Models

In the treatments of growth and development, parts V and VI used an overlapping-generations framework in a way that sidestepped exchange between age groups by assuming two generations—adults and their children—with the former making the choices for the family as a whole. Samuelson's original overlapping-generations model was designed specifically to explore the more general problem of exchange between age groups within a population. Gale (1973) provided an elegant exegesis of Samuelson's ideas. There followed an immense literature with many variations in the model assumptions. As an early example, one may cite Diamond (1965). When Jess Benhabib and I began our collaboration in 1978, he chose the Gale model as a starting point. This was the origin of two of our joint papers (Benhabib and Day, 1980, 1982) demonstrating the existence of chaos in economic settings. Perhaps the most widely cited of all early studies of chaos in overlapping-generations models is Grandmont's (1985) paper on "Endogenous Competitive Business Cycles." Other authors have since contributed further analyses, for example Reichlin (1986) and Julien (1988). Still others continue to be produced.

In all of these studies, the focus of attention is on the existence and character of sequential competitive intertemporal equilibrium in which expectations are self-fulfilling. Grandmont and Laroque have investigated an alternative model of sequential competitive *temporary* equilibria, a model much in the spirit of the Leontief-Day-Lin model of chapter 17 but incorporating exchange between young adult and older generations.

25.2.6 Cournot Processes and Adaptive Games

The possible emergence of chaos in adaptive competitive processes was first suggested in a note by Rand (1978), who used some ad hoc reaction functions. This idea was pursued by Dana and Montrucchio (1987), and by Puu (1997) for Cournot's sequential "best response" (or adaptive economizing) strategies. Recent laboratory experiments by Rassenti (et al.) suggest that those results may be empirically relevant for explaining boundedly rational, out-of-equilibrium behavior in gamelike settings. Important and extremely interesting results have also been found in repeated prisoner's dilemma games. This is clearly an important frontier for work in the field.

25.2.7 Adaptive Preferences

Georgescu-Roegen (1950) had argued that behavior based on adaptive preferences would be unpredictable. Maurice Peston (1967) subsequently produced a study of the model deriving cyclic preferences. Then Jess Benhabib and I (1981) derived generic chaos for such a model. Later, I studied a pure exchange economy whose agents possessed adaptive preferences that led to stationary states when they were isolated but generated chaotic trade patterns when they engaged in exchange (Day, 1986). This finding is analogous to that of the behavior of coupled oscillators whose components are stable in isolation but whose interactions lead to fluctuation, another of the many seminal insights that Richard Goodwin (1947) contributed to our discipline. Various scholars have investigated adaptive preferences when their dependence on experience is nonlinear, including Vendrik (1993).

25.2.8   Chaos in Experimental Studies

Mention was made above of a laboratory experiment carried out by Rassenti et al. (2000) in a Cournot-like setting in which the subjects' output choices appeared to follow highly erratic paths. A considerable body of further experimental studies has also been conducted by Sterman (1989) and Kampmann (1992), who asked experimental subjects to make economic decisions in highly nonlinear environments. These studies present compelling evidence that under such conditions people fail to learn the true structure they face and persist in using nonoptimal adaptive tactics that, in interaction with their environments, perpetuate chaotic economic behavior. The implications of this work would seem to be profound.

25.3   General References

In addition to individual studies mentioned in the previous pages, a great many expositions have been aimed at broad scientific or general audiences. In the former category, for example, James Gleick's *Chaos* (1987) has been widely read; Prigogine (1980, 1996) provides stimulating nontechnical interpretations for the philosophically minded reader; and Ivar Ekeland (1988) provided an exceptionally elegant exposition that emphasizes the emergence of the theory of complex economic dynamics from the fountainheads of Newton and Poincaré.

It is often the case that new ideas, when first introduced, are not entirely welcome in the academic journals, which tend to emphasize variations on well-established themes and widely practiced methods. Seminal work often appears in the proceedings of conferences, as in Blackwell's papers, purposely eclectic journals, as in Karlin's "Dynamic Programming Theorem" (1959), which appeared in the *Naval Logistics Quarterly*, or in collections put together by more adventurous editors, as in Seymour Harris's (1950) early volume on the economics of Keynes.

Much of the literature on complex economic dynamics has appeared in similar outlets. Examples include Prigogine's conferences, reported in a special volume of the *European Journal of Operations Research* edited by Peter Allen (1987), a series of proceedings of conferences held in Italy, including Gori, Geronazzo, and Galeotti (1993), volumes edited by Velupillai (1990, 1996), a special issue of the *Journal of Economic Theory* edited by Jean-Michel Grandmont (1986), a special issue of *Economic*

Theory edited by Mukul Majumdar (1994), collections edited by Barnett, Geweke, and Shell (1989), Baumol and Benhabib (1988), and Day and Chen (1993), and several special issues of the *Journal of Economic Behavior and Organization* also devoted to complex dynamics (volume 10, 1984, volume 16, 1991, and volume 31, 1997).

Mathematical, interdisciplinary, and economics-oriented journals focused on nonlinear dynamics and related topics have now been established in recognition of the field's relevance and of the growing stream of research devoted to it. These include *Discrete Dynamics in Nature and Society, Chaos, Solitons and Fractals, Nonlinear Economics and Econometrics*, and the *International Journal of Chaos and Bifurcation Theory*.

Recent single-authored or dual-authored volumes of considerable interest include those of Abraham-Frois and Berrebi (1995), Azariadis (1993), Brock and Malliaris (1989), Gabisch and Lorenz (1987), Goodwin (1990), Hommes (1991), Lorenz (1993), Medio (1992), and Rosser (1993).

26 Implications for Policy and Economic Science

I really think that the progress of society consists of irregular movements and to omit the consideration of causes ... is to omit the causes of the wealth and poverty of nations—the grand object of all inquiries in Political Economy.
—Malthus to Ricardo, January 26, 1817[1]

In the ... Age of Civilization so far, we can discern no cumulative progress towards ... permanent law and order. We can only see chaotic fluctuations of which the outcome is not yet in sight.
—Arnold Toynbee, *Change and Habit: The Challenge of Our Time*

Chaos demands to be recognized and experienced before letting itself be converted into a new order.
—Hermann Hesse[2]

When Malthus wrote the passage quoted above, he did not have available quarterly reports of industrial businesses or the elaborate statistics published by various modern trade organizations, or the government indexes of aggregate production, capital utilization, employment, and the general level of prices we hear so much of today. But any astute observer of daily life was aware of the turbulent motion of commodity quantities and prices, and anyone over twenty years of age would have noticed the changes in production and transportation that were transforming the cities and the countryside of England.

Although archaeology was not yet a science, Malthus must have had a classical education. The Greek and Roman writers knew about the spread of city-states and the rise and fall of empires. An educated man had to know that life was not a stasis. And, of course, Malthus had Adam Smith to inform him. Anyone interested in economics had to know that a nation flourished when its people invested in capital accumulation, when its labor force was healthy and well educated, when its methods of manufacturing favored specialization, and when its institutions of resource allocation allowed individual discretion and initiative and facilitated voluntary exchange. They knew that competition within such a market system directed capital to those uses where demand was potentially greatest and adjusted prices in response to imbalances of supply and demand, which in turn stimulated compensating changes in production and consumption. They also knew that such a system was capable of inflation, of speculative bubbles, of financial panics, and they knew of the vicissitudes of individual fortunes in the face of changing technologies and market conditions. In short, they had to know that economies were evolving systems.

Yet, in the intervening two centuries, understanding economics from the dynamic, nonlinear, evolutionary point of view has advanced sporadically. People in general are often too bound up with everyday life, too focused on what is happening, and too involved in what should be done now to concern themselves with the span of events beyond a few months or years. As a result, we fail to recognize the great movements of which we are a part, which are carrying us along and which will affect our lives or those of our descendents.

Economists in particular suffer this myopia. Too many of us have ignored a study of the causes of society's irregular progress. Without an adequate understanding of it, our ability to influence events must inevitably be faulty, and without an adequate understanding of economic process, economic policy must inevitably fail. It is the task of dynamical economic science to understand economic process, including the roles of both foresight and myopia, both equilibria and disequilibrium in that process.

This book has been devoted to that task. It has developed and illustrated some of the basic concepts and methods of economic dynamics, emphasizing the analysis of irregular economic movements and evolving economic structure. A handful of purely logical theorems about simple and complex dynamics have been seen to apply in a wide variety of particular economic settings. The burden on the economic theorist is to determine under what economic conditions the theorems apply and whether or not they do so generically or only for a particular set of unlikely circumstances. In pursuit of this task, conditions were identified in models of market exchange, of macroeconomic business fluctuations, and in economic growth and development that lead to the generic existence of all the kinds of simple and complex economic behavior.

In a sense, the upshot of it all is that in economics anything can happen. But there is a different way of putting this: economic theory can explain much more than was ever thought possible only a few years ago. It can still explain hypothetical equilibria and periodic cycles. It can also explain erratic business fluctuations; not just growth trends, but fluctuating growth rates; not just endless growth, but many of the qualitative varieties of structural change that have characterized economic evolution over the entire span of our species insofar as we have knowledge of it.

In spite of serious limitations (which have been pointed out as we went along), the models investigated here introduce questions that need to be addressed and illustrate the types of answers we can expect to derive from more general investigations. Even at this stage of development, however, it seems to me that some clear and important implications emerge. In this chapter I outline my personal view of what these implications are. I first consider the implications for policy, then turn to those for scientific method, for our analysis suggests a reorientation in the way we specify economic models and how we test their empirical relevance.

26.1 Implications for Policy

Let us look first at the models of individual markets discussed in part III.

26.1.1 Dynamics of Competitive Markets

Real-world consumers and producers do not know equilibrium prices, or equilibrium strategies, or, indeed, much about how the economy as a whole works. They must base their decisions on currently available information and must adapt their behavior to price, profit, and quantity signals that indicate promising directions for improving performance. Several models representing quantity and price adjustment mechanisms were studied in this book. In the introduction, Walras's producers' tatonnement was used to describe the adjustment of quantities to profits, and in part III Walras's consumers' tatonnement was considered. Two additional models of out-of-equilibrium competitive market models were also taken up in part III. In an extension of Walras's consumers' tatonnement, market mediators respond to inventory changes that reflect excess demand or excess supply and suggest the right direction for changing prices. In an extension of Walras's producers' tatonnement, producers attempt to maximize current profit opportunities within limits determined by their working capital and by their willingness to be flexible in the face of uncertainty.

In all of these models the several types of simple and complex dynamics were found to be generic, the conclusion being that convergence to equilibria cannot be taken for granted. Moreover, it was found that the possibility of instability and of chaotic fluctuations increased as the extent of the market increased or if price and quantity adjustments were not cautious enough. In such conditions, both adequate capitalization and sufficient caution are needed to maintain viability. But no one knows what level of capitalization is sufficient or just how flexible or cautious to be. Excessive capitalization ties up a resource that could be used elsewhere; inadequate capitalization leads to "gambler's ruin." Excessive caution can delay profitable responses; excessive flexibility can lead to debilitating overshoot and fluctuations with excessive and potentially ruinous amplitude.

The task of economic policy makers then is to design and install institutions for recapitalizing bankrupt enterprises if and when the need arises, for—failing this—firms and, in the extreme, an entire industry can self-destruct. Of course, business failure can also be caused by incompetent or corrupt management. When this happens, the bankruptcy laws, which force a transfer of ownership, play a positive role. If, in spite of normal market forces and reasonable rules of management, financial disaster occurs because of causal effect reversal and inadequate capitalization, then some form of bailout through government loans or subsidies may be in order. In practice it is often difficult, no doubt, to distinguish these cases. Certainly, however, the role of government in buffering such extreme vicissitudes should not be ruled out without careful consideration.

26.1.2 Macroeconomic Fluctuations

The real/monetary business cycle theory developed in part IV is based on the intrinsic interaction of the monetary and real sectors. When the combined response of real investment and monetary demand to interest rates is strong enough, fluctuations can occur and are robust. The negative correlations between interest rates and investment and between interest rates and demand deposits assumed in the theory is reflected in the facts. The asymmetric, irregular fluctuations derived in the model also bear a passing resemblance to data, as can be seen in the periodic reports of the various Federal Reserve banks and the widely available computer data banks.

The implications include the following possibilities. First, through a range of tax rates and for changes in the money supply and government expenditures, fiscal and monetary policies may modify the amplitude and duration of business fluctuations and reverse their asymmetry without substantially altering the chaotic nature of the fluctuations. Second, macroeconomic performances averaged over the cycle may exceed what could occur at a stationary state, even though the cycle is chaotic and even though sufficiently tight monetary policy or sufficiently stringent fiscal policy could stabilize the economy. Third, policy instruments can themselves exhibit causal effect reversal, in the sense that increases in a given instrument might improve macroeconomic performance at first, then diminish performance after some point is reached. These possibilities would seem to imply sources of uncertainty in discretionary policy making that have not been recognized before. They provide an explanation of why the effects of economic policy often run counter to intention and intuition.

Does this imply that the government should abstain from attempting to stabilize the economy? Perhaps. Certainly, it implies that economic policy should be tempered with caution. Nonetheless, the social costs of recession, unemployment, unused capacity, bankruptcy, etc., will usually induce political responses. Here, it seems to me, we can infer appropriate guidelines from policies designed for other irregular, unpredictable disasters, such as fires, typhoons, earthquakes, and wars. For such contingencies, stocks of human and physical resources are maintained at various places that make possible a measured response when a disaster strikes. The costs of maintaining and using these stocks are borne through routine taxation and voluntary contributions.

Recessions, it seems to me, should be dealt with in a similar vein, not by attempting to prevent them altogether but rather by accepting their inevitable occurrence in a market economy—part of the price for the market's contribution to viability and freedom of choice—and by having standby policies that can be implemented as the need arises. Employment offices could be maintained more or less like (perhaps as part of) local draft boards. Planning boards at local, state, and national levels of government could prepare, maintain, and bring up to date provisions for public goods *that are not provided by private businesses in normal times*, but ones that play a crucial role for business productivity and human welfare in the long run. Those unfortunate workers and business managers who cannot find employment in the private sector could be allocated to publicly financed—but perhaps privately managed—projects. When unemployment is relatively low, such projects could be small and local; when unemployment is high, larger-scale projects could be initiated. As the private business sector recovers, tax revenues will automatically increase, enabling the deficits incurred from satisfying the public demand for work and the public need for goods to be reduced. Health and life insurance, retirement, and similar benefits could be required of all such publicly financed production so that relatively minimal income-earning opportunities could be maintained for all those willing to work. Direct government welfare transfers could be eliminated for all except the disabled. A business cycle might still persist in the private sector, and there might still be considerable uncertainty and substantial costs of reallocating labor and capital. But access to the market would be maintained, the social cost of rapid change reduced, and fluctuation of output and employment somewhat moderated.

The economics profession and politicians have shifted from this general prescription, which originated during the Great Depression and in the years following World War II. It had dominated fiscal policy until Europe and America shifted from government-funded jobs programs to income entitlements funded by government transfers. This development was followed by a shift in macroeconomic theory from the out-of-equilibrium adjustments point of view to that of viewing the economy *as if* it were always in a thoroughgoing competitive equilibrium, in effect assuming away the potential for active monetary and fiscal policy. The out-of-equilibrium adjustment process involving real/monetary interaction seems to me to be a more plausible theory of the business cycle and therefore a more appropriate basis for formulating macroeconomic policy.

26.1.3 Growth Theory and Long-Run Fluctuations

The policy implications of the chapters on growth theory do not seem to me to be as obvious as those of the chapters on market mechanisms and aggregate business cycles. The models studied in part V do, however, alert us to the great difference between explaining long-run fluctuations on the basis of somewhat plausible (if simplified) representations of behavior and rationalizing them on the basis of axioms of optimality and equilibrium. The fact that mathematical models exist that satisfy these axioms and that mimic some of the real-world complexity is interesting and perhaps insightful. Yet it does not tell us much about why our own world behaves as it does, because we *know* that our own world does *not* satisfy the axioms of optimal growth theory. The other models (the behavioral ones of chapter 16 and the adaptive economizing ones of chapter 17), crude as they are, have assumptions closer to what we know of our own world, and therefore serve an explanatory purpose, in particular showing how forecasting errors of rates of return can induce overinvestment and under-

investment, bringing about medium- or long-term fluctuations in output
and capacity utilization.

By contrast, the theory of optimality and equilibrium identifies a kind
of potential. It embodies the economist's vision of a perfectly coordinated
exchange based on a particular criterion for comparing possibilities. Both
adaptive economizing and optimal growth approaches in the sector model
explain how considerations for the future lead to capital accumulation
and economic growth. But the former provides a more realistic explanation for the irregular growth fluctuations that persist in the data. In
theory, the possibility of such fluctuations is enhanced by increased emphasis on the future or by a decreased capital elasticity of production,
both of which increase the error in forecasting the rate of return on
savings. As in the case of the business cycle model of part IV, plausible
parameter values based on empirical studies seem to be quite consistent
with the appearance of irregular growth fluctuations, thus lending further support to the judgments (i) that the complex behavior of macroeconomic data arises at least in part from adaptations to out-of-equilibrium
signals, and (ii) that appropriate institutions are needed to buffer and
moderate the social cost of private, out-of-equilibrium behavior.

26.1.4 Development and Economic Evolution in the Very Long Run

When growth models incorporate structural change, infrastructure, and
social and environmental space, these factors are seen to play crucial roles
in determining viability and possible patterns of economic evolution, including regime switching and reswitching and turbulent periods before
lasting transition occurs. We begin to see why the human record has not
been one of steady improvement in welfare with orderly transitions from
one more advanced culture to the next, why our ancestors—and we ourselves—have not been able to orchestrate technology and socioeconomic
organization so as to make possible such a utopian march from savagery
to sophistication. Social scientists and philosophers have yet to meet their
greatest challenge, to so design the engines of economy and polity that
intermittent chaos and catastrophe can be avoided and law and order
might prevail. From the theoretical perspective of the very long run we
saw how daunting this challenge must be, just as Toynbee surmised in his
descriptive essay of long-run history quoted at the head of this chapter.

From an empirical perspective and using a generational time scale,
human population, human production, and human productivity—despite

all their vicissitudes—are growing explosively on this earth. If there are limits, and there surely must be ultimate limits to human numbers and to resource utilization, then we have been heading toward them at accelerating speed. The multiple-phase theory of development tells us that in these conditions, the probability of overshooting equilibrium, plunging into chaos, or collapsing altogether becomes ever greater unless the braking effect of external diseconomies becomes important soon enough or unless society can stabilize population before the limits are exceeded.

Of special importance for interpreting policy is the implication that regime shifts can occur suddenly relative to the time spent *within* regimes. That is why very-long-run evolutionary forces are relevant for explaining what happens in the short run. The theory tells us that successful growth may be followed by a catastrophic decline which can be prevented only if a new "more advanced" sociotechnical system can be adopted before the collapse. Thus, in addition to the desirability of population control and resource conservation, adequate infrastructural provisions must be provided. In the absence of adequate population control, the only solution to the problem of collapse is successful basic research that can provide the groundwork for designing more advanced sociotechnical regimes accompanied by mechanisms that can mobilize the infrastructural resources needed for each transition.

26.1.5 Summary

The common implications for policy drawn from all our models is the potential role for institutions outside the market system itself—in buffering change, enhancing viability of the market system, and moderating the social costs of rapid change. In fact, the market is a set of institutions designed in part, authorized in part, and regulated in part by the institutions of the state. Thus, both public and private institutions interact and in a very real sense *coevolve*. The grand dynamics of this coevolution of market and state is a phenomenon whose analysis exceeds the capacity of the models to which the present book is confined. It demands a consideration of political economy and economic history in a very broad way.[3]

Nonetheless, a further development of economic theory in the directions suggested in this book can play a significant role in that broader mission. The methods of comparative dynamics and global analysis, applied to models that allow for alternative policy strategies and that are based on assumptions which approximate salient features of real-world decision making, can have important applications as well as interesting theoretical properties.

26.2 Implications for Science

26.2.1 Mathematical Theory and Economic Science

Except for those defining optimal growth in chapter 18, the models of this book were not meant to represent an economy as a perfect balance of forces. Instead, they were designed (again with the exception of optimal growth models) to explain salient features of economic life as it has been experienced in the past and as it is being experienced in our own time. Assumptions were not arbitrary or chosen merely to satisfy abstract axioms of individual rationality or social efficiency. Rather they were intended to reflect, at least in an approximate way, aspects of real economic structure. In the numerical examples, whenever possible, plausible parameter values were chosen that were related at least crudely to empirical information.

Obviously, not too much should be made of this plausibility, because all the models are simple. All have limits and all cry out for generalization by including more variables and more detailed representations of economic structures. But simplicity has its benefits. It has enabled us to derive, for the models under consideration, an understanding of behavior for all the possible parameter configurations.

This approach reflects a scientific methodology that deserves some further elaboration. The advantage of mathematical theory is its clarity: the primitives of an argument are either unambiguous or they are not; the results based on them are either mathematically correct or they are not. By couching a theory in formal, symbolic terms and deriving its implications with precision, one is enabled to eliminate unnecessary logical disputes.

But science must go beyond pure logic. Its assumptions are intended to be informed by observation, and its implications tested by their consistency with factual data. Yet the clarity of mathematical theory is partially lost when it is used to explain phenomena. Obfuscation creeps in and differences of opinion lead to contrasting and conflicting scientific schools of thought. In few other disciplines than in economics do more contrasting interpretations arise in making the connections between theory and fact. This is not only because of problems of observation, measurement, and inference, but also because the investigator may often see the world as he would like to see it and not the way it really is. These difficulties must have been behind Malthus's admonition that "the first task of philosophy is to see things as they are."

Consider then the nature of fact, the starting point for any science. Facts are accumulated by careful observation and measurement. They can never be totally objective, because observations are filtered and measurements processed, so that much of what we consider to be fact is but a particular and possibly distorted representation. Nonetheless, in science our theories are at the mercy of the facts, whose acquisition is therefore of fundamental importance.

The careful observation and accurate description of what is and what was is the basis for the construction of history, that is, time lines of system states. Such time lines are what a dynamical science is intended to explain—in economics as in physics, in biology, and in the other sciences of human behavior.

Careful observation also leads to a related but somewhat different category of fact: intuitions about *how things work*. Such intuitions lead to models that explain the time lines of observed behavior. What are the properties of time lines that can be explained? Ideally, one would like an exact explanation of an exactly objective fact. Better yet, one would like an exactly correct prediction of future events in the time lines. Since facts are seldom, if ever, exact in an objective sense, such ideals are not attainable.

Facts, however, may be more reliable in reflecting objective *qualitative* characteristics of real-world time lines, such as trends, cycles, irregular fluctuations, evolving structures. The present study is an example of the use of mathematical economic theory to explain qualitative properties of factual time lines on the basis of assumptions that reflect intuitions and facts about how economies work. In principle, the models can generate exact numerical trajectories. In actual practice, numerical simulations can only approximate the state that emerges from its preceding approximated value. The theory of complex dynamics tells us that, as a consequence, these computations should not predict factual time lines accurately very far into the future—even if our models were exactly "true." Numerical error is compounded, and the computed path will depart from the "true" path very rapidly (perhaps returning close to it but departing away from it again). This is particularly important in economics, where factual time lines are not objectively accurate in a numerical sense but may reflect salient qualitative features of the real world. Thus, *we should not reject theories for their inaccurate numerical predictions but rather for their failure to exhibit the qualitative properties of the data.* Many of the numerical examples used throughout this book were chosen to illustrate this methodological approach.

I have emphasized the plausibility of the assumptions on which most of the models in this book are based. These assumptions encompass the basis of all economic theory, namely the microfoundations of technology, preferences, and economizing choice, and the macrofoundations of supply and demand. The models of this book, derived as they are from the founders of classical, neoclassical, and modern economic theory, all rest on these foundations. But I have emphasized that economic choice is adaptive and at best boundedly rational, and that in general economic actions are not perfectly coordinated. These foundations reflect the facts about how economies actually work. Stationary or steady states exist in most of our models, occuring when markets clear and when expectations are self-fulfilling. These stationary states satisfy conventional properties of economic equilibria. But they were shown to be generically unstable, so that convergence to them cannot be taken for granted.

26.2.2 Statistical Estimation and Inference

Qualitative judgments of the kind discussed above for formulating and evaluating economic theory are necessary but need to be buttressed wherever possible by more precise methods of estimation and inference. Advances in statistics and econometrics are improving the prospects for doing so. The basic task is to estimate and establish the statistical significance of the natural nonlinearities that are specified in complex economic dynamic models. Various iterative techniques have been available for many years, but shockingly little has been done to apply them in the dynamic context. Recent progress has been made for the piecewise linear case. An example of the latter that has direct application to the behavioral stock market model of chapter 11 was produced by Srinivasan (1993), who gives references to the relevant literature. The difficulties inherent in direct structural estimations have been cogently illustrated by Geweke (1993).

A more indirect approach is to "calibrate" a given model, as was done above in the empirical business cycle and growth models of chapters 13 and 17, in more or less the same way, for example, as in the famous real business cycle model of Kydland and Prescott (1982). Then one generates a sample trajectory of the calibrated model and compares it with relevant factual data. For the reasons outlined above, we would not expect to explain the data points or predict their future values at all accurately. However, we should demand of the model that it explain and predict the data in terms of trends, standard deviations from trends, and, more generally, autocorrelations and spectral decompositions.

Years of work on the statistical analysis of economic time series data led by Clive Granger and his colleagues have shown that many economic data series appear to have been generated by stochastic processes, in particular by autoregressive moving averages and linear difference equations with variously specified lags among the state variables and the assumed random terms. See Hatanaka (1996) and the collection edited by Engle (1995). The results of Radunskaya, referred to in the preceding chapter, seem to be especially important in this context. The potential observational equivalence of deterministic nonlinear and stochastic processes suggests that a test of a given theoretical model can be based on fitting Markov processes to both model trajectories and factual data. The point of view here is that the Markov process is not a theory of the underlying generating process but a statistical characterization of its trajectories, a characterization that should be at least approximately shared by the empirical and the theoretical data.

An approach for inferring if nonlinearity is involved in the processes generating observed data is not based on estimating the structure of specific models; rather, it is based on developing methods for answering the general question, Can one infer from a given irregular time series—without specifying a model at all—if it has been generated by a deterministic, nonlinear process or by a stochastic, linear one? This approach, which has received far more attention than that of structural estimation, was originated by Takens (1980) and applied by Scheinkman and LeBaron (1989), Ramsey, Sayers, and Rothman (1990), Chen (1988), and many others. More powerful tests for discriminating nonlinearity have been developed by Hinich (1982) and by Brock and Dechert (1987). Using these methods, considerable but perhaps not overwhelming evidence has been accumulated that many economic data series have indeed been generated by nonlinear processes. Several useful reviews of the various methods and the issues concerning them have appeared, including Chen (1993) and Barnett and Hinich (1993).

Further progress in this direction is likely to be limited, for three reasons. First, many economic time series are too short for statistical tests to possess much power. That is, they may find it relatively easy to reject the hypothesis of nonlinearity when it is false, but relatively difficult to accept it when it is true. Second, we know that many forces and interactions not included in our models—even the most elaborate ones—actually are at work in the real-world economy. Many of these forces will impinge on the economy in an irregular way and will have an effect much like the purely random shocks assumed in stochastic processes. This will confound the statistical tests. Third, the fact that a large class of chaotic models can generate trajectories observationally equivalent to those of stochastic Markov processes implies that a fundamental and possibly insurmountable identification problem exists. This implies that the structural estimations of model components using calibration methods that draw on data other than the estimated state trajectories must inevitably be employed. This suggests in turn that the proper test is that of comparing the stochastic properties of model-generated trajectories and factual time series, as outlined above.

But suppose, as the result of statistical analysis, that the real data (GNP, the Dow index, etc.) do appear to follow a linear stochastic process. Could we forget about nonlinearity and just use linear models for practical work? Bifurcation studies amply illustrated in this book provide a definite answer: No! The reason is that we ultimately want to use models to identify policy instruments that can be manipulated to modify the behavior of the real system. However, even small changes in parameters can not only change the time path of the system, but can also drastically shift the long-run stochastic behavior (in terms of densities) of the system. This implies that each parameter shift would require reestimation of the underlying parameters of the system, but reestimation and the new policy regime would require time for the system to generate new data.

One could therefore understand the policy effects only by studying the model with its crucial nonlinearities intact. This would appear to be analogous to the Lucas critique in macroeconomics, which points out that predictions that do not incorporate the full interactive effects of private/ public agent decision making are bound to fail. On this ground, Lucas argues for a full game-theoretic analysis of perfectly informed strategic decision making by all agents in the economy. Here the issue is one of whether the crucial endogenous nonlinearities should be explicitly incorporated. It is the omission of salient nonlinearities that confounds prediction on the basis of parametric bifurcation studies.

26.2.3 The Frontiers of Complex Economic Dynamics

Although much has been accomplished in this field so far, much more needs to be done. In the realm of mathematical methods, the complex dynamics of many-state-variable nonlinear systems needs to be studied so that the kinds of analyses described in this book can be extended to a wider class of models that can take into account salient interactions that have to be omitted in the single-state-variable case.

In the realm of economic theory, work in this direction is being carried out for example by Pintus, Sands, and Vilder (1996), Grandmont, Pintus, and Vilder (1995), and Vilder (1995). Increased effort needs to be directed toward modeling adaptive economizing, out-of-equilibrium, and regime-switching processes, and toward identifying the role played by viability-inducing mediation mechanisms. As more general, empirically informed theory is developed, more general econometric methods of estimation and inference must also be sought along the lines of the qualitative methods outlined above.

Those of us who have been developing complex economic dynamics during the last two decades have had the satisfying experience of establishing a new way of understanding aspects of the real world that in former times seemed to lie beyond the dynamic principle. The next decades of research should belong to those who will extend this way of understanding to a level of generality that has been accomplished already in optimization, equilibrium, and game theory, making it as econometrically based as the work in linear statistics and time series analysis, and as practically relevant as the work of the great empirical model builders such as Leontief, Tinbergen, Klein, Modigliani, Tobin, and Jorgenson.

With these developments it should be possible to reestablish the relevance of economic theory for practical policy applications.

Epilog

During a break while preparing the final revision of this book, I was struck by the words to a popular country tune:

Cause and effect
Chain of events
All this chaos makes perfect sense
When you spin around, things come undone
Welcome to Earth, third rock from the Sun.

Wallace Stegner quoted Henry Adams: "Chaos, he told me, is the law of nature; order is the dream of man." We no longer think of humans as separate from nature but rather as a realm of nature, interacting within itself and with the other natural realms in a complex web of causal effect. We know that chaos occurs within our realm, and, now that we know where to look for explanations, it makes perfect sense. To find explanations is the task of dynamical economic science. To formulate them coherently and rigorously is the purpose of dynamic economic theory. As we progress in this task, we may hope for a better realization of order in the human realm.

Appendix: Background Theorems

The following concepts and theorems are discussed in volume I, part II. They are reproduced here, without their accompanying text, for convenience, as they are used again and again in the present volume. The section numbering is that of volume I, as is the equation numbering.

4.1.1 Difference Equations and Domains

Begin with a map or function $\theta : D \to \mathbb{R}$ where D is a subset of the real numbers $\mathbb{R}$ called the *domain of admissible* or *feasible* states. Then

$$x_{t+1} = \theta(x_t), \quad x_t \in D, \ t \in \mathbb{N}^+$$

is the first-order difference equation where $\mathbb{N}^+$ is the set of nonnegative integers. The pair (θ, D) is a *system*. The *null domain* is the set $D^0 := \mathbb{R} \backslash D$. It represents the part of the real numbers where states are not defined or allowed.

4.2.1 Iterated Maps and Semiflow

The recursive application of the difference equation yields the sequence

$$x_0 = x$$
$$x_1 = \theta(x)$$
$$x_2 = \theta(\theta(x))$$
$$x_3 = \theta(\theta(\theta(x)))$$
$$\vdots$$
$$x_t = \theta(\dots(\theta(x))\dots).$$

In this way, the state of the system for any period can be derived starting from an arbitrary initial condition $x_0 = x$.

Define the *identity map* by $\theta^0(x) := x$ for any x. Then define $\theta^{t+1}(x) := \theta(\theta^t(x))$ for $t = 1, 2, 3, \dots$ for any x.

4.2.2 Trajectories and Orbits

A recursively generated sequence

$$\tau(x) := (x, \theta(x), \theta^2(x), \dots, \theta^t(x), \dots)$$

is called a *trajectory*. Because θ is a single-valued function, *any finite history from x and the trajectory from x are unique*. The *orbit* of a trajectory

$\gamma(x)$ is the set of points through which the trajectory passes; that is, $\gamma(x) = \{x, \theta(x), \theta^2(x), \ldots\}$. If a trajectory repeats any point after a finite number of time intervals, then $\gamma(x)$ is a finite set.

4.2.5 Semidynamical Systems

Consider two iterated maps θ^s and θ^t beginning from two points x and y with $z = \theta^s(y)$ and $y = \theta^t(x)$. By substitution, $z = \theta^s(\theta^t(x))$. Because y is the state that occurs t periods after x and z occurs s periods after y, evidently z occurs $s + t$ periods after x, that is,

$$z = \theta^s(\theta^t(x)) = \theta^{s+t}(x)$$

where θ^{s+t} is just the $(s + t)$th iterated map. The set of maps $\{\theta^0, \theta^1, \theta^2, \ldots, \theta^n, \ldots\}$ is a *semigroup* with the group operation defined by (4.6) and the identity element θ^0. This set of maps determines the unique trajectory from any initial condition. A closed system and its associated semigroup of iterated maps is called a *semidynamical system*, which we shall also denote by (θ, D).

5.1.1 Fixpoints and Stationary States

A trajectory $\tau(\tilde{x})$ from a state $\tilde{x}$ such that $\theta^t(\tilde{x}) = \tilde{x}$ for all t is called *stationary* and $\tilde{x}$ is called a *stationary state*. In particular $\tilde{x} = \theta(\tilde{x})$, so a stationary state of a system (θ, D) is a fixpoint of the map θ that lies in D.

5.2.1 Cycles and Fixpoints

A $y \in D$ such that

$$y = \theta^p(y) \quad \text{and} \quad y \neq \theta^n(y), \ n = 1, \ldots, p - 1$$

for some integer $p > 1$ is called p-cyclic. Note that *a p-cyclic state is a fixpoint of the p-th iterated map.*

THEOREM 5.1 *Let θ be continuous on D. If there exist $y, z \in D$ such that $\theta(y) \leq y$ and $\theta(z) \geq z$, then there exists a stationary state $\tilde{x} \in [\min\{y, z\}, \max\{y, z\}]$ of the difference equation (4.1).*

THEOREM 5.2 *Let $\theta : D \to \mathbb{R}$ be continuous on D and let $I = [a, b] \subset D$. If*

(i) $\theta(I) \subset I$ or

(ii) $\theta(I) \supset I$

then there exists a fixpoint $\tilde{x} \in I$ and $\tilde{x}$ is a stationary state of the system (θ, D).

THEOREM 5.3 (Diamond)   *Let (θ, D) be a closed continuous system and suppose there exists a set A such that*

$$A \cap \theta(A) = \varnothing,$$

$$A \cup \theta(A) \subset \theta^2(A).$$

Then there exists a cycle of every order $n = 1, 2, 3, \ldots$ in D.

THEOREM 5.4 (Li-Yorke)   *Let (θ, D) be a closed continuous system and suppose there exists a point a such that*

$$\theta^3(a) \leq a < \theta(a) < \theta^2(a)$$

or conversely, such that

$$\theta^3(a) \geq a > \theta(a) > \theta^2(a).$$

Then there exists a cycle of every order $n = 1, 2, 3, \ldots$ in D.

THEOREM 5.5 (Švarkovskii)   *Suppose θ is continuous on a closed, bounded set D. Let $P(k)$ be the property that a periodic orbit of order k exists. Then*

$$
\begin{aligned}
P(3) \quad &\Rightarrow \quad P(5) \quad \Rightarrow \quad P(7) \quad \Rightarrow \quad \cdots \\
\cdots P(2 \cdot 3) \quad &\Rightarrow \quad P(2 \cdot 5) \quad \Rightarrow \quad P(2 \cdot 7) \quad \Rightarrow \quad \cdots \\
\cdots P(2^n \cdot 3) \quad &\Rightarrow \quad P(2^n \cdot 5) \quad \Rightarrow \quad P(2^n \cdot 7) \quad \Rightarrow \quad \cdots \\
\cdots P(2^m) \quad &\Rightarrow \quad P(2^{m-1}) \quad \Rightarrow \quad \cdots \quad \Rightarrow P(2) \Rightarrow P(1)
\end{aligned}
$$

5.3.1   Asymptotic Stability

The idea of converging trajectories can be stated for a general system (θ, D). Let $N(x, \delta) := (x - \delta, x + \delta)$ be a δ-neighborhood of x in D. A trajectory $\tau(x)$ is called *asymptotically stable* if and only if there exists positive δ such that for all $y \in N(x, \delta)$,

$$\lim_{t \to \infty} |\theta^t(y) - \theta^t(x)| = 0.$$

THEOREM 5.6   *Let (θ, D) be a continuous system. A stationary state $\tilde{x} \in D$ is asymptotically stable if and only if there exists a $\delta > 0$ such that*

$$|\theta(y) - \tilde{x}| < |y - \tilde{x}|$$

for all $y \in N(\tilde{x}, \delta)$.

THEOREM 5.7 *If θ is differentiable at a stationary state $\tilde{x}$ of (θ, D), then $\tilde{x}$ is asymptotically stable if*

$$|\theta'(\tilde{x})| \le \delta < 1.$$

THEOREM 5.8 *Let θ be differentiable almost everywhere and in particular at the p-periodic points $x \in \gamma(y)$ where y is p-cyclic. A sufficient condition that the cyclic points $x \in \gamma(y)$ are asymptotically stable is*

$$\times_{x \in \gamma(y)} |\theta'(x)| \le \delta < 1.$$

THEOREM 5.9 *Let $\theta(\cdot)$ be differentiable almost everywhere on D and in particular at the p-periodic points $x \in \gamma(y)$ where y is p-periodic. Then a sufficient condition for the periodic trajectories $\tau(x), x \in \gamma(y)$ to be unstable is that*

$$\times_{x \in \gamma(y)} |\theta'(x)| \ge \delta > 1.$$

In particular, if $\tilde{x}$ is a stationary state, then

$$|\theta'(\tilde{x})| \ge \delta > 1$$

is sufficient for $\tau(\tilde{x})$ to be unstable.

THEOREM 5.10 *Let θ be differentiable almost everywhere on D and assume that there exists an integer $m \ge 1$ such that*

$$\left| \frac{\theta^m(x)}{dx} \right| \ge \delta > 1$$

for all $x \in D$ where the derivative is defined. Then all trajectories in (θ, D) are unstable. In particular, if

$$|\theta'(x)| \ge \delta > 1$$

where the derivative is defined, then (θ, D) is unstable.

THEOREM 7.1 (Chaos) *Let $\{\theta, D\}$ be a continuous dynamical system and suppose there exists a least integer $m \ge 1$ and a nonempty compact set X such that*

$$X \cap \theta^m(X) = \varnothing,$$

$$X \cup \theta^m(X) \subset \theta^{2m}(X)$$

(i) Then there exists an uncountable set S such that $\theta(S) \subset S$, i.e., S is closed (nonexpanding) under θ and for all $x \in S$ the trajectory $\tau(x)$ is nonperiodic.

(ii) There exists a set P such that for each $p = 1, 2, 3, \ldots$, there is a point of period mp in P.

(iii) Any trajectory in S wanders away from any other trajectory in $S \cup P$, no matter how close it may come.

(iv) All trajectories in S move close to every other one infinitely often.

THEOREM 7.2 (Li-Yorke)   *Let $\{\theta, D\}$ be a continuous dynamical system. If there is a point $x \in D$ and an integer m such that*

$$\theta^{3m}(x) \leq x < \theta^m(x) < \theta^{2m}(x)$$

or

$$\theta^{3m} \geq x > \theta^m(x) > \theta^{2m}(x)$$

then the results of Theorem 7.1 hold.

THEOREM 7.3 (**LIMPY I**)   *Let $\{\theta, D\}$ be a continuous, compact dynamical system. Suppose there exists a point x and an odd integer $m \geq 3$ such that*

$$\theta^m(x) < x < \theta(x)$$

or

$$\theta^m(x) > x > \theta(x);$$

then there exists a cycle with odd period k not greater than m such that k divides m i.e., m/k is an integer ($m \bmod k = 0$). Moreover, by Theorem 7.4 below the chaos properties hold.

DEFINITION 7.1   The iterates $\theta^i(x)$, $i = 0, \ldots, n$ are said to have no division if there exists no $y \in D$ such that either

$$x_j < y \quad \text{for all even } j \quad \text{and} \quad x_j > y \quad \text{for all odd } j$$

or

$x_j > y$ for all even j and $x_j < y$ for all odd j.

THEOREM 7.4 (**LIMPY II**)   *Let $\{\theta, D\}$ be a continuous, compact dynamical system and suppose there exists a sequence $(\theta^i(x))$, $i = 0, 1, \ldots, n$ in D with no division and such that one or other of the inequalities of Theorem 7.3 is satisfied. Then there exists a cycle of odd period and the chaos properties hold.*

PROPOSITION 7.4 (Stretchable Maps)   *Let (θ_μ, D) be a continuous compact dynamical system depending on the parameter $\mu \geq 0$. Assume there exists a nondegenerate open interval $I := (x', x'') \subset D \subset \mathbb{R}^+$ such that*

$$\theta_1(x) > 0 \quad all \quad x \in I, \quad \theta_1(x') = \theta_1(x'') = 0$$

and assume μ is stretchable, i.e.,

$$\theta_\mu(x) \equiv \mu\theta_1(x) \quad all \quad x \in D.$$

Then there exists a value of μ, say μ^c, such that the system has the chaos property for all $\mu > \mu^c$.

THEOREM 8.1 (Poincaré Recurrence Theorem)   *Let (X, Σ, μ) be a probability space and let the measure $\mu(\cdot)$ be invariant under θ. Let A be any set of positive measure. Then almost all points of A return to A infinitely often.*

THEOREM 8.2 (Birkhoff–von Neumann Mean Ergodic Theorem)   *Let (D, Σ, μ) be a probability space and let θ be measure preserving and ergodic. Let $g(\cdot)$ be an integrable function. Then*

$$\lim_{n \to \infty} \frac{1}{n} \sum_{i=0}^{n-1} g(\theta^i(x)) = \int_D g d\mu \quad for \; almost \; all \quad x \in D.$$

COROLLARY 8.1   *Let (D, Σ, μ) be a probability space and let θ be measure preserving and ergodic on D. Then for μ-almost all x in $A \in \Sigma$, $\tau(x)$ will visit every measurable set proportionally to its measure.*

DEFINITION 8.5   A measure μ is said to be absolutely continuous with respect to Lebesgue measure if there exists an integrable function f called the density of μ such that

$$\mu(X) := \int_X f(x)\,dx$$

for all $X \in \Sigma$.

DEFINITION 8.6 (Strongly Ergodic Dynamical Systems) A dynamical system (θ, D) where $a = \inf D$ that is ergodic with respect to an absolutely continuous measure μ defined on $\mathbb{R}$ will be called strongly ergodic. For a strongly ergodic system with density f, the measure is equivalent to the cumulative distribution function (c.d.f.)

$$F(x) := \mu([a, x]) = \int_a^x f(u)\,du.$$

THEOREM 8.4 (Lasota and Yorke 1973) *Let $\theta : D \to D$ be piecewise C^2 where D is an interval. If*

$$|\theta'(x)| \geq \delta > 1, \quad \lambda\text{-almost everywhere in } D,$$

then there exists an absolutely continuous invariant measure.

THEOREM 8.5 *Let (θ, D) be a dynamical system where D is an interval and the map θ is piecewise strictly monotonic on each piece of partition of interval pieces D_i, $i = 1, \ldots, n$, such that for each $i = 1, \ldots, n$, θ_i restricted to the interior of D_i is continuously differentiable and expansive. Then there exists a finite collection of sets $L_1, \ldots, L_m$ where each L_i, $i = 1, \ldots, m$, is a finite union of closed intervals, and a set of absolutely continuous probability measures $\mu_1, \ldots, \mu_m$ invariant under θ, such that*

(i) each L_i contains at least one turning point of θ in its interior (which implies that $m \leq n - 1$);

(ii) $\mu_i(L_i) = 1$, $i = 1, \ldots, m$, i.e., each μ_i is ergodic with respect to L_i, hence $d\mu_i$ is positive almost everywhere there;

(iii) every measure invariant under θ can be written as a linear combination of the μ_i. (That is, the μ_i form a basis in the space of invariant measures.)

COROLLARY 8.3 *Given the hypotheses of Theorem 8.5, there exists a partition $\{B_i, i = 1, \ldots, m\}$ such that*

(i) each B_i is a finite union of intervals;

(ii) $B_i \supset L_i$, $i = 1, \ldots, m$;

(iii) each B_i is the basin of attraction for L_i, i.e., $\omega(x) = L_i$ for λ-almost all $x \in B_i$.

COROLLARY 8.4   *Given the hypotheses of Theorem 8.5, if $n = 2$ there exists a unique, ergodic absolutely continuous invariant measure with a unique attractor that is the union of closed intervals for λ-almost all $x \in I$.*

COROLLARY 8.5   *If a map $\theta(\cdot)$ does not satisfy the assumptions of Theorem 8.5 but there exists an integer, say p, such that the map $\theta^p(\cdot)$ satisfies them, then the theorem holds.*

COROLLARY 8.6   *Suppose (θ, D) satisfies the assumptions of Theorem 8.5 and let $\{B_i, i = 1, \ldots, m\}$ be the partition of D into basins of attraction as in Corollary 8.3. Moreover, let $f_i = d\mu_i$ for each absolutely continuous invariant ergodic measure μ_i. Then for all $x \in B_i$*

$$\lim_{n \to \infty} \frac{1}{n} \sum_{j=1}^{n} g(\theta^j(x)) = \int_D g(u) f_i(u) \, du,$$

and in particular, for all $x \in B_i$,

$$\bar{x}_i = \lim_{n \to \infty} \frac{1}{n} \sum_{j=1}^{n} \theta^j(x) = \int_D u f_i(u) \, du$$

and

$$\sigma_i^2 = \lim_{n \to \infty} \frac{1}{n} \sum_{j=1}^{n} [\theta^i(x) - \bar{x}]^2 = \int_D (u - \bar{x})^2 f_i(u) \, du.$$

THEOREM 8.6 (Misiurewicz)   *Let θ, I be piecewise strictly monotonic on an interval I with an interval partition of pieces $c\ell I_i = [a_{i-1}, a_i]$, $i = 1, \ldots, n$. Let $A := \{a_i, i = 0, \ldots, n\}$ be the set of endpoints of the intervals. Assume that*

(i) any cyclic point in I is unstable;

(ii) there is a neighborhood N_A of A such that

$$\gamma(y^i) \subset A \cup (I \backslash N_A).$$

(Recall that $(\gamma(y^i)$ is the orbit through $y^i \in A$. This means that the points of every orbit through any endpoint are eventually cyclic, or they belong to a set whose points are all a finite distance from any endpoint.)

Moreover, assume that in the interior of each set I_i, $i = 1, \ldots, n$,

(iii) θ_i is continuously differentiable; and

(iv) $|\theta_i'(x)|^{-\frac{1}{2}}$ is a convex function.

Then the results of Theorem 8.5 and Corollaries 8.3–8.6 hold.

THEOREM 8.7 (Divergence from Periodic Trajectories and the Appearance of Deceptive Order)   *Let $\{\theta, D\}$ be a continuous dynamical system that satisfies the assumptions of either Theorem 8.5 or Theorem 8.6. Then for each invariant ergodic set L_i, there exists a denumerably infinite set of cyclic points of odd order above some odd integer, say m, and every even integer order. Let P_i be this set of cyclic points in L_i. Then for all $y \in P_i$ and μ_i-almost all $x \in B_i$,*

$$\liminf |\theta^n(x) - \theta^n(y)| = 0$$

$$\limsup |\theta^n(x) - \theta^n(y)| > 0.$$

THEOREM 8.8 (Chaos Almost Everywhere)   *Let (θ, D) be a dynamical system that satisfies the assumptions of either Theorem 8.5 or Theorem 8.6. Let B_i be the basin of attraction for the attractor L_i. Then almost any trajectory in B_i will approximate periodic cycles of all even orders and all odd orders above some odd integer and will also approximate finite segments of any trajectory in the scrambled set.*

THEOREM 8.9 (Hofbauer and Keller 1982, Ziemien 1985)   *Let θ satisfy the assumptions of Theorem 8.5 or Theorem 8.6. Let μ_i be the absolutely continuous invariant ergodic measure with corresponding support L_i, $i = 1, \ldots, k$. Then for almost all x the time averages converge in distribution to a normal distribution $N(m_i, \sigma_i^2)$ with mean m_i and variance σ_i^2, or, alternatively, the normalized averages*

$$\sqrt{N} \left(\frac{\bar{x}^p(N) - m_i}{\sigma_i} \right)$$

converge in distribution to the standard normal $N(0, 1)$ for some i when $P \to \infty$ and $N \to \infty$.

THEOREM 8.10 (Pianigiani and Yorke 1979)   *Let θ be a piecewise C^2 transformation as defined in Theorem 8.6. If θ is strongly expansive, then there exists an absolutely continuous measure conditionally invariant with respect to the Lebesgue measure.*

Notes

13 The Real/Monetary Business Cycle Theory

1. This chapter draws on Day and Shafer (1985) and Day and Lin (1992). Classic discussions of the dynamic theory will be found in Keynes (1936), Goodwin (1943), and Hicks (1950, chapter 4). For balanced texts, see Branson (1989) or Blanchard (1997). For a series of developments that refine and extend the analysis, see the discussion in chapter 25, below.

2. For an eloquent exegesis of this view, see Lucas (1987).

3. Early and still relevant mathematical renditions are Modigliani (1944) and Samuelson (1947).

4. This assumption enables us to stay within the analytical framework common to all the models discussed in this book. A more realistic assumption would be to suppose that interest rates adjust with a lag. This is done in more advanced analysis. See, for example, Flaschel, Franke, and Semmler (1997).

5. For an elementary discussion of the implicit function theorem, see Courant (1934, p. 482).

6. For a classic discussion of lags responsible for the adjustment process, see Metzler (1965), who refers to related literature of the time. The Swedish School, following Wicksell and especially Lunberg in the 1930's, had already emphasized the role of lags, as had Robertson in England. It was the latter's influence that led to the term "Robertsonian lag."

7. Due to the implicit function theorem, in the same manner as the function (13.2).

8. What I have here called a fixed price equilibrium is a competitive *dis*equilibrium if (13.3) is satisfied as a strict inequality. Benassy (1986) calls it a "non-Walrasian equilibrium." Because the labor market does not clear, it could also be called a "Keynesian disequilibrium," as suggested in the work of Clower (1963) or Leijonhufvud (1968). In any case it is assumed here that the money market clears and that supply adjusts to demand.

9. For recent research that removes these simplifying assumptions, see chapter 25.

10. On stability, asymptotic stability, and global stability, see volume I, §5.3 and §5.4.

11. For a good discussion of the qualitative properties of money demand, see Branson (1989, chapters 12 and 13). For an early discussion of the supply of money function, see Smith (1967). For a classic analysis of the speculative demand for money, see Goodwin (1943), drawing on a seminal article by Williams (1936).

12. For example, Hansen (1949), Ackley (1961), or Branson (1989).

13. The classic statement is Hicks (1937). See Branson (1989) for a thorough development.

14 Plausible Parameters, Counterfactual Histories, and the Robustness of Chaos

1. For standard texts that use the linear model see Gordon (1978) or Hall and Taylor (1986). Quantitative policy analyses such as Hall (1977) and purely theoretical studies such as Smyth (1974) and Sargent (1986) almost always use the linear model.

2. This chapter draws on Day and Lin (1992) and Day and Shafer (1987).

3. Another way of interpreting equation (14.3) is as follows. Suppose investment depends on the difference between the marginal rate of return, ρ, and the real money rate, r, the cost that investors face for financing investment, so that $I = \gamma(\rho - r - d)$ where d is a deduction for uncertainty. In the one good economy with excess capacity, a unit of fixed capital yields $\rho = Y/K$. Then we get (14.3) where $Y' = dK$ and $\gamma = \beta K$.

4. It is an empirical fact that, in spite of changes in the nominal tax schedule, in the United States the average (per capita) tax rate on income, including federal, state, and local taxes, has been remarkably stable for half a century, varying roughly between .2 and .22.

5. A value of .75 was chosen for α, which is roughly midway in the range found in the literature. See Hall (1977), Branson (1989), Morley (1983), and Ackley (1961). Hall, for example, estimated an adjusted marginal propensity to consume (a) of .36, which, given an average tax rate of .20, implies an *un*adjusted marginal propensity to consume of .45. Branson gives a value for the MPC of .71, while Morley gives a value of .65. Ackley reports values ranging from .5 to .95 depending on the length of the data series, the independent variables included, and the econometric methods used.

For the investment function Hall estimated the base values $\beta = 1.36$ and $\gamma = 83.8$. He considered alternative values representing possible fractions of complete adjustment of investment possible within a given year. This is similar in the present context to a choice of values of μ between 0 and 1. Hall considered values of $\mu = .125, .25, .50,$ and $.75$. Given our estimates for a and β, if $\mu = .25$, then the marginal effect of income on aggregate demand in regime 2 is $a_2 = a + \mu\beta = .7$. Klein asserted in the same place that it was "an econometrically established fact" that, instead, a_2 was about 1.5, a value that would imply a μ of roughly .6. Lin and I used this value but chose a more conservative estimate for β of 1.16 (Day and Lin, 1992).

Hall also estimated a linear demand curve for money $L^0 + \kappa Y - \lambda r$ with $\kappa = .135$ and $\lambda = 2$, which gives a slope to the rising portion of the LM curve of $\kappa/\lambda = .06$. We used lower values for λ which give the rising portion of the LM curve a much steeper slope than Hall's. (Our values are .95, .665, and .191 for the three periods, respectively.) Remember that this implies a longer flat portion of the LM curve.

Recalling that the interest effect on investment increases as capital stock grows, and using values of capital stock for our three base periods, Day and Lin (1992) got values for the marginal effect of interest, γ, of 11, 21, and 27 for the three periods, respectively. See note 3.

6. Discussions with David Lilien were helpful in the preparation of these estimates. Our value of $\beta = 1.16$ is conservative, given Klein's more extreme estimate. (See note 5.) The value for κ of .13 is not controversial, but both γ and λ, which are the marginal effects of interest on investment and money demand, respectively, were given widely varying estimates by the experts. Using our values for β and κ, we find that the monetary interaction σ is negative if

$$\gamma/\lambda > 9.$$

Consequently, the marginal influence of interest on investment (in the interest-sensitive phase) must be much stronger than that for money. Hall's estimate for γ and λ (of 83.8 and 2 respectively) satisfies this relation, and so do ours.

7. By setting $1 - y = x$ and substituting in (14.33), we get (14.34) except that b is replaced by a and y by x. We could, therefore, confine attention to Cases I and II (or III) as the canonical forms. It is convenient to distinguish Case II and Case III because it is virtually always assumed by macroeconomists that $0 < a < 1$ while it is recognized that b could exceed unity (and does in some of our examples). Case II is therefore the interesting one.

15 Comparative Monetary and Fiscal Policy

1. For examples, see the references in chapter 14, note 5.

2. This chapter is based on Day (1989). All of the numerical experiments were performed by T. Y. Lin.

3. Note that changes in G are equivalent in effect to changes in autonomous investment and autonomous consumption.

4. See Day (1989).

16 Capital Accumulation, Balanced Growth, and Growth Cycles

1. My analysis uses a discrete time version of the model that originated with Solow (1956), Swan (1956), and Tinbergen (1958). The Tinbergen article was originaly published in German during World War II.

2. Solow (1956) considered a variable savings rate but did not emphasize the possibilities for instability.

3. See Phelps (1961), an early contributor to the vast literature on "optimal" growth theory. Bellman (1957) and Pontriagin et al. (1962) provided the mathematical foundations of modern optimal growth theory.

4. The rationalization theorem is due to Boldrin and Montrucchio (1986a, 1986b).

5. This is because various neoclassical authors formalized notions of marginal utility and marginal productivity using smooth, differentiable relationships, and based the equilibrium theory of income distribution on the homogeneity thus postulated.

6. See, for example, Courant (1934), volume 1, p. 126.

7. A variable rate of population growth is taken up in chapter 19.

17 Adaptive Economizing: Generic Properties

1. The behavior of the economy over time is thus described by a sequence of recursively connected economizing decisions. This formulation is an example of a "recursive programming model." A general formulation is given in Day and Cigno (1978, chapters 1–3) along with many examples.

The origin of this specific example is a graphical note by Leontief (1958), who attributed the basic idea to Irving Fisher. Mathematical analyses were given in Day (1969) and Day and Fan (1976), but they did not consider the full range of possibilities. The analysis of it below draws on Lin (1988), Lin, Tse, and Day (1992), and Day and Lin (1992) but is entirely new.

2. The concept of a flexible asset was explored by Koopmans (1964) and discussed further in my (1967b) exploration of the present theory.

3. I considered the perfect knowledge case in the previously cited paper.

4. This is a special case of the general formula for *adaptive expectations*, which, using our notation, is

$$r_t^1 = r_{t-1}^1 + \lambda(r_t - r_{t-1}^1), \quad 0 \le \lambda \le 1.$$

If $\lambda = 1$, expectations are adjusted completely to experience, which has been assumed in (17.8). This is the extrapolative case. If $\lambda = 0$, experience does not influence expectations. The more general case where $0 < \lambda < 1$ is explored in Lin (1988) and Day and Lin (1992).

5. Equation (17.11) can be derived by substituting (17.8) into (17.5), using (17.6), then rearranging and collecting terms to get

$$c^1 = y - rk + \rho[y - c + (1 - \delta)k]$$
$$= (1 + \rho)y - [r - \rho(1 - \delta)]k - \rho c.$$

By using the fact that $r = (1 + n)\rho + n + \delta$, the middle term is seen to be equal to $(1 + \rho)(n + \delta)k$, from which equation (17.11) follows.

6. Taking the total differential of (17.1) and setting $du = 0$ gives the marginal rate of substitution between the future sustainable standard of living and present consumption, $\frac{dc^1}{dc} = -\frac{u'(c)}{\psi u'(c^1)}$.

7. The finding that $g'(k)$ is positive on $(0, k^0)$ justifies the representation $g^a(k)$ given in figure 16.3a, except that the function may have some wiggles as it increases.

8. This in spite of the fact that Europe had almost achieved a zero population growth (ZPG) rate. With the classical "generation" of 25 years as the unit time period and an annual growth rate of, say, .014, population would double every half-century. On the generational scale this gives $n = .414$, a rate that has been roughly approximated for the world as a whole toward the end of the twentieth century. It would be interesting to see how growth in the model would be influenced if the latter figure could be reduced to the ZPG level of $n = 0$.

As for the rate of depreciation, Solow (1964, p. 87) chose a working figure of 4% on an annual basis, which yields a generational rate of roughly $\delta = .64$. According to this figure, after a quarter-century nearly two-thirds of the capital stock available at the beginning would be worn out or obsolete. Kydland and Prescott (1982, p. 1361) use an annual rate of 10%, which gives a generational value for δ of just over .9 so that nearly all capital stock wears out (or becomes obsolescent) in a generation. At the other extreme, if one includes social capital, such as schools, roads, parks, hospitals, irrigation canals, aqueducts, sewage disposal systems, railroad beds, etc., these figures may be too high. It might be reasonable to consider a much lower value, say .25, so that only a quarter of the capital stock is "consumed" in a generation. For illustration purposes these three values for δ, .25, .64, and .9, should serve well enough; the middle value conforming roughly to standard estimates, the former and latter providing values at the edges of the plausible range.

Turning to the production function, Solow (1964) settled on a value of $\beta = .36$ for the U.S., while for Germany a value of .67 was suggested. These probably provide a useful range pertaining to modern conditions. A much lower value might be relevant for earlier epochs predating the industrial revolution. To represent this possibility a value of $\beta = .20$ will be used.

18   Optimal Growth

1. The Golden Rule of savings was introduced by Phelps (1961).

2. Classic contributions include Cass (1965) and Koopmans (1965).

3. It is the approach to macroeconomics advocated by Lucas (1987) and is the foundation of the "Real Business Cycle" school.

4. Phelps (1961) derived these results using a continuous time argument.

5. Recall the discussion of the historical and planning time indexes in §17.1.2.

6. An early analysis is Strotz (1956). An elaborate analysis is Koopmans (1965).

7. The formulation of intertemporal optimization theory in terms of the principle of optimality was originated by Richard Bellman in a series of papers produced in the 1940s and 1950s. His first book (1957) describes this work. Elegant mathematical treatments of the theory were given by Karlin (1959) and by Blackwell (1965). A definitive treatment that builds on and extends this early work aimed specifically at students of economics is Stokey and Lucas (1989); see parts I and II, especially pp. 8–16, 66–87, 92–95, 131–139.

8. It should be emphasized that the term "optimal" is always made with respect to a specified objective or utility function. The Golden Rule already discussed provides an alternative definition. Many others are possible. For a profound discussion, see Koopmans (1965).

9. See note 7, especially Stokey and Lucas (1989).

10. A procedure originated by McKenzie (1986).

11. See Stokey and Lucas (1989) and Boldrin and Montrucchio (1986a).

12. See Stokey and Lucas (1989).

13. Samuelson (1947) introduced this idea in formal terms. Its use in what follows was originated by Boldrin and Montrucchio (1986b). My analysis here makes use of their paper and the corresponding material in Stokey and Lucas (see note 7).

14. Recently, in a yet unpublished work, Dawid and Sorger have shown that utility functions incorporating wealth as well as consumption can rationalize paths. Again, however, such a utility function is not the same as the utility function generating the adaptive economizing model.

15. My colleague Timur Kuran (1995) has dealt extensively with the phenomenon of preference falsification, a closely related concept. On cognitive dissonance, see Akerloff and Dickens (1982).

19   Population, Productivity, and Generational Welfare

1. Substantial empirical research has provided evidence that population cycles are at least in part caused by an interaction between net birth rates and per capita income, just as Malthus argued. See Easterlin (1973), Lee (1976), Day, Kim, and Macunovich (1989).

2. Throughout our discussion we will treat population size and the net birth rate as real numbers. Since people do not come in fractions, our interpretation must be that the birth rate gives the average number of children per family (of either sex).

3. In this section I have used as literal an interpretation of Malthus as possible. In the *Essay on the Principle of Population*, Malthus (1963, p. 5) assumed that output was bounded above by a linear trend. In his *Principles of Political Economy*, however, he included in the analysis, like Smith before him and like Ricardo, what we recognize now as a production function with diminishing returns. Early formal explorations of the classical model include Samuelson (1947, pp. 296–298) and Baumol (1970, pp. 266–268). My treatment in the next section was first outlined in Day (1982). It differs from these earlier studies in its explicit inclusion of Malthus's natural growth constraint and in its derivation of irregularly fluctuating population, as Malthus conjectured.

4. Let $S := \{(Y, x) \mid x \geq 0, Y \leq BF(x)\}$. Let $F(x)$ be a *strictly concave function* on an interval $I \subset \mathbb{R}^+$. Then for all $x, y \in I$ with $x < y$ and for all $\lambda \in (0, 1)$, $F(z) > (1 - \lambda)F(x) + \lambda F(y)$ where $z = (1 - \lambda)x + \lambda y$. Correspondingly, the chord connecting any two points in S belongs to the interior of S, and to any boundary point of S there corresponds a unique tangent line. This by definition means that S is *strictly convex*. Thus, $F(\cdot)$ strictly concave $\Rightarrow S$ strictly convex.

5. For the graphs, $B = 10$ and $\beta = 1/2$.

6. Malthus, *Essay on the Principle of Population*, chapter 2.

7. Easterlin (1973) gave such a threshold a prominent place in explaining demoeconomic fluctuations. Other aspects of modern behavior would add further modification of the basic birth function. Of particular importance is the propensity for birth rates to fall at relatively high levels of income. It can be shown that this phenomenon does not change our results very much. See Day, Kim, and Macunovich (1989).

8. It would be interesting to consider a model in which the income distribution given by $\omega(x)$ could be modified whenever an absolute decline in population is implied. Such a model could have much different and more stable behavior than the present one.

9. A histogram that illustrated the ergodic character of this trajectory, and bifurcation diagrams that show how the nature of trajectories change as η/γ increases when β and n are fixed, will be found in Day and Min (1996).

20 Household Preferences, Social Infrastructure and Production Diseconomies

1. The practice of infant exposure is known from the classical era. On herbal spermicide, see Riddle, Estes, and Russell (1994). The evidence cited there is controversial.

2. On the household fertility theory, see Becker (1981), Schultze (1981), and Day, Kim, and Macunovich (1989).

3. The key role of infrastructure has recently been emphasized by the World Bank (1994). It is important to distinguish between public goods and infrastructure, although the latter tends to include many of the former.

   Malthus (1817, republished 1963, pp. 406–407) observed: "Every society must have a body of persons engaged in personal services of various kinds,... statesmen to govern it, soldiers to defend it, judges and lawyers to administer justice,... physicians and surgeons to cure diseases and heal wounds.... No civilized state has ever been known to exist without a certain portion of all these classes of society in addition to those who are directly employed in production."

4. Boserup (1981, p. 6), who coined the term "administrative technology," and North (1981) have given infrastructure a crucial role in their discussions of economic development.

5. Empirical measurement of the contribution of infrastructure to aggregate production is progressing. Examples include Eliasson (1990) and Pinnoi (1994). See also the World Bank Report (1994).

6. Infrastructure was introduced into economic growth theory in Day and Walter (1989) and Day and Zou (1994).

7. For a classic statement of these sources of diseconomies, see A. G. Robinson (1931, revised 1958).

8. Ester Boserup's term; Boserup (1981, p. 6).

9. This is because of breastfeeding practices in the hunting and food-collecting bands, problems of sanitation, and deficiencies in medical knowledge.

10. These regularity conditions are (i) that the utility function is continuous and quasi-concave, that is, with convex upper contour sets, and (ii) that the correspondence $\Gamma(q, y)$ is continuous or nonempty for all $q > 0$, $y \geq 0$. Note that the strategies $c(y)$ and $b(y)$ are not dynamic programming (intertemporally optimal) strategies. For the theory of inter-temporally optimal population growth, see, for example, Dasgupta (1969), Pitchford (1974), and Benhabib and Nishimura (1986).

11. All of these results can be established for demoeconomic functions that are compatible with smooth utility functions. Moreover, demoeconomic functions with declining family size after income gets high enough can also be incorporated into the theory, but these possibilities involve details of analysis that add very little to what has been learned so far. See Day, Kim, and Macunovich (1989).

12. Let $F(x)$ be a continuous function mapping an interval $x \rightarrow \mathbb{R}$ where $x \subset \mathbb{R}$. Define S as in chapter 19, note 4. If S is strictly convex, then $F(\cdot)$ is said to be *strictly quasi-concave* on x. On pseudo-concavity, see chapter 23, note 3.

13. The switch points are continuous functions of the parameters $x^i(\eta/B)$ for all $i = \ell, u$ and $x^i(\zeta/B)$, $i = r, s$ where, remember, $\zeta = \eta + (q/\alpha)(1 + n)$. The following properties are readily derived:

$$\frac{\partial x^i}{\partial \eta} > 0, \quad \frac{\partial x^i}{\partial B} < 0, \quad \frac{\partial x^i}{\partial M} > 0, \quad i = \ell, r \tag{c}$$

$$\frac{\partial x^r}{\partial q} > 0, \quad \frac{\partial x^r}{\partial \alpha} < 0, \quad \frac{\partial x^r}{\partial n} > 0 \tag{d}$$

$$\frac{\partial x^i}{\partial \eta} < 0, \quad \frac{\partial x^i}{\partial B} > 0, \quad \frac{\partial x^i}{\partial M} < 0, \quad i = s, u \tag{e}$$

$$\frac{\partial x^i}{\partial q} < 0, \quad \frac{\partial x^s}{\partial \alpha} > 0, \quad \frac{\partial x^i}{\partial n} < 0 \tag{f}$$

$$\lim_{\gamma \to 0}(x^r - x^\ell) = 0, \quad \lim_{\gamma \to 0}(x^u - x^s) = 0. \tag{g}$$

The intuition behind the partial derivatives in (c)–(f) and the limiting statements in (g) is revealed by moving the parameters η and ζ in figure 20.4.

14. Note that when $\eta < y^M < \zeta$, $\mathscr{D}^n = \varnothing$ and $\mathscr{D}^s = (x^\ell, x^u)$. When $y^M < \eta$, $\mathscr{D}^n \cup \mathscr{D}^s = \varnothing$.

15. The following comparative static results can be derived.

(i)

$$\frac{\partial \tilde{x}^\ell}{\partial \eta} > 0, \quad \frac{\partial \tilde{x}^\ell}{\partial q} > 0, \quad \frac{\partial \tilde{x}^\ell}{\partial \alpha} < 0, \quad \frac{\partial \tilde{x}^\ell}{\partial n} = 0, \quad \frac{\partial \tilde{x}^\ell}{\partial B} < 0, \quad \frac{\partial \tilde{x}^\ell}{\partial M} > 0$$

$$\frac{\partial \tilde{x}^u}{\partial \eta} < 0, \quad \frac{\partial \tilde{x}^u}{\partial q} < 0, \quad \frac{\partial \tilde{x}^u}{\partial \alpha} > 0, \quad \frac{\partial \tilde{x}^u}{\partial n} = 0, \quad \frac{\partial \tilde{x}^u}{\partial B} > 0, \quad \frac{\partial \tilde{x}^u}{\partial M} < 0.$$

(ii)

$$\lim_{\gamma \to 0} x^\ell = \lim_{\gamma \to 0} \tilde{x}^\ell = \lim_{\gamma \to 0} x^r$$

$$\lim_{\gamma \to 0} x^r = \lim_{\gamma \to 0} \tilde{x}^u = \lim_{\gamma \to 0} x^u.$$

21 Macroeconomic Evolution

1. I have lost track of the specific source of this quotation from one of Georgescu-Roegen's works. It will probably be found in one of the essays collected in Georgescu-Roegen (1966) or in his book (1971).

2. See Dahmén (1986) for an excellent discussion.

3. On the key role of infrastructure in economic development, see chapter 20, note 3.

4. It is a convention of much contemporary growth theory to maximize a utility function over an infinite horizon as described above in chapter 18. Such a procedure would provide an alternative "global" switching criterion that would define intertemporal equilibrium and optimal regime switching. While certainly of technical interest, in my view such an approach has little if any relevance for understanding the facts of economic history—or of current events.

5. Reference here is to Arrow (1962).

6. Recall the definition of §5.5.2.

7. As the phase structure for each regime depends on the state of the economy, equation (21.7) provides a formal statement of Trygve Haavelmo's (1956) assertion that "the form of equations of a realistic model may ... be ... a function of the variables involved."

8. The technology potential is a scale parameter. Dividing both sides of (21.10) by $\tilde{B}$, we get

$$z_{t+1} = z_t + \rho z_t(1 - z_t)$$

where $z_t = B_t/\tilde{B}$. The unique positive stationary state is $\tilde{z} = 1$. We can think of z_t as the *relative productivity index*.

22   A Grand Dynamics of Economic Development

1. Baumol (1970, p. 13).

2. See, for example, Butzer (1977) or Martin (1971). For the outbreak of fluctuations, see Zubrow (1975).

3. While Herodotus's description is disputed so far as exact details of settlement are concerned, it is nonetheless generally representative of the process of colonization by Mediterranean peoples during the epoch of early civilization, which resumed in the Renaissance with the settlement of Europeans in various parts of the globe. Herodotus also tells of a city near the Bosporus whose citizens claimed that they were founded by a colonial expedition from Egypt.

4. Scientists have attempted to estimate an ultimate bound for the earth as a whole, obtaining values ranging from 5 to 25 billion people.

5. Nissen (1988) describes how this process began at the very dawn of complex society and civilization in the ancient Near East. Observe that "Athens was, until the 18th century B.C., just a cluster of farming villages. A dramatic population explosion during this period ... was accompanied by the political unification of the independent villages of Attica." Scarre (1988).

6. See Myers (1994, p. 41). Silverman (1994, p. 3) wrote of this period that "traditional land patterns of Judea were changing ...small holdings were bought up by aristocrats and priests, condemning their former owners to lives as tenant farmers or hired laborers."

See Nissen (1988) for the similar process that took place earlier in Mesopotamia. Also see Iseminger (1996), who summarizes recent findings on pre-Columbian North America: "In a broad plain east of St. Louis during the years 9500–600 B.C., hunter-gathers set up seasonal villages. During the Woodland period 600 B.C.–800 A.D., coop cultivation developed and the population settled into larger communities. The number of settlements and population grew slowly until more intense farming based on corn permitted a more rapid increase. At its apex about 1200 A.D. the region was dominated by a substantial city, Cahokia, surrounded by dozens of satellite communities and scores of smaller villages. Some time after 1200 A.D. decline set in and by 1400 Cahokia was abandoned entirely and no positive ties have been established between the great city and any historical tribe."

7. See Nissen (1988) and Saggs (1989).

8. These fascinating examples are described in Sagan (1985).

9. For a discussion of the Indian case see Kenoyer (1998). There is considerable evidence to suggest that events such as these transpired in the pre-Columbian societies of Central and South America. See Sabloff (1975).

An alternative to the integration of entire economies is the process of emigration and immigration. Some people may leave one society and join another. In this way, a small, very productive economy could grow while a larger, less productive society could slow, cease, or reverse growth so as to maintain or even increase its well-being. This process seems to have begun at the very dawn of complex society and civilization in the ancient Near East. See Nissen (1988). A good example from ancient history is provided by the Greek colonies in Sicily, which continued to absorb immigrants from the homeland for several centuries and which quickly rivaled Athens in the size and splendor of their economy. The explosive growth of the New World over the last four centuries has been due in considerable part to the shedding and assimilation of millions of European emigrants.

10. Further references to the archaeological literature related to the present theory will be found in Day and Walter (1989). A splendid, boldly synthetic, nontechnical survey of human socioeconomic evolution that vividly portrays its dynamic character will be found in Barraclough et al. (1984).

11. An implication of these facts is that

$$\omega_*^{S/A}(x) \geq \omega_*^{F/F}(x) \quad \text{for all} \quad x \in \mathcal{X}.$$

12. A classic division of human history into similar grand systems is given in Childe (1951). For related references, see chapter 24.

13. There are many references to the "sea people" and the "dark age" of Greece, for example, Toynbee (1966).

14. See note 4 above.

23   Existence of Evolutionary Scenarios

1. The formal investigation of these questions was initiated in Day and Walter (1989). The present discussion gives a more complete analysis.

2. Notice that $\theta_i^{-s}(S)$ for $S \subset \mathcal{D}^i$ can be empty for some $r \geq 1$ for all $s \geq r$. In particular, it can happen that $\theta_i^{-1}(S) = \varnothing$ for all $S \subset \mathcal{D}^i$. This would imply that $E^i = \mathcal{D}^i$. Of course, $\theta_i^{-s}(S) \subset \theta^{-s}(S)$, $S \subset \mathcal{D}^i$.

3. *Concavity, quasi-concavity, pseudo-concavity*. The following definitions are used. Consider the $f : I \to \mathbb{R}$ where I is an interval in $\mathbb{R}$. Then

(i) f is strictly concave if for all $x, y \in I$ such that $x < y$,

$$f[\lambda x + (1 - \lambda)y] > \lambda f(x) + (1 - \lambda)f(y) \quad \text{for all} \quad \lambda \in (0, 1);$$

(ii) f is strictly quasi-concave if for all $x \in I$, the set

$$\{y \in I \mid f(y) > f(x)\}$$

is strictly convex;

(iii) f is pseudo-concave if and only if

$$f'(y)(x - y) \leq 0 \Leftrightarrow y$$

is a maximizer on the set

$$[\min\{x, y\}, \max\{x, y\}].$$

It can be shown that

(a) f concave $\Rightarrow$ f quasi-concave;

(b) f concave $\Rightarrow$ f pseudo-concave;

(c) f pseudo-concave $\Rightarrow$ f quasi-concave;

(d) f pseudo-concave $\Rightarrow$ a local maximum over the entire domain is a unique global maximum;

(e) f pseudo-concave $\Rightarrow$ f strictly quasi-concave.

See Mangarsarian (1969). Note that (d) implies that f is either strictly monotonic or strictly bitonic (i.e., single-peaked).

25   Precursors and Ongoing Developments

1. As will be evident in very recent studies such as Reed and Kraske (1996), there is still plenty to be gained by using linear mathematics in dynamic analysis.

2. The term "chaos" is of ancient origin. In Greek it means a vast chasm or void. In the Bible it was used to connote "formless, primordial matter," and in common parlance it signifies "a study of utter confusion or disorder." In modern science it is used to connote behavior governed by deterministic laws but that is unpredictable and apparently random. The *New Oxford Dictionary* states that chaos is due to "sensitivity to initial conditions." But this is a property rather than a cause of chaos, which is due to causal effect-reversing nonlinearity as explained in chapter 2.

3. An indelible memory from graduate school was Gerschenkron's denumeration and systematic devastation of the several stages-of-growth theories. All fell to his lucid counterexamples. Some of what he had to say will be found in his essays.

26   Implications for Policy and Economic Science

1. Quoted in Keynes (1956).

2. This quotation from Hesse was sent to me by my friend John Maney; I have not been able to find its source in Hesse's writings.

3. I have discussed this general consideration in various places, for example Day (1998).

Bibliography

Abraham-Frois, Gilbert, and Edmond Berrebi. 1995. *Instabilité, Cycles, Chaos*. Paris: Economica.

Ackley, Gardner. 1961. *Macroeconomic Theory*. New York: Macmillan.

Akerloff, George, and William T. Dickens. 1982. "The Economic Consequences of Cognitive Dissonance." *American Economic Review*, 72, 307–319.

Allen, Peter (ed.). 1987. *European Journal of Operations Research*, volume 30.

Antoniou, I., and K. Gustafson. 1997. "From Irreversible Markov Semi Groups to Chaotic Dynamics." *Physica A*, 236, 296–308.

Antoniou, I., I. Prigogine, and S. Tasaki. 1996. "New Spectral Representation of Mixing Dynamical Systems." In V. Lakshmikantham (ed.), *World Congress of Nonlinear Analysts, '92*. Berlin: Walter de Gruyter.

Arrow, Kenneth. 1962. "The Implications of Learning by Doing." *Review of Economic Studies*, 29, 155–173.

Arrow, Kenneth, H. D. Block, and Leo Hurwicz. 1959. "On the Stability of Competitive Equilibrium." *Econometrica*, 27, 82–109.

Arrow, Kenneth, and Frank Hahn. 1971. *General Competitive Analysis*. San Francisco: Holden-Day.

Arrow, Kenneth, and Leo Hurwicz. 1962. "Competitive Stability under Weak Gross Substitutability: Nonlinear Price Adjustment and Adaptive Expectations." *International Economic Review*, 3.

Aubin, Jean-Pierre. 1997. *Dynamic Economic Theory*. Berlin: Springer-Verlag.

Aubin, Jean-Pierre, and Helené Frankowska. 1990. *Set Valued Analysis*. Boston: Birkhäuser.

Azariadis, Costas. 1993. *Intertemporal Macroeconomics*. Cambridge, MA: Blackwell.

Baierl, Gary, Kazuo Nishimura, and Makoto Yano. 1998. "The Role of Capital Depreciation." In Special Issue, Multisectoral Models, *Journal of Economic Behavior and Organization*, 33, 467–479.

Bala, Venkatesh, and Mukul Majumdar. 1992. "Chaotic Tâtonnement." *Economic Theory*, 2, 437–446.

Barnes, Julian. 1984. *Flaubert's Parrot*. New York: McGraw-Hill.

Barnett, William A., and S. Choi. 1989. "A Comparison between the Conventional Econometric Approach to Structural Inference and the Nonparametric Chaotic Attractor Approach." In Barnett, Geweke, and Shell (1989).

Barnett, William A., John Geweke, and Karl Shell (eds.). 1989. *Economic Complexity: Chaos, Sunspots, Bubbles, and Nonlinearity*. Proceedings of the Fourth International Symposium in Economic Theory and Econometrics. Cambridge: Cambridge University Press.

Barnett, William A., and Melvin J. Hinich. 1993. "Has Chaos Been Discovered with Economic Data?" In Day and Chen (1993).

Barraclough, G., et al. (eds.). 1984. *The Times Atlas of World History*. Rev. ed. Maplewood, NJ: Hammond.

Batten, David, John L. Casti, and Börje Johansson (eds.). 1987. *Economic Evolution and Structural Adjustment*. Berlin: Springer-Verlag.

Baumol, William J. 1970. *Economic Dynamics*. 3d ed. New York: Macmillan.

Baumol, William J., and Jess Benhabib. 1988. "Chaos: Significance, Mechanism, and Economic Applications." *Journal of Economic Perspectives*, November.

Becker, Gary. 1960. "An Economic Analysis of Fertility." *Demographic and Economic Change in Developed Countries*. Princeton, NJ: National Bureau of Economic Research.

Becker, Gary S. 1981. *A Treatise on the Family*. Cambridge: Harvard University Press.

Bellman, Richard. 1957. *Dynamic Programming*. Princeton, NJ: Princeton University Press.

Benassy, Jean-Pascal. 1986. "A Non-Walrasian Model of the Business Cycle." In Day and Eliasson (1986).

Benhabib, Jess. 1992. *Cycles and Chaos in Economic Equilibrium*. Princeton, NJ: Princeton University Press.

Benhabib, Jess, and Richard H. Day. 1980. "Erratic Accumulation." *Economics Letters*, 6(2), 113–117.

Benhabib, Jess, and Richard H. Day. 1981. "Rational Choice and Erratic Behavior." *Review of Economic Studies*, 48, 459–471.

Benhabib, Jess, and Richard H. Day. 1982. "A Characterization of Erratic Dynamics in the Overlapping Generations Model." *Journal of Economic Dynamics and Control*, 4, 37–55.

Benhabib, Jess, and Kazuo Nishimura. 1979. "The Hopf-Bifurcation and the Existence and Stability of Closed Orbits in Multisector Models of Optimal Economic Growth." *Journal of Economic Theory*, 21, 412–421.

Benhabib, Jess, and Kazuo Nishimura. 1986. "Endogenous Fluctuations in the Barro-Becker Theory of Fertility." Paper delivered at Conference on Demographic Change and Economic Development, September 1986, Fern University, Hagen.

Blackwell, David. 1965. "Discounted Dynamic Programming." *Annals of Mathematical Statistics*, 36, 226–336.

Blanchard, Olivier. 1997. *Macroeconomics*. Upper Saddle River, NJ: Prentice-Hall.

Boldrin, Michele. 1989. "Paths of Optimal Accumulation in Two-Sector Models." In Barnett, Geweke, and Shell (1989).

Boldrin, Michele, and Luigi Montrucchio. 1984. "The Emergence of Dynamic Complexities in Models of Optimal Growth: The Role of Impatience." Working Paper #7, Rochester Center for Economic Research, University of Rochester.

Boldrin, Michele, and Luigi Montrucchio. 1986a. "Cyclic and Chaotic Behavior in Intertemporal Optimization Models." *Mathematical Modelling*, 8, 627–700.

Boldrin, Michele, and Luigi Montrucchio. 1986b. "On the Indeterminancy of Capital Accumulation Paths." *Journal of Economic Theory*, 40, 26–39.

Borel, E. 1908. "Les Probabilités denombrables et leurs applications arithmétiques." *Rendiconti Circ. Mat. Palermo*, 27, 247–271.

Boserup, Ester. 1975. *The Conditions of Agricultural Growth*. Chicago: Aldine.

Boserup, Ester. 1981. *Population and Technological Change*. Chicago: University of Chicago Press.

Boserup, Ester. 1996. "Development Theory: An Analytical Framework and Selected Applications." *Population and Development Review*, 22, 505–515.

Branson, William. 1989. *Macroeconomic Theory and Policy*. 3d ed. New York: Harper and Row.

Brock, William A. 1986. "Distinguishing Random and Deterministic Systems: Abridged Version." *Journal of Economic Theory*, 40, 168–194.

Brock, William A., and G. Chamberlain. 1984. "Spectral Analysis Cannot Tell a Macro Econometrician Whether His Time Series Came from a Stochastic Economy or a Deterministic Economy." Working paper, Department of Economics, University of Wisconsin, Madison.

Brock, William A., and W. Davis Dechert. 1987. "Theorems on Distinguishing Deterministic and Random Systems." In W. Barnett, E. Berndt, and H. White (eds.), *Dynamic Econometric Modeling, Proceedings of the Third International Symposium in Economic Theory and Econometrics*. Cambridge: Cambridge University Press.

Brock, William A., and A. G. Malliaris. 1989. *Differential Equations, Stability and Chaos in Dynamic Economics*. Amsterdam: North-Holland.

Buccola, Steven T., and Vernon Smith. 1987. "Uncertainty and Partial Adjustment in Double Auction Markets." *Journal of Economic Behavior and Organization*, 8, 587–602.

Burmeister, E., and R. Dobell. 1970. *Mathematical Theories of Economic Growth*. London: Macmillan.

Butzer, K. 1977. "Environment, Culture, and Human Evolution." *American Scientist*, 65, 572–584.

Carlsson, Sune. 1939. *A Study on the Pure Theory of Production*. Rpt. New York: Augustus Kelley, 1965.

Cass, David. 1965. "Optimum Growth in an Aggregate Model of Capital Accumulation." *Review of Economic Studies*, 32, 233–240.

Cassavillan, Guido, Teresa Lloyd-Brager, and Patrick A. Pintus. 1997. "Multiple Steady States and Endogenous Fluctuations with Increasing Returns to Scale in Production." Working paper.

Chen, Ping. 1988. "Empirical and Theoretical Evidence of Economic Chaos." *System Dynamics Review*, 4, 81–108.

Chen, Ping. 1993. In Day and Chen (1993).

Chiarella, Carl, and Peter Flaschel. 1996. "Real and Monetary Cycles in Models of Keynes-Wicksell Type." *Journal of Economic Behavior and Organization*, 30, 327–352.

Chichilnisky, Graciela, Geoffrey Heal, and Yun Lin. 1995. "Chaotic Price Dynamics, Increasing Returns and the Phillips Curve." *Journal of Economic Behavior and Organization*, 27, 279–291.

Childe, V. Gordon. 1951. *Man Makes Himself*. New York: Times Mirror. (Originally published 1936, slightly revised 1941 and 1951.)

Chomsky, N. 1966. *Cartesian Linguistics*. New York: Harper and Row.

Clower, Robert W. 1963. "The Keynesian Counter-Revolution: A Theoretical Appraisal." *Schweizerische Zeitschrift für Volkswirtschaft und Statistic*, 99, 8–31. Rpt. in D. W. Walker (ed.), *Money and Markets: Essays by Robert W. Clower*. Cambridge: Cambridge University Press, 1984.

Clower, Robert, and Daniel Friedman. 1986. "Trade Specialists and Money in an Ongoing Exchange Economy." In Day and Eliasson (1986).

Cohen, Joel. 1995. "Population Growth and Earth's Human Carrying Capacity." *Science*, 269, 34–36.

Cohen, M. 1977. *The Food Crisis in Prehistory*. New Haven: Yale University Press.

Collet, P., and J. Eckmann. 1980. *Iterated Maps on the Interval as Dynamical Systems*. Basel: Birkhäuser.

Courant, Richard. 1934. *Differential and Integral Calculus*. New York: Nordemann. Rpt. New York: Wiley, 1970.

Dahmén, Eric. 1986. "Schumpeterian Dynamics: Some Methodological Notes." In Day and Eliasson (1986).

Dana, Rose-Anne, and P. Malgrange. 1984. "The Dynamics of a Discrete Version of a Growth Cycle Model." In J. Ancot (ed.), *Analyzing the Structure of Econometric Models*. The Hague: Nejhoff Publishing.

Dana, Rose-Anne, and Luigi Montrucchio. 1987. "Dynamic Complexity in Duopoly Games." In J.-M. Grandmont (ed.), *Nonlinear Economic Dynamics*. Boston: Academic Press.

Dasgupta, Partha S. 1969. "On the Concept of Optimum Population." *Review of Economic Studies*, 36.

Dawid, Herbert, and M. Kopel. 1998. "On Optimal Cycles in Dynamic Programming Models with Convex Return Functions." *Economic Theory*.

Day, Richard H. 1963. *Recursive Programming and Production Response*. Amsterdam: Elsevier North-Holland.

Day, Richard H. 1967a. "Profits, Learning, and the Convergence of Satisficing to Marginalism." *Quarterly Journal of Economics*, 81, 302–311.

Day, Richard H. 1967b. "A Microeconomic Model of Business Growth, Decay, and Cycles." *Unternehmensforschung*, 11(1), 1–20.

Day, Richard H. 1968. "A Note on the Dynamics of Cost Competition within an Industry." *Oxford Economic Papers*, August.

Day, Richard H. 1969. "Flexible Utility and Myopic Expectations in Economic Growth." *Oxford Economic Papers*, 21, 299–311.

Day, Richard H. 1978. "Modelling Economic Change: The Recursive Programming Approach." In Day and Cigno (1978).

Day, Richard H. 1982. "Irregular Growth Cycles." *American Economic Review*, 72, 406–414.

Day, Richard H. 1983. "The Emergence of Chaos from Classical Economic Growth." *Quarterly Journal of Economics*, 54, 201–213.

Day, Richard H. 1984. "Disequilibrium Economic Dynamics: A Post Schumpeterian Contribution." *Journal of Economic Behavior and Organization*, 5, 57–76.

Day, Richard H. 1986. "On Endogenous Preferences and Adaptive Economizing: A Note." In Day and Eliasson (1986).

Day, Richard H. 1989. "Comparative Monetary and Fiscal Policy Dynamics." In E. Nells and W. Semmler (eds.), *Financial Dynamics and Business Cycles: New Perspectives*. Armonk, NY: M. E. Sharpe.

Day, Richard H. 1992. "Complex Economic Dynamics: Obvious in History, Generic in Theory, Elusive in Data." *Journal of Applied Econometrics*, 7, 10–23.

Day, Richard H. 1995. "Multiple-Phase Economic Dynamics." In T. Maruyama and W. Takahashi (eds.), *Nonlinear and Convex Analysis in Economic Theory: Lecture Notes in Economics and Mathematical Systems*. Berlin: Springer-Verlag.

Day, Richard H. 1996. "Balanced Budgets: Economic Nirvana or Fiscal Chaos?" *Contemporary Economic Policy*, 14, 15–25.

Day, Richard H. 1998. "An Evolutionary Theory of Democratic Capitalism." In G. Eliasson and N. Karlson (eds.), *The Limits of Government*. Stockholm: City University Press.

Day, Richard H., and Ping Chen (eds.). 1993. *Nonlinear Dynamics and Evolutionary Economics*. New York: Oxford University Press.

Day, Richard H., and Alessandro Cigno (eds.). 1978. *Modelling Economic Change*. Amsterdam: Elsevier North-Holland.

Day, Richard H., and Gunnar Eliasson (eds.). 1986. *The Dynamics of Market Economies*. Amsterdam: Elsevier North-Holland.

Day, Richard H., and Yiu-Kwan Fan. 1976. "Myopic Optimizing, Economic Growth and the Golden Rule." *Hong Kong Economic Papers*, 10, 12–20.

Day, Richard H., and Kenneth Hanson. 1986. "Adaptive Economizing, Technological Change and the Demand for Labour Disequilibrium." In P. Nijkamp (ed.), *Technological Change, Employment and Spatial Dynamics*. Berlin: Springer-Verlag.

Day, Richard H., and Kenneth Hanson. 1991. "Cobweb Chaos." In T. K. Kaul and J. K. Sengupta (eds.), *Contributions to Economic Analysis. Economic Models, Estimation, and Socioeconomic Systems: Essays in Honor of Karl Fox.* Amsterdam: Elsevier North-Holland.

Day, Richard H., and Kyoo-Hong Kim. 1987. "A Note on Nonperiodic Demoeconomic Fluctuations with Positive Measure." *Economics Letters*, 23, 251–257.

Day, Richard H., K. H. Kim, and D. Macunovich. 1989. "Complex Demoeconomic Dynamics." *Journal of Population Economics*, 2, 139–159.

Day, Richard H., and Tzong-Yau Lin. 1992. "An Adaptive, Neoclassical Model of Growth Fluctuations." In A. Vercelli and N. Dimitri (eds.), *Macroeconomics: A Survey of Research Strategies.* New York: Oxford University Press.

Day, Richard H., Samuel Morley, and Kenneth Smith. 1974. "Myopic Optimizing and Rules of Thumb in a Micro Model of Industrial Growth." *American Economic Review*, 64, 11–23.

Day, Richard H., and Giulio Pianigiani. 1991. "Statistical Dynamics and Economics." *Journal of Economic Behavior and Organization*, 16, 37–83.

Day, Richard H., and Wayne Shafer. 1985. "Keynesian Chaos." *Journal of Macroeconomics*, 7, 277–295.

Day, Richard H., and Wayne Shafer. 1987. "Ergodic Macroeconomic Fluctuations." In A. Medio (ed.), *Advances in Dynamic Economics*, special issue of *Journal of Economic Behavior and Organization*, 8, 339–362.

Day, Richard H., and Herbert Tinney. 1969a. "A Dynamic von Thunen Model." *Geographical Analysis*, 1, 137–151.

Day, Richard H., and Herbert Tinney. 1969b. "Cycles, Phases and Growth in a Generalized Cobweb Theory." *Economic Journal*, 79, 90–108.

Day, Richard H., and Jean-Luc Walter. 1989. "Economic Growth in the Very Long Run: On the Multiple-Phase Interaction of Population, Technology, and Social Infrastructure." In Barnett, Geweke, and Shell (1989).

Day, Richard H., and Min Zhang. 1996. "Classical Economic Growth Theory: A Global Bifurcation Analysis." In T. Puu (ed.), *Chaos, Solitons and Fractals*, 7, 1969–1988.

Day, Richard H., and G. Zou. 1994. "Infrastructure, Restricted Factor Substitution and Economic Growth." *Journal of Economic Behavior and Organization*, 23, 149–166.

Dechert, W. Davis, and Kazuo Nishimura. 1983. "A Complete Characterization of Optimal Growth Paths in an Aggregated Model with a Non-Concave Production Function." *Journal of Economic Theory*, 31, 322–354.

Deevey, E. S. 1960. "The Human Population." *Scientific American*, 203, 194–205.

Deneckere, Raymond, and Steve Pelikan. 1986. "Competitive Chaos." *Journal of Economic Theory*, 40, 13–25.

Devaney, R. L. 1989. *An Introduction to Chaotic Dynamical Systems.* 2d ed. Redwood City, CA: Addison-Wesley.

Diamond, Peter. 1965. "National Debt in a Neoclassical Growth Model." *American Economic Review*, 55, 1126–1150.

Dunford, Nelson, and Jacob T. Schwartz. 1958. *Linear Operators, Part I: General Theory.* New York: Interscience. Rpt. New York: Wiley, 1988.

Easterlin, Richard A. 1973. "Relative Economic Status and the American Fertility Swing." In E. B. Sheldon (ed.), *Family Economic Behavior: Problems and Prospects.* Philadelphia: Lippincott.

Easterlin, Richard A. 1987. *Birth and Fortune: The Impact of Numbers on Personal Welfare.* Chicago: University of Chicago Press.

Eberts, R. W. 1986. "Estimating the Contribution of Urban Public Infrastructure to Regional Growth." Working Paper 8610, Federal Reserve Bank of Cleveland.

Eckmann, J., and D. Ruelle. 1985. "Ergodic Theory of Chaos and Strange Attractors." *Reviews of Modern Physics*, 57, 329–356.

Einstein, Albert. 1902. "Kinetic Theory of Thermal Equilibrium and the Second Law of Thermodynamics." Trans. Anna Beck. Rpt. in *Collected Papers of Albert Einstein*, vol. 2. Princeton: Princeton University Press, 1987ff.

Eisner, Robert. 1994. "Real Government Saving and the Future." *Journal of Economic Behavior and Organization*, 23, 111–126.

Ekeland, Ivar. 1988. *Mathematics and the Unexpected*. Chicago: University of Chicago Press.

Eliasson, Gunnar. 1990. "The Firm as a Competent Team." *Journal of Economic Behavior and Organization*, 13, 275–298.

Engle, Robert F. 1995. *Arch: Selected Readings*. Oxford: Oxford University Press.

Flaschel, Peter, Reiner Franke, and Willi Semmler. 1997. *Nonlinear Dynamics and Economic Theory*. Cambridge: MIT Press.

Ford, Joseph. 1981. "Ergodicity for Economists." In *New Quantitative Techniques for Economic Analysis*. New York: Academic Press.

Franke, Reiner, and Asada. 1994. "A Keynes-Goodwin Model of the Business Cycle." *Journal of Economic Behavior and Organization*, 24, 273–296.

Gabisch, Günter, and Hans-Walter Lorenz. 1987. *Business Cycle Theory*. Berlin: Springer-Verlag.

Gale, David. 1973. "Pure Exchange Equilibrium of Dynamic Economic Models." *Journal of Economic Theory*, 6, 12–36.

Georgescu-Roegen, Nicholas. 1950. "The Theory of Choice and the Constancy of Economic Laws." *Quarterly Journal of Economics*, 64, 125–138.

Georgescu-Roegen, Nicholas. 1951. "Relaxation Phenomena in Linear Dynamic Models." In T. C. Koopmans (ed.), *Activity Analysis of Production and Allocation*. New York: Wiley.

Georgescu-Roegen, Nicholas. 1966. *Analytical Economics*. Cambridge: Harvard University Press.

Georgescu-Roegen, Nicholas. 1971. *The Entropy Law and the Economic Process*. Cambridge: Harvard University Press.

Geweke, John. 1993. In Day and Chen (1993).

Gibbs, J. Willard. 1981. *Elementary Principles in Statistical Mechanics*. Woodbridge, CT: Ox Bow Press. (First published 1910.)

Gleick, James. 1987. *Chaos: Making of a New Science*. New York: Penguin.

Goeree, J. K., Cars Hommes, and C. Weddepohl. 1997. "Stability and Complex Dynamics in a Discrete Tâtonnement Model." *Journal of Economic Behavior and Organization*, 33, 395–410.

Goodwin, Richard M. 1943. "Keynesian and Other Theories of Interest." *Review of Economics and Statistics*.

Goodwin, Richard M. 1947. "Dynamical Coupling with Special Reference to Markets Having Production Lags." *Econometrica*, 15.

Goodwin, Richard M. 1951. "Nonlinear Acceleration and the Persistence of Business Cycles." *Econometrica*, 19.

Goodwin, Richard M. 1978. "Wicksell and the Malthusian Catastrophe." *Scandinavian Journal of Economics*, 80, 190–198.

Goodwin, Richard M. 1982. *Essays in Economic Dynamics*. London: Macmillan.

Goodwin, Richard M. 1990. *Chaotic Economic Dynamics*. Oxford: Clarendon Press.

Goodwin, Richard M. 1993a. "A Marx-Keynes-Schumpeter Model of Economic Growth and Fluctuations." In Day and Chen (1993).

Goodwin, Richard M. 1993b. "My Erratic Progress toward Economic Dynamics." Remarks made at banquet, April 18, 1989; in Day and Chen (1993).

Gordon, Robert. 1978. *Macroeconomics*. Little, Boston: Brown.

Gori, Franco, Lucio Geronazzo, and Marcello Galeotti. 1993. *Nonlinear Dynamics in Economics and the Social Sciences*. Berlin: Springer-Verlag.

Grandmont, Jean-Michel. 1985. "On Endogenous Competitive Business Cycles." *Econometrica*, 53, 995–1046.

Grandmont, Jean-Michel. 1988. Introduction to J. M. Grandmont (ed.), *Temporary Equilibrium: Selected Readings*. Boston: Academic Press. Originally published as a special issue of the *Journal of Economic Theory*, 1986.

Grandmont, Jean-Michel, Patrick Pintus, and Robin de Vilder. 1995. "Capital-Labor Substitutions and Competitive Nonlinear Endogenous Business Cycles." Working paper.

Greenwald, Bruce C., Meir Kohn, and Joseph E. Stiglitz. 1990. "Financial Market Imperfections and Productivity Growth." *Journal of Economic Behavior and Organization*, 13, 321–345.

Gumowski, Igor, and Christian Mira. 1980. *Recurrences and Discrete Dynamical Systems*. Berlin: Springer-Verlag.

Haavelmo, T. 1956. *A Study in the Theory of Economic Evolution*. 2d ed. Amsterdam: North-Holland.

Haberler, Gottfried. 1937. *Property and Depression*. Geneva: League of Nations, Geneva. 3d ed., Lake Success, NY: United Nations.

Hahn, Frank H. 1973. *On the Notion of Equilibrium in Economics*. Cambridge: Cambridge University Press.

Hall, Robert. 1977. "Investments, Interest Rates, and the Effects of Stabilization Policies." *Brookings Papers in Economic Activity*, 1, 61–121.

Hall, Robert, and John Taylor. 1986. *Macroeconomics*. New York: Norton.

Hansen, Alvin H. 1949. *Monetary Theory and Fiscal Policy*. New York: McGraw-Hill.

Hansen, Alvin H. 1953. *A Guide to Keynes*. New York: McGraw-Hill.

Harris, Seymour (ed.). 1950. *The New Economics*. New York: Knopf.

Hatanaka, Michio. 1996. *Time-Series Based Econometrics*. New York: Oxford University Press.

Helleman, R. (ed.). 1981. *Nonlinear Dynamics*. New York: New York Academy of Sciences.

Hicks, John R. 1937. "Mr. Keynes and the Classics: A Suggested Interpretation." *Econometrica*.

Hicks, John R. 1950. *A Contribution to the Theory of the Trade Cycle*. London: Oxford University Press.

Hinich, Melvin. 1982. "Testing for Gaussianity and Linearity of a Stationary Time Series." *Journal of Time Series Analysis*, 3, 1969–1976.

Hommes, Cars. 1991. *Chaotic Dynamics in Economic Models*. Gronigen: Wolters-Noordhoff.

Hommes, Cars. 1994. "Dynamics of the Cobweb Model with Adaptive Expectations and Nonlinear Supply and Demand." *Journal of Economic Behavior and Organization*, 24, 316–336.

Huang, Weihong. 1995. "Caution Implies Profit." *Journal of Economic Behavior and Organization*, 27, 257–277.

Iseminger, William R. 1996. "Mighty Kohokia." *Archeology*, May/June, 31–37.

Jensen, R. V., and R. Urban. 1984. "Chaotic Price Behavior in a Nonlinear Cobweb Model." Yale University, Department of Applied Physics.

Julien, Bruno. 1988. "Competitive Business Cycles in an Overlapping Generations Economy with Productive Investment." *Journal of Economic Theory*, 46, 45–65.

Kaas, Leo. 1998. "Stabilizing Chaos in a Dynamic Macro Model." *Journal of Economic Behavior and Organization*, 34, 313–332.

Kaizouji, Taisei. 1994. "Multiple Equilibria and Chaotic Tâtonnement: Applications of the Yamaguti-Matano Theorem." *Journal of Economic Behavior and Organization*, 24, 357–362.

Kampmann, Christian. 1992. "Feedback Complexity and Market Adjustment: An Experimental Approach." Ph.D. dissertation, Massachusetts Institute of Technology, Cambridge.

Karlin, Samuel. 1959. "Dynamic Programming Theorem." *Naval Logistics Quarterly*.

Kenoyer, Jonathan Mark. 1998. "Birth of a Civilization." *Archeology*, 1, 54–61.

Keynes, John Maynard. 1936. *The General Theory of Employment, Interest and Money*. New York: Harcourt Brace.

Keynes, John Maynard. 1956. "Robert Malthus." In *Essays and Sketches in Biography*. New York: Meridian Books.

Klein, Lawrence. 1977. Brookings Papers on Economic Activities, 1.

Koopmans, Tjalling C. 1964. "On Flexibility of Future Preferences." In Maynard W. Shelley II and Glenn L. Bryan (eds.), *Human Judgements and Optimality*. New York: Wiley. Also in *Scientific Papers of Tjalling C. Koopmans*. Berlin: Springer-Verlag, 1970.

Koopmans, Tjalling C. 1965. "On the Concept of Optimal Economic Growth." In *The Econometric Approach to Development Planning*. Amsterdam. Also in *Scientific Papers of Tjalling C. Koopmans*. Berlin: Springer-Verlag, 1970.

Kopel, M., H. Dawid, and G. Feichtinger. 1997. "Periodic and Chaotic Programs of Intertemporal Optimization Models with Non-Concave Net Benefit Function." *Journal of Economic Behavior and Organization*, 33, 435–448.

Kuran, Timur. 1995. *Private Truths, Public Lies*. Cambridge: Harvard University Press.

Kydland, F. E., and E. C. Prescott. 1982. "Time to Build and Aggregate Fluctuations." *Econometrica*, 50, 1345–1370.

Lasota, A., and M. C. Mackey. 1985. *Probabilistic Properties of Deterministic Systems*. Cambridge: Cambridge University Press.

Lasota, A., and G. Pianigiani. 1977. "Invariant Measures on Topological Spaces." *Bulletins U.M.I.*, 14(B), 592–603.

Lasota, A., and J. Yorke. 1973. "On the Existence of Invariant Measures for Piecewise Monotonic Transformations." *Trans. of the American Mathematical Society*, 186, 481–488.

Lee, Ronald. 1976. "Demographic Forecasting and the Easterlin Hypothesis." *Population Development Review*, 2, 459–468.

Leijonhufvud, Axel. 1968. *On Keynesian Economics and the Economics of Keynes*. New York: Oxford University Press.

Leontief, Wassily. 1934. "Delayed Adjustment of Supply and Partial Equilibrium." Rpt. in W. Leontief (ed.), *Essays in Economic Theories and Theorizing*. London: Oxford Economic Press, 1966.

Leontief, Wassily. 1953. *Studies in the Structure of the American Economy*. New York: Oxford University Press.

Leontief, Wassily. 1958. "Theoretical Note on Time, Preference, Productivity of Capital, Stagnation and Economic Growth." *American Economic Review*, 48, 105–111.

Li, T. Y., and J. A. Yorke. 1975. "Period Three Implies Chaos." *American Mathematical Monthly*, 82, 985–992.

Lin, Tzong-Yau. 1988. "Studies of Economic Instability and Irregular Fluctuations in a One-Sector Real Growth Model." Ph.D. dissertation, University of Southern California, Los Angeles.

Lin, Tzong-Yau, Wai-man Tse, and Richard H. Day. 1992. "A Real Growth Cycle with Adaptive Expectations." In Dimitri B. Papadimitrious (ed.), *Profits, Deficits and Instability*. Houndmills, NY: Macmillan.

Lorenz, Eduard N. 1963a. "Deterministic Nonperiodic Flow." *Journal of the Atmospheric Sciences*, 20, 130–141.

Lorenz, Eduard N. 1963b. "The Predictability of Hydrodynamic Flow." *Transactions of the New York Academy of Sciences*, series II, 25, 409–432.

Lorenz, Eduard N. 1964. "The Problem of Deducing the Climate from the Governing Equations." *Tellas*, 16, 1–11.

Lorenz, Hans-Walter. 1993. *Nonlinear Dynamical Economics and Chaotic Motion*. 2d ed. Berlin: Springer-Verlag.

Lucas, Robert E. 1987. *Models of Business Cycles*. Oxford: Basil Blackwell.

Lundberg, Erik. 1968. *Instability and Economic Growth*. New Haven: Yale University Press.

Magill, Michael J. P. 1979. "The Origin of Cyclic Motion in Dynamic Economic Modeling." *Journal of Economic Dynamics and Control*, 1, 199–218.

Majumdar, Mukul (ed.). 1994. "Chaotic Dynamical Systems." Special issue, *Economic Theory*, 7, 5.

Majumdar, Mukul, and Tapan Mitra. 1997. "A Note on Controlling Chaotic Tâtonnement." *Journal of Economic Behavior and Organization*, 33, 411–420.

Malinvaud, Edmund. 1980. *Profitability and Unemployment*. Cambridge: Cambridge University Press.

Malthus, Thomas. 1817. *An Essay on the Principle of Population*. 5th ed. Rpt. Homewood, IL: Richard D. Irwin, 1963.

Malthus, Thomas. 1820. *Principles of Political Economy*. London: John Murray. Rpt. in Piero Sraffa (ed.), *The Works and Correspondence of David Ricardo*, volume 2. Cambridge: Cambridge University Press, 1970ff.

Mandelbrot, Benoit. 1982. *The Fractile Geometry of Nature*. San Francisco: W. H. Freeman.

Mangasarian, Olvi L. 1969. *Nonlinear Programming*. New York: McGraw-Hill.

Martin, P. S. 1971. "The Revolution in Archeology." *Science*, 36, 1–8.

May, R. M. 1976. "Simple Mathematical Models with Very Complicated Dynamics." *Nature*, 261, 459–467.

May, R. M., and G. F. Oster. 1976. "Bifurcations and Dynamic Complexity in Simple Ecological Models." *American Naturalist*, 220, 573–599.

McKenzie, Lionell. 1986. "Optimal Economic Growth, Turnpike Theorem and Comparative Dynamics." In K. Arrow and M. Intrilligator (eds.), *Handbook of Mathematical Economics*. Amsterdam: North-Holland.

Medio, Alfredo. 1992. *Chaotic Dynamics: Theory and Application*. Cambridge: Cambridge University Press.

Mera, K. 1975. *Income Distribution in Regional Development*. Tokyo: University of Tokyo Press.

Metzler, Lloyd. 1941. "The Nature and Stability of Inventory Cycles." *Review of Economic Studies.*

Mincer, J. 1963. "Market Prices, Opportunity Costs, and Income Effects." In C. Christ et al. (eds.), *Measurement in Economics.* Stanford, CA: Stanford University Press.

Misiurewicz, M. 1980. "Absolutely Continuous Measures for Certain Maps of an Interval." *Publications Mathématiques*, 53, 17–51.

Mitra, Tapan. 1998. "On the Relationship between Discounting and Complicated Behavior in Dynamic Optimization Models." *Journal of Economic Behavior and Organization*, 33, 421–434.

Modigliani, Franco. 1944. "Liquidity Preference and the Theory of Interest and Money." *Econometrica*, 12, 45–88.

Montrucchio, Luigi. 1986. "Optimal Decisions over Time and Strange Attractors: An Analysis by the Bellman Principle." *Mathematical Modelling*, 7, 341–352.

Morishima, Michio. 1996. *Dynamic Economic Theory.* Cambridge: Cambridge University Press.

Morley, Samuel A. 1983. *Macroeconomics.* Chicago: Dryden Press.

Moser, Jürgen. 1973. *Stable and Random Motions in Dynamical Systems.* Princeton: Princeton University Press.

Myers, Eric M. 1994. "Galilee in the Time of Jesus." *Archeology*, 47, 41.

Nerlov, Marc. 1993. "Toward a New Theory of Population and Economic Growth." *Journal of Political Economy*, 82, 200–218.

Nicolis, G., and I. Prigogine. 1977. *Self-Organization in Nonequilibrium Systems: From Dissipative Structures to Order through Fluctuations.* New York: Wiley.

Nikaido, Hukukane. 1968. *Convex Structures and Economic Theory.* New York: Academic Press.

Nishimura, Kazuo, and Makoto Yano. 1995. "Durable Capital and Chaos in Competitive Business Cycles." *Journal of Economic Behavior and Organization*, 27, 165–182.

Nissen, Hans J. 1988. *The Early History of the Ancient Near East, 9000–2000 B.C.* Trans. Elizabeth Latzeier and Kenneth J. Northcott. Chicago: Chicago University Press.

North, Douglass. 1981. *Structure and Change in Economic History.* New York: Norton.

North, Douglass, and Robert Paul Thomas. 1973. *The Rise of the Western World: A New Economic History.* Cambridge: Cambridge University Press.

Nusse, Helene, and James Yorke. 1995. *Dynamics: Numerical Exploration.* New York: Springer-Verlag.

Peston, M. 1967. "Changing Utility Functions." In M. Shubik (ed.), *Essays in Mathematical Economics in Honor of Oskar Morgenstern.* Princeton, NJ: Princeton University Press.

Phelps, Edmond. 1961. "The Golden Rule of Accumulation: A Table for Growthness." *American Economic Review*, 51, 638–643.

Pianigiani, Giulio. 1979. "On the Existence of Invariant Measures." In V. Lankshmikartan (ed.), *Applied Nonlinear Analysis.* New York: Academic Press.

Pianigiani, Giulio. 1980. "First Ribom Map and Invariant Measures." *Israel Journal of Mathematics*, 35, 32–48.

Pianigiani, Giulio. 1981. "Conditionally Invariant Measures and Exponential Decay." *Journal of Mathematical Analysis and Application*, 82, 75–88.

Pinnoi, Nat. 1994. "Public Infrastructure and Private Production: Measuring Relative Contributions." *Journal of Economic Behavior and Organization*, 23, 127–148.

Pintus, Patrick, Duncan Sands, and Robin de Vilder. 1996. "On the Transition from Local Regular to Global Irregular Fluctuations." Working paper dated October 16, 1996.

Pitchford, John. 1974. *Population in Economic Growth*. Amsterdam: Elsevier North-Holland.

Pohjola, Matti. 1981a. "Stable, Cyclic and Chaotic Growth." *Zeitschrift für Nationaleökonomie*, 41, 1–2, 27–38.

Pohjola, Matti. 1981b. "Built-in Flexibility of Progressive Taxation and the Dynamics of Income: Stability, Cycles, or Chaos?" Department of Economics, Tampere, Finland (February).

Pontriagin, L. S., et al. 1962. *The Mathematical Theory of Optimal Processes*. Trans. K. N. Trinogoff, ed. L. W. Neustadt. New York: Wiley-Interscience.

Prigogine, Ilya. 1980. *From Being to Becoming*. New York: W. H. Freeman.

Prigogine, Ilya. 1996. *The End of Certainty*. New York: Free Press.

Prigogine, Ilya, and Isabelle Stengers. 1984. *Order out of Chaos: Man's New Dialogue with Nature*. Toronto: Bantam Books.

Puu, Tönu. 1997. "The Chaotic Duopolists Revisited." *Journal of Economic Behavior and Organization*, 33, 385–410.

Radunskaya, Amy. 1994. "Comparing Random and Deterministic Time Series." *Economic Theory*, 4, 765–776.

Ramsey, James B., C. L. Sayers, and P. Rothman. 1990. "The Statistical Properties of Dimension Calculations Using Small Data Sets: Some Economic Applications." *International Economic Review*, November.

Rand, D. 1978. "Exotic Phenomena in Games and Duopoly Models." *Journal of Mathematical Economics*, 5, 173–184.

Rassenti, Stephen, Stanley S. Reynolds, and Ferena Szidarovsky. 2000. *Journal of Economic Behavior and Organization*, 41: 2 (forthcoming).

Reed, Irving S., and Wolfgang F. Kraske. 1996. "Reflections, Spinors, and Projections on a Minkowski Space Underlie Dirac's Equation." *Linear Algebra and Its Applications*, 239, 227–262.

Reichlin, P. 1986. "Equilibrium Cycles in an Overlapping Generations Economy with Production." *Journal of Economic Theory*, 40, 89–102.

Riddle, John M., J. Worth Estes, and Josiah Russell. 1994. "Ever since Eve ... Birth Control in the Ancient World." *Archeology*, 47, 29–37.

Robertson, D. H. 1940. *Essays in Monetary Theory*. London: P. S. King and Staples.

Robinson, E. A. G. 1958. *The Structure of Competitive Industry*. Chicago: University of Chicago Press.

Rosser, Barkley. 1993. [to come].

Rössler, O. 1976. "Different Types of Chaos in Two Simple Differential Equations." *Zeitschrift für Naturforschung*, 31, 1664–1670.

Ruelle, David. 1980. "Strange Attractors." *Recherche*, 108.

Ruelle, David, and F. Takens. 1971. "On the Nature of Turbulence." *Communication of Mathematical Physics*, 20, 167–192.

Saari, Donald. 1991. "Erratic Behavior in Economic Models." *Journal of Economic Behavior and Organization*, 16, 3–36.

Saari, Donald, and Carl P. Simon. 1978. "Effective Price Mechanisms." *Econometrica*, 46, 1097–1125.

Sabloff, Jeremy A. 1975. "A Model of a Pre-Columbian Trading Center." In J. A. Sabloff and C. C. Lamberg-Kaslovsky (eds.), *Ancient Civilizations and Trade*. Albuquerque: University of New Mexico Press.

Sagan, Eli. 1985. *At the Dawn of Tyranny: The Origins of Individualism, Political Oppression and the State*. New York: Alfred A. Knopf.

Saggs, H. W. F. 1989. *Civilization before Greece and Rome*. New Haven: Yale University Press.

Samuelson, Paul A. 1947. *Foundations of Economic Analysis*. Enl. ed., 1983, Cambridge: Harvard University Press.

Samuelson, Paul A. 1948. "Dynamic Process Analysis." In Howard Ellis (ed.), *A Survey of Contemporary Economics*. Philadelphia: Blakiston. Rpt. Homewood, IL: Richard D. Irwin, 1952.

Samuelson, Paul A. 1958. "An Exact Consumption-Loan Model of Interest with or without the Social Contrivance of Money." *Journal of Political Economy*, 66, 467–482.

Sargent, Thomas J. 1986. *Macroeconomic Theory*. New York: Academic Press.

Sărkovskii, A. N. 1964. "Coexistence of Cycles of a Continuous Map of a Line into Itself." *Ukranian Mathematics Journal*, 16, 61–71.

Scarre, Chris (ed.). 1988. *Lost Worlds: The Times Atlas of Archeology*. Maplewood, NJ: Hammond.

Scheinkman, J. A., and B. LeBaron. 1986. "Nonlinear Dynamics and Stock Returns." *Journal of Business*, University of Chicago.

Scheinkman, J. A., and B. LeBaron. 1989. "Nonlinear Dynamics and GNP Data." In Barnett, Geweke, and Shell (1989).

Schinasi, Garry J. 1982. "Fluctuations in a Dynamic, Intermediate-Run IS-LM Model: Applications of the Poincaré-Bendixson Theorem." *Journal of Economic Theory*, 28, 369–375.

Schultze, T. Paul. 1981. *Economics of Population*. Reading, MA: Addison-Wesley.

Schumpeter, Joseph. 1934. *Theory of Economic Development*. Cambridge: Harvard University Press.

Sen, Amartia (ed.). 1970. *Growth Economics*. Harmondsworth, UK: Penguin.

Silverman, Neil Asherman. 1994. "Searching for Jesus." *Archeology*, 49, 30–37.

Simon, Herbert. 1951. *Trigger Effects in Resource Allocation*. In T. C. Koopmans (ed.), *Activity Analysis in Economic Production and Allocation*. New York: Wiley.

Smith, Warren L. 1967. "Time Deposits, Free Reserves, and Monetary Policy." In G. Pontecorvo, R. P. Shay, and A. G. Hart (eds.), *Issues in Banking and Monetary Analysis*. New York: Holt, Rinehart and Winston.

Smyth, David J. 1974. "Built-in Flexibility of Taxation and Stability in a Simple Dynamic IS-LM Model." *Public Finance*, 29, 111–114.

Solow, Robert M. 1956. "A Contribution to the Theory of Economic Growth." *Quarterly Journal of Economics*, 57, 65–94.

Solow, Robert M. 1964. *Capital Theory and the Rate of Return*. Amsterdam: North-Holland.

Sorger, Gerhard. 1997. "Imperfect Foresight and Chaos: An Example of a Self-Fulfilling Mistake." *Journal of Economic Behavior and Organization*, 33, 363–384.

Sparrow, Colin. 1982. *The Lorenz Equations: Bifurcation, Chaos and Strange Attractors*. New York: Springer-Verlag.

Srinivasan, Rajesh. 1993. "Econometric Analysis of Nonlinear Dynamics in a Behavioral-Institutional Model of Stock Price Fluctuations." Ph.D. dissertation, University of Southern California, Los Angeles.

Sterman, John. 1989. "Deterministic Chaos in an Experimental Economic System." *Journal of Economic Behavior and Organization*, 12, 1–28.

Stokey, Nancy, and Robert Lucas. 1989. *Recursive Methods in Economic Dynamics*. Cambridge: Harvard University Press.

Strogatz, Steven H. 1994. *Nonlinear Dynamics and Chaos*. Reading, MA: Addison-Wesley.

Strotz, Robert. 1956. "Myopia and Inconsistency in Dynamic Utility Maximization." *Review of Economic Studies*, 23, 165–180.

Stutzer, M. 1980. "Chaotic Dynamics and Bifurcations in a Macro Model." *Journal of Economic Dynamics and Control*, 2, 353–376.

Swan, T. W. 1956. "Economic Growth and Capital Accumulation." *Economic Record*, 32, 334–361.

Takens, F. 1980. "Detecting Strange Attractors in Turbulence." In D. Rand and L. Young (eds.), *Dynamical Systems and Turbulence, Warwick 1980*. Lecture Notes in Mathematics, no. 898. Berlin: Springer-Verlag.

Takens, F. 1983. "Distinguishing Deterministic and Random Systems." In G. Borenblatt, G. Iooss, and D. Joseph (eds.), *Nonlinear Dynamics and Turbulence*. Boston: Pitman.

Takens, F. 1984. "On the Numerical Determination of the Dimension of an Attractor." Unpublished manuscript.

Tinbergen, Jan. 1958. "A Theory of the Trend." [To come].

Tobin, James. 1975. "Keynesian Models of Recession and Depression." *American Economic Review*, 65, 195–202.

Toynbee, A. 1966. *Change and Habit: The Challenge of Our Time*. London: Oxford University Press.

Udwadia, Firdaus E., and Robert E. Kalaba. 1996. *Analytical Dynamics*. Cambridge: Cambridge University Press.

Ulam, S. M., and John von Neumann. 1947. "On Combinations of Stochastic and Deterministic Processes." *Bulletin of the American Mathematics Society*, 53, 1120.

Uzawa, H. 1961. "The Stability of Dynamic Processes." *Review of Economic Studies*, 12.

Velupillai, K. (ed.). 1990. *Nonlinear and Multisectoral Macrodynamics: Essays in Honor of Richard Goodwin*. New York: New York University Press.

Velupillai, K. (ed.). 1996. *Nonlinearities, Disequilibria and Simulations: Essays in Honor of Bjorn Thalborg*. London: Macmillan.

Vendrik, Maarten. 1993. *Collective Habits and Social Norms in Labour Supply*. Maastricht: Universitare Pers Maastricht.

Vilder, Robert Gerard de. 1995. *Endogenous Business Cycles*. Tinbergen Institute Research Series no. 96. Amsterdam: Amsterdam Thesis Publishers.

Walras, Léon. 1926. *Elements of Pure Economics or the Theory of Social Wealth*. Trans. William Jaffé. Homewood, IL: Richard D. Irwin.

Weddepohl, C. 1995. "A Cautious Price Adjustment Mechanism: Chaotic Behavior." *Journal of Economic Behavior and Organization*, 27, 293–300.

Williams, John Burr. 1936. *The Theory of Investment Value*. Cambridge: Harvard University Press. and the carryover *Quarterly Journal of Economics*.

Williams, John Burr. 1967. "The Path to Equilibrium." *Quarterly Journal of Economics*, 81, 241–255.

Woodford, Michael. 1988. "Expectations, Financial Constraints and Aggregate Instabilities." In M. Kohn and S. C. Tsiang (eds.), *Finance Constraints, Expectations and Macroeconomics.* New York: Oxford University Press.

Woodford, Michael. 1989. "Imperfect Financial Intermediation and Complex Dynamics." In Barnett, Geweke, and Shell (1989).

World Bank. 1994. *Infrastructure for Development.* World Development Report, 1994. New York: Oxford University Press.

Zou, Gang. 1991. "Economic Growth and Economic Development." Ph.D. dissertation, University of Southern California, Los Angeles.

Zubrow, Ezra. 1975. *Prehistoric Carrying Capacity: A Model.* Menlo Park, CA: Cummings Publishing Company.

Index

Names

Abraham-Frois, Gilbert, 343
Ackley, Gardner, 371, 372
Akerloff, George, 375
Allen, Peter, 329, 342
Antoniou, I., 329
Arrow, Kenneth, 333, 334, 377
Aubin, Jean-Pierre, 334
Auden, W. H., v
Azariadis, Costas, 343

Bala, Venkatesh, 334
Barnes, Julien, 247
Barnett, William A., 333, 343, 357
Barraclough, G., 379
Batten, David, 340
Baumol, William J., 247, 343, 375, 378
Bellman, Richard, 142, 338, 373, 374
Benassy, Jean-Pascal, 371
Benhabib, Jess, 338, 340, 341, 343, 376
Berrebi, Edmond, 343
Blackwell, David, 342, 374
Blanchard, Olivier, 371
Block, H. D., 333
Boldrin, Michele, 150, 338, 373, 375
Boltzmann, Ludwig, 328
Borel, E., 330
Boserup, Ester, 195, 340, 376
Branson, William, 371, 372
Brock, William, 333, 343, 356
Bücher, Karl, 339
Burmeister, Edwin, 337

Carlsson, Sune, 335
Cass, David, 338, 374
Casti, John, 340
Chamberlain, Gary, 333
Chen, Ping, 329, 333, 343, 356, 357
Chiarella, Carl, 336
Chichilnisky, Graciela, 334
Childe, V. Gordon, 379
Cigno, Alessandro, 373
Clausius, Rudolf, 328
Clower, Robert, 334, 371
Collet, Pierre, 331
Courant, Richard, 371, 373
Cournot, Augustin, 337, 341

Dana, Rose-Anne, 336, 341
Dasgupta, Partha, 376
Dawid, Herbert, xvi, 338, 375
Day, Barbara Gordon, xvi

Day, Richard H., 329, 332, 334–341, 343, 371, 372, 373, 375, 379, 380
Dechert, W. David, 356
Deneckere, Raymond, 338
Devaney, R. L., 331
Diamond, Peter, 340
Dickens, William T., 375
Di Matteo, Massimo, xvi
Dobell, Rodney, 337
Dunford, Nelson, 328

Easterlin, Richard A., 159, 195, 375
Eckmann, Jean-Pierre, 331
Einstein, Albert, 328
Ekeland, Ivar, 327, 329, 342
Engle, Robert F., 356

Fan, Yiu-Kwan, 373
Fischer, Wolfram, 339
Fisher, Irving, 373
Flaschel, Peter, 336, 371
Ford, Joseph, 330
Franke, Reiner, 336, 371
Friedman, Daniel, 334
Frisch, Ragnar, 335

Gabisch, Günter, 343
Gale, David, 340
Galeotti, Marcello, 342
Georgescu-Roegen, Nicholas, 221, 331, 341, 377
Geronazzo, Lucio, 342
Gerschenkron, Alexander, 339, 380
Geweke, John, 343, 355
Gibbs, Willard, 328
Gleick, James, 342
Goeree, J. K., 334
Goodwin, Richard M., 331, 335, 336, 340, 341, 343, 371
Gordon, Robert, 371
Gori, Franco, 342
Grandmont, Jean-Michel, 341, 342, 358
Granger, Clive, 356
Greenwald, Bruce, 335
Gumowski, Igor, 331
Gustafson, K., 329

Haavelmo, Trygve, 332, 377
Haberler, Gottfried, 335
Hahn, Frank, 333, 334
Hall, Robert, 371, 372
Hansen, Alvin H., 371
Hanson, Kenneth, 335
Harris, Seymour, 342

Topics